PHILOPONUS

On Aristotle's
"On the Soul 1.1-2"

PHILOPONUS
On Aristotle's
"On the Soul 1.1-2"

Translated by
Philip J. van der Eijk

Cornell University Press

Ithaca, New York

Preface © 2005 by Richard Sorabji
Introduction, Translation and Notes
© 2005 by Philip J. van der Eijk

All rights reserved. Except for brief
quotations in a review, this book, or parts
thereof, must not be reproduced in any form
without permission in writing from the publisher.
For information address Cornell University Press,
Sage House, 512 East State Street, Ithaca, New York 14850.

First published 2005 by Cornell University Press.

ISBN 978-0-8014-4482-1

Acknowledgments

The present translations have been made possible by generous and imaginative funding from the following sources: the National Endowment for the Humanities, Division of Research Programs, an independent federal agency of the USA; the Leverhulme Trust; the British Academy; the Jowett Copyright Trustees; the Royal Society (UK); Centro Internazionale A. Beltrame di Storia dello Spazio e del Tempo (Padua); Mario Mignucci; Liverpool University; the Leventis Foundation; the Arts and Humanities Research Board of the British Academy; the Esmée Fairbairn Charitable Trust; the Henry Brown Trust; Mr and Mrs N. Egon; the Netherlands Organisation for Scientific Research (NWO/GW); Dr Victoria Solomonides, the Cultural Attaché of the Greek Embassy in London. The editor wishes to thank Matthias Perkams, Pamela Huby, Robert Todd and William Charlton for their comments, John Sellars for preparing the volume for press, and Deborah Blake at Duckworth, who has been the publisher responsible for every volume in the series since the beginning.

Printed and bound in Great Britain

Librarians: Library of Congress Cataloging-in-
Publication Data are available.

Contents

Preface	vii
Acknowledgements	x
Introduction	1
Deviations from the Text of M. Hayduck	11
Translation	13
Prooemium	15
Chapter 1	36
Chapter 2	82
Notes	115
Bibliography	145
English-Greek Glossary	163
Greek-English Index	177
Index of Names	207
Subject Index	209
Index of Passages	215

Preface

Richard Sorabji

The commentary by Philoponus on Aristotle *On the Soul* is taken from the seminars of his teacher, Ammonius, with additions of his own. This opening volume contains an important overview in the Prooemium, which first distinguishes the different faculties of the soul and then argues for the soul's incorporeality, but also analyses its relation to fleshly and non-fleshly bodies. I shall concentrate on the Prooemium, because it makes a number of striking points.

At 4,22, Philoponus explains Aristotle's idea at *An. Post.* 1.31, 88a12-17; 2.2, 90a26, that one might be able to recognise from a single observation that all lunar eclipse is due to the earth's shadow, or that all glass is transparent because it contains pores. Philoponus takes the example of inferring from the sphericity of the moon that all heavenly bodies are spherical. But what he adds is that it requires knowing that they all have the same essence and then using discursive reason (*dianoia*).

At 5,16, it is no accident that Philoponus talks in a commentary on Aristotle of opinion being *reminded* (*anamnêsthênai*) by seeing a single instance that all members of a given species have two feet. For he ascribes to Aristotle Plato's theory that we are *reminded*, or *recollect*, what we knew before birth, when he says in *De Intellectu* p. 40,36 Verbeke, that the child's potential intellect has innate knowledge suppressed by the process of birth.

At 5,3, Philoponus makes opinion (*doxa*) project concepts (*proballein logous*) that it retains within of perceptible objects. This was already postulated by Proclus as the method by which opinion recognises the essences of sensible things, *in Tim.* 1, 251,4-9, a reference I owe to Matthias Perkams. Elsewhere Proclus describes the projection of concepts onto the screen of imagination as like projection of images onto a mirror, rather in the manner of the modern cinema, *in Eucl.* 1, 121,1-7; 141,2-19.

In Philoponus, we find the Platonist tendency to blur Aristotle's sharp distinction between intellectual and perceptual functions. At 5,34-6,10, he equates imagination, which receives impressions (*tupoi*) from the senses, and which Aristotle treats as a perceptual faculty, with passive *intellect*. This blurring of the perceptual and intellectual was already present in an earlier commentator Themistius, who at *in DA*

98,35-99,10, made potential intellect into a storehouse of impressions from perception. And Proclus already reports that passive intellect and imagination had been equated, *in Eucl. 1*, 51,10-52,20.

Turning to the practical faculties, at 5,24-33, Philoponus evinces an attitude to deliberate choice (*proairesis*) closer to that of the Neoplatonist Iamblichus than to Aristotle's. For Aristotle, deliberate choice had been the centrepiece of his ethics. The human being had been equated with this faculty, *EN*, 6.2, 1139b5. By Iamblichus, by contrast, deliberate choice is criticised precisely because it can turn either way (*rhepein pros amphotera* is like Philoponus' *epamphoterizein*), and so side against reason. It is useful only in the world of becoming, and, unlike the wish for the good (*boulêsis*), of which Philoponus also speaks, it would be shed by the purified soul, Iamblichus *On the Mysteries of the Egyptians*, 1.10, 36,1-5; 1.12, 41,3-4.

The incorporeality of soul is argued partly on the basis that sight has to receive opposite qualities, both black and white, and no physical object can at the same time receive opposites in the same place, 12,34-13,20. The gradual dematerialisation of the senses by Aristotle's commentators, because of the need to avoid collision of opposites like black and white, started with an earlier commentator, Alexander, and has been traced in my 'From Aristotle to Brentano: The Development of the Concept of Intentionality'.[1]

Self-awareness also depends on the incorporeality of some faculties. At 14,31-2, Philoponus uses a term for self-awareness that is already found in the Stoic Epictetus, *epistrephesthai*, to turn in on oneself, and he refers to the point made by the Neoplatonist Porphyry, *Sentences* 41, 52,7-53,5, that a body cannot engage in this self-penetration. The only faculties which can do so are rational faculties, because they can operate independently of body. At 14,36ff., Philoponus gives as a reason for believing that rational faculties are self-aware the same reason as was given by Aristotle *DA* 3.4, 430a2-4; *Metaph.* 12.7, 1072b19-21, and repeated by Alexander *DA* 86,14-23 and Plotinus 5.3 [49] 5 (42-8). According to Aristotle, the thinking intellect is identical with the objects of its thought as they act upon it. So the objects which it thinks are, in a way, itself. Hence it is self-thinking.

Philoponus says in 14,33-5 that it is the rational soul that is aware of our perception, whereas Aristotle had said it was the central perceptual faculty, *On Sleep* 2, 455a15-22, called by the commentators the common sense. The preference for reason had started among Platonists before Philoponus. It is found in Plutarch of Athens ap. 'Philoponus' *in DA* 3, 464,24-465,31 (I have sought to explain divergent reports in *The Philosophy of the Commentators, 200-600 AD*, vol. 1, *Psychology*, 4(c) [London & Ithaca, NY 2004]); Proclus *in Tim.* 1, 254,31-255,20. In a final twist, Philoponus' contemporaries in Athens combine the idea that the common sense is responsible with the idea that a rational faculty is responsible for self-awareness, by blurring Aristotle's distinction of the perceptual and the intellectual further, and making Aristotle's common sense into a rational faculty; Priscian, *On Theophrastus* 21,32-22,23; 'Simplicius' (who I now incline to think was Priscian) *in DA* 187,27-188,35; 173,3-7.

Philoponus tells us in 17,19ff. about the Platonist theory that the soul is housed not only in our fleshly body, but also in two finer bodies, called vehicles, which interpenetrate the fleshly body and outlast it. The idea of a vehicle for the soul comes from Plato, *Phaedrus* 247B, *Phaedo* 113D, and *Timaeus* 41D-E. A vehicle for the soul is needed, according to Philoponus, to permit punishment after death (a problem for Christian accounts of Purgatory), and to permit the materialisation of ghosts and demons. The coarser pneumatic vehicle could be shed by a purified soul, but not the luminous vehicle, as Proclus had already said, *in Tim.* 3, 236,31ff.; 298,12ff.; *ET* 196; 207-9; *PT* 3.5. Proclus reports, however, that there had been other views on the impermanence of the pneumatic vehicle, *in Tim.* 3, 234,8-235,9. Our need to keep our soul vehicles healthy is said by Philoponus at 19,27 to have implications for diet.

Philoponus shows himself aware of medical developments since Aristotle. In 19,19ff., unlike Aristotle, he is aware that the brain, not the heart, is the seat of consciousness, and he knows about its membranes and about the suppression of consciousness by pressure on the membranes, and about the optic nerve. He may have known about this through the works of the great doctor, Galen, but later in the commentary he opposes some of Galen's physicalistic conclusions. Galen has a treatise called *That mental states follow the states of the body*. Philoponus, like Alexander before him, objects to the talk of following (*hepesthai*) and of being a result (*apotelesma*). Borrowing a word used by Alexander he says that mental states merely supervene (*epiginesthai*) on bodily states, 51,13-52,1.

Philoponus finishes the Prooemium by saying that Aristotle in *On the Soul*, just as in the *Physics* and *Metaphysics*, concludes his treatise by moving to the highest principles, in this case to the immortal rational soul, 20,31ff.

Philoponus was a Platonist, but also a Christian and an expounder of Aristotle. What strikes me about this Prooemium is how much it is the Platonism that comes to the fore, including the repeated Platonist reinterpretation of Aristotle. One would not predict from reading this Prooemium on its own that Philoponus would later launch a whole book attacking the pagan Platonist, Proclus, on behalf of Christianity. This may reflect the extent to which the Prooemium represents the views of Philoponus' teacher Ammonius.

Note

1. *Oxford Studies in Ancient Philosophy*, supp. vol. 1991, 227-59.

Acknowledgements

Philip J. van der Eijk

I am deeply grateful to the editor, Richard Sorabji, for his support, his advice on many points of translation and interpretation, and for his generous patience during the preparation of this volume. I am further indebted to Frans de Haas for commenting on an early draft of a section of Chapter 1; to the anonymous readers of the translation who provided many valuable suggestions for improvement; to William Charlton for allowing me access to his translation of Book 2 before it was published; to Sarah Francis for her assistance with the preparation of the Glossary and the Indices and with correction of the proofs; to Inna Kupreeva and John Sellars for their assistance with the final preparation of the manuscript; and to my wife Arachne for her invaluable personal support.

I should further like to express my gratitude to the Wellcome Trust for its financial support of the project from which this translation has arisen; to the University of Newcastle upon Tyne for providing a most supportive and stimulating working environment; to the Royal Netherlands Academy of Arts and Sciences (KNAW) for awarding me a fellowship at the Netherlands Institute for Advanced Study (NIAS), where part of the work for this translation was done; and to Leiden University for its institutional support in the very early stages of this project.

Introduction

Philip J. van der Eijk

The present commentary on Aristotle's *On the Soul* is attributed to John Philoponus, or John the Grammarian, the Christian Neoplatonist thinker and polymath who worked in Alexandria in the sixth century AD,[1] and who also wrote commentaries on Aristotle's *Physics*, *Prior* and *Posterior Analytics*, *Meteorologica*, *On Coming-to-be and Perishing*, and the *Categories*.[2] His authorship of Books 1 and 2 of the present commentary, and of the very substantial Prooemium that precedes it, has to my knowledge never been questioned – and indeed, they present striking connections with Philoponus' famous and influential commentary on Chapters 4-8 of Book 3 of Aristotle's *DA* dealing with the highest soul faculty, the Intellect.[3]

The commentary is presented as being 'based on the seminars of Ammonius, son of Hermeias, with some additions of his own'. Other commentaries by Philoponus have similar headings.[4] This suggests that what we have here is Philoponus' written account of Ammonius' exegesis based on the latter's oral teaching,[5] supplemented with observations by Philoponus himself. There has been considerable scholarly discussion about what Philoponus' 'own additions' consisted of,[6] whether they are especially to be found in the Prooemium or in other sections, whether there were differences of opinion between teacher and pupil, and to what extent in the commentary (and the Prooemium) Philoponus has actually and in all respects 'appropriated' Ammonius' ideas. Yet although Ammonius wrote commentaries himself (those on Porphyry's *Isagôgê* and on Aristotle's *De Interpretatione* are extant, as are his 'Prolegomena' to the *Categories*), none on the *DA* survives and we have hardly any independent evidence for his views on the soul.[7] Most of this must therefore remain speculation, and in what follows I shall treat the commentary as an exposition of Philoponus' ideas.

Philoponus was, of course, not the first to write a commentary on the *DA*.[8] Indeed, he himself refers frequently to earlier exegetes, most notably to Alexander of Aphrodisias, whose commentary on the *DA* is now lost but on which Philoponus provides us with a considerable amount of information.[9] Philoponus often disagrees with Alexander, while on other occasions he reports Alexander's interpretation without explicit endorsement or disapproval; only rarely does he express agreement or approval (e.g. in 35,10). He also refers several times to the fourth-century Neoplatonist Plutarch of Athens,[10] and more generally to 'the Attic interpreters',[11] by whom he presumably means the Athenian tradition of Plutarch, Syrianus, Proclus and Damascius (none of whose commentaries on *DA* have survived). He was clearly aware of Themistius' (extant) Paraphrase of the *DA*,[12] but whether he was familiar with the important surviving commentary on *DA* attributed to Simplicius is uncertain: there are no clear signs of interaction, and the works may well be roughly contemporary.[13]

In relation to these earlier exegetes, Philoponus takes several interesting new lines of interpretation, most notably concerning his identification of 'imagination' (*phantasia*) with the passive intellect,[14] his assumption of two 'vehicles' of the soul, the 'pneumatic' and the 'luminous' or 'astral' body,[15] his views on the interconnectedness between the various faculties of the soul by means of 'sympathetic reaction',[16] and his insistence on the 'suitability' of the bodily substrate to the reception of the forms;[17] and further examples can be found in his interpretation of particular sections of Plato's *Timaeus* in Chapters 2 and 3. These interpretations clearly reflect Philoponus' own philosophical views on the soul, some of which, at least at the stage when he wrote this commentary, were profoundly influenced by Proclus.[18] The *in DA* belongs to that group of (presumably early, or at least pre-517) works of Philoponus in which he is not concerned with the exposition and defence of Christian theological ideas and where, apart from occasional references to 'angels', his Christian beliefs hardly ever shine through.[19]

Of course, Aristotle's psychological views as expounded in the *DA* are not easily reconcilable with a Neoplatonist framework.[20] Unlike Aristotle, Philoponus believes in the Platonic doctrine of the pre-existence and immortality of the (rational) soul; and although he says that Providence rules and sends us 'here' with a purpose, viz. embellishing the material world (6,21), he still regards the soul's incarnation in the body as the undesirable result of a metaphysical 'fall' (18,18) out of the soul's blessed state of separateness from the material and physical world.[21] He believes in the existence of a higher, superior, transcendent reality, where the soul comes from and to which it is to return. The highest human good is not to be found in this earthly life; rather, the purpose of human life is to prepare for this return by means of 'cathartic' virtues and a frugal life-style that neutralises the influence of the body; and as part of this preparation the immortal soul must, after the death of the physical body, go through a period of 'purification' in which it is cleansed from the evils of the material world before it can be re-united with the higher transcendent reality. It goes without saying that a good deal of flexibility is required to make Aristotle's work fit in with these views. Philoponus' (and others') attempts to harmonise Plato and Aristotle are therefore often guided by a rather selective emphasis on the more 'Platonising' tendencies in Aristotle's thought, such as Aristotle's views on the Intellect, on the primacy of form over matter, on contemplation as the highest human activity, and on the Unmoved Mover as the ultimate principle of movement in the universe. In the Prooemium, we see Philoponus engaged in a long argument eagerly trying to prove with passages from Aristotle's own works (one of which is quoted twice) that Aristotle, like Plato, believed in the separability and immortality of the rational soul (10,9-11,29). And a further striking example in the present volume can be found in 37,19ff., where Aristotle is credited with the belief that universals are the ideas in the mind of the Platonic Craftsman.[22]

That the Neoplatonists unashamedly used their commentaries on Aristotle (and, to a lesser extent, on Plato) as vehicles for the exposition of their own philosophical views has by now become an established scholarly view,[23] and it should therefore come as no surprise to see Philoponus uninhibitedly reading his own ideas into Aristotle's text. For the use of his commentary, however, and indeed for that of most Neoplatonist commentaries, this has important implications which are less easily appreciated by the modern reader. These commentaries were not meant to be used selectively as a reference work allowing the reader to see what Philoponus or Simplicius had to say on specific Aristotelian passages; rather they were to be read and studied from beginning to end as continuous expositions with a clear structure, sequence and coherence. This explains why many parts of Philoponus' commentary on the *DA* can only be understood properly against the background of what he has said earlier on, especially in the Prooemium, and indeed he often refers to, or takes for granted, things set out in the Prooemium or in an earlier section of the commentary.[24]

These considerations also make it easier to understand why Philoponus, like other commentators, devotes so much attention to Book 1 of Aristotle's *DA*[25] – a book in which Aristotle, in characteristically aporetic fashion, deals with preliminary methodological issues and with the views of his predecessors, while expressing his own views only tentatively or at best implicitly. At first sight, this might seem an unpromising starting point for a Neoplatonist. In fact, however, it provides Philoponus with numerous opportunities to draw attention to philosophical issues of major importance, and his commentaries on the successive lemmas of the Aristotelian text sometimes read as a series of philosophical mini-essays, complete with cross-references from the one to the other.

Thus in Chapter 1, which is aporetic and methodological and concerned with questions about the right procedure in discussing the soul, Aristotle's text prompts Philoponus to dwell on the status of the study of the soul and its importance to other areas of philosophical inquiry such as ethics, theology and physics,[26] on the primacy of form over matter,[27] on the hierarchy of souls and soul faculties,[28] on modes of inferential reasoning,[29] etc. Of particular interest in this chapter is Philoponus' extensive and sustained commentary on Aristotle's discussion of the relationship between body and soul, especially concerning the so-called 'affections' or 'experiences' (*pathê*) of the soul in 403a16ff. As is well known, Aristotle concludes (albeit provisionally) that all such affections have a material/corporeal aspect as well as a formal/non-corporeal aspect: they are 'enmattered formulae' (*logoi enuloi*, 403a25), and should therefore be discussed and defined both from a formal and a material aspect (403b9). For example, anger, Aristotle argues, would have to be described and indeed defined both as a desire for retaliation and a boiling of blood in the region of the heart. The implication is that these descriptions are complementary, and that it is only their combination that makes the natural philosopher's analysis of an affection such as anger complete.

In his lengthy comments on this passage (44,18-63,14), Philoponus is torn between conflicting tendencies. On the one hand, he cites medical evidence in support of the corporeal aspect of all mental processes, including rational activities like thinking. He refers to 'doctors' who argue that 'the faculties of the soul follow the mixtures of the body' (50,25ff.). Philoponus may be alluding to Galen here, although the idea itself was wide spread and of much older origin. The effects of the bodily constitution on moral and intellectual behaviour had been discussed by Plato in *Tim.* 86B-87B, and also Aristotle himself had attributed great significance to the influence of the bodily 'constitution' (*phusis*) and 'mixture' (*krasis*) on human ethical and cognitive performance.[30] Even Plotinus had recognised the possibility of the soul's giving in to the force of base emotions as a result of the 'mixture' (*krasis*) of the body (3.1.34-6).[31] There further was the increasing 'materialisation' of cognitive and emotional processes in early Peripatetic, Hellenistic and early Imperial philosophical thinking. And parallel to this, somehow connecting medical and philosophical ideas, there was the physiognomical tradition, which stressed the close correspondence between mental states, character, and physical appearance.[32] Philoponus was well aware of these traditions. He cites the 'physiognomists' somewhat later in his commentary, in connection with the same view that 'the faculties of the soul follow the mixtures of the body'.[33] And Philoponus took the results of medical science seriously enough. His work displays a strong interest in anatomical and physiological issues, e.g. the location of specific mental functions in different parts of the brain and the role of the nerves in transmitting intelligence and consciousness to the rest of the body. He seems well aware of the medical literature of his time, and willing to take its results on board in the interpretation of the Aristotelian text.[34] That in itself makes the present commentary of interest not only to philosophers, but also to historians of medicine and science. There are even two works on medical topics attributed to Philoponus (one *On Pulses*, another *On Fevers*),[35] and fragments of a commentary on Galen's

On the Usefulness of the Parts survive in Arabic translation.[36] Indeed, in Arabic sources he is often cited as an authority in medicine.[37] Not all of this evidence is free from difficulties, and it has been argued that his name may have been confused with another medical writer named John of Alexandria.[38] However this may be, it is by no means inconceivable that a man with the breadth of interest and learning of Philoponus would have written on medical topics. His later contemporary Stephanus, who wrote commentaries on Aristotle's logical works alongside commentaries on Hippocrates' *Aphorisms* and *Prognosticon* and Galen's *Therapeutics to Glauco*, would present a good parallel.[39] More generally, the close connection between medicine and philosophy in late antiquity would make such a combination of interests quite plausible.[40]

On the other hand, Philoponus is anxious to resist the materialist, 'bottom-up' implications of the medical theory and to preserve the non-corporeality and separability of the rational soul (51,15ff.). This prompts him, with an appeal to 'the Attic interpreters', to make an exception for the highest rational function, the Intellect (although interestingly not for *dianoia*, 'discursive thinking' which, according to a passage somewhat later on, *is* subject to bodily influence).[41] Living a life devoted to philosophy in accordance with the Intellect sets one free from the influence of the bodily mixture, he insists (51,20ff.): we are no slaves of our bodily constitution or the whims of our temperaments, there is something 'within our control'. At this point (51,35; 52,4ff.), Philoponus inserts ideas set out in the Prooemium, and we suddenly find ourselves presented with an elaborate Neoplatonic picture, in which the Aristotelian discussion is set in the context of a metaphysical account of the origin of the 'affections' and their basis in the material world. Philoponus' procedure here is an interpretive *tour de force*, in which the Aristotelian text, medical authorities, and his own Neoplatonic ideas are all explicitly brought to bear on this piece of Aristotelian reasoning.

In the immediate sequel, Philoponus dwells at considerable length on the inconclusive passage at the end of this paragraph, in which Aristotle discusses the various definitions of anger but apparently without being able to make up his mind about the final answer to the question as to how the student of nature should proceed. Philoponus interestingly insists on the relevance of three aspects of the definition: the form, the matter, and the cause why this particular form is in this particular matter (54,20-21). Thus a state of boiling of the blood around the heart which is not caused by a desire for retaliation is not anger, and vice versa. He also dwells for several pages on the different kinds of definition of mental affections according to the disciplines one is coming from, and he dismisses dialectical definitions as 'empty' from the point of view of the study of nature.

A further example of the interest of this commentary follows in the next chapter, where Aristotle begins with his discussion of the views of his predecessors. In his characteristic manner, he divides them into two groups, those who concentrated on the soul's capacity to cause movement and those who were primarily concerned with its cognitive aspects. Like some modern scholars,[42] Philoponus does not read Aristotle's account as a genuine attempt at intellectual historiography, but rather as a systematic and didactically useful survey of different positions one can take. He thus displays a remarkable insight in the strategy and methodology underlying Aristotle's 'doxographic' treatment of the views of his predecessors (e.g. in 82,12ff.). He is not so much interested in the question to what extent Aristotle's portrayal of earlier thinkers' views is historically correct and faithful, but rather in the rationale of his procedure and methodology here. And it is striking that his own listing of the positions of earlier thinkers in the Prooemium (9,3ff.) presents some very close verbal similarities with his comments on Aristotle's characterisations of some of the Presocratic thinkers later on in Chapter 2. It is therefore not surprising that for the study of Presocratic philosophy, the information Philoponus provides here is rather disappointing. There is little in what he says about thinkers such as Democritus or Anaxagoras, at least in *in DA*, that goes beyond what Aristotle says or that appears to reflect access to sources of additional information. But again, to expect otherwise would be to misunderstand the purpose and methodology of Philoponus' text.

In the present volume, the most interesting, and also most difficult example in this respect is found in the section where Philoponus provides a summary report of Aristotle's account (as given in his work *On Philosophy*, now lost) of Plato's unwritten doctrines (75,32ff.). In comparison to the relevant sections in Themistius' and (Ps?-)Simplicius' commentaries on the Aristotelian passage (404b18-27), Philoponus' account is considerably longer and more elaborate. Yet whether Philoponus had access to Aristotle's *On Philosophy* and/or to other sources of information on Plato's unwritten doctrines is very doubtful, and it has proved extremely difficult, if not impossible, to disentangle genuine 'Platonic' elements in this report from their Neoplatonic and Neopythagorean wrapping.[43] Yet to a reader coming to this report from what has preceded it, especially after digesting Philoponus' own ideas on the hierarchy of cognitive functions as set out in the Prooemium, the report makes better sense and fits in well with what has been presented so far.[44]

This commentary therefore contains much that is of interest for philosophers, historians of ideas, and historians of interpretation. In terms of influence, Philoponus' commentary on the *DA* was paraphrased by the Byzantine scholar Sophonias in the thirteenth to fourteenth centuries and thus was accessible to late Byzantine thinkers such as Pletho and Gennadius. Parts of it were translated into Latin by William of Moerbeke in the thirteenth century, and may have served as a source of inspiration for Thomas Aquinas' *Expositio* on the Soul.[45]

Text and translation

This translation is based on the edition by Michael Hayduck in the *CAG* series (vol. 15, Berlin 1897). In his Preface, Hayduck discusses the main witnesses for the textual transmission of the work (the MSS D, R, A, Pal., and a lost manuscript that seems to have constituted the basis for Trincavelli's edition of Venice 1535, indicated by 't'). For the Prooemium, there is also a paraphrase version by Psellus in *PG* 122, col. 1030-1076 (variants listed by Hayduck, pp. xiv-xix; see Leemans [1932]); and there are a number of excerpts preserved in the Suda lexicon (Suid.). I have followed Hayduck in leaving out what appear to be explicative additions preserved in one or more of the MSS. Hayduck prints these in his apparatus, and I have printed corresponding translations in the notes. Apart from these, there are relatively few problems of textual constitution, and only on a few occasions, listed below, have I found reason to prefer a reading not favoured by Hayduck or to propose an emendation. In terms of presentation, I have sometimes printed as separate lemmas passages which are discussed by Philoponus as separate lemmas but not presented as such by Hayduck.[46]

In accordance with the conventions of this series, in the translation of the Aristotelian lemmata square brackets surround words that are not quoted by Philoponus but added to provide a continuous Aristotelian text. Words in angle brackets are explicative additions (not textual emendations, which are indicated in the notes).

Notes

1. For some recent general characterisations of Philoponus' life, work and intellectual development see Sorabji (1987a) and Verrycken (1998), where references to the older literature can be found. For a discussion of Philoponus' activity as a commentator, in particular on Aristotle's *On the Soul*, see Blumenthal (1996) *passim*, but esp. 47-51 and 51-62.

2. And possibly (though this is uncertain) the *Metaphysics*; see Blumenthal (1996) 60-1. The extant commentary on *Generation of Animals* (*CAG* 14.3) attributed to Philoponus is believed by Hayduck to be by Michael of Ephesus (but this requires a fresh examination). For a full list of works by Philoponus, which include writings on medicine, astronomy, mathematics, grammar, cosmology and Christian theology, see Sorabji (1987b) 231-5.

3. These chapters survive in a Latin translation, edited by Verbeke (1966) and translated for the present series by Charlton (1991). They differ significantly from the Greek version of the commentary on Book 3 as printed in Hayduck's *CAG* edition, which has been widely believed not to be by Philoponus himself, although controversy still surrounds the identity of its real author. For a translation of Book 3 and a survey of the discussion see Charlton (2000a) and (2000b), who favours Stephanus as author; see also Lautner (1992); Wolska-Conus (1989); Blumenthal (1996) 61-5. An indirect witness to the lost chapters of Philoponus' commentary on *DA* 3 is Sophonias' Paraphrase of the thirteenth/fourteenth century (*CAG* 23.1), on which see van Riet (1965). Parallels

between the Prooemium, 1.1-2, and the chapters on the intellect are listed in the notes.

4. Those on *An. Pr., An. Post.* and *GC*.

5. In the titles of some commentaries (though not those of Philoponus) the expression 'from the voice' (*apo phônês*) of Ammonius is used (e.g. Asclepius *in Metaph.*); on this phrase see Richard (1950) 193.

6. For a useful overview see Blumenthal (1996) 59-61.

7. For a case where it may be possible to identify a difference of opinion between Ammonius and Philoponus regarding the sense of smell see Sorabji (1991) 233-5. See also Blumenthal (1986) 326-7.

8. For a survey of earlier commentaries on *DA* see Blumenthal (1996) 36-51.

9. For a discussion of the surviving evidence see Moraux (2001) 317-53. For references see the Subject Index.

10. See 21,21 with note.

11. See 21,28 with note, and Immisch (1904); Blumenthal (1986) 320 notes that no direct evidence for Iamblichus or Proclus' exegetical activity on Aristotle's *DA* is attested.

12. cf. *in DA* 2.11, 408,25, 410,1, and 418,25; *On the Intellect* 6, 78,13-80,56. For a translation of Themistius' Paraphrase see Todd (1996).

13. See Blumenthal (2000) 10. The question of the authorship of this commentary has been vigorously discussed; for an overview see Blumenthal (2000) 1-7; Urmson and Lautner (1995) 2-10; Steel in Huby, Steel and Lautner (1997) 105-40. Iamblichus is quoted in (Ps?-)Philoponus *In DA* 3, 533,26, but not in Philoponus' commentary on Books 1 or 2, but his work *On the Soul* may well have been available. See Finamore and Dillon (2002).

14. See 6,1-2 with note; see also the discussion above by Richard Sorabji in the Preface.

15. See 18,17-28 with note; see also the discussion above by Richard Sorabji in the Preface.

16. *sumpatheia*: see 8,22-3.

17. *epitêdeiotês*: see 14,5-28.

18. cf. Steel (1978) 19 n. 60, who suspects the influence of Proclus in the Prooemium, esp. in pp. 15-20 Hayduck (cf. Proclus *ET* 16, 44, and 186).

19. Even though this is now no longer interpreted as evidence for a 'conversion' of Philoponus from Neoplatonism to Christianity, there is an undeniable tension between some of the views expounded in these earlier works and later works such as the *Against Proclus On the Eternity of the World*. This has led some scholars to the assumption of a development in Philoponus' thought in two (or more) stages, sometimes indicated by 'Philoponus I' and 'Philoponus II', most notably by Verrycken; see esp. his (1985) and (1994). See also Évrard (1953) 350 and Blumenthal (1988) 104.

20. See Blumenthal (1983) and (1996).

21. For an overview of Philoponus' psychological views in general see Verbeke (1966), Introduction, and (1985). See also Verrycken (1985) and (1994). For the 'fall' of the soul see also Philoponus, *in DA* 2.3, 255,9-15 (with Verbeke's comments, [1966] xxviii).

22. We will see a further remarkable case of harmonisation of Plato and Aristotle with regard to the question of the soul's movement in Chapter 1.3 in the forthcoming translation of *Philoponus: On Aristotle On the Soul 1.3-5* in this series.

23. This has been pointed out especially by Blumenthal in several publications; see e.g. his (2000), Introduction.

24. The continuity between the Prooemium and the Commentary has been

Introduction 9

stressed by Verbeke (1985) 451-5, who points out that the Prooemium is very different in content, 'agenda' and structure from most other prefaces to Neoplatonist commentaries on Aristotle's works, which deal with the usual introductory issues of the philosophical curriculum (cf. Hadot [1987b]). The continuity between Prooemium and Commentary is also indicated by crossreferences in Philoponus' *in DA* 1.5, 200,2, *in DA* 2.1, 203,5, and *in DA* 2.2, 241,36.

25. See Blumenthal (1996) 79-89.
26. 25,9-16; see also Prooemium 12,15, where the importance of self-knowledge is stressed. See Blumenthal (1996) 3-5.
27. 25,9-16.
28. 36,30-37,17.
29. 40,18ff.
30. *Phys.* 246b4-5: 'the virtues of the body, such as health and handsomeness, we posit in a mixture and balance of hot and cold'; *EN* 1154b11-14: 'The melancholics by their nature require treatment all the time; for their bodies are constantly irritated by their mixture, and they are in a state of intense desire'; *GA* 744a30-2: in man the brain has more moisture and is greater than in other animals, because in man the heat in the heart is most pure: 'This good proportion is indicated by man's intelligence: for man is the most intelligent of all animals'; and *Pol.* 1327b35: '(Among the Greeks), some groups have a one-sided nature, others are well-blended with regard to both these characteristics (i.e. intelligence and courage).' Cf. also *Probl.* 954a15: 'the melancholic humour is a mixture of hot and cold, for from these two the nature (of the body) is constituted'. For a discussion of this see Tracy (1969), van der Eijk (1990) and (1997) and Sorabji (2003) and (2004a) 182-204.
31. cf. Blumenthal (1983) 76.
32. cf. the (Ps?-)Aristotelian *Physiognomonica* 805a1-3: 'that mental dispositions follow the bodies and that they do not exist in themselves being unaffected by the movements of the body'.
33. *in DA* 1.4, 155,22-3; see n. on 50,25 and Sorabji (2003) 157-8.
34. A good example is his reference to 'medical theory' (*ho iatrikos logos*) about sensory nerves in 89,16-17 to reject the theory that sense perception is effected by the blood. See also Prooemium, 19,8-10 (with note). On Philoponus' knowledge of medical ideas see Todd (1977) and (1984), and Kupreeva (forthcoming). Considering Philoponus' medical interests attested elsewhere, it is possible that they reflect one of the 'additions of his own' to Ammonius' teaching (see above, p. 1); but this remains, as noted, speculation.
35. For a discussion see Schiano (2003) and Garofalo (2003).
36. On this see Adnouf (1995) and Strohmaier (2003).
37. See Ullmann (1970) 89-91.
38. See Meyerhof (1931) and Pormann (2003).
39. See Charlton (2000a) and Wolska-Conus (1989).
40. See Westerink (1964).
41. 155,4-35.
42. See e.g. Mansfeld (1986) and Viano (1996).
43. See nn. 492-5 on pp. 139-40.
44. cf. the hierarchy of cognitive faculties in 78,25, and the striking reference to *phantasia* there, which makes sense only to an audience that has been through the preceding discussion in the Prooemium.
45. See Verbeke (1966); Schissel von Fleschenberg (1932); Karamanolis (2002). On the reception of Philoponus in the Arabic world see Steinschneider (1869).

46. An earlier English translation of the Prooemium was published by Dudley (1974/5); German translations of short sections of the Prooemium and of Chapters 1 and 2 can be found in Böhm (1967) and in Scholten (1996), as follows: 12,10-15,8: Böhm 233-6; 16,2-12: Böhm 236-7; 17,6-20,22: Böhm 237-41; 50,14-52,25: Böhm 241-4; 65,32-66,14: Scholten 208-09; 75,11-15: Böhm 245. A number of short passages in the Prooemium are translated into French by Aujoulat (1998).

Deviations from the Text of M. Hayduck (*CAG* 15)

3,15: Reading *peri* (with Pal. and t) instead of *epi* (D).
5,17-18: Reading *panta gar haper* (with t) instead of *pan gar hoper* (D Pal.).
7,17: Reading *homoion hautôi auto* (with t) instead of *hoion auto* (D).
7,19: Reading *homoion hautôi* (with t) instead of *hoion auto* (D).
8,19: Omitting the first *kai* in line 19 (with t).
10,1: Reading *rhêseis* (with t) instead of *khrêseis* (favoured by Hayduck in his Add. et corr.).
10,26-7: Read *tais tou sômatos energeiais* (with Pal.).
13,25, 26 and 30: Reading *phutikoi* (with t) for *phusikoi* (D R Pal.).
39,2: Omitting *ekeina* (with R t).
68,29: Reading *sumbainei* (e conj.) instead of *sumbainein*.
70,11: Reading *phêmi* (e conj.) instead of *phêsi*.

PHILOPONUS
On Aristotle
On the Soul 1.1-2

Translation

Lecture notes of John of Alexandria on Aristotle's
On the Soul, based on the seminars of Ammonius,[1]
son of Hermias, with some additions of his own

Prooemium

As we are about to listen to the lectures on the soul, it is necessary before doing so[2] to speak about the faculties of the soul, <and to state> into how many[3] they are divided and what name each of these individually has obtained, and next how many[4] doctrines of the ancients there exist about these, and in addition to these things to mark out the true doctrine about these things on the basis of division.[5]

<The faculties of the soul>

<The rational faculties of the soul>
First, the faculties of the soul admit of a division into two: some of them are rational, others non-rational.[6] Each of these <groups of> faculties is in its turn divided into two: of the rational faculties some are concerned with life and appetite,[7] others with cognition; and likewise also for the non-rational faculties.[8] Again, the rational and cognitive faculties of the soul are divided into three: one of these is opinion, the other discursive thinking, the third intellect. Now opinion is concerned with the universal in the perceptible objects, for this is the object of its knowing.[9] It knows that all white is capable of widening[10] vision, and that every human being has two feet. Furthermore, it also knows the conclusions of objects of discursive thinking[11] but without giving account <of them>; for it knows that the soul is immortal, but why it is immortal it does not know also: the latter is the function of discursive thinking, whereas the function of opinion is just to know the fact.[12] This is why the Eleatic stranger correctly defines it <i.e. opinion> in the dialogue the *Sophist* as the final result of discursive thinking.[13] For while discursive thinking concluded that the soul is immortal, opinion grasps this conclusion and only knows the fact that it is immortal. For the functioning of discursive thinking is something like completing a journey by moving from premises to conclusions, which is where it has got its name from.[14] For instance, discursive thinking seeks to know on what ground it is that the soul is immortal; next, starting from things that are <relatively> more clear,[15] it proceeds to what is being sought by saying that the soul is

self-moved, and that what is self-moved is also always in motion, and that this is immortal, and that consequently the soul is immortal.[16]

The activity of the intellect[17] is to grasp intuitively things by means of straightforward apprehensions[18] in a way that is superior to demonstration.[19] For just as sense perception, by coming into contact with what is white or with a particular shape, gets to know this in a way that is superior to demonstration (for it does not require syllogistic proof that this particular object is white, rather it knows this by straightforward apprehension), likewise the intellect, too, gets to know the intelligible objects by straightforward apprehension in a way that is superior to demonstration. This activity of the intellect occurs only to those who have arrived at the extreme end of purification and knowledge,[20] those who by means of purifying virtues[21] have got accustomed to activating <the intellect> without imagination[22] and apart from sense-perception. For the intellect is, somehow, the most perfect state of the soul. This is why Plotinus says about it <i.e. the intellect> that 'anyone who has once activated it knows what I mean, since such a state is not capable of being communicated in words'.[23] The intellect is concerned with the intelligible objects, which Timaeus has defined by saying that they are grasped by intellection[24] with the aid of reason,[25] whereas discursive thinking is concerned with the objects of thinking, and opinion with the objects of opinion, which Timaeus calls objects of opinion as such by saying that they are known by opinion with the aid of non-rational sense-perception.[26] Of these faculties the intellect takes the first rank, and opinion the last, and discursive thinking the middle, which is also particularly appropriate to our soul, since that, too, takes the middle rank in the universe.[27] And by means of this, I mean thinking, our soul is lifted up to the contemplation of the intelligible objects, which is the perfection of the soul.[28] For since our soul is of the same kin and origin as the perceptible objects, it is incapable, because it is accustomed to the senses, of lifting itself upward to the contemplation of the intelligible objects, which are without matter, and instead it believes that even these are bodies and have magnitude, and it imagines all that belongs to perceptible objects <as applying to> this area <i.e. the intelligible domain> too. This is also what Plato states in the *Phaedo*,[29] when he says that this is the most difficult of the things within ourselves, that when we have a little freedom from the distractions of the body and want to be free for the contemplation of divine things, imagination[30] comes in between and stirs up confusion in us, by making us suppose that the divine is a body and has magnitude and shape, and it <i.e. imagination> does not allow us to think of God without reference to body or shape. For this reason it is necessary for the soul that is on its way to its own perfection first to activate thinking, which is concerned with the intermediate objects.[31] Of this nature are the objects of thinking, and also our soul and the study of it are of this kind, and furthermore the study of mathematics which – I mean the mathematical objects – have their <mode of> being without matter, even if not their <mode of> existence,[32] so that <our soul>, having grown accustomed to being activated in[33] these without matter, proceeds on its way and reaches the things that are completely separate from matter, I mean the divine objects. This is why Plotinus says: 'The young must be guided through the intermediary of mathematics to <the state of> being accustomed to incorporeal nature.'[34] And whenever thinking draws conclusions also about intelligible objects, it does not do so by itself but by being intertwined with the intellect,[35] just as when it draws conclusions about[36] perceptible objects while being intertwined with imagination.

Even if the majority of people do not have any share in this intellect, yet traces and manifestations[37] <of it> have penetrated also to us; these are the common insights,[38] which we all know without demonstration, or rather in a way that is superior to demonstration, for instance that things that are equal to the same thing are equal to each other, or that if one subtracts the equal from the equal, the result is equal, or that in every case either the affirmation or the negation is true, or that everything yearns for the good, etc.[39] For in order to be persuaded of these things we do not require proof, on the contrary, we know them by means of primary intuitive apprehension which is superior to demonstration. These common insights, then, as we have said, which reach all <men>, are evidently manifestations of the intellect.[40] Concerning this, Aristotle has spoken also in the works *On Demonstration* against those who believe that there is no such thing as <scientific> knowledge, <saying> that we not only claim that there is <scientific> knowledge, but also that there is a starting point of knowledge, by which we know the determining principles <of things>,[41] where by determining principles he means either the common insights and the definitions in the syllogisms (for every syllogism has to get its starting point from common insights which, as we said,[42] come from the intellect also to us; for we know without demonstration that this is a man or a soul or something like that), or by determining principles he means the intelligible objects in the sense of the limits of things.[43] For a determining principle,[44] as the geometrician says, is the limit of something.[45] Therefore he <i.e. Aristotle> says that the intellect is the starting point of knowledge; for by it we possess the common insights; and on the basis of this, in as much it is based on principles, discursive thinking produces scientific demonstrations. More properly speaking, it is the intelligible objects which he calls determining principles; for, indeed, they are the extremes of things. We say then, he says, that the intellect, which he has called the starting point of knowledge, is that by which we know the intelligible objects; for they are determining principles, in as much as they are limits. Since we have said[46] that opinion knows the fact that, but does not know the reason why, and since we also said that it <i.e. opinion> knows the universal in the perceptible objects, and furthermore indeed also the conclusions of objects of reasoning, it is worth asking from where opinion gains the knowledge of the universal in perceptible objects. For on the strength of the demonstration by what <faculty> does opinion accept the conclusion that each man has two feet and holds on to it, just as in the case of objects of discursive thinking, when thinking has demonstrated that the soul is immortal, opinion accepts this conclusion and holds on to it? For it is not thinking that has demonstrated this, I mean that every human being has two feet or every horse is capable of whinnying and all that kind of thing. For it is not possible to prove the universal from individual instances. For it is not that since Xanthus and Balius[47] have four feet, and the horses in this place and those in that, too, one can actually say that all of them do, nor is it actually possible to say that every Ethiopian is black because this particular Ethiopian is black and that one too.

That it is not thinking that demonstrates what is perceptible, is clear; and that it is not imagination or sense perception either, is also very clear, and when we discuss them,[48] this will become even clearer; for each of these knows something individual. What, then, is the basis for opinion knowing the universal of perceptible objects? Well, our answer is that, first of all, there is a certain way by which it is possible for thinking to draw conclusions about the universal that is in the perceptible objects, as Aristotle did in the case of the stars when he wanted to show that they are spherical, proving this on the basis of one <star>, the moon.[49] For if, in the case of objects that are identical in essence, what applies in one case necessarily also applies to all, and if all stars are identical in essence, and if it has been demonstrated that the moon is spherical, it is clear that the other <stars>, too, will be spherical. And someone who has seen smoke concludes that there is fire in that place in the following way: there is smoke in this place; now all smoke comes from fire; therefore there is fire in this place. Perhaps, then, as I said,[50] it is possible also concerning certain <types of> perceptible objects[51] to draw universal conclusions, if not for all; however, I say[52] that the rational soul has the formal principles of things joined with its own substance, and because they have descended in matter they have, as it were, been encapsulated,[53] like the spark that is hidden in the ashes.[54] Just, then, as when someone pokes a little in the ashes, the spark immediately lights up, and it is not that the person who has done the poking has created the spark, but only that he has stopped things which prevented it <from doing so>, likewise opinion, provoked by sense perception, projects the formal principles of things.[55] In this way it is also said that teachers do not put knowledge into us, but they bring to light the knowledge that is already in us and as it were hidden.[56] For if the formal principles of things were not in us, by means of what <faculty> are we aware[57] of it when someone is saying things that are contrary to the nature of things? For example, when two people are talking about the soul and we reject the one and refute him for not speaking in accordance with the nature of things, but assent to the other one and say that it is he, rather, who is speaking the truth, by what <criterion> would we compare what is said by them, and say that the one speaks the truth while the other does not, if we did not have a single formal principle of things? Well, it is clear that we say that they speak the truth or falsehood by comparing <what they say> to the insights about things that are hidden in us and provoked by those who speak to us.[58] In this way, then, I say that when sense perception learns that this or that person has two feet, opinion, too, is provoked by this and reminded that all that is of the same nature has two feet. And it is more germane to say that these, too, are common insights and adumbrations[59] of the intellect; for all things[60] that we know in a way that is superior to demonstration, we know these by means of a common insight. Yet as to those things which require demonstration in order to be known by us, to know the conclusions of these without demonstration is the function of opinion. For example, it knows without reason that the soul is immortal, because the knowledge of this is <arrived at> by means of demonstration, and not in a way that is superior to demonstration, as we know without demonstration that every man is capable of laughing.

<Practical faculties>[61]
Of the rational faculties of the soul, then, the cognitive ones have now been subjected to division; the practical ones are wish and deliberate choice.[62] Wish is concerned only with what is good, whereas choice goes in two directions.[63] Wish belongs to the rational soul itself and by itself, choice to the <soul> that is intertwined with non-rationality. For when the soul is outside the <domain of> becoming, it is active in accordance with wish only; for it is in what is good only;[64] but when it gets into the <domain of> becoming,[65] since the non-rational faculties get intertwined with it by causes which we will speak of,[66] then it holds the faculty of choice because of its being interwoven[67] with the non-rational soul, because <then> it sometimes proceeds from non-rationality, sometimes from reason, and it prefers the one over the other.[68]
These, then, are the rational faculties of the soul.

<The non-rational faculties of the soul>
As for the non-rational faculties of the soul, some are cognitive, others are concerned with life and appetite; and the cognitive ones are imagination[69] and sense perception. They differ from each other in that sense perception extends to what is external, whereas imagina-

tion has its knowledge from within. For sense perception knows only what is present and that which it apprehends from outside, whereas imagination receives from sense perception the impressions[70] of the perceptible objects and re-shapes these within itself, which is why Aristotle also calls it a passive intellect:[71] 'intellect' in so far as it has the object of knowledge within itself and grasps it by straightforward apprehension, as does the intellect, and not by means of proof, and 'passive' because its knowing is accompanied by impressions and does not occur without it giving shape <to the objects imagined>.[72] It is called imagination because it is as if it is a bringing to a halt of light:[73] for imagination is the standstill of things that have been brought to light: for it brings the external appearances to a halt within itself. Each of these two <i.e. sense perception and imagination> extends to individual things; it knows this particular <instance of> white, but not all white. They differ in that the one <i.e. sense perception> knows what is outside, whereas the other <i.e. imagination> knows what is inside; and imagination receives the impressions of the five senses, whereas each of the senses only knows its own proper object of perception.[74]

As for the <faculties> concerned with appetite and life, one of these is spirit,[75] the other is desire.[76] Now someone may ask what we mean when saying that desire and spirit are contradistinguished. Tell me, <he may ask>, does not also spirit desire retaliation against someone who has previously caused pain?[77] And tell me further, <he may ask>, does not also reason desire the objects of learning and theoretical study? My response to this is that the word desire is used both in a general and in a specific sense. For just as the word 'disposition'[78] is used generally and with regard to the state <something is in>, but also used more specifically as contradistinguished from this state, likewise the word desire is used both generally for all faculties of the soul, but it is also used more specifically as contradistinguished from spirit. For since Providence has sent us here in order to embellish things here,[79] it has also entrusted to us that share which it wants us to preserve;[80] and in order that we do this, since there are many things that defile this share, and since it is naturally subject to change and passing away, <Providence> has given us spirit and desire, in order that by means of the one <.i.e. spirit> we scare away what defiles it, and by means of the other <i.e. desire> weave anew what passes away.[81] These, then, are the rational and the non-rational faculties of the soul.

Over and above these are the so-called vegetative[82] faculties, and these are three: the one concerned with nutrition, the one concerned with growth, and the one concerned with generation. They are called vegetative, because in plants they are the only ones that can be seen; for plants feed themselves when they are watered, and when they are manured they grow, and they generate something similar to themselves; for a vine comes from a vine[83] and an olive tree from an olive tree.[84]

To sum up, then, we say that we are humans and living beings and ensouled; in our capacity as humans we have the rational faculties we enumerated, in our capacity as living beings we have the non-rational faculties, and in our capacity as ensouled beings we have the vegetative faculties. 'Ensouled' is what we also say of plants; for it is characteristic of ensouled beings to grow and to feed themselves and to generate <beings> similar to themselves. For plants, at any rate, too, are said to be alive or dead; and life and death come about by the presence or the absence of the soul. Now those <beings> that have the higher <forms of> life necessarily also have the lower ones,[85] but the reverse is not the case; for it is not possible to have the rational faculties without having the lower ones first. Obviously in the case of the senses, too, it is not possible to share in one that is higher without sharing in the lower one;[86] at any rate all those <beings> that share in vision also share in hearing and the remaining <senses>, and those that share in hearing also share in smell and taste and touch, yet not necessarily in vision, as in the case of the mole. Of course there are some <living beings> that share only in touch, such as sponges. Therefore it is not possible to share in the superior <senses> without sharing in the lower ones. This is not because the higher ones need the lower ones in order to exist, but conversely the body cannot have a share in the higher ones if it has not previously received a share in the lower ones; for the body cannot receive a share in the non-rational <soul> if it has not previously received a share in the vegetative soul, nor can it receive a share in the rational soul if it has not received a share in both of these. For since none of the species[87] should perish, lest the universe should be incomplete (for the universe is the fullness of the forms), and since it was impossible for those <beings> here[88] to remain numerically the same, since they are subject to coming to be and passing away, they, too, got a share of eternity according to their ability, since all things yearn for the eternity of the first[89] as the proper principle, and each has a share in this in accordance with its own measures. For this reason, then, the things here, because they are unable to be numerically[90] eternal, have a share in eternity by each generating <an individual> like itself;[91] and this is the most suitable work of nature, that each of the natural <beings> generates another one like itself.[92] Since, therefore, we need generation, and since the generative faculty comes about in <something of> a defined magnitude, for this reason we need growth. And since growth comes about through nutrition, we need the faculty of nutrition. This is why we share in the vegetative faculties as well as the non-rational animals. Therefore, when we activate these faculties, we are active in the way of plants, and when we activate spirit and desire, as non-rational animals; only when we use reason are we active in the manner of humans. This is also why Plotinus made that most divine statement when he said that all those who activate their nutritive faculties in an obsessive manner are in danger of turning into trees.[93]

It is worth examining what the difference is between desire and the vegetative faculties, both the generative and the nutritive. For we do not see the activity of desire being concerned with anything else except food and the generative faculties, so that desire seems to be identical to the vegetative faculties.[94] What, then, do we say in response to this? It is not identical, for desire is activated together with sense perception, yet the vegetative faculties do not involve sense perception. This is also why in non-rational animals as soon as they see a female their sexual appetite is aroused; this shows that desire is accompanied by some sort of knowledge. Yet this is not so with the vegetative activities: even while asleep, we actually often emit seed without any perception or imagination causally preceding it, obviously because our vegetative faculties are activated. For just as when reason is enslaved by non-rationality and reason itself sets every mechanism in motion in order to fulfil its need for food[95] and sexual activity, we do not therefore claim that reason is identical to the vegetative faculties, likewise we do not claim this regarding desire either. Yet it is peculiar to the vegetative faculties to yearn simply for food and sex, without perceiving <anything>, and for desire to yearn for such and such food and such and such sex, and simply for what is pleasant. Well then? Is the final result of the two faculties one and the same, of desire as well as of the vegetative faculty? My reply is that it is not one, but of the vegetative faculty it is simply food and sex, whereas the purpose of desire is pleasure. This is the purpose of desire, in order that, as I said,[96] by this yearning we preserve our share[97] and the succession of our kind.

As for reason, whenever it is made subservient to desire, I am denying that there is a peculiar purpose served by this activity, since such an activity is contrary to its nature, and things that are contrary to nature do not in any way look to a purpose. For just like a servant, it does not prepare its own purpose but that of desire, viz. pleasure.

Now let no one raise this trivial difficulty: 'Well then, do we have three souls and are we managed by three souls?' My response is that just as the soul, when united with this body, seems to be constituting one thing, whereas in reality it is not one thing, likewise <the soul[98] that is> connected with the non-rational and vegetative soul[99] creates one continuum because of the connection between them (after all, the non-rational soul has been attached to the rational soul and is connected with it, and so is the vegetative soul with the non-rational soul), and because of the sympathetic affection[100] that arises from this connection we speak of one soul and say that the rational soul uses the other faculties as instruments. Of these faculties, I mean the non-rational ones and the vegetative ones, some are in closer proximity to the rational soul, others less so; the non-rational ones are in closer proximity, because it is their nature to obey reason;[101] this is why we calm them down by chastising their desires: 'beating his breast he calmed his heart with the following words',[102] and again 'endure, my heart, this thing, for you have endured worse things',[103] and again 'accustom yourself to controlling anger, pleasure and pain', etc.[104] And why do I speak about our level? Many wild animals, too, get calmer as a result of reason. Since the vegetative faculties do not obey reason, they are at a greater distance from the rational soul; for it is not possible to instruct the nutritive faculty to feed itself only up to a point, or the faculty of growth to cause growth only up to a point. Nor is this possible with the generative faculty: this is why we often emit semen in sleep without wishing it; and even if we make the generative faculty more moderate, it is clear that we check not simply the faculty itself but the desire; for the faculty remains no less present even if it is not activated. These, then, are the faculties of the soul, both the rational and the non-rational and the vegetative ones.

<*The incorporeality of the soul*>

<*The views of earlier philosophers*>
In general, some say that the soul is incorporeal, others that it is a body; and of those who say it is a body, some say it is a simple body, others that it is a composite body; and of those who say it is a composite body, some say that it is composed of bodies that are connected with each other, others that it is composed of bodies that are not connected with each other. Of those who have said that the soul is a simple body,[105] some have said that it is an aetherial body, which is the same as saying that it is a celestial body, as did Heraclides of Pontus,[106] while others said that it is fire, such as Heraclitus,[107] for he said that the principle of things is fire, <and he said that> in this way, then, the soul was fiery, too, because of its being easily moved. Others say that it is airy, such as Anaximenes[108] and some of the Stoics, yet others that it consists of water, such as Thales[109] and Hippo, who is nick-named the atheist;[110] for since they saw that seed consists of a moist substance, therefore they believed that the principle of things should actually be water. No one has ventured to say that it is earth, because earth is by nature heavy and difficult to move.[111] These, then, are the ones that say that the soul is a simple body, since these five are also the only simple bodies; and these are also the only ones of those who say that it is a body who are capable of saying that it is immortal.

Of those who have conceived of the soul as composite some have supposed that it consists of unconnected elements, such as Democritus and Leucippus[112] and, generally speaking, those who introduce the atoms; they used to say that atoms and void are the principles of things, and that the soul, therefore, consists of spherical atoms because of its being easily moved. Others have supposed that it consists of elements that are connected to each other, as did Critias, one of the Thirty;[113] he said that the soul is blood: 'For in humans thought is the blood that is in the region of the heart.'[114]

Of those who have adhered to the opinion that the soul is incorporeal, some say that it is separable from bodies, others that it is inseparable. And of those who say that it is inseparable, some said that it is the proportion of the mixture,[115] for example that, if one mixes twice as much fire with water or one-and-a-half as much or something like that, this produces the soul, the proportion that happens to be two to one or one-and-a-half to one being the soul. Others say that it is the mixture itself,[116] yet others that it is the actuality;[117] for the actuality is the perfection and the form of the substrate. The proportion is different from the mixture; for the proportion is viewed in the quantity itself, in one-and-a-half as much or in twice as much or in some other quantity, and, generally speaking, the quantitatively determined relation of the one to the other is the proportion of the things that are mixed; but the mixture is a quality that is the final product of the mixture of the qualities; for example, from hot and cold, tepid arises as a kind of mixture, or from white and black, grey. And the actuality is the completeness of the substrate, that is, the form that supervenes on the matter from the particular combination of the elements, as, for example, the form of the earthen vessel supervenes on the clay.

Of those who have said that the soul is separable from the body, some have said that the whole soul is separable, both the rational and the non-rational and the vegetative soul, such as Numenius,[118] who was led astray by some of the aphorisms of Plato, who says in the *Phaedrus*, 'All soul is immortal',[119] clearly speaking about the human soul; for that he is aware that the soul of the non-rational beings is mortal we shall show clearly when we shall quote what he actually says.[120] Others say that the whole soul is inseparable <from the body> and for this reason mortal, as does Alexander of Aphrodisias, who in fact tries to pull down Aristotle towards his own doctrine.[121] Others say that the rational soul is separable, but the non-rational and the vegetative are inseparable. Of these, some say that both are inseparable from our solid body,[122] others that only the vegetative soul is inseparable from this whereas the non-rational soul is separable from this but inseparable from another body, I mean the pneumatic;[123] and this is also the true doctrine, as we shall show, which both Plato and Aristotle heralded.

Indeed, that Aristotle, too, is of this opinion and is aware that the one soul is separable, whereas the other is inseparable, can be shown clearly on the basis of many passages;[124] at any rate at the end of the treatise *On the Parts of Animals*,[125] which immediately precedes the present treatise,[126] he says that each of the parts of the animals is characterised by a specific vital activity, e.g. the heart, the liver, the brain etc., and then he says that the question needs to be asked whether one should call this activity soul or a part of soul or <something that does> not <take place> without soul. This shows that he is aware that there is a great width, or rather depth, of souls.[127] And <there is the question>, he says, whether the student of nature is to discuss the whole soul or not the whole soul but only that which is not without matter.[128] Therefore, he is aware that soul is separable from matter. For if the student of nature is to speak about the whole soul, he says, it is clear that he will also speak about the intellect; but if he is also to speak about the intellect, he will of necessity also speak about the intelligible objects. For the intellect is intellect of intelligible objects,[129] as sense perception is perception of perceptible objects; for they are relational things. But to discuss the intelligible objects is the task of the first philosopher. It will therefore follow from this that the student of nature will cover all things, which is absurd, both perceptible objects because of sense perception, and intelligible objects because of intellect.[130] And in this very treatise *On the Parts of Animals* he says: 'It seems that the intellect enters from outside and is divine; for its activity has nothing in common with the activities of the body.'[131] And again in the present book, having stated with regard to the affections of the soul, spirit and desire and the others, that they are inseparable from the body, he says: 'And for this reason it is in fact the task of the student of nature to study the soul, either in its entirety or the soul that is of this kind',[132] i.e. in as far as it is not without matter; therefore, he knows soul to be separable from matter. And in the second book, while investigating the other faculties of the soul <and considering> whether each of them is a soul or a part of the soul, he says: 'As for the intellect and the faculty of contemplation this is not yet clear, but it seems that this is a different kind of soul, and that this alone is capable of being separated, as what is eternal from what is perishable.'[133] And again in the third book he says: 'If, then, thinking is like perceiving, it is some kind of being affected by the intelligible object or something else of the sort; therefore it has to be impassive.'[134] And a little later: 'Only when separated is this what it <truly> is, and this alone is immortal and eternal. Yet we do not remember this, for it is impassive, whereas the passive intellect is perishable.'[135] It is therefore clear from these passages that he says that the intellect is impassive and immortal and eternal and separable in itself, whereas imagination, which he has called passive intellect,[136] is perishable: <he has called it> intellect, because it has the object of knowledge within itself, and passive, because it is accompanied by impressions. And again in the same book he says: 'Therefore what is called the intellect of the soul (by intellect I mean that by which the soul thinks and forms beliefs) is none of the things in actuality before it thinks them. This is why it is reasonable <to hold> that it is not in a state of mixture with the body.'[137] And a little later, while distinguishing sense perception from the intellect, he says that whereas sense perception, when grasping the larger perceptible objects, cannot grasp the more dull objects, the intellect, in as much as it grasps the larger objects of thought, to that extent can grasp the smaller ones more easily.[138] The reason for this is, he says, that 'the faculty of sense perception is not without body, whereas the intellect is separable.'[139] And again: 'This intellect is essentially separable and unmixed and impassive.'[140] Indeed, even before these <statements> he says in the first book: 'The intellect seems to enter <in us> as a substance, and not to perish; it would be particularly likely to perish as a result of the dulling in old age.'[141] And again: 'What kind of part <of the body> the intellect will hold together, or how <it will do this>, is difficult even to imagine.'[142] And again: 'As for the intellect and the faculty of contemplation this is not yet clear, but it seems that it is a different kind of soul, and that this alone is capable of being separated, as what is eternal from what is perishable.'[143] This shows that he wants it to be separable from the body and to be active without the body and also to be eternal.[144] There are many <passages> which one could produce in order to show that Aristotle is aware that the rational soul is immortal and that it is separable from all body, but what has been said suffices.

That surely Plato, too, is aware that the rational soul is immortal, is superfluous to say; and that he is also aware that the non-rational soul is mortal, is shown sufficiently by what is said in the *Timaeus*.[145] For when, he says, the Craftsman had created the whole divine nature, both the visible and the invisible one, he <i.e. Plato> says, he <i.e. the Craftsman> said to them[146] that three mortal kinds were still required for the arrangement of the universe, meaning those that live on land, those that live in the air and those that live in water, and if those did not come into being the world would be incomplete. 'If it were through me that these things came into being and got a share in life, they would become equal to gods. In order, then, that they be mortal and that this universe be, as it should be,[147] a whole, you must turn, in accordance with your nature, to the creation of mortal[148] animals, imitating the power I have used for your coming into being. And that <part of> them for which it is appropriate to be called by the same name as the immortal beings, which is called divine and which rules in them,[149] I have sown and initiated and I will hand it over to you; for the rest, you must weave something mortal to what is immortal and create animals.' This clearly shows that he says that the non-rational soul is woven as something mortal to reason, whereas <that part> which is ruling is divine and immortal, in so far as it is rational in mortal animals, just as everywhere else he calls that which rules reason.[150]

Thus it is clear that both Plato and Aristotle think that neither the whole soul is separable from the body nor that the whole soul is inseparable, but that the rational soul is separable, whereas the remaining <soul> is inseparable.

<Demonstration of the incorporeality of the soul>
Yet one should not leave it at the statements of the ancients, but rather produce the demonstrations for all these things; for these doctrines have a bearing on our whole life.[151] Besides, what is more appropriate for us than the knowledge of ourselves? We shall demonstrate, then, everything that has been said, that the whole soul is incorporeal and that only the rational soul is separable from all body and therefore immortal,[152] and that the non-rational soul is separable from this solid body but inseparable from the *pneuma*,[153] and furthermore, whether this very pneumatic body exists at all, and that it continues to exist for some time after the departure from this body, and that the vegetative soul has its being in this solid body and perishes together with it.

Since all doctrines that say that the soul is a body, whether a simple or a composite one, are false, we shall produce the refutation that is common to all of them, in order that we do not have to refute them one by one.

That it is possible for no soul whatsoever to be a body is clear from the following. Each body is dissoluble by its own nature and capable of being divided indefinitely. That is why it is in need of something that holds it together. Now since that which holds it together is either soul or some other faculty, is this a body or is it incorporeal? If it is a body, this will in turn also need something that holds it together. Again, therefore, we will ask concerning this, too, whether it is a body or incorporeal, and so on *ad infinitum*. It is therefore necessary that the faculty that holds the bodies together is <itself> incorporeal. Now, in the case of ensouled bodies, that which holds them together is the soul. Therefore the whole soul is incorporeal.

In the present book Aristotle has in many ways refuted these <earlier> doctrines, and he adds the following in particular:[154] What do I say concerning the other <faculties of the soul>? The lowest cognitive faculty of the soul is sense perception, and this is shown by geometrical necessity to be incorporeal. If, then, the lowest faculty is incorporeal, so much the more will this be true for the superior ones. How, then, does he demonstrate this? No body, he says,[155] can apprehend opposite <qualities> during one and the same moment and in one and the same part; the finger cannot simultaneously and in its entirety take part in[156] both white and black, nor can it simultaneously and in the same part become both hot and cold. Yet sense perception apprehends simultaneously and at the same moment opposite qualities: for during the process of reading, it apprehends both white and black; this is also why it knows that the one is first and the other second, by distinguishing the black from the white. How, then, does vision apprehend opposites during one and the same moment? Does it do so in the same part or does it apprehend black in one part, white in another? If it does so in the same part, it is clear that it apprehends them without being divided and that it is incorporeal; but if it does so in different parts, it is similar, he says, to 'if I perceive this, and you that', just as if, he says, 'you were to say that what I saw is different from what you saw'.[157] For what discerns must be one and the same and apprehend the objects it discerns in the same part. And a body cannot simultaneously in the same part grasp opposites, or simply, different objects; yet sense perception does grasp white and black during one and the same moment; therefore it grasps things without being divided, and for this reason it is incorporeal. For if it apprehended black and white by different parts, it would be unable to distinguish white from black; for no one distinguishes what is seen by himself from what is seen by somebody else.

That imagination, too, is incorporeal and undivided, is clear from the following. Why do impressions that are formed later not make those that were already there earlier invisible? Which is what would happen if it were corporeal, as in the case of wax: for in the case of wax, the impressions that are formed later make the ones that were already there earlier invisible. Yet even the vegetative soul, which is inferior even to sense perception, and indeed the vegetative formal principles,[158] are clearly shown to be undivided and therefore incorporeal. For in each part of the seed the same vegetative formal principles are present without being divided that are also present in the seed as a whole, viz. the principles concerned with nutrition, those concerned with growth, and those concerned with formation; for just as every seed that is emitted, if the uterus holds on to it, produces a perfect living being, no less will it do so even if it does not make perfect the whole but just the part. If, then, the vegetative formal principles of the living being were a body, it would be impossible for the principles of the head and the feet and all other parts to be present simultaneously in the same part. As it is, however, as they are all present in this, likewise all are present in another one too; therefore they are all present in every part without being divided; therefore they are incorporeal; for what is undivided is incorporeal. At any rate, just as the faculties of nutrition, growth, and generation are present in a tree as a whole, likewise they are present also in the branches or in the cutting and indeed in the kernel itself.

But perhaps someone might raise the problem what the origin of monstrosities is. Is this not as a result of a deficiency or a surplus on the part of the seed? And why is it that, if a part were cut off from the grain, the remaining part no longer sprouts? Why do the bark or the leaf or that sort of thing no longer grow? And yet these are parts of the tree. My response concerning the monstrosities is that it is the matter which is the cause, since there is also a need for a certain suitability[159] of the matter, both in quantitative and in qualitative respects; and the menstrual blood is the matter of living beings; therefore, when this is in excess or deficient or has been made contrary to nature, it is the cause of monstrosities. And, generally speaking, these faculties, even if they are incorporeal, still have their being in the body as their substrate, and in order for them to exist they need to have their substrate commensurate in quality as well as quantity. For instance, the circle and, generally speaking, the mathematical figure, is shown itself and by itself to be without quantity and without magnitude and, generally speaking, incorporeal; yet it would not exist if it did not in addition assume a substrate that is commensurate to it in magnitude and quality; for instance, a circle cannot exist in a small and momentary body,[160] nor in a body that is moist and fluid. In this way, then, I state also with regard to the present subject that even if the formal principles are by themselves undivided, still, since they have their being in a body as a substrate, yet not generally speaking every body or a body of any kind is capable of receiving the formal principles, it also for this reason requires a suitability of the substrate. And if, generally speaking, the faculties in the whole tree are all found to be present also in the parts without any deficiency, it is clear that <this is> for no other reason than that they are in themselves undivided. For if they were bodies, they would not be present wholly in the branch that is cut off, and the tree would be mutilated. And if someone said: 'Yet one can say that they are homoeomerous bodies that extend through the whole, and of homoeomerous bodies the same form that is present in the part is also present in the whole, as is the case with flesh; for the part of flesh is flesh', our response to this, then, will be that if they were homoeomerous bodies, they would not in their entirety penetrate the entire substrates; for it is impossible for one body to penetrate another.

If, therefore, the lower faculties of the soul are incorporeal, so much the more will this also be the case with the rational part of the soul, which is by far superior. For that this, too, is incorporeal, has been shown both by means of general arguments, and we state it also in particular and with regard to this <part> in the following way. None of the bodies knows itself nor does it turn in on itself;[161] for the hand does not know itself, nor does any of the other parts know itself. Yet neither do the non-rational faculties, even though they are incorporeal, know themselves: for vision does not know itself, nor does hearing or, generally speaking, sense perception, nor does it seek <to know> of what nature it is: rather it is reason that seeks to know this about them. However, the rational soul itself knows itself; it, at any rate, is what is seeking, and it, too, is what is being sought; it is what discovers, and it is what is being discovered; it is what knows and what is being known.[162] Therefore it has clearly been demonstrated to be incorporeal.

15,1 Moreover, the faculties that are present in the body as in their substrate gain strength with the body and again weaken with it; such, at any rate, are sense perception, spirit, and desire; yet the rational soul, by contrast, gains strength while the body wastes away; therefore it is not present in the body as in a substrate. Furthermore, nothing seeks to destroy its own substrate, for all things yearn to be; yet the rational soul despises the body, it subdues it by virtuous efforts and often casts it away as a whole; therefore it does not have its being in the body as in its substrate.[163] In this way, then, it has been shown that not a single faculty of the soul is a body.

In addition to these things, we need to demonstrate that whilst the rational soul has its being separate from all body, the others have their being in the body; and one of these, the non-rational, has its being in the *pneuma*,[164] while the vegetative has its being in this one.[165] In order to demonstrate these things, let us first, to begin with, accept the following point.

<*The relationship between the non-rational parts of the soul and the body*>
In the introduction to the present book[166] Aristotle presents us with a rule that was accepted by all philosophers in common, both those who supposed the soul to be mortal and those who supposed it to be immortal. This rule is the following.[167] We must, he says, judge the essence[168] <of something> on the basis of its activities, since every essence has its corresponding activity. Every essence, then, he says, that has not a single activity separable from the body will necessarily also have its <own> essence not separable from the body; for if it, while having its essence separable, has not a single activity separable from the body, it will, when it is separated from the body, have nothing in respect of which it will be active; consequently, it will be in vain. Yet neither God nor nature does anything in vain.[169] Therefore it is impossible for that which has its essence separable not to have a single activity without the body.

Again, another rule is this.[170] Every essence that has its activity separable from the body will itself necessarily also be separable from the body; but if it were not separable, the consequence would be that what is caused is superior to what causes it and what is inferior would be superior to what is superior, which is absurd, for what causes something always has to be superior to what is caused by it and what is prior by nature has to be superior to what comes after it; and what is prior by nature is superior.[171] How, then, is this the case? For we know that every activity arises from a faculty,[172] and every faculty from an essence; therefore, the activity has the third rank after the essence. If, then, the essence of something is inseparable from the body, while its activity is separable, and what is separable is superior to what is inseparable,[173] the activity will be superior to the essence, and it will be the same thing to say that what is caused is superior to what causes it and what is secondary, or rather tertiary, to what is naturally prior, which is absurd. Therefore it is impossible for an activity that is separable from the body not to proceed from an essence which itself also is separable. These, then, are the Aristotelian rules. Of these, the latter is of use to us for our discussion of the rational soul, and the former for our discussion of the other souls. Let us therefore speak, to begin with, about the rational soul.

If no single essence that is inseparable from the body has its activity separable – and we will show in the case of the soul that its activity is separable from the body – it is absolutely necessary that it, too, will itself be separable. When, therefore, the soul examines the intelligible objects and directs itself towards insights about God, it is clear that it has such an activity separable from all body. Likewise this is also the case when it seeks itself; for in such things it in no way needs either the co-operation of the body, nor is its activity concerned with the body, and therefore such an activity will in all respects be separable from the body, even from imagination itself. Yet if its activity is separable, its essence will of necessity also be separable; and if its essence is separable, it will of all necessity also be eternal; for this is commonly agreed by all, that every essence that is separable from bodies is also eternal. For look, if it, being separable, is not eternal but has come into being and is subject to passing away, it was, before coming into being, either capable of coming into being or it was not capable <of this>. Now if it were not capable, it would not have come into being; for what is impossible does not come into being;[174] and if it were capable, it would on all accounts be material. For this, i.e. being capable of being an individual thing at a certain time or not, is a characteristic of matter; yet if things that are separable are without matter, they will not be as a result of <a state of> potentiality <changing> into <a state> of actuality, but they will always be in <a state of> actuality.

Another <way of showing this> is like this. Everything that passes away, passes away in <one of> two ways,[175] either that of bodies by their dissolution into the elements, or that of incorporeal things when the form is extinguished by the lack of internal harmony of the substrate in which it has its being, just like a harmony when the strings are loosened.[176] Now in neither of these two ways is it possible for the rational soul to pass away, neither the way of bodies (for it is incorporeal), nor that of things that are incorporeal yet have their being in a body as a substrate; for it has been demonstrated to be separable from the body. Therefore, if it has been demonstrated to be separable from the body, it has at the same time been demonstrated to be also eternal.[177] So much for the rational soul.

In addition to these things, let us also discuss the other <souls>, both the non-rational and the vegetative one. That these are inseparable is clear from the rule that has been mentioned. For if we show that they have not a single activity that is separable from a body, there is every necessity that they themselves, too, are inseparable. All activities of these, therefore, are present in a body and are concerned with a body; for the faculties of nutrition and of growing and of generation are present in a body and are activated through a body and are concerned with bodies. The same applies to spirit and desire: for the one stirs up the blood in the region of the heart,[178] the other brings the liver in a certain condition.[179] They are present in a body, then, and take place through a body, but they are also concerned with a body: for desire is either an appetite for foods or money or simply corporeal things, and spirit is an appetite for retaliation against the one who has done us harm in any of these things. Therefore, if the activities of these <faculties> are not without a body, this will of necessity also apply to their essence. For what would their activity be for when being separated? What would they nourish, or cause to grow, or generate? Whom would they retaliate? Yet desire, too, will not have any of the pleasant things that stir it towards longing; consequently, they will be in vain. And if this is impossible, that something is in vain, the essence from which such activities proceed will be inseparable from the bodies. As it is, however, the vegetative <soul> is inseparable from the solid <body> and perishes with it; this is evident from the fact that its faculties are also present in plants, in which the pneumatic body is not found.[180] After the departure of the soul they evidently remain for a short time in the relevant body, for[181] nails and hair will also grow on corpses.[182] But if even after death there is still clearly a trace of the faculty of growth in the body, it is necessary that there will also be a trace of the faculty of nutrition; for nutrition is for the sake of growth. From this, therefore, it is clear that these faculties have their essence in this <body>; and if they do, of necessity the faculty of generation will do so, too; for it belongs to the same series, for where the former two are, there of necessity the third also appears. One might say that there is a trace even of this in a dead body because of the living beings that come into being from corpses, such as wasps, bees, grubs, etc.

<The pneumatic body>

Yet the non-rational soul no longer has its being in this <i.e. the dead body>: it persists also after the departure of the soul from this <body>, having as its vehicle and substrate the pneumatic body,[183] which itself is also composed of the four elements but is called pneumatic because of the element that is in excess, air, just as our present body is called earthy as a result of the element that is in excess there. How then is it evident whether non-rational life has its being in this? Or rather, we ought to ask first how it is evident that there is a pneumatic body at all. For it is proper to ask first whether it exists at all, and then to show that non-rational life is in it.

How, then, is it evident that there is *pneuma*? It is agreed, or rather demonstrated, that our soul after its departure from this body arrives in Hades, where it receives punishment for the ways in which it has not led a good life.[184] For Providence is not only concerned with our being but also with our well-being. This is why the soul is not neglected when it slides away into what is contrary to nature, but it receives the attention that is appropriate to it, and when it has erred because of readiness to indulge, its purification necessarily also involves pain. Here, too, healing takes place by opposites.[185] For this reason the soul that is being purified suffers pain in the places of punishment in the underworld through chastisement. Yet if the soul is incorporeal, it cannot be affected. How then is it chastised? At least some sort of body must in any case be attached to it, which by undergoing immoderate <internal> expansion or contraction[186] as a result of immoderate cooling or heating, causes pain to the soul by sympathetic affection,[187] just as here, when our present body suffers, the soul has pain because of the physical bondage and the sympathetic affection that arises from this; for in itself the incorporeal is not affected by anything.

Of what kind, then, is this body that is attached to it? It is not, of course, like our present body, for this had disintegrated into the elements it was composed of. Rather, it is what we call the pneumatic body.[188] In this, therefore, spirit and desire are present at any rate as in a substrate, and they are inseparable from it. How is this evident? From the fact that after the departure of the soul from this solid body, spirit and desire must still be present in the soul, for if they were not and the soul at its departure from the body was also separated from these affections, it would be completely pure and liberated from <the domain of> becoming. Yet having been liberated from <the domain of> becoming and from these affections it would have ascended and it would not enter the places of punishment in the underworld. For as we said,[189] when it descended into <the world of> becoming, these affections were given to it for the reasons mentioned;[190] yet it is impossible for it to be separated from <the world of> becoming without purifying itself. Since it moves itself and fell out of the good of its own accord, it must, in order to be lifted up again, purify itself. The places of punishment in the underworld cannot lift it upward, but only cause it to turn in on itself to such an extent that it ends up condemning itself and is purified by its own initiative and casts off willingly <the things> with which it was willingly bound by sympathetic affection. This is why they say[191] that after the places of punishment in the underworld it comes back here for as long as it takes for it to purify itself,[192] and is lifted upwards, liberating itself from <the world of> becoming, and then it does away also with spirit and desire together with this vehicle, I mean the *pneuma*; but <they say that> after this there is yet another body eternally attached to it, which is celestial and therefore eternal, which is called luminous or astral.[193] For as <the soul> belongs to the cosmic entities, it must have a share assigned to it which it manages, being part of the cosmos;[194] and if it is always in motion and always has to be active, it must have a body eternally attached to it which it will keep alive always; this is why they say the soul always has the luminous body, since this is eternal. Because of what has been said, then, the pneumatic body must exist, and spirit and desire must be inseparable from it.

It is clear that, just as the vital and appetitive faculties of the non-rational soul are present in the *pneuma*, likewise this is also the case with the cognitive faculties: for if the inferior faculties are separable from the solid body, so much the more will this be the case with the superior ones; and the cognitive ones, by which I mean imagination and sense perception, are superior.[195] However, even if the non-rational faculties of the soul have their being in this <i.e. the pneumatic body>, yet certain traces proceed from this also to the solid body,[196] just as we have said that the common insights proceed from the intellect to all <people>.[197] For that illuminations of the non-rational soul proceed even as far as this body, is clear. For spirit stirs up the blood in the region of the heart and causes there to be some sort of boiling, while desire brings the liver in this or that condition according to its own movements,[198] and all senses illuminate the brain;[199] for it is from there that the sensitive faculty is supplied to the sense organs through the nerves, and when the brain is affected, the senses become numb, as is shown by doctors;[200] for when what is called the membrane-protector[201] is put upon the cerebral membrane, the animal becomes insensitive and immobile (the membrane is a kind of skin that protects the brain), and when the back part has been affected, the higher part of the person affected has the benefit of perception, while the lower parts become insensitive because the sensitive faculty is no longer supplied by the brain when the organ, I mean the nerve, has been affected; and if the nerve is bound, the lower part in turn becomes insensitive, whereas the upper part remains sensitive.[202]

It is therefore clear also from what we have said that there is such a thing as the pneumatic body, and that spirit and desire are inseparable from it. And this has become even clearer from the evidence of the facts themselves. Where do the shadowy appearances come from that manifest themselves around tombs?[203] For the soul does not have a shape nor is it visible at all. Yet they say that unpurified souls after their departure from this body wander for a while with the *pneuma* and exhibit this <i.e. the pneumatic body> around the tombs. This is why one needs to take care to lead a good life; for they say that because this *pneuma* is solidified as a result of an unhealthy regimen, the soul is dragged down towards the emotions. And they say that it also has something of the life of plants: for <they say that> these are nourished, yet not nourished in the way this <solid> body is, but by means of vapours, and not part by part but as a whole by the whole, so to speak, in the way in which sponges absorb vapours.[204] This is why serious people apply themselves to a light and rather dry regimen, because <by this regimen> the *pneuma* is not solidified but becomes lighter.[205] To this end, they say, they even adopt purgatives;[206] while this <solid> body is washed by water, this <pneumatic body> is cleansed by purgatives that operate by means of vapours; for it is nourished by some vapours, but purged by others.[207] They say that it is not equipped with different organs, but is active as a whole and throughout by means of the senses and apprehends the objects of perception.[208] This is why Aristotle in the *Metaphysics* says that sense perception, properly speaking, is one, and the sense organ, properly speaking, is one,[209] where by sense organ he means the *pneuma* in which the sensitive faculty as a whole and entirely apprehends the various objects of perception. How, then, is it sometimes evidently equipped with different organs when it manifests itself around tombs and sometimes has a human-like shape, sometimes even the shape of another animal?[210] To this they answer first this: it often happens that it has its human-like shape because it <the *pneuma*> has been solidified because of a bad regimen and compressed together with the surrounding body, as happens with ice; for this is compressed into the form of the vessels in which it is frozen.[211] What, then, is the origin of the different shapes it evidently has? Perhaps, they say, when the soul wishes to show this, by stirring up imagination it moulds <this pneumatic body> along with it, or even, perhaps, with the assistance of demons being involved as well,[212] it appears and again disappears as it becomes more compact and again widens; for being airy, when it gets more compact and contracts it becomes visible, and again it becomes invisible as a result of extension and widening.

In response to all this someone will raise the question whether it is human souls at all which, by means of their own *pneuma*, appear around tombs and whether it is not some sort of wandering demons, which naturally can change into anything because of the flexible nature of their pneumatic bodies that are attached to them, when they evidently do this continuously. And how could <human> souls, too, be moulded here for a short time? Do they do this of their own accord or not? For if they did this of their own accord, it <i.e. the soul> would never move to a different place; for <as it is>, it moves to the places of punishment below the earth. Yet if it is not of its own accord but because it is forced by Providence to remain <where it is>, how then will its power towards evil increase and be capable of more than it is here? Yet if it lays off the burden of the solid body, it ought rather to be relieved of heaviness and in a state of consciousness <of its own faults> and having been, so to speak, close to the places of punishment below the earth, become more moderate. As it is, it does the evil things which it could not do even here.[213]

<Transition to the commentary>
In the first book he <i.e. Aristotle> discusses the opinions about the soul of those before him; he will expound their doctrines, and he will accept those doctrines that were correct, and refute them if something they thought about the soul was wrong. In the second book, he will expound his own doctrine of the soul, and he will discuss it first more in general and in rough outline, next individually according to each faculty of the soul. Also in the second book, after discussing the soul in general, he will discuss individually the vegetative and the non-rational soul, and in the third book the rational soul;[214] he mentions the rational soul also in book two and the non-rational in book three. As he is used to doing in all his treatises on natural subjects, towards the end of the treatises lifting himself up to the transcendent causes of natural things, he does so here, too. For also in the *Physics*,[215] towards the end, when he discusses movement and is seeking the cause of movement, he lifts himself up to the first cause and principle of movement, and he says that the first mover has to be unmoved; for if that were moved, not even the things that are moved would remain in their <state of> being moved. Consequently, if there are things that are always in motion, it is necessary that what causes their movement is unmoved. Next, having sung its praise by saying that it is incorporeal and eternal and omnipotent, he says: 'On such a principle, then, the heavens and the world depend.'[216] For the complete student of nature must, after stating the natural causes, ascend to the transcendent causes and not remain in these <i.e. the natural ones>. This is what he has done in his *On Coming-to-Be and Perishing*.[217]

<Chapter 1>

402a1 Considering knowing[218] to belong to the things that are fine and valuable ...

The introduction contains an eulogy on the study of the soul and an encouragement to obtain knowledge of it, or rather an encouragement for those who are serious about it and are worthy of this kind of study, but a discouragement for those who are the opposite of these.[219] It seems that by having two introductions he encourages by means of the one, but discourages by means of the other: by saying that knowing is fine and valuable and that the study of the soul is most valuable and most exact, he seems to encourage all people to it; on the other hand, by saying that 'it is in all respects and in all senses most difficult to obtain some plausible conviction about it' (402a10-11), he seems to discourage people from it. Consequently, by means of these two introductions it is made clear that he encourages to the lectures on the study of the soul only those who are serious about it. After this praise and encouragement he adds the reason why the study of the soul is difficult, and then he sets out a number of problems that ought to be examined with a view to the account of the soul.

Now, Alexander, as Plutarch says,[220] while in fact wanting to give a display of his own doctrines and to pull Aristotle's doctrines down to his own, pretended to comment on this treatise as well.[221] While setting forth his own distorted view based on introductions[222] he interpreted the introduction itself in a distorted way by saying that the words 'considering knowing to belong to the things that are fine and valuable' are elliptical: 'Considering what?', he says. 'One should understand "that it is fine and valuable" in addition.'[223] Thus Alexander.

The Attic interpreters[224] have interpreted this phrase more naturally: 'Knowing', they say, 'we consider to be one of the things that are fine and valuable.' Moreover, it is quite normal for Aristotle to praise knowing in this way; for this reason, too, in the *Metaphysics* he begins like this: 'All men naturally long for knowing; a sign of this is the delight they take in the senses.'[225]

It is important to ask what he means when saying that knowing is fine and valuable. For instance, is all knowing good, even knowing evil things themselves? I reply: Yes, even knowing evil things is good, genuine knowing; for, as Plato says, and correctly says, knowledge[226] of evil causes us to avoid it, but ignorance of the good causes us to fall into what is evil.[227] Consequently, ignorance of evil, conversely, causes us to get involved in what is evil, but knowledge of what is good causes us to cleave to good.

The word 'knowing' is used in three ways: either in the sense of scientific understanding,[228] as Plato says in the *Phaedo*, 'For knowing is that someone after gaining understanding of something holds on to it and has not rejected it',[229] and in the *Gorgias*;[230] or it means knowledge in general outline and broadly speaking, as he <i.e. Aristotle> himself says in the *Physics*, 'Since knowing and understanding are concerned with all branches of scientific understanding',[231] for by 'knowing' he signifies knowledge in general outline, by 'understanding' he signifies exact knowledge; or it has the common meaning of every kind of knowing, which he also adopted in the passage of the *Metaphysics* mentioned above.

402a1 ... but one kind <of knowing> more so than the other, either in exactness or because it is concerned with things that are superior and more admirable; for both of these reasons we may reasonably rank the inquiry into the soul among the things of primary importance.

The whole idea of the introduction is as follows. All knowledge, he says, we consider to be fine and valuable, but one kind to be more valuable and fine than the other for two reasons, either because the subject matter with which the knowledge is concerned is superior, or because the knowledge is more exact. Astronomy,[232] for instance, is finer than medicine because it is concerned with a more valuable subject; for the one is concerned with the heavenly bodies, the other with human bodies. Yet astronomical knowledge is also superior to medicine in being more exact; consequently, in both respects astronomy is more valuable than medicine, both in subject matter and in the kind of knowledge. Again, geometry is more valuable than mechanics in both respects,[233] because geometry is concerned with a subject that is without matter (for geometrical figures are in themselves without body and without magnitude; for if the circle had magnitude, it would always be finite, say, a cubit in size; and if that were the case, there would not be a circle of two cubits or of three cubits or any other circle apart from the one which has a magnitude of one cubit; and if it were a body, it would always be finite; for example, if it were of bronze, there would not exist an iron or wooden circle or in general none made of any other body than the bronze; consequently, the subject matter of geometry as a whole is without matter). Mechanics, however, is concerned with bodies and magnitudes. Therefore geometry is more valuable than mechanics. It is so also as far as the kind of knowledge is concerned, for the former is infallible, the three angles of every triangle being always equal to two right angles, not just broadly speaking but with complete exactness and without the slightest variation, the hypotenuse always being asymmetrical with the side. However, the theorems of mechanics are not exact, since it is concerned with bodies and magnitudes.

A similar relation exists between arithmetic and harmonics:[234] since arithmetic deals with relations between numbers, its subject is also superior, this being without matter, whereas the other is concerned with a body, viz. with strings and magnitudes of sounds, and for this reason arithmetical knowledge is more exact. Since that form of knowledge is finest that is superior in either of these two respects, and since both respects are seen to apply to the soul, the study of the soul therefore is valuable and fine in both respects.

The study of the soul is valuable because it is concerned with an awesome subject, the soul itself, which is the finest of all things here.[235] But the study of the soul is also more valuable in being more exact. In what way the study of the soul is more exact, we may learn as follows. In *On Demonstration*[236] Aristotle supplies us with two rules by which we can distinguish what is more exact. If, he says, there are two sciences and you want to know which one is more exact, there are two ways of knowing this. If the one demonstrates the principles of the other, then the one which demonstrates the principles is more exact, as physics is more exact than medicine, for physics demonstrates the principles of medicine.[237] Again, geometry is more exact than mechanics, for geometry demonstrates the principles of mechanics. Arithmetic is more exact than harmonics, for the principles of harmonics are demonstrated in arithmetic. First, philosophy is more exact than all sciences together, for it demonstrates the principles of all sciences. Again, he says, the more exact science is the one that is concerned with a subject that is without matter, such as geometry, arithmetic, and theology.[238] For this reason he says in the *Metaphysics* that the study of the intelligibles is both very easy and difficult.[239] It is very easy because it is concerned with the objects that are stable and always the same; the divine objects are clearest, because they are unchanging in respect of being, in respect of potentiality, and in respect of actuality all at once.[240] For this reason it is very easy, but it is difficult because of our weakness, for being embodied and subjected to emotions we do not have the power to look into their light, just as what happens with bats: the sun being the clearest, they cannot look into its rays because of the weakness of their eyes.[241] It would seem, then, to them that the light of the stars is brighter, since it is commensurate to them. The same applies to our relation to the intelligible objects.

Since that science is more exact which is concerned with a subject that is without matter or which demonstrates the principles, in which of both ways is the study of the soul more exact? Evidently in that it is concerned with a subject that is without matter; for it does not demonstrate the principles of other sciences. If the soul is without matter in all respects, it is also immortal in every way. This is the ground on which Alexander actually regards this passage as spurious; he says that the sentence 'but one kind <of knowledge> more than the other, either in exactness or because it is concerned with things that are superior and more admirable' does not belong to the text and was added to it, in order to prevent the interpreter of this passage from being compelled to say that the study of the soul is more exact because it is concerned with a subject that is without matter, viz. the soul itself, in accordance with the Aristotelian rules;[242] having conceded that the soul is without matter, he will necessarily also grant that it is immortal.[243]

'Superior and more admirable' (402a2-3): 'superior' with a view to the nature of the object, 'more admirable' with a view to our judgement.

'For both of these reasons we may reasonably rank the inquiry into the soul among the things of most primary importance' (402a3-4): 'For both of these reasons', Alexander says, 'means because it is fine and because it is valuable', since he regards the adjoining passage as spurious. By 'for both of these reasons', he <i.e. Aristotle> means: because of the exactness of the study and because of the awesomeness of the subject-matter. He says 'inquiry' instead of knowledge, because people who possess scientific knowledge we call inquirers.[244]

'... we may rank <the inquiry into the soul> among the things of most primary importance' (402a4): He does not say 'of supreme importance', but of most primary importance,[245] for it is the study of the intelligible objects, which are in all respects unchanging in being, in potentiality and in actuality, that is of supreme importance; the study of the soul comes second because, even though its being is unchanging, its actuality is not.[246] For this reason Plato said that the soul is identical to the immortal beings in name only, because only what is unchanging in all respects is immortal in the proper sense.[247] The soul, however, does change with respect to its actuality, and for this reason it is identical to the immortal beings in name only. Likewise one may call the heavenly bodies identical to the immortals in name only, for they change, too, in place, if not in being.[248] 'Of primary importance', then, clearly means primary to what comes after it; for the soul occupies the first rank after the intelligibles.

402a4 Moreover, it would seem that the knowledge of the soul contributes greatly to truth as a whole.

The knowledge of the soul, he says, is admirable and valuable in itself, and also, he says, because it contributes to truth as a whole, i.e. to philosophy as a whole; for saying 'truth' is the same as saying 'philosophy', since genuine wisdom is truth; for there is no falsehood in it. Consequently, if it contributes to philosophy as a whole, it is evident that it contributes to ethical, theological, and natural philosophy. It contributes to ethical philosophy because it is impossible for us to adorn our character without having studied the faculties of the soul. If virtue is adornment of the soul, and if adornment is a fine arrangement of the faculties of the soul, and if someone who has not studied their nature cannot arrange them, the ethical philosopher will also discuss the soul, as he <i.e. Aristotle> himself says in the *Ethics*.[249]

It also contributes to theology, for a question we are examining regarding the separate intellect that is in us is whether it, too, is immortal.[250] Since the intellect is intellect[251] of intelligible objects, and since concerning relational things the person who knows the one will also know the rest, it is evident that the study of our intellect contributes greatly to theology as well. For this reason he says in the treatise *On the Parts of Animals*[252] that the student of nature cannot discuss the soul as a whole, for if he were to discuss the soul as a whole, he should also have to discuss the intellect, and if that is the case, also the intelligible objects, for the intellect is the intellection of the intelligible objects. However, this belongs to theology and to first philosophy.

Again, if it is the task of the student of nature to discuss bodies and their forms and faculties, and if among the forms embedded in bodies the soul is finest, it also contributes to our study of nature.

402a6 ... especially with regard to nature.

He has added 'especially with regard to nature' because what contributes is different from that to which it contributes.[253] Now it does not contribute by being a part of the treatment of ethics or of that of theology; rather, the study of the soul is a study of the subject in question of its own accord. When dealing with theology, it <i.e. the soul> turns in to the intelligible and the divine objects, and it examines the rank orders there, and when it turns in on the intelligible objects it also turns in on itself and it will deal with its own being and rank; for the soul is the lowest species of the intelligible and divine objects.[254] On the other hand, when it deals with characters and studies the ranks of the virtues, it will also deal with its own faculties, to which the virtues belong. Yet by being a part of the study of nature it contributes, for nature and soul are different things.[255] In what way it contributes, he adds now:

402a6 For it is, in a way, the principle of living beings.

It is a principle both in the sense of a productive and a formative and a final principle, for these are the principles in the proper sense. The soul is a principle in the sense of a productive principle, in that it sets the living being in motion by means of its wishing only, and does not require any kind of dislodgement; in the sense of a formative principle, in that it is the soul that defines the form of the living being and, simply speaking, of all ensouled beings; for ensouled forms are said to be what they are just in virtue of their soul, for what is superior in each of the natural objects, Aristotle himself says,[256] is the form of each object; and in ensouled beings this is the soul. It is a final principle, in that it is that for the sake of which the body exists; for the body exists for the sake of something, and the soul is that for the sake of which it exists. For this reason, the way in which living beings are equipped with organs[257] is different according to the peculiar nature of the soul that is in each of them: it is different in humans, different in birds, different in land animals, different in animals that live in water, and in each of these <kinds> there is a great depth,[258] since each kind of animal is equipped according to the faculty of the soul that masters it; they are different in respect of being characterised by the spirited part or by the desiring part, on which it is not now the time to speak. He has added 'in a way', because the proximate principle of living beings is their nature, not the soul.

402a7 We seek to view it and to get to know both its nature and its essence ...

'View'[259] might roughly be taken to mean 'intuitively grasping what is said about it', whereas 'getting to know'[260] means 'searching for it accurately'. For we say that we view a particular thing when we simply grasp it, but that we get to know it when in addition we learn its attributes. By 'nature and essence'[261] we have to understand either pleonastically the same thing, in that the second term explains the first, i.e. 'I use the term "nature" instead of "being"', or by nature he means the genus to which the soul belongs, by being its definition, e.g. under what genus is it ranked, substance or quantity or quality? Those who say that the soul is a mixture might say that the soul is ranked under quality, those who say that it is a proportion that it is ranked under quantity.[262] Thereafter, having grasped its genus, we should also learn the differentiae that constitute it and thus give its definition, for the definition signifies the essences of things.

402a8 ... and after that its attributes.

He does not mean that one should look for the things that belong to it accidentally,[263] as white belongs to a body accidentally, but the things that accompany it essentially. This, then, is the way in which we have to understand 'its attributes', just as in the definition the conclusion of the syllogism <is expressed>. 'For a syllogism', he says, 'is a statement in which, some things being given, something different from the things that are given necessarily follows.'[264] Just as in this passage he does not mean that the conclusion belongs accidentally to the premises, but the words signify that which in itself necessarily follows from them, likewise it should be understood in the present passage.

402a9 Some of these are believed to be affections peculiar to the soul, others to be common[265] <to the soul and to the body> and to be attributes of living beings in virtue of the soul.

As for the things that necessarily accompany the soul, some accompany the soul alone, others accompany the whole living being, I mean the living being that consists of a soul and a body; the affections[266] of the soul are thinking (for this is peculiar to the rational soul itself in itself), the other affections are perceiving, imagining, being angry, desiring, and anything else of this nature; these are common to the composite.[267] For he takes the whole soul as one thing and says that some of its affections are peculiar to it, not to all kind of soul without further qualification, but to the soul roughly speaking, it being evident that they are peculiar to the rational soul; for the rational soul, too, is in the soul taken without further qualification. As for the other souls, no affection is peculiar to them, since their essence is not separate either. The word 'affection' is used in two meanings: it means either affection which leads to destruction or affection leading to perfection.[268] For we say that wood is affected by fire, but in the sense that this leads to its destruction; yet we also say that the senses are affected by the objects of perception: it is evident that this is in the sense of being perfected and being brought from potentiality to actuality. In this way Plato says in the *Sophist* of the whole that the whole is not one, but is affected by the one,[269] thereby evidently meaning being affected in the sense of being perfected; for the whole is not the same as the one, since the whole is a whole consisting of parts, and the parts are many, not one; consequently, the whole is not one, since it has its being in many things, but it has the one as something by which it is affected; for it has been affected by the one, thereby adopting its proper perfection.

On the basis of this passage we can refute Andronicus of Rhodes,[270] who declared *On Interpretation* spurious: since Aristotle there says that thoughts are affections of the soul, as it is said in *On the Soul*, Andronicus says that this is nowhere stated in *On the Soul*, so that either *On the Soul* or *On Interpretation* must be spurious; but *On the Soul* has been agreed to be by Aristotle; therefore, *On Interpretation* is spurious. We reply that in this passage by affections peculiar to the soul Aristotle means nothing else than thoughts, so that this is what he referred to in *On Interpretation*.[271]

402a10 In all respects and in all ways it is most difficult to obtain a plausible conviction about it.

We have said that in the introduction he praises the study of the soul and encourages the more serious people to it, but discourages those who take a more indifferent attitude to it. On this basis, then, in order to achieve this, he wants to show that the study of the soul is difficult. In what way it is difficult, he has already said earlier, viz. in that we want to view its nature and its essence, i.e. we want to discover what the definition of the soul is. This search for the definition, he says, is most difficult, both in general with respect to all things, and in particular with respect to the soul: in general, he says,[272] as far as definitions are concerned, one has to examine, first, whether there is one method according to which it is possible to give definitions of all things, or many; and if there is one method, one has to find out what this method is; and if there are many, one has to find out how many they are in number and of what nature they are. Moreover, when we have found out that there are so many, say two methods, and of what nature they are, viz. description and definition,[273] then in addition to these we have to face a third question, viz. what kind of methods we have to use for what kind of things. Furthermore, even when we have discovered this, a further question presents itself: since a definition consists of genera and differentiae, what is the genus of the present thing and what are its differentiae by which the genus is divided? We must ask this in order to know, with regard to the present subject, what the constitutive[274] differentiae are so that by combining these with the genus we state its definition. This is the general reason why it is difficult to obtain the definition of the soul, since these problems apply to every definition; in particular, for the soul, an even greater difficulty is presented by the account of the soul, as he expounds in the next sentence.

402a11 Since this question is common to many other <areas> ...

The search for a definition, he says, is common to many things. He says 'many', as it is not possible to give definitions of all things (neither the most general things nor things which cannot be divided); rather, these things are signified by means of description, the most general things by the properties which are essential to them, the indivisible things by means of their proper attributes.

402a12 ... I mean the inquiry into its being and into what it is ...

Since the word 'being' has many meanings ('genus', 'matter', 'definition', sometimes also 'existence'[275] in all its forms), for this reason, after saying 'the inquiry into being' he explains this by adding 'and into what it is', in order to signify the definition.

402a13 ... one might easily think that there is one method that applies to all things in respect of which we want to know their being, just as we want <to know> a demonstration[276] of its proper attributes [and the consequence of this would be that we would have to seek this method].

There is a difference between 'accidental' and 'attribute'.[277] 'Accidental' is what is the opposite of essence, which is not present by itself nor belongs to things in virtue of their essence, but which is added to them from outside, just as black and white are added to bodies; but 'attribute' is what accompanies beings necessarily, as we say that the conclusion is attributed to the premises,[278] not because the conclusion is accidental to the premises, but because it follows from them necessarily. We apply the word 'accidental' to things of this kind, because it is added to other things, even in those cases where it belongs to them necessarily and because they are as they are. But accidental in the proper sense does not follow from the fact that things are as they are; one may, at least, think even of a white raven. In this case, then, one may also give the name 'proper attributes'[279] to those <attributes> that belong to things primarily and by themselves and whose elimination also eliminates the things to which they belong and vice versa; for instance, it is an attribute of man to be capable of receiving knowledge, and of every triangle to have three angles that are equal to two right angles or for its two sides to be longer than the remaining <third>. These things are said to belong to the things <in question> primarily and by themselves, primarily because they immediately belong to those things only and to no other thing, by themselves, because they are essential <to the things they belong to>. This is also the reason why they can be reversed: if something is a man, then it is capable of receiving knowledge and vice versa, and if something is a triangle, then necessarily the three angles are equal to two right ones and the two sides are longer than the remaining <third>, and vice versa. This, then, he calls 'proper attributes'. This is also primary and by itself; 'by itself' means 'in virtue of the essence <of the thing to which they belong>'. Not that, if something <belongs to something> by itself, it also <belongs> primarily; for in most cases 'by itself' is part of 'primarily'. For 'living being' is an attribute of man by itself, but not primarily; therefore, even if something is not a man, it may still be a living being, so that it does not belong to human being primarily. Similarly shape belongs to triangle by itself, but not primarily; for even if something is not a triangle, it may still be a shape. And why do I talk of shape? Indeed, not even does 'rectilinear' belong primarily to the triangle, although it does belong to it by itself. For something may be rectilinear, even if it is not a triangle. This is what he means by being a proper attribute, the things that belong to something primarily, which belong to the thing exclusively, and to every <individual instance of the thing> and always and by itself, so that it can be reversed. Concerning these matters he says in the *On Demonstration* that demonstration is concerned with these <attributes> only, neither with what is accidental to a thing nor with what, though belonging by itself, does not belong primarily.[280] And this is reasonable, for demonstration is scientific knowledge, and scientific knowledge is infallible and stable because it is always concerned with the same things and remains the same, and for this reason it is impossible that there should be demonstration of things that are accidental and which are different in different circumstances and which come and go. Again, if demonstration is concerned with what is disputed, and the things that belong to something by themselves and not primarily are agreed on for the most part, e.g. that 'living being' belongs to man and 'shape' to triangle, demonstration of these will not be demonstration in the proper sense. He shows in these passages that there is no demonstration of the most general genera, since there is no definition either, but we signify them by means of description; for every proper demonstration is what proves the things caused on the basis of the causes, and the things that are parts on the basis of the whole. For instance, how do we demonstrate that man is a substance? Through the middle term 'living being': because every living being is a substance. Consequently, the cause of man's being a substance is that every living being is a substance. This is more general too: that every living being is a substance is more general than that man is a substance. Again, given that something is a triangle, for this reason its three angles are equal to two right angles, and again, given that it is a triangle, its two sides are longer than the remaining one; but it is not that, because its angles are equal to two right ones, for that reason it is also a triangle. This, then, is demonstration proper.

There is also a form of demonstration called inferential, which proves the causes on the basis of the things caused, as Aristotle practises himself in the *On the Heavens*, where he uses the illumination of the moon as a demonstration that it is spherical.[281] Yet what ought to be demonstrated was, conversely, that it is spherical and that for that reason it was illuminated in that way. We use this way of demonstration when what is caused is clearer to us than the cause, as is the case with the moon: the thing caused, the illumination, is clearer to us than the cause, the fact that it is spherical. We know that twice a month it becomes crescent-shaped, when it has been in conjunction <with the sun> and when it is about to get into conjunction, and twice a month it becomes semicircular, twice gibbous and once full; this is because it is spherical. If it were a flat plate, it would either be illuminated completely or not be illuminated at all; as it is, since the sun is higher, when its position is diametrically opposed to the moon, we can see, because of our middle position, that the complete semicircle which is turned to us, with which it comes into contact, is illuminated, but as it comes closer the illumination of the part we are facing is constantly reduced, while the illumination of the part that is beyond our sight is increased, since, as I said, the sun is higher than the moon; and in this way, little by little, until it has reached the same perpendicular as the moon, so that we are no longer in a middle position between both of them, but both are at one and the same side of us, it causes the side facing us to be unilluminated, but it illuminates the side beyond our sight. Proof of this is also to be obtained from our common experience. If someone were to create a large ball, and he would colour the one hemisphere white, the other black, and then throw the ball high up into the air, and something would turn it aside a little, while the white hemisphere happens to be upward and the ball is subsequently turned sideway, it will be seen as becoming a slender, crescent-shaped figure, and then, when the ball is partially turned sideway, we see the other shapes occur, and finally, when the white hemisphere is turned downwards completely, if it is at great height, the white hemisphere will be seen as having the shape of a flat plate. This, then, by way of digression from the present subject.

A similar inferential demonstration we call 'if there is smoke here, there is fire too'. For smoke is an indication of fire. The irrefutable sign is an indication, as smoke is of fire, just as the moon being illuminated in a particular way is an indication of its being spherical. What is refutable is not called an indication, but a sign;[282] that is, when what is caused is not in all circumstances accompanied by the cause, as in the following: she is pale, because she has given birth; for being pale is not always accompanied by having given birth. It is refutable, and therefore it is not an indication but a sign, just as standing near a freshly slaughtered body is a sign of having killed it. Now demonstration is concerned with the proper attributes, of which we said that they belong <to things> primarily and by themselves. One might therefore suspect, he says, that just as there is one demonstrative method of these things, likewise there is one method for grasping the definition of each particular thing. But even if there is one, we must find out of what nature it is.

402a16 But if there is not one common method concerned with what something is, our discussion will be even more difficult; for then we have to grasp concerning each particular thing what the method is.

If there were one method, the only question would be what it is; but since there are more than one, there are more questions: how many they are in number, of what nature they are in kind, and which one we must use for what thing. For the words 'We will have to grasp concerning each particular thing what the method is' mean what kind of method should be adopted concerning what kind of thing.

402a19 And even if it is clear whether this is demonstration or division or some other method, [there are still many problems left and scope for error ...]

This he says *ex hypothesi*. If after finding all that has been listed, he says, it actually becomes clear to us that this is the method by which we reach definitions, say, demonstrative or by means of division or

48   *Translation*

definition, then another problem follows not smaller than the ones mentioned; what this problem is, he adds:

10   **402a21** ... as to the question from what basis the inquiry should proceed, (he says).[283] For every inquiry has a different starting point, as is the case with numbers and planes.

That is to say, under what genus shall we rank the present subject, since there is not one genus of beings but ten, and one thing is ranked under one genus, another under another.[284] 'As is the case with numbers and planes', he says. As starting-points for these he mentions, of number, the definite quantity, and of plane, the continuous, or otherwise one could mention as starting-points of these, of number the monad, of plane the line or the point; for when these things are in flux, the latter yields the line, the former the plane figure.[285] However, these starting-points are connected and as it were elementary starting-points, but the continuous and the definite are dissociated. Again, connected starting-points often contribute to our statement of definitions, as with numbers: we say that a number is a plurality consisting of monads. Now what we look for, he says, is under what genus the present subject should be brought (for of many things the genus is disputed), so that, when we have discovered this and have divided it into its proper differentiae, in this way we can state the definitions.

402a23 First, then, it may well be necessary to analyse <it and to say> to which of the genera it belongs and what it is.

Having finished with the problems he raised about definitions in general, which evidently also present themselves with the soul, he now starts with the problems concerning the soul with regard to acquiring its definition. Concerning the soul, too, he says, we must raise the question under what genus we shall rank it; for there is great controversy about this. Some rank it under the heading of substance, others under quantity. Among these is Xenocrates; the soul, he says, is a number moving itself,[286] and number is brought under quantity, if that is what he means rather than something different to which he refers by these words in the form of a riddle. Others say that it belongs under quality. Among these are the doctors who say that it is a mixture;[287] to this group belong also those who say that it is an actuality;[288] for we shall learn in what way Aristotle calls the soul actuality. Those who say that it is a proportion of the elements would seem to rank it under the <category of> relative; for the twofold or the one-and-a-half belong to the category of relative, for twofold is of something. So far, then, the genus remains controversial.

Yet when we find[289] that it is a substance, a further question arises, viz. whether it is corporeal or incorporeal and, if it is corporeal, whether it is simple or composite, and if it is incorporeal, whether it is separable or inseparable; and whether there is one soul in each <living being> or many, and if there is one, whether it has one form or many different faculties, and what the difference between the faculties is; and if there are many, whether they are many in number or also in species, and if in species, whether they are different in genus as well or not; for what is different in species is not in all cases different in genus, e.g. man and horse, whereas what is different in genus is necessarily also different in species, such as stone and living being. These questions, and others in addition to these, must be examined in order to obtain the definition of the soul.

'First, then, it may well be necessary to analyse <it and to say> to what genus it belongs and what it is.' (402a23) That is, one must learn its genus on the basis of division, the genus that belongs to the category of what-it-is. We learnt in the Introductions[290] that the genera belong to the category of the what-it-is.[291] For when we are asked what a man is, we say: a living being. And if someone who does not know what a date-palm is and asks it, we reply that it is a tree. First of all, therefore, we should know what the soul is; for just as divine Plato says in the *Phaedrus*,[292] there is one starting-point of good planning: one should know what it is one is planning about, or else one necessarily fails completely. In our inquiry into the soul, therefore, if we have not learnt first what it is, whether it is a substance or a quantity, and if it is a substance (which it is) but instead of calling it a substance we called it quantity or quality or any other of the categories, then, if we drew our conclusions in accordance with our starting-point, we would inevitably fail completely, because we look for one thing instead of the other. Moreover, Aristotle says in the *Physics*: 'Since in all methods of inquiry which are concerned with starting-points or causes or elements, having knowledge and scientific understanding are achieved by getting to know these <starting-points, etc.>'.[293] Now in order to know things there is a need to know the starting-points, and since these differ from one area to another, we must find out what the starting-point of the soul is, and much more so in as much as the question of the starting point is much more problematic with regard to the soul than in other fields.

402a25 Moreover, <we should analyse> whether it belongs to what is potentially or whether it rather is some sort of actuality. [For the difference between these is not small.]

Still proceeding according to the method of division, he takes the correct section of the division and subdivides this. Having asked whether it is a substance or a quantity or a quality or any other of the categories, he has passed over the others and assumed that it is a substance; then he finally subdivides this into corporeal and incorporeal. For instead of saying corporeal or incorporeal, he says 'whether it belongs to what is potentially or whether it rather is some sort of actuality'. By what is potentially he means the corporeal, by actuality he means the incorporeal. For generally speaking, every body is potentially,[294] and potentially in respect of substance or quantity or quality or change of place. Now all bodies subject to coming to be and passing away are potentially, in accordance with all meanings of 'potentially'; we are potentially humans in the seed and in the menstrual blood,[295] and being children we potentially have the size of a man. Similarly with regard to 'potentially' in the qualitative sense: while being hot, we are potentially cold, and while sitting, we potentially move. The celestial bodies have potentiality only with regard to change of place: when the sun rises, it is potentially in the centre of the heavens, and when it has got there in actuality, it is potentially setting; the same applies to the other celestial bodies. Now we observe that all bodies have potentiality, and this is the reason why he <i.e. Aristotle> referred to the body by means of the word 'potentially'. However, when saying 'what is potentially' instead of 'the body', why, in the case of the incorporeal, does he not say 'actually' in the dative, but 'actuality' in the nominative?[296] For 'potentiality' and 'potentially' are different,[297] and similarly 'actuality' and 'actually' are different. For matter is only potentiality; for it is potentially everything, but actually nothing. Form is only actuality; now, what consists of matter and form is both potentially and actually. These things accompany each other, and that which is potentially is also actually. For all forms are potentially in matter, which actually becomes now this, then that. Being potentially a man now, at some point it will actually become a man. Or rather, it has both 'potentially' and 'actually';[298] since it is never deprived of form, this form actually is a particular thing, but potentially it is something else: the form of the seed is potentially man. Well, since what is actually, is also in what is potentially, and since in the things divine and incorporeal 'potentially' does not occur, since there is no matter, for that reason 'actually' does not occur there either (for it is not that they are actually a particular thing, but they are actualities themselves,[299] being pure forms without matter, just as he says in *On Interpretation* that things that lack potentiality are actualities, whereas he does not say that they are actually),[300] for this reason, therefore, by contrasting the immaterial and incorporeal with the material and composite nature, he says 'whether it belongs to the things that are potentially', i.e. the bodies, 'which are potentially', i.e. in matter, 'or some sort of actuality', i.e. some sort of pure and immaterial form; 'for this makes no small difference', i.e. the difference between corporeal and incorporeal is not small.

402b1 One must also examine whether it is divided or undivided.

This 'divided or undivided', as Alexander also thinks,[301] we may take as applying to the faculties of the soul, i.e. whether it consists of many faculties or whether it is undivided. Democritus claims that it is undivided and not consisting of many faculties, for he says that thinking is the same as perceiving and that they proceed from one faculty.[302] We can also understand the passage in the following way, whether the soul in its unqualified sense is one in each <living being>, or divided into different souls, so that there are more souls in each <living being>. It is obvious that it is possible to say both <that there are> more and <that there is> one; 'more', because the soul of plants and the non-rational soul differ from one another in kind, and likewise the non-rational and the rational soul, and they are separate from one another; but 'one', because of the kinship and the sympathetic relationship[303] between them. For indeed, also from reason activities penetrate as far as the soul of plants, and their movements and lives, so to speak, bring reason into harmony with themselves.[304] In this way, then, it is both one and not one. But it is better to interpret the words 'divided or undivided' as follows, viz. that he says whether there is one soul in all ensouled beings or many, and if there are many, whether they differ in species only or also in genus. Those who say that it is a mixture[305] are likely to say that it is one, and that it is changed in relation to the peculiarity of the mixture which is present in each individual, just as the air which is common and inhaled by all is one in relation to the peculiarity in each of the living beings. But these people turn what is higher into what is lower and make what is caused more powerful than the causes; for <what they say is that> the unensouled body is the cause of soul, the lifeless of life, the unmoved of what has the capacity to move, the non-rational of what is not non-rational, and so forth.

402b1 ... and whether the whole soul is of one and the same kind or not; and if it is not of one and the same kind, whether it is different in species or in genus.

Following the question 'many or one', given that there are many, we must investigate whether it is of one and the same kind or not. This is not meant as being said in relation to the plurality of souls that are in each individual, but without qualification about every soul that is in living beings, which is also wider: the following sentence makes this clear. Those who were investigating the soul, he says, investigated only the human soul; thus it is clear that the argument is about every kind of soul. Also, then, the phrase 'divided or undivided' is rather to be taken in this way. These souls, then, he says, that are present in living beings in an unqualified sense, do they differ in species or also in genus? Indeed he once again assumes what is true and agreed upon by means of division, that they differ in species.

402b3 For in actual fact those who speak of the soul and examine it, appear to look <only> at the human soul.

Some say (and Alexander is one of them)[306] that he alludes to Plato here; but it seems that Plato, also in many other places but especially in the *Timaeus*, discusses also the non-rational soul.[307] Perhaps, then, he alludes to the natural philosophers in the circle of Democritus and the others. We could indeed speak in their defence: for they can say that in the human soul one finds every faculty of the soul; hence when discussing this, we are likely to be discussing it in its entirety.

402b5 One should be careful not to ignore the question whether the account of it <i.e. the soul> is one, as it is <with the account> of a living being, or whether it is different according to each <species>, such as <the account> of horse, dog, man, god.

Having asked whether the souls are homogeneous or heterogeneous, at this point he says again with regard to their genus, if indeed it is a genus, that one should be careful and examine whether it is possible to give one definition for every kind of soul or not. One definition would be given if they had the genus in common, as one definition is given of horse, man, and the other species, since living being is the genus <and that definition would be> an ensouled substance endowed with sense perception, <a definition> which fits the individual living beings because of the genus they have in common; but if they did not have one genus in common, one single definition of them could not be given. Now souls do not have one. Why is this? Because in the case of souls some things are prior by nature, others posterior by nature, and where there is prior and posterior, there is no genus by which they are commonly designated. Prior by nature is that which eliminates the other thing, but which is not itself eliminated,[308] and that which is brought into the common stock, instead of bringing it in.[309] Now, in the case of souls there is prior by nature and posterior; for where there is the rational soul, there is also the non-rational and the vegetative, and where there is the non-rational, there is also the vegetative;[310] yet it is not that where there is the vegetative soul, there are the others as well, or that where there is the non-rational soul, there is the rational soul as well; and once the vegetative soul is eliminated, it also eliminates the remaining souls from its substrate. Consequently, in souls there is prior by nature and posterior; for the vegetative soul is prior, not in dignity but in that without it the others cannot be, and similarly the non-rational soul is prior to the rational soul.³¹¹ Now, if there is prior and posterior in souls, there will therefore not be a genus by which they are commonly designated, I mean the soul, but <such a term> will be an homonymous term just as things <whose name> comes from one thing and are related to one thing.³¹² Consequently, there is not one definition of these, since there is not one of any of the homonymous terms, but rather the definitions of the souls are different, as there is a different definition for man, dog, and horse. This is why he <i.e. Aristotle> himself, too, when intending to give an account of the soul that is common <to all kinds of soul>, said 'if one ought to render something common that applies to every kind of soul' (412b4),³¹³ not with the purpose of rendering one definition, but out of some sort of analogy, so that we would understand, it being clear that there is no common definition.

402b7 The living being in general either is nothing or something posterior. [And one could make a similar point with regard to any other common characteristic one might predicate of it.]

Some have thought that here³¹⁴ he speaks of the Forms, alluding to Plato. But this is not the case. For Aristotle, too, thinks that the genera and species exist prior to the plurality <of individual instances>. At any rate, in the *Metaphysics* he says that, just as orderly arrangement is twofold, the one type being in the commander, the other in the soldiers,³¹⁵ and that the orderly arrangement in the soldiers is derived from that of the commander, and health, too, is twofold, the one being in the doctor, the other in the body that is being restored to health, and the health that is in the doctor is productive of that of the body,³¹⁶ likewise the orderly arrangement in the universe has come into being as a result of the orderly arrangement in <the mind of> the Craftsman. Consequently, he also is aware of the transcendent formal principles of things. Again, in the present treatise he says: 'The active intellect is the things',³¹⁷ and 'Those who have spoken of the soul as a place of forms were right'.³¹⁸ Again, in the *Metaphysics*, when discussing the divine intellect, he says that the forms of all things are present in it;³¹⁹ at any rate, he says that when seeing itself it sees all things, and when seeing all things it sees itself. And there are numerous other statements by him that one could compare, which all express the same thought. Therefore the discussion here is not about the forms that are prior to the many, but about the things that come into being later. This is why he does not say without qualification that the living being is not, but he has added 'in general', thereby making it clear that as a substance the living being exists and is defined, but that as a general kind it has no existence; for there is no such thing as a general unqualified living being which is not one of the individual beings. Consequently, as a universal and as a genus the living being is either nothing or something later, that is, it exists in thought only; for it has its existence in its being the object of thinking, yet as something existing by itself it is nothing. Indeed, when defining man and horse, one does not define these in so far as there is something common seen in a plurality of indivisible objects, but in so far as it is a natural being and a substance. For their plurality is because of their matter, not because of their form. Indeed, that living being and man are defined in so far as they are a substance, not in so far as they are used as designations for a plurality of things, is evident. For even if there were just one man, likewise the definition of man will fit, as will that of the living being. This is the interpretation of Alexander.[320]

Now, since Aristotle has mentioned the living being in general by saying that perhaps there is not one definition of every kind of soul as there is of the living being,[321] for this reason he has added that the living being is nothing when viewed as a universal, or something that is posterior. If he wishes the definition of a living being to apply universally, and the definitions do not concern the genera that are prior to the plurality <of individual instances> (for it is not even possible to define these, since they <i.e. these genera> are creative formulae),[322] and since we define the things that exist in thought only[323] (for what we express in the definition is the notion we have about the things), and since these things came into being later, we have been right in saying that he says these things in relation to the things that came into being later.

402b9 Furthermore, if there are not many souls but parts <of the soul>, <the question is whether> we have to examine the whole soul first or its parts. [It is difficult in these things as well to specify what kind of parts are different from each other. Also, one should examine whether one should study the parts of the soul first or their functions, for example, thinking or the intellect, and perceiving or the faculty of sense-perception, and similarly with regard to the others. And if the functions should be studied first, one might again raise the question whether one should study their objects first, e.g. the sense-object prior to the sense faculty, the thought-object prior to thought.]

Having asked whether <the soul> is one or many, and said that, if there are many, <we should examine> whether they are different in species only or also in genus, he now considers the other part of the division. For he says 'if there are not many souls but parts'. As for 'not many', we shall again understand this in a twofold sense analogously to the things mentioned above. For either <he means that> in each of us and, in general, in each living being there is not a plurality of souls, e.g. as if in man there were the vegetative soul and the non-rational

soul and the rational soul and their parts, but rather one soul, and
that these are its parts, that is to say, different faculties; or <he
means> that the soul in its unqualified sense is not divided as a kind
into many species of souls, into reason, spirit, desire, and the other
souls, so that each of these would be soul, which is what his words
'whether it is divided or undivided' would amount to; for the genus is
divided into its species. Consequently, in each of the living beings
there is not soul but a part or parts of soul, the soul in its unqualified
sense being a whole, not a genus. 'If, then', he says, 'there are not a
plurality of souls but of parts of souls', i.e. there are many faculties.

Whether you understand this in the latter way or in a different
way, he says, the account will again contain many difficulties. For we
have to examine whence to start with our exposition or theoretical
study, whether from the parts or from the whole. For either will seem
to be reasonable: one might assume that one should start from the
whole as from something that is clearer, the whole being clearer than
the parts; but again it might seem that one should rather start from
the parts as from something that is more simple; for someone who
intends to know something that is composite needs to know first that
of which it consists.[324] Again, since the faculties have certain functions to fulfil, I mean the activities (for each activity comes from a
faculty), again we have to examine whether we should start from the
activities or from the faculties. Now, given that the essences of things
are obscure, but their activities are evident, for this reason we should
start from what is evident. For we fathom the dispositions on the
basis of the activities, the dispositions being obscure, and when we
have learnt the dispositions – which is the same as the faculties – we
fathom on the basis of them also the essences; for each faculty arises
from an essence, and each activity from a faculty.[325] But even, he says,
when we have discovered this, that we should start from the activities
– since the activities are among the things that are relational, e.g.
thinking is relative to the thinkable, and sense perception to what is
perceptible, and imagination to what can be imagined, and discursive
thought to what can be the object of such thought, and similarly also
with the other activities – since, then, they are among the things that
are relational, and since the person who knows the things that are
relational should also know in relation to what, it is, again, he says,
necessary to examine whether one should start from the activities or
from the objects with which their activities are concerned. And since
that concerning which they are active is clearer than the activities
(for the perceptible is clearer than perception, the object of opinion
clearer than opinion itself, and the other things in the same way), we
should therefore start from them. There is a difference only in the
case of the intellect and the intelligible; here, the intelligible is less
clear than the intellect; for the intellect is ours, whereas the intelligible is beyond us. This is why the person who wishes to know about

the intelligibles should also have knowledge first as to what the intellect is. This, at any rate, is what Aristotle does on this point only: he teaches first about the intellect, and after that about the intelligibles.[326]

'It is difficult in these things as well to specify what kind of parts are different from each other.' (403b10-11)[327] For it is obscure whether imagination and perception are the same or different, or imagination and locomotion, and similarly with regard to the others.

'Also, one should examine whether one should study the parts of the soul first or their functions' (402b11-12), parts being their faculties, functions their activities.

'For example, thinking or the intellect' (402b12-13), with the intellect being the faculty, thinking the activity.

'And perceiving or the faculty of sense-perception' (402b13), with perception, again, being the activity, perception the faculty.

'And similarly with regard to the others' (402b13-14), i.e. faculties and activities.[328]

'And if the functions should be studied first, one might again raise the question whether one should study their objects first' (402b14-16) or their functions, i.e. the actualities; for we have said that the perceptible and perception are opposites for the functions, and the others similarly; for they are opposites in the way of the relational things: for perception is perception of the perceptible. For example, 'the sense-object prior to the sense-faculty, the thought-object prior to the thought'. He should have said: the sense-object prior to sense-perception and the intelligible to thinking, for these indicate the activities. But as it is, he has expressed himself rather improperly by saying the sense-faculty and thought, which indicate the faculties.

402b16 It seems that not only to know the what-it-is is useful in order to study the causes of the attributes of the substances
...

After expounding the problems that must be examined, both in general for every definition and in particular for that of the soul, he now wants to provide us by means of these words with a method and to put us in a good position to find these definitions. This method is as follows. Not only, he says, do the definitions of things contribute to our getting to know the essential attributes of things – as is the case, for example, whenever we say that the soul is a self-moving substance:[329] for because of this we conclude that it is also immortal, and we have learned from the definition that immortality is an essential attribute of the soul; and again, after getting to know what a triangle is, we find out from this that its two sides are longer than the remaining one, and that it has its three angles equivalent to <that of>

two right angles. Not only, then, he says, do definitions contribute to our discovering the essential attributes of things, but sometimes it is also the other way round: in order for us to get to know what the definition of the present object is, it often helps if we know the essential and primary attributes of the things. This is what he means here by 'essential attribute', as we already said earlier.[330]

But if this is so, it might seem as if the demonstration is circular; for if we get to know the attributes through the definitions and the definitions through the attributes, the demonstration is circular. Now, my response to this is that it is not circular. For in either case he is not talking about the same attributes, but of some which we get to know through the definitions, and again of others through which we are well supplied with regard to the definitions. For attributes that are clear and grasped on the basis of what is evident contribute to our understanding of definitions we do not yet know, whereas the definitions contribute to the grasping of attributes that are not plain on the basis of what is evident, as indeed he often does himself. For when wishing to give a definition of place, since that was obscure, he said: 'Let us first assume as a kind of criterion of the definition that is to be given those things that according to common insight[331] are attributes of place, such as the encompassing of what is in a place, being equal to it' and all the other things he summed up there. 'And if', he says, 'the definition given is such that it suits all the things that according to common insight are attributes of place, this will be a sound thing; and if not, it will not'.[332] In this way he proceeds also concerning the infinite, the void, and time;[333] and in this way in the *Meteorologica*, too, he searches for the cause of a hailstorm by searching for what is commonly agreed to be an attribute of it, viz. its occurring in autumn and in spring, and in warm places also in winter.[334] 'Next', he says, 'let us give a cause for this which corresponds to all these'. In this way, then, he says also now, since we are seeking the definition of the soul, and this is obscure, let us grasp this on the basis of what evidently accompanies it essentially and primarily, i.e. imagination, locomotion, reproduction, and all such things, so that from these we get on the right track towards grasping its definition; for these are peculiar to the soul, and this is why after its departure these and similar <faculties> do not activate the body.

402b18 ... just as in mathematics <knowledge of> the straight and[335] the curved, or what a line is or a plane, helps us to discover to how many right angles the angles of a triangle are equal[, but also, conversely, the attributes contribute for a large part to knowing what something is].

This is an example of discovering on the basis of the definitions the essential attributes of things, for getting to know on the basis of definitions the things that follow from it is generally speaking inevitable in the case of mathematics, since in this area we cannot grasp any of the attributes on the basis of perception, but we need to know first what a triangle is, and next we can thus conclude from this what follows from this. By means of this example he makes it clear that here by 'attributes' he means the things that belong to something essentially and primarily. For it belongs essentially and primarily to a triangle that its three angles are equivalent to two right angles. For this belongs to a triangle only, and to every triangle. It contributes to the knowledge of such things, he says, to know what a line is or what a plane is, whether it is straight or curved. He says this hypothetically for the purpose of the example, not as if these things, either all of them or they only, contribute to knowing that the three angles are equal to two right ones; for neither the definition of the curved nor of the plane contributes anything, rather, one should also take the definitions of certain other things in addition. Now in these subjects, in order to grasp the attributes, one requires the prior grasping of the definition, since we cannot say anything about them on the basis of what is manifestly visible. Concerning other things one sometimes needs knowledge of the attributes for the grasping of the definition, as is the case with place, time, void, and the infinite, as now with the soul, because the definition is obscure, whereas the attributes are evident on the basis of perception.

402b22 For when we can give an account in accordance with the appearance about its attributes, either about most of them or about all of them ...

By appearance[336] he means either cognition in general or the appearances and the manifest, calling it appearance after it being apparent.

402b24 ... then we shall also be in a position to give an excellent account of its essence.

For if we know many of the attributes that belong essentially and primarily to the things, we can as it were trace them and through these find the definition of the thing. By essence he means all simple things and the definition and all else that belongs to essence; having found the definition through it we shall also find all that belongs to the essence. This is what he wanted to make clear when he continues:

402b25 For the starting point of every demonstration is the what-it-is.

By this he shows that even if it is on the basis of what is evident that we have some knowledge of the attributes of substances, we have this knowledge on the basis of perception and not in the form of demonstrative knowledge. But if we know the definition, we can obtain knowledge of these <attributes> in a scientific way by using the definitions as starting points. Now, surely it is not with regard to simply all the attributes of the substances that this needs to be adopted (by attributes, as I already said, I mean those things that belong primarily and essentially), so that the demonstration does not appear circular, if indeed through the attributes we get to know the definition and through the latter the former. Rather, is it that there are some things through which we get to know the definitions, i.e. those things we get to know of through perception, such as the fact that simultaneously with being present it gives life to bodies (this is peculiar to the soul), the fact that it is cause of nutrition, growth, generation, the fact that for animals it is the cause of movement sideways; these things are known to us through perception. But there are other things which are obscure and which we infer on the basis of the definitions, such as the rational soul's being immortal; for once we find in its definition that <the soul> is a self-moving substance, we could infer the immortal from the self-movement. For the definition is grasped on the basis of the essential attributes of things, but it does not encompass all the essential attributes but <only> all those that are sufficient to distinguish essentially the underlying nature from the others.

Either this, then, is the way in which the phrase 'For the starting point of every demonstration is the what-it-is' is to be understood, or alternatively as I said, and as is more true and as is also Alexander's opinion,[337] he <i.e. Aristotle> says that the definition is the starting point of all the things that once for all belong essentially to the things. For how is it possible to have knowledge based on demonstration as to what the essential attributes of a thing are for someone who does not know its definition? For it is possible to learn from perception at least some of the attributes of things, from which we also find the starting points towards the definition. But it is impossible to have scientific knowledge of these things for someone who does not know the essence of the thing, i.e. the definition. For there truly is one starting point for the person who is about to plan well; he should have knowledge about what he is going to plan on, otherwise he will inevitably fail completely.[338] Now that imagining, perceiving, discursive thinking, etc. are attributes of the soul, we know from perception; but what the nature of these is, and whether they are the same or different, and all the questions that are being examined about these, we do not know; rather, only then do we have scientific knowledge of these things when we know the essence of the soul. But the demonstration is not circular here. For in every field there are four problems, whether it is, what it is, of what nature it is, and through what it is.[339] Now that these attributes are, we learn from what is manifest, and the what-it-is and the definition <we learn> from these; from the definition we do not learn that the attributes are, but we do learn what they are and of what nature they are and through what cause. Consequently, from what the attributes are, we learn the what-it-is of the definition, and through the what-it-is of the definition the other problems that are raised regarding the attributes; consequently, the demonstration is not circular. This is not in any sense absurd, to demonstrate certain things through each other and not according to the same thing, but different things through different things. That this is what Aristotle has in mind is indicated by what follows.

402b26 Therefore definitions in virtue of which it does not follow that one gets to know the attributes, and which do not even allow conjecture about them, have been stated for dialectical purposes and are devoid of content.

This is in accordance with what has been said before. If the what-it-is is the starting point of every demonstration, it is absolutely inevitable that, if the definition given of the thing is not of such a kind that through this knowledge is produced concerning all the essential attributes of the thing as through a starting-point, or not even some conjecture is adopted, it is inevitable, he says, that, since not all essential attributes of a thing become manifest in the definition, such a definition is dialectical and is stated in vain, i.e. it floats in a void and does not touch the nature of the thing, and thinking finds as it were no support in the thing but is floating high up in the sky. 'Dialectical', that means not in accordance with <a thing's> nature but simply looking at appearance and at seeming to say something, of the kind which he is going to mention himself a little bit further down when he says that anger is a desire for retaliation.[340] This definition is not based on nature, for it does not make clear what the essence of anger is, rather it cuts something that has its being in something <else> away <from this> and defines it on its own, but from this one cannot get to know the attributes of anger,[341] as one would from someone who says that anger is a boiling of the blood in the region of the heart because of a desire for retaliation. The latter definition does make the following attributes known, viz. that a certain palpitation of the heart accompanies those who are angered, and that heat gathers around these parts and that those who are angry redden. This is because of the movement of the blood. Of this kind is also the definition of the soul given by Xenocrates: 'It is a self-moving number', he says.[342] Someone who hears this will not be able to suspect or grasp from this any of the things that belong to the soul or to the living being. By means of these <examples> Aristotle provides us with a rule for the rendering of definitions, viz. that they should be such that all <attributes> that belong essentially to the things can be concluded through these as from some starting point. This is the most perfect definition.

403a3 A further problem is posed by the affections of the soul, whether these are all common to that which has soul, or whether there is one that is peculiar to the soul itself; it is necessary to grasp this, but not easy.

Having stated the problems that need to be examined in the discussion of the soul, and having said next that the knowledge based on the perception of its essential attributes puts us in a good position to grasp its definition, he now says that this very point, viz. to undertake a study of the affections of the soul as a procedure towards its definition, is precisely what is most difficult. That, he says, is because we cannot discern on the basis of sense perception whether all affections of the soul are common to the composite <of soul and body>, I mean the living being, or whether it has certain affections that are peculiar to it <i.e. the soul>; indeed, he says, it is absolutely necessary to establish this in advance in order to know the essence of the soul, yet it is most difficult to establish. If it just uses the body as an instrument and has its activities peculiar to itself, there is no need also to refer to the body for the definition – after all, an axe does not complete the essence of a carpenter – but if the soul has its being in the body, so that its activities belong to the composite, it is necessary also to refer to the body in the definition, just as we have mentioned in relation to anger.[343] Establishing these <matters>, then, is necessary, but not easy.

'Affections' is a more general term he uses here for the activities of the soul.

403a5 It seems that with most of these <the soul> neither experiences them nor brings them about without the body, [for example, getting angry, being courageous, desiring, and perceiving in general].

This is because most affections are accompanied by the body and are concerned with bodies; for when people are angry, or suffer pain, or desire, or are courageous or frightened, indeed, with all such things the body is brought in a certain condition as well and is moved together <with the soul>. Moreover, the activities involved in these affections are concerned with bodies. Consequently, such things belong to the composite and are not peculiar to the soul.

403a8 Thinking in particular seems to be something peculiar <to the soul>.

Look, he has again called thinking[344] an affection. This relates to Andronicus of Rhodes,[345] who declared *On Interpretation* spurious because there Aristotle says that thoughts are affections of the soul,[346] as has been said in *On the Soul*, yet evidently nowhere in *On the Soul* has he called thoughts affections, Andronicus believed. In that case look just at this text, where he says 'Thinking in particular seems to be something peculiar', i.e. a peculiar affection. If, then, he says, the soul has an affection peculiar to it, it is thinking.

403a8 Yet if this, too, is a kind of imagination, or at least does not take place without imagination, it, too, will be unable to be without body.

If thinking, he says, either is a kind of imagination or does not occur without imagination, it is absolutely necessary that thinking is not peculiar to the soul either, but rather belongs to the composite, since imagination is tied with sense perception (for this is where it derives its impressions from), and sense perception belongs to the composite. And in this passage, indeed, he speaks as if he is dealing with problems;[347] but in the third book he clearly says that thinking is without imagination. He speaks as follows: 'As for the primary thoughts, what makes them different from images? Or is it that the other thoughts are not images either, but that they are not without images?',[348] where by primary thoughts he means those that are concerned with intelligible objects, which he has said are not products of imagination. Now 'not without' is used in three senses:[349] either in the sense of causing neither harm nor benefit, as we say that a body in the sunlight is not without shade (for shade neither benefits nor harms a body) or in the sense of necessity as an instrument or something like that, as we say that Achilles excelled in battle, but not without his ashen spear (he necessarily needed the spear for his excelling in battle; he could not excel deprived of it), or in the sense of that which is an impediment, as we say that someone sailing in a storm was saved, but not without danger; here, we take 'not without' in the sense of something that is able to impede. So in the statement 'Or is it that the other thoughts are not images either, but that they are not without images', he has adopted <the expression> 'not without' in the sense of being able to impede. In the present passage 'if this, too, is a kind of imagination, or at least does not take place without imagination' he uses 'not without' in the sense of 'necessarily', as if the intellect required the imagination as a kind of instrument to fulfil its own activities. This is why he has added: 'it, too, will be unable to be without body'; but the argument is hypothetical.

403a10 Now if a certain activity or affection of the soul is peculiar <to it>, it will be possible for it <i.e. the soul> to be separated; but if there is nothing that is peculiar to it, it will not be separable.

There has been much wavering among interpreters about this passage. They thought that the philosopher is using a conversion with opposition, and they understandably queried the fact that the philosopher used the conversion badly, viz. on the basis of the antecedent, whereas he should have used the conversion on the basis of what follows.[350] For, they say, he speaks as follows: 'If there is some kind of affection that is peculiar to the soul, it <i.e. the soul> will be separable'. Next he took the opposite of what was thought and proved the opposite of what follows, 'if there is no affection peculiar to the soul, it will not be separable either', whereas he should have reversed it from what follows: 'if it is not separable, it will not have an affection peculiar to it'.

The Attic interpreters[351] rightly said that here he does not use conversion at all, but he takes two specific conditionals, and produces through these two specific rules, which we have mentioned before basing ourselves on this passage,[352] viz. that of those bodies whose activities are separable, the essences will also be separable, and that of those bodies whose activities are inseparable the essence will inevitably also be inseparable. For if the activities are inseparable, whereas the essence is inseparable, since the activities are based on the potentialities, while the potentialities are based on the essences, then, whenever the activity is separated, if indeed it is separable, there will have to be an activity without essence or without potentiality, and this is impossible; for every activity is based on a potentiality, and every potentiality is based on an essence. When, therefore, the activity is separable, the essence also has to be separable; and if that is the case, it will of necessity be immortal and imperishable. Why? Everything that perishes, perishes in two ways, either through dissolution into its own elements, such as our bodies, or by extinction in the substrate, because <the latter> becomes unsuitable <for it>, just as a harmony is destroyed when the strings lose their tension.[353] Now, since perishing, then, is twofold, either as in the case of bodies or as in the case of incorporeal <beings> having their being in an underlying body, if the soul was shown to be incorporeal and separable from the body, it will not in any way perish. Again, since the activities are inseparable, the essences also have to be inseparable; and if the essences are separated, they will be unable to be activated and without purpose. But neither God nor nature act without purpose,[354] so that it is absolutely necessary that when the activities are inseparable, the essences are so as well.

Now these rules are accepted jointly by those who say that the soul is mortal and those who say it is immortal. But against these rules the following objections are raised, one against each. Against the former, they say: 'What does Aristotle mean by saying that if there is a specific affection that is peculiar to the soul, and if he says the same about the activity, does it also have its essence separable? For look', they say, 'the eye has its peculiar activity, viz. seeing, and yet it does not have an essence that is separable; for it is impossible for the eye to be separated from the body.' What is our reply to this? That 'peculiar' has a twofold meaning, either in the sense that something can be peculiar as to a part, as we say that it is peculiar to a foot to walk – after all, we do not say that walking is peculiar to the foot in the sense that it does not require the whole <it is part of> (for it does require the whole body), but in the sense that it is peculiar to this particular part apart from the other parts – or alternatively, <'peculiar'> is used in the sense of that which does not require the whole for its presence, just as if someone were to say that the fattiness of diluted olive oil is peculiar to olive oil or the sweetness in oenomel[355] is peculiar to honey. Such a statement does not simply state the peculiar as being <peculiar to> a part, but as something not in need of the whole for its existence; for sweetness does not require oenomel for its existence, but it is separable from the whole; for it is only in the honey. Something like this is what Aristotle means by peculiar, which is also separable in being; for the sweetness of the honey is separable from the composite, being peculiar to the honey. The eye, however, is said to have its peculiar power not as something not requiring the whole, but in opposition to the other parts, since it does require the whole for its existence; it requires the brain and the optic nerves and *pneuma* and other things like that.[356] Consequently, the activity of the eye is peculiar in relation to the other bodily parts, but not peculiar in relation to the whole; for it requires wholeness for its substance.[357]

The objection against the other rule is the following. 'What', they say, 'does he mean by saying that those things whose activities are not peculiar but belong to the composite – which is identical to saying they are inseparable – that the essence of these things is not separable either? For look', they say, 'the activity of the steersman is inseparable from the ship, but his essence is separable; for the steersman is separable from the ship.'[358] Now we say that the steersman exercises activity both as a steersman and as a human being; and his activities as a steersman are inseparable from the ship and are not peculiar to the steersman, but his activities as a human being are peculiar to the steersman in his capacity of human being. This is why also the essence is separable. For we do not say that the separable essence has to possess all activities as its peculiar activities, and even if it does not have them all, it will not be separable, but if it generally has a certain activity that is separable, its essence will under any circumstances have to be separable as well, whereas in the case that the essence is inseparable, all activities under any circumstances have to be common and therefore inseparable as well.³⁵⁹ This, then, is why the steersman, since while being on the ship he would also be exercising activities in his capacity as a human being, such as thinking, conversing, eating and drinking, and in general experiencing all a living being experiences, for this reason his essence would also be separable from the ship; and since the rational soul, too, that is in the body, has two activities, it has some of these in its capacity of being in the body (for it, too, is in some way like a steersman of the body), whereas it has others as being peculiar to the rational soul. Now, the activities it has in its capacity of being in the body are inseparable from the composite, such as setting the body in motion, and reproduction; it is obvious that it has these activities in so far as it is in the body, for if it was separable from all body, what would cause movement, what would reproduce? On the other hand, its activities in its capacity of a rational essence, such as discursive thinking, intuitive thinking, since these do not require the body in any way, are peculiar to it and therefore show that its essence is also separable. This is why Aristotle, when giving a definition common to all soul, or rather an account analogous to a definition, and saying that it is the actuality of a natural body possessing organs that potentially has life, seeks to know in what sense we speak of actuality. 'Is the soul', he says, 'like an inseparable actuality or is it like the sailor of a ship?' So he himself also knows that actuality is something separable, and accordingly he wants the soul to be an actuality. Again, they ask, what makes him infer that, having said 'if a certain activity or affection of the soul is peculiar', 'it will have to admit of being separated'? For he should have said that it is necessary for it to be separated. We, therefore, say that he has said this in relation to the whole relationship³⁶⁰ of the soul to the body or indeed to bodies. For since it is a fact that when it is in the body it is inseparable from the body, for this reason he says that it is possible for it to be separated from the body, even if it will come into being again in the body and does not completely remain for an infinite length of time without this solid body <that it now has>.³⁶¹ That which comes into being in something also departs from this, when nature allows this, just as heating and cooling, sitting down and standing. Therefore, as I said, he has expressed himself in this way with attention to the whole relationship <of the soul> to the body. Perhaps he extends his account also beyond this to the so-called luminous body,³⁶² which they say is eternally attached to it, and he may have used the word 'possible' in this sense, saying 'in so far as it is up to its own nature, it would be separated from it, even if it is not necessary for the soul to be separated from it'. This is what 'possible' means: that from which, while not being necessary, but when it is given, nothing impossible follows.[363] In so far as it is in its own nature, it could be separated from this, too. In addition to this we say that 'what is possible', as he says himself in *On Interpretation*,[364] is also applied to what is necessary; for we say 'it is possible for the sun to enter into Aries', although it will get there necessarily. Here, too, it is possible, then, to take 'what is possible' to refer to what is necessary.

403a12 But just as what is straight has many attributes, in so far as it is straight, such as its touching a bronze sphere at a point, yet straightness separated will not touch it, [for it is inseparable, if indeed it is always joined with some sort of body].

He has introduced unclarity in what he says by using an identical term <twice> without distinguishing the different meanings. For in one way he takes that which is straight as that which is participated in, I mean straightness itself, but in another way in the sense of that which participates, namely the composite, I mean the straightened body, e.g. a rod. This is an example of the fact that when the activity is inseparable, the essence will also have to be inseparable. So what does he mean? We say that the straight line touches the bronze sphere at a point (for it has been demonstrated in geometry that the plane touches the sphere at a point and similarly the straight line touches the circle), and it is not that, because we say that the straight line is affected by this,[365] we say that it is affected by this on its own, but it is obvious that we are talking about the straightness in the bronze or stone or in some material of this sort. In the same way we will never say about the soul, when we say that it is affected, that it is affected on its own, but we are talking about the composite. This is why he has added 'the bronze sphere', so that we do not take his words in the sense of the bronze straight line, as those who teach mathematics do. For the geometrician shows that a sphere touches a plane at a point, but he does not add any material, but demonstrates the definitions in themselves. Now by saying 'as to what is straight, in so far as it is straight', he understands that which exists in material; but in saying 'straightness separated will not touch it' he refers to straightness itself. This, then, he says, when separated from its substrate, will no longer be affected in this way nor will it touch the bronze sphere, since it does not exist independently. He takes the straightness as an analogy to the soul, and the straight body to the composite, and the bronze sphere to the perceptible things which the soul apprehends. For if the soul apprehends perceptible objects in this way, as the straight line touches the bronze sphere, it is obvious that the soul, when separated from the body, will no longer be able to apprehend perceptible objects, but will directly disappear. We say, then, that just as the perceptible straight line touches the perceptible sphere, likewise the intelligible straight line touches the intelligible sphere; and the soul, then, when separated from the body, even if it does not apprehend the perceptible forms, does apprehend intelligible and immaterial ones. As for the phrase 'has many attributes', <this refers>, so to say, to its having all its points lying in a sequence, its coinciding with another straight line, and similar things.

403a16 Moreover, it would seem that in all affections of the soul the body is involved [, e.g. spirit, gentleness, fear, pity, courage, and also joy and loving and hating; in all these, the body is also affected].

That the affections[366] of the soul are not peculiar to it, but to the composite,[367] is demonstrated by Aristotle on two grounds.[368] First, on the ground that in all cases they are accompanied by movements of the body: anger is accompanied by a movement of the blood in the region of the heart, and desire by a condition of the liver; shame causes the face to blush, because blood is dispersed at the plane, whereas fear causes paleness as a result of a contraction of blood towards the deeper parts of the body. Generally speaking, in the case of every affection <of the soul> the body is brought into a certain condition <along with the soul>. And if the affections of the soul are accompanied by movements of the body, it is evident that they are not peculiar to the soul alone, but to the composite. In one respect, then, this is evident from the above, but in another from the fact that when people who have a natural <bodily> mixture of a particular kind are moved by affections, they naturally behave according to the mixture in which their bodies are held.[369] Thus we see that there are people who are prone[370] to anger because they have a corresponding <bodily> mixture, whereas other people are not easily moved by this affection because they have the opposite mixture. Similarly, in the case of the other affections we see that when people are drunk they are prone to get angry, cowardly, reckless or ruthless. Diseases, too, may cause a man to be prone to anger, and particular kinds of food stimulate the desire for sexual intercourse, whereas other kinds extinguish it. Hence the doctors' saying that 'the faculties of the soul follow the mixtures of the body'.[371] For this reason they say that people with a particular mixture are prone to anger, e.g. those who have a tendency to melancholic affections,[372] and that those who have a tendency to a hot and moist condition are prone to sexual intercourse; generally speaking, with any single affection, they attribute its cause to a certain quality of the mixture. They even extend this to the higher cognitive faculties and claim that people whose brain has a dryer mixture have better memories, but are slower in thinking,[373] whereas those people who have the opposite mixture are confronted with the opposite affection, and similarly with imagination and the other affections. Moreover, the effect produced by the original mixture may also be produced by the regimen which leads to this mixture. For this reason, people who lay claim to knowledge are careful to be moderate when it comes to food, and drink moderately, whence the saying comes that 'a fat belly does not produce a subtle mind'.[374] That is why, when we are drunk, we cannot think the things we thought when we were not drunk. This holds good for eating moderately or immoderately as well. In general, people turn out to be better talented[375] and more sharp-witted or, on the contrary, dull-witted, according to the corresponding mixture. This, then, is the ground for the doctors' saying that the faculties of the soul follow the mixtures of the body.

In reaction to this the Attic interpreters[376] say the following. Just as these doctors state that because the corresponding impulses[377] of the soul follow the mixtures of the body, therefore the soul is in the body as in its substrate, likewise we, too, will prove the opposite by means of the opposite. If the soul is inseparable from the body for the very reason that its impulses follow the body's mixture, then, if it does not follow the body's mixture, it will be separable. Now we observe that with some people, even though they have a bad mixture, their impulses do not follow these mixtures because of the influence of philosophy; on the contrary, they have gained mastery over these, which would not have happened if the <soul's> faculty was in the mixture as in its substrate in the same way as being white, pale, or black, which occurs as a result of a corresponding mixture, cannot be held under control, not even by numerous philosophical occupations, as long as the mixture is not adapted accordingly. Thus it is absolutely necessary that, if such and such an impulse of the soul is as if it were a result[378] of a mixture, a man who is inclined to anger cannot keep his anger under control, and similarly in other cases. Yet we see that this is not the case; therefore, the impulses of the soul do not necessarily follow the mixtures of the body. This is even conceded by the doctors themselves, for after saying that the faculties of the soul follow the mixtures of the body they have added: 'except for the occupations of philosophy'.[379] Consequently, if philosophical occupations are able to cause the impulse of the soul not to follow the mixtures of the body, there is indeed something which is in our control, and they do not follow <the body> necessarily. Consequently, they do not have their being in the mixture, for if they had, how would a man resist affections? What would be the basis for the irreconcilable battle between reason and the affections? For nothing battles against the body that preserves it,[380] nor does it have any ambition to battle with its cause.[381] Therefore, if the mixture were the cause of all the movements of the soul, it would never battle with itself; for things which battle are each other's contraries. That the rational soul, then, is in fact separable from the body,[382] is sufficiently demonstrated by people who lead a successful life by holding their bodies in contempt.

Yet nothing deprecates its own substrate, indeed, it rather wants to preserve it.[383] However, the soul evidently does the opposite.[384]

Since the affections are given to the soul as it descends into <the domain of> becoming as a result of the causes mentioned above,[385] and since they have their being in *pneuma*[386] as in a substrate and penetrate, as we said,[387] even into the solid body, they do not come into being without a mixture of a particular kind, just as a harmony does not come into being without strings. Nevertheless it is not simply a result of a mixture, on the contrary, just as the musician under all circumstances needs strings of a particular kind, while harmony comes into being in the particular suitability of the strings as a result of the formal principles in the <mind of the> musician,[388] likewise we say that the affections, too, do not occur without a mixture of a particular kind, yet without being themselves a mixture or a result of a mixture,[389] on the contrary, <they are> just like things growing spontaneously that need in all cases soil of a certain nature, as well as rain, yet this is not enough for them to come into being, but it is their formal principles which originate from the whole of creation <that cause them to come into being>.[390] Likewise <in the present case> we say that the formal principles originating from the whole of creation[391] cause the formal principles of these affections to come into being in a mixture of a particular kind, according to the dignity[392] of each singular rational soul. Therefore, just as the form that comes into being in the things that grow spontaneously neither originated simply from a mixture[393] of earth and water, nor came from outside after having existed before in a mode of existence of its own, but were created and moulded by the creative formal principles in a particular suitability of the elements, <likewise the creative formal principles create and mould> the forms of the affections <in a particular suitability of the mixture>.[394] One should not think that the causes are inferior to the things that are caused, for if, as we have said before,[395] the mixture is a cause of anger and desire and of perception and of imagination, what is lifeless will be the cause of life (for these affections are lives) and what is unensouled, of soul, and what lacks perception will be the cause of knowledge, which is absurd.

Perhaps the following is worth investigating as well. If the non-rational soul and the vegetative soul have their existence in the body as in a substrate, and if what has existence of its own is superior to what exists in something else, and if the body has existence of its own, then the body will be superior to the souls of this kind. What then shall we say to this? Well, that these souls are not in the body as in a substrate, but as form in matter; for the soul is the form of the living being.[396] Now, without exception the form is superior to the matter, for neither with the form of flesh, nor with that of fire or of any other body does the fact that they cannot exist on their own make them inferior to their matter, since not even formless matter itself has existence of its own, but it is always viewed in combination with a form. As for the proximate matter, even if it has existence by itself, as the wood of a board, it still does not exist as mere matter, but as a particular form of the wood; and whenever wood becomes the material of the board, then it is evident that the wood is inferior to the form of the board, since one of them is for the purpose of something, whereas the other is that for whose purpose it is. What then is the difference between being as form in matter and being in a substrate? Well, it is by being coupled with the matter that the form produces the being of one thing, just as the form of the board coupled with the wood produces the board, and similarly the form of the flesh coupled with the elements or the humours produces the flesh, and it is just the same in other cases. Yet what is in something else as in its substrate, when being coupled with the substrate, does not produce one being, just as the white, being coupled with the body, does not produce another species: for white does not co-operate with the body to produce being, neither when it is present, nor when it is absent.

403a19 This is indicated by the fact that sometimes as a result of strong and powerful affections[397] no excitement or fear is brought about [, while sometimes it is moved by only small and faint such incentives].

That, as he states, these affections are not peculiar to the soul but to the composite, is evident from people who suffer increase and decrease <of emotion> because their bodily disposition is of a certain kind. There are people who have such a <bodily> mixture that in spite of the presence of numerous exciting factors they are not moved to anger, because in them the blood in the region of the heart is in a cold condition and difficult to move, whereas others are inclined to this affection so that even when the exciting factors are very slight and feeble, they are immediately provoked to anger because their disposition is of such a kind that the blood in the region of the heart is always boiling. For this reason, too, people who are inclined to getting beside themselves are confronted with this affection because the blood boils over. Again, as for cowardice or recklessness, some people similarly remain hardly impressed even by strong fears, whereas other people are often moved to fear and cowardice easily, even though nothing fearful is present, because their <bodily> mixture is of the same kind as that which occurs to people who are in a state of fear;[398] for with those people the heat is contracted towards the deeper parts of the body, whence they become pale: 'Pallor seized his cheeks.'[399] Now when a man has got this mixture from the beginning, he is easily moved towards this affection. Consequently, if these affections were peculiar to the soul, they should not be dependent on the body nor have their origin in its disposition, but whatever the state of the body is, the soul should similarly[400] be moved or not be moved to the affections. Yet, as it is, also a man's age may alter the form of the affections and may cause them to change accordingly, for the obvious reason that his mixture has changed accordingly over time. It follows that they belong to the composite, for if the non-rational and the vegetative soul used the body as an instrument, it would not be moved by it; for the craftsman is not moved by any of his instruments, but they are moved by him. Nor when the instruments change do they change the desires of the craftsmen accordingly, but a body which has such and such a mixture does change the faculties of this kind along with it.

403a21 ... when the body is in a state of anger and is in such a state as when a man is angry.

That is, when the body has a mixture of such a kind that it is inclined to anger; and it will be like that, if it has a mixture of the same kind as the one that is found with people who are angry. For then such a man will be easily moved to anger.

403a22 Even clearer is the following case: though nothing fearful happens, it nevertheless happens that people are seized by the same affections as someone who is afraid.

These are really powerful demonstrations that these affections are not peculiar to the soul: cases when a man suffers the same as anyone else will suffer because of strong fears, even though in his case there is nothing which moves him from outside, but he is moved to fear because of the strong proneness of his body to this affection.

403a24 If this is the case, it is evident that the affections are enmattered formal principles [and therefore the definitions will have to correspond, e.g. being angry would be defined as a certain movement of a certain body or of a bodily part or of a faculty of it, on account of this or that and for the purpose of this or that].

'If this is the case', he says, i.e. if these affections are not peculiar to the soul but to the composite, 'then they are enmattered formal principles',[401] i.e. they are forms which have their being in matter and are not separable. Consequently their definitions are of this kind, 'e.g., being angry is a kind of movement of a body of a particular kind, or of a part or a power of the body, being a result of this or that and being for the purpose of this or that.' If it is the task of the student of nature to discuss enmattered forms, i.e. some forms in this matter, others in that, it is therefore necessary for the student of nature to render definitions which are based on the matter and the form and the cause by which the form occurs in the matter. When discussing the form he will necessarily discuss the matter as well, for they both belong to <the category of> relative. Moreover, if the student of nature is an expert, and if expertise[402] should know the reasons of the things it deals with, he will of necessity also discuss the cause by which a particular form is in a particular matter. 'For I will not call expertise', Plato says, 'anything which does not have a rational explanation'.[403] Thus he <i.e. Aristotle> roughly sketches the form of physical definitions: 'a movement', he says, such as we call the boiling in the case of anger (for boiling is a movement), 'of a body of a particular kind', i.e. of a natural organ, 'or part'. The affection we want to define is often found in the whole of the body, e.g. when we want to define touch: for that we will call a movement of the whole body. As for a movement of a part of the body, this is as with anger, for we say that anger is a boiling of the blood in the region of the heart. 'Or of a power', like when we do not call anger a boiling of the blood in the region of the heart, but a boiling of the heat in the region of the heart. It is evident that by the blood in the region of the heart the heat is signified, and by the heat the blood. 'As a result of this or that and for such and such a purpose.' Evidently as a result of an agent causing pain and for the purpose of retaliation. Having said, then, 'through a desire for retaliation' we have signified both; for retaliation signifies both the agent causing pain and the revenge.

403a27 And for this reason it is in fact the task of the student of nature to study the soul, either in its entirety or the soul that is of this kind.

Since the natural kinds which the student of nature is investigating are of this kind, and since the natural definitions are also of this kind and take the matter into account, it is the student of nature's task to discuss such souls that are not without matter. For to discuss the immaterial and intellectual souls would, as he points out in *On the Parts of Animals*, be the task of the first philosopher;[404] for he who discusses the intellect must also discuss the intelligibles, and this is the task of theology. But as we already said,[405] the complete student of nature will lift himself up and will also ascend to the transcendent causes of natural things, as he himself says in the *Physics*, when after his discussions about movement he has discussed the unmoved cause: 'On such a principle, therefore, the heavens and the universe depend.'[406] Similarly also in *On Generation*[407] and in the present passage, since he will also discuss these as natural causes; for he has already said about the rational soul that it is in a word a principle for living beings. This is why he says here 'either in its entirety'.

403a29 A student of nature and a dialectician would give a different definition of each of them [, for example, of what anger is: the latter would define it as a desire for retaliation or something of the sort, the former as a kind of boiling of the blood and the heat in the region of the heart].

Having said that the affections of the soul are enmattered formal principles and that because of this it is the task of the student of nature to study the soul either in its entirety or at least not without its matter, he next wants to show by means of the following what kind of definition of the soul would be appropriate for the student of nature. Now since these are the three things in the natural things, matter, form, and the cause by which the form is in the matter, there are five methods of investigation concerning these: physics, the individual sciences, dialectic, mathematics, first philosophy. He now examines how each of these methods will define the present subject. Let us first say what kind of subjects each of these methods is concerned with. The task of the student of nature is to discuss all the things mentioned, the matter of the natural things as well as their form, and the cause by which the form is in the matter; for example, as to what is the matter of the celestial bodies, he will say that it is not the four elements but a fifth body which is different from them; as to the question what is the form, that they are spherical; as to the question why they are spherical, he will give the cause of this that corresponds to them and which is based on the structure which they had in relation to what preceded them, as does Plato in the *Timaeus*, when he asks why the heavens are spherical:[408] because, he says, that which was to receive everything and to encompass everything had to contain the most spacious of shapes; now, the most spacious among the plane figures is the circle, and among the solids the sphere. He demonstrates this by the fact that of figures with equal circumference that which has more angles is most spacious, and for this reason the figure without angles is the most spacious of all. For example, if a room has four angles, and there is another figure that has many angles, for instance, eight angles, each of them will have a circumference of four cubits, and if there is another figure which is circular, i.e. a circle, that has a circumference of the same four, the plane of the figure with six angles will be larger than that of the figure with four sides, and that of the circle will be larger than that of the figure with six angles. Similarly, in solid figures, I mean a cube and an octahedron or a dodecahedron, and a sphere etc., the figure with many angles will have a larger surface than the cube, and the sphere will have a larger surface than the polygon figure. Aristotle also gives a natural cause of the figure: he says that the spherical shape is appropriate for something that is to become eternal, which has neither beginning nor end but is turned towards itself;[409] and Plotinus

<infers> the natural cause of the shape of the heavens from the disposition they have in relation to the things that precede it;[410] and proximate to them, beyond the celestial things, are the intelligible substances; and that which is caused must be as similar as possible to the proximate cause and convey its image and imitation. This is why, he says, the heavens are moved in a circle, because they imitate the intellect. For it is peculiar to the intellect to turn in on itself; for it is both seeing and what is seen; seeing the forms it sees itself,[411] and seeing itself it has viewed the forms, for it is a fullness[412] of forms and a form of forms.[413] Thus the heavens have their spherical shape because of the circular movement, and they have this because of their assimilation to the intellect. There is also another way in which it imitates the intellect, which is completely undivided; just as the intellect is at the same time everywhere, likewise the heavens get everywhere. They imitate what is everywhere by getting everywhere; for the turning in and the assimilation to the higher things is a fulfilment of things that are inferior. In this way, then, the student of nature gives account of the matter as well as the form and the cause of all natural things, and for this reason he gives a definition consisting of the matter and the form and the cause through which the form is in the matter.

The subject-specific expert that is concerned with the particular is also concerned with all these things, but he differs from the student of nature in that he is concerned with a partial thing. For example, the doctor is concerned with human bodies, the carpenter with bricks and timber. He, too, will state the definition taking account of the matter and the form and the cause. But he differs from the student of nature also in this respect, that the subject-specific expert only gives the most proximate causes, whereas the student of nature will also give the primary causes. For example, the doctor will give as cause of coming into being and passing away the right proportion between the humours and the elements as the cause of the right proportion, but the student of nature will go beyond these to the matter and the form. For the subject-specific expert, too, has to know the cause. 'For I', Plato says, 'do not call expertise anything which does not have a rational explanation.'[414]

The dialectician will state definitions both on the basis of the form and on the basis of the cause; for he is concerned with these. He will not be examining these as a cause, but simply as a thing or as a form, e.g. that anger is a desire for retaliation. Here he gives us nowhere a notion of the essence of anger, he only gives us the cause through which it is: in order that the person who has first been caused pain retaliate. Aristotle says that this is empty for the reason that it does not touch on the <actual> thing. That in stating the cause he does not render it as the cause but simply as a thing is clear from the fact that he does not mention what is caused. That which is caused by the desire is the boiling of the blood in the region of the heart; since he wishes to retaliate, this is why he moves the blood in the region of the heart. Consequently, if the dialectical definition, although it states the cause, does not mention what is caused, and since it is absolutely inevitable that the person discussing the cause will also mention that which is caused (for this belongs to the relational items), it will be obvious that he does not mention the cause as cause, but, as I said, as something in its own right.

The mathematician, too, is concerned with the forms that are inseparable from their matter, though not with all of them but only with those that can be conceptually separated. These are the so-called common objects of perception, such as magnitudes and shapes.[415] The form of flesh and bone and similar things cannot even be separated from their matter conceptually; for when the soft and the moist and the red and anything else of which the form of flesh is made up are being thought of, their appropriate matter is being thought of simultaneously, and when their matter is being subjected to abstraction, they too are subjected to abstraction. The mathematician, then, states the definitions of the forms in themselves, as they are the result of abstraction, not by taking account of the matter, but by stating them in themselves. This is also why he does not mention the cause in the definition; for if he also defined the cause, he would inevitably also include the matter. Since, then, he does not deal with matter, for this reason he will not mention the cause either. For example, what is a triangle? A shape encompassed by three straight lines. What is a circle? A shape encompassed by one line. In these definitions he does not mention matter, and hence he does not mention the cause through which this form is in this matter either – unless, perhaps, he will mention the causes of the concomitant attributes that necessarily belong to the figures, for example, <he will state the cause> why the three angles of the triangle are equivalent to two right angles.

The first philosopher will discuss the forms that are completely separate from matter. For among the enmattered forms there are also the formulae in our soul, yet there are also transcendent formulae in the creative intellect. Of those in the soul, those that are in the imagination have extension, but those that are in the rational part of the soul are undivided and without extension. Now the geometrician discusses the extended forms in the imagination; for he uses the imagination as a kind of reckoning board, exercising activity in individual parts and measuring and dividing distances. But the first philosopher discusses both the forms that are in the rational part of the soul and those that are in the creative intellect.[416] These forms differ in that those in the soul are images of the first things and provide knowledge of things, whereas the others are archetypes[417] and creative. When discussing the creative forms,[418] he will exercise activity as a theoretical student, but when discussing those that are in the soul, as a purgative; he is active as a purgative when he turns in on himself and knows the essence of the soul, for then there will be truly and scientifically purgation of the emotions and of ignorance. Knowing the essence of the soul, he will know that it is a fullness of forms, and for this reason he will say that processes of learning are in fact processes of recollection.[419]

The one who says 'desire for retaliation' is obviously the dialectician; this is the cause and the end of the movement of heat. The one who says 'boiling of the blood or heat in the region of the heart' is the student of nature; he proceeds from the matter; for the blood in the region of the heart, or simply the heat, is the matter. What do we mean when we say that he proceeds from the matter? For he would seem to be proceeding both from the matter and from the form. For he said it was a boiling, and this is the form of anger, whereas the matter is the blood in the region of the heart, and the cause, as it were the final cause, is through a desire for retaliation. But I say that the boiling is not simply the form of anger, for then as often as the blood in the region of the heart would be boiling, also through other causal triggers, this would be anger; rather it is the boiling that takes place through this particular cause that is the form of anger, as he himself said just now, I mean through the person who has caused pain. Consequently, the simple boiling of the blood would be as it were the proximate matter underlying the boiling that takes place through the person causing pain. When, then, have we mentioned the form? When we added 'a desire for retaliation'. For in saying 'for retaliation' he has mentioned both the boiling having been set in motion through the aggrieving person, and because of the desire to retaliate; for retaliate refers also to the one who has first caused pain.

403b1 Of these the one states the matter, the other the form and the definition.

The student of nature has stated the matter, the dialectician the form or the cause. For the cause is, as it were, the form that characterises the emotion of anger selected here as an example. For as I said, the blood in the region of the heart will also be moved by other causes of some kind, but not towards retaliation, for this is characteristic of anger. Consequently, this cause will also be the form. Here he says, in rather rough outline, that the student of nature states the definition proceeding from the matter, but next he queries and examines more accurately what the definition given by the student of nature is, and he says that it is the one that states, together with the matter, also the form that is connected with the cause.

403b2 For the one is a definition, the other[420] is of the thing.

A comma has to be put between the connecting particle and 'the other', so that it runs as follows: 'For the one is a statement of the definition and is the cause or the form of anger, the other is a definition of the thing, that is of the essence and the matter.'

403b3 It has to be in matter of a particular kind, if it is going to be <at all> …

This definition, he says, that proceeds from the form, if it is going to be in existence and not empty or inapplicable to any existing thing, has to be in matter; consequently, the person who is going to give a complete definition will also have to mention the matter.

403b3 … just as the definition of a house is of this particular kind, e.g. a shelter that protects against decay through wind and rain and heat. But the other person will say that it is bricks and timber.

This is an example of the same things. The one definition, he says, that says 'a shelter that protects against etc.' is dialectical, rendering the final cause of the house, whereas the one saying that it is brick and mortar and timber renders the matter. Of what kind, then, is the form of the house? Now the cause, as I already said, is a form too, except that you might call this particular combination of words a form that is proximate to the house, whereas its matter is things such as timber and bricks and mortar; for it is not any chance thing.

403b6 Again, another will define it as the form realised in such and such for the purpose of such and such.

Having given two definitions, the one based on matter and the other based on form, he now says that there is also another kind of definition, which will cover the matter and the form and the cause, for instance, 'a house is a shelter present in this particular combination of bricks, mortar, and timber'. Next he gives also the reason why this form is in this particular matter, viz. 'it protects against decay through winds and rain and heat'. For it does not suffice to say that it is a shelter protecting against decay etc. in order to establish a house: for by that token a cave or a tent could also be a house. One should add the quality of the material and the combination.

403b7 So which of these is the student of nature? (And of the three definitions, he says, of what nature shall we say the

definition of the student of nature is?)⁴²¹ The one concerned with
the matter which ignores the verbal account, or the one concerned with the verbal account only? Or rather the combination of both?

By saying 'or rather the combination of both' he adds to the division simultaneously the remaining part of the division and he connects the concluding decision. He says 'of both', although there are three <components> of the student of nature's definition, the matter, the form, and the cause, since, as I have said many times now, the cause is also a form.

403b9 Which of these two? Or is it rather someone concerned with the attributes of the matter that are not separable, nor in so far as they are separable.

Having said in the beginning that it is the dialectician's task to give definitions on the basis of the form, the task of the student of nature <to give definitions> on the basis of the matter, and then moving on and correcting his argument by saying that the definition of the student of nature is the one consisting of both, he now understandably asks about the other two definitions, the one based on the matter only and the one based on the form only, to which scientist each definition belongs. As for the fact that the definition based exclusively on the form belongs to the dialectician, he says nothing, for he has already said it; as for the definition based on the matter only, he says that there is not a single science that is concerned with the matter only. For each science aims to add a form to the matter that has been subjected to it, hence there is no science that will give a definition on the basis of the matter only. Yet he does not simply say that there is no science that is concerned with the matter only, but 'with the affections of the matter that are not separable, nor in so far as they are separable', because no practitioner of a science deals with matter without further qualification, but always with a particular kind of matter, to which a particular kind of attribute essentially always belongs. The student of nature, too, even if he discusses matter without further qualification, will at the same time also discuss matter of a particular kind, e.g. what matter belongs in the higher regions of the atmosphere, both in general and in the particular cases of hail, snow, etc.; and similarly also concerning the things on earth, the matter of animals, metals, etc. Now since the discourse of an expert in a particular science is about matter of a certain kind, it has itself and by itself certain affections belonging to it, which the experts are particularly concerned with, and for this reason he has also added 'concerning the attributes of the matter'. For the carpenter, for the purpose of fitting a door, looks for straight planks of wood, and if he was asked why, he would reply, 'because they fit each other'. And the shipbuilder does not look for, say, ebony, because it is compact and does not float upon water, nor for any oak, but for looser types of wood such as cypress, etc.; likewise, the architect is concerned with the properties of his own materials, e.g. that one should not use, say, pumice-stones, since these are brittle; and similarly with all experts in other sciences. He adds 'not separable, nor in so far as they are separable', although they are not separable, e.g. the properties of the <types of> wood listed, or rather of all wood, in so far as it is wood, are inseparable. For instance, width of wood is an inseparable property of the matter of ships, or density of bricks of the matter of a house.

As for the phrase 'nor in so far as they are separable', this means to the extent to which they cannot be separated even in definition; for some properties are separable in definition, such as figures and all the mathematical objects; we can separate these conceptually; yet we can view neither the width of the wood nor the density, not even conceptually. These are properties of the matter, which cannot be separated even conceptually, since they are included in the definition of the matter; for, say, the loose wood is the whole matter; but the figures are not properties of the matter but of a body; they supervene on the body that has been informed by forms, but not in so far as it is a natural body, which is why they are also separable in definition. All these properties of natural bodies are inseparable, such as the wide, the dry, the heavy. Thus nor can the boiling of anger that takes place in the blood be separated, not even conceptually. So this whole, the boiling of the blood in the region of the heart, is the matter of anger. Thus there is no science, he says, which is concerned with the properties of the matter only without any definition or cause. Hence Plato says rightly 'I do not call anything which is without a rational explanation a science'.[422] If this is the case, no one will render a definition on the basis of the matter only.

403b10 But the student of nature is concerned with all that is a function and a property of such-and-such a body and such-and-such a matter. [All that are not of this kind, another person <should discuss>. The subject-specific expert will deal with some things as the case may be, e.g. the carpenter or the doctor.]

By saying 'concerning all', he distinguishes the student of nature from the subject-specific expert; for each of these is concerned with a part; and by saying 'of such-and-such a body' he distinguishes him from the mathematician; for the latter does not look at the figures as belonging to this particular body, and hence he does not include the matter in the definitions. Again, he would distinguish him from the dialectician and from the first philosopher; for neither of these examines these affections as belonging to such-and-such a body or as being in such-

and-such matter, as we already said. Thus it is the task of the student of nature to deal with all these things that belong to such-and-such a body; for he will not only deal with a body, but also with this particular body; concerning all, he says, through which each body is a substance. 'And of such-and-such matter'. Of each he gives the proximate matter together with the properties or activities that are peculiar to it; for all enmattered bodies are being viewed in their capacity of acting or being acted upon. Now, 'functions or properties', as Alexander says, <is used> instead of 'he will deal with the affections that are in the matter and in the body together with the verbal account of them, i.e. their cause'.[423]

'All that are not of this kind, another person <should discuss>', i.e. not such things as he has listed. For if the subject-specific expert is concerned with the things mentioned, clearly he will not be concerned with everything; thus next to the things mentioned, the subject-specific expert will deal with some things, as the carpenter will be concerned with the straightness or dryness of timber, and the doctor with certain things, viz. with bodies that are ill.

403b14 ... and the things that are not separable, but in so far as they are affections of such-and-such a body and <in so far as they are known> by means of abstraction, are the business of the mathematician.

The mathematician, too, deals with inseparable forms, but not in so far as they are affections of this body which is of such-and-such a kind, i.e. not in so far as they are affections of bronze or wood or something of this kind, but as it were by stripping them of their matter (this is what is meant by 'by abstraction'), and thus he examines these by themselves. The form of flesh and wood and similar things is inseparable and is an affection of a such-and-such a body, e.g. of such-and-such a configuration of elements and such-and-such a mixture, and therefore cannot be separated, not even conceptually. But mathematical forms, I mean figures, are inseparable from their matter too, yet not in so far as they belong to the body underlying them in so far as this body is such-and-such, and for this reason the same forms belong to most objects, to timber, bricks, and most other things, whereas this is not the case with flesh or bone. Hence, since they are not affections of such-and-such a body, because of this they can actually be separated conceptually without the matter in which they exist impeding it.

403b15 And in so far as they are separable, it is the task of the first philosopher.

Those who wish the philosopher to know[424] the forms clutch on this passage. 'Look', they say, 'he does know of the forms that are separable from the things here, and he says that the first philosopher deals with these'. And they also adduce other things he says elsewhere as testimony to this, viz. that he says that orderly arrangement is twofold, the one in the commander, the other in the army, and that the orderly arrangement in the commander is productive of the orderly arrangement in the army.[425] Again, he says that health is twofold, one in the doctor in the sense of producing health and according to the theory, the other the health that resides in the healthy body; therefore he knows also the separate forms. But those who do not accept that he speaks of the forms say that by separate forms he means the divine substances themselves, which are separated from matter in respect of their completeness, as he also says elsewhere, that they are actualities without potentiality.[426]

403b16 But we should return to where our discussion started. We have said that the affections of the soul are inseparable from the natural matter living beings are made of, in so far as they belong to them, being what they are, such as anger and fear, and not in the way in which a line and a plane are.

He has said that the affections of the soul are enmattered formal principles and that for this reason it is not the task of the student of nature to discuss the soul in its entirety, but only in so far as it is not without matter. Because of this, he was forced to say in how many ways the enmattered things should be defined and what kind of definition the student of nature would use; and then he went on and said which kind of persons would use the other types of definition, which did not contribute anything to the present discussion. He now returns to the discussion of the affections of the soul and reminds us of what he has said, that in order to find the definition of the soul we need the affections of the soul. Now we know, he says, that the affections of the soul are not peculiar to the soul alone but to the composite, and they are inseparable from this and cannot even be separated from it conceptually as in the case of a line and a plane; for the latter, even though their existence is inseparable from the bodies they belong to, can still be separated conceptually. The affections of the soul, therefore, are not inseparable in the same way as a line and mathematical figures, but in such a way that they cannot even be separated from their matter conceptually. For it is impossible to represent the essence of anger in a statement without mentioning the matter, and the same thing applies to the other affections: this is what is meant by 'in so far as they belong to them'. For anger, in so far as it is anger, is inseparable from the body: it is a boiling of the blood in the region of the heart; and similarly with the others. But the line and the triangle and such things, in so far as they are like this, can be separated, even if their existence is inseparable. This is why their definitions are given without reference to the matter. Since anger exists both in reason and in the *pneuma*,[427] it also exists in the living body, for example, reason instructs desire by means of *pneuma*, and *pneuma* sets the blood in the region of the heart in the living being in motion through desire,[428] as in the case of the ruler and the commander and the soldiers (the ruler instructs the commander to attack these people, and the commander sets the soldiers in motion and they start attacking).[429] Now, since anger is threefold, to prevent us from thinking that when he says that anger is inseparable from the living being he is talking about anger as a formula (for this is separate from all body), or about anger in the *pneuma* (for this, too, even if it is not separated from the whole body, is separate from the earthy material), for this reason he says 'in so far as they are such-and-such', i.e. in so far as they are a boiling of the blood in the region of the heart; for this anger is clearly inseparable from the living body.

<Chapter 2>

403b20 In examining the soul, it is necessary at the same time to raise the problems that we must know the answers to as we proceed [and to call to our aid the views of all those of our predecessors who had something to say about it, in order that, if some of their statements were correct, we adopt these, and if some were wrong, we be on our guard against them].

What he means is this: while inquiring into the essence of the soul and raising problems prior to its actual discussion, since the starting point of knowing the answers is raising the questions, as he says both here and elsewhere,[430] we must raise questions about the soul in order to know the answers, and we must start by dealing with what has been said about it by the ancients. He also mentions the reason for this: 'in order that, if some of their statements were correct, we adopt these, and if some were wrong, we be on our guard against them.' This is what he means here; yet, since the syntax has made the expression rather unclear, one should slightly transpose <the words> by putting <them> as follows: 'While examining the soul it is necessary first to deal with the doctrines of our precursors and at the same time raise the problems that must be solved, and therefore we must call to our aid all who have discussed it, etc.' For since the present aim <of inquiry> is the soul, he says, we should start our discussion by listing the doctrines of our precursors and call them to our aid in our discussion, and be on our guard if an earlier statement is wrong, but adopt it if an earlier statement was right.

403b24 To begin with our inquiry, we must set out <those things that> are particularly believed to belong to it <i.e. the soul> by nature. [The ensouled being is generally believed to differ from the unensouled in two respects, movement and perception; and these are more or less the things about the soul we have also adopted from our predecessors.]

65,1

He now does what he had proposed to do,[431] viz. finding the definition of the soul on the basis of its essential attributes. He had said that we not only learn the essential attributes <of something> from its definition, but often also the reverse happens, i.e. we learn the definition from the attributes when these are clearer than the definition.[432] He therefore adopts <those aspects that> are believed to belong to the soul, i.e. causing movement and perception. He proves this <belief> on the basis of what is posterior by nature but is clearer to us, since even what is posterior by nature gets known to us earlier, I am referring here to the ensouled being; for what is ensouled is by nature posterior to the soul. He claims, then, that that by which the ensouled is found to be different from the unensouled is likely to be characteristic of the soul. For if the same thing which is now ensouled were to become unensouled, whereas previously it was perceiving and moving in respect of place when it was ensouled, it will, when it has become unensouled, no longer move or perceive; hence movement and perception are activities of the soul. And for the time being he says that these are attributes of the soul in an unqualified sense, not because he himself adheres to this statement, but because all his precursors were of this opinion.

5

10

15

He is about to list the doctrines of his precursors and says that these are the two attributes of the soul we have adopted from the ancients; this is why he has not said 'those that particularly belong to it by nature' but 'those that are particularly believed to belong to it'. Since he does not yet reveal his own opinion but exhibits that of the ancients, for this reason he says that perception and movement belong commonly to the soul. As a matter of fact, they do not belong to all <kinds of> soul: they do not belong to the vegetative, but <only> to animals. At any rate, when he <i.e. Aristotle> in the sequel gives his judgement and sets out his own doctrine,[433] he says that what belongs to the soul in general is living: it causes those in which it is present to live, and living is what living beings that feed themselves and grow and generate beings similar to themselves do; for life can be perceived in each of these faculties. This, then, is, in general, peculiar to all soul; as for animals, he says that <their peculiar attributes are> thinking, judging, and perceiving.

20

25

In the present passage, however, he follows the ancients and says that perception and movement belong to the soul, meaning by 'movement' locomotion, and within this the kind of movement that is

30

generated by an impulse of the soul, with the entity that is being moved having the origin of the movement within itself.[434] For natural bodies move, too, but not by nature nor because they have the principle of movement within themselves, but because they are set in motion from outside by something else. For it does not naturally belong to a lump of earth to move downwards, rather it has this kind of movement towards what is natural when it is in a place that is contrary to <its> nature. For each <thing> is stable in its own main mass; for indeed, whole masses tend either to be stable or to move in a circle, because circular movement, too, is a kind of stability.[435] The movement of the fiery sphere and the air surrounding it[436] that are moving together with the universe is by force, although it does not deviate from the natural movement; for things that move in a circle keep their own place; they do not enter into what is contrary to nature, i.e. the area surrounding the earth, but they have their own designated share even when moving in a circle. But the individual fire and the individual air and water, when forced to deviate from their natural <place> by an external agent, move back in the direction of their natural <place>. In so far as it is moved, it is contrary to nature, since it is in an alien environment and outside its own main mass. Therefore, the movement towards the natural place is not natural, and the movements of their main mass are not of this kind. And nature ought to become more manifest in the main mass;[437] these movements in the <individual> parts are therefore not natural, but they are ways[438] towards the natural. For the celestial beings, circular movement is natural, and the whole undergoes the same as the <individual> parts, and it is in the whole rather than in the parts that circular movement becomes manifest; for the circular movement of the whole is fastest. In this way, then, such movements are not natural, but they are ways towards what is natural. However, people can mean 'by nature' in a different way, just as we say that healing is natural, whereas sickening is contrary to nature, since the one leads to what is natural, the other to what is contrary to nature. In this way, then, he says, the ancients have said that perception and movement belong to the soul, and they did so rightly, even if not to all soul; yet in the sequel they drew the wrong conclusions from this. Since they thought that everything that causes movement is moved, they say that if the soul causes movement, and if everything that causes movement is itself also moved, the soul itself, too, will undergo locomotion; and in this they were wrong. For if what causes movement were corporeal, it would actually be moved itself, as the stick that moves the door or the hand that moves it and the whole body that moves the hand and the soul that moves the body; yet, if the primary source of movement is incorporeal, it is not necessary for it to undergo movement, I mean locomotion, itself, since the divine that moves the universe is unmoved too, having a stable mode of being and power and activity.[439] Besides, none of the objects of desire that cause movement are themselves moved: the hay moves the donkey towards desire without being moved itself, and likewise the image moves the lover.

403b28 For some say that the soul is primarily and particularly the source of movement. [They believed that what is itself not in motion cannot move anything else, and thus they regarded the soul as something that is in motion.]

He has rightly added 'primarily'; for the stick moves the door, but not primarily; nor does the hand move primarily, nor does even the whole body, but the soul does; that, then, which moves particularly and primarily, he says, is the soul.

403b31 Which is why Democritus[440] says that it is some kind of fire and something hot; [for he said that there is an infinite number of shapes and atoms, and he called the spherical ones fire and soul, similar to the so-called motes in the air, which become visible in the sunbeams that enter through windows].

Having said that we have adopted from our predecessors these two attributes of the soul, movement and sense perception, he first sets out the doctrine of Democritus. The latter said that atoms and void are the principles of natural bodies; for, <he says>, there are in the universe an infinite number of indivisible bodies[441] differentiated by an infinite number of shapes, the gathering and dissolution of which constitute coming to be and passing away. Furthermore, <according to Democritus>, the differences between natural bodies correspond to the shapes of the atoms of which bodies consist, and also with their position and arrangement, as we have expounded at greater length in the *Lectures on Physics*.[442] Democritus, then, holding that movement is characteristic of the soul, said that it is fire, since fire moves very easily and quickly; and he says that fire consists of spherical atoms, because what is spherical moves most easily of all shapes, since it touches a plane <only> at a point. Now since the soul causes movement, and what causes movement must itself also be moved (for the more easily it is itself moved, the more easily it causes movement), for this reason he says that the soul and fire must consist of the atoms that move most easily, the spherical ones. Consequently, in this respect, viz. in saying that the soul is fire, Democritus goes in the same direction as Heraclitus; but he differs in that, whereas the latter said that this fire is a continuous body, as is also our view, Democritus says that the atoms are not continuous but are kept apart by void, 'just as the so-called motes in the air, which become visible because of the sunbeams that enter through windows'. Democritus did not mention these dusty shavings that are seen through windows

as if to say that the soul and fire consist of these, or in general that these are what the atoms are; rather, he says, just as these are in the air, but because they are made of such small parts they appear not to
25   be there because they cannot be seen, yet are exposed as real by the rays of the sun whenever they dash through windows, likewise, he says, there are the atomic bodies that are fine and invisible because they are so small; and he held these to be the principles of natural bodies, just as doctors think the four elements are the principles of composite bodies;[443] and of these, <he said>, the spherical atoms constitute the soul and fire.

404a4 And the seed-medley of all these <atomic bodies>, he says, is the element[444] of the whole of nature [and a similar view was held by Leucippus ...[445]]

By 'seed-medley[446] of all these' he means the plurality of shapes; for just as in a seed-medley there is both wheat and barley and the other seeds, likewise in the atomic bodies there is a seed-medley of all shapes. He further says that Leucippus held this doctrine too; he was a companion of Democritus.

68,1   **404a6** [... and of these the spherical <bodies> are the soul, <he says>,] because such 'shapes' <*rhusmous*> have a particular ability to penetrate everything [and being themselves in motion, to set other things in motion too. They assume that it is the soul that imparts movement to living beings].

Rhusmos is an Abderite expression, which means 'shape'.[447] Indeed, it is clear that one should not let those have it their way who try to explain this etymologically by saying, e.g., that it has to do with
5   flowing.[448] For if the spherical shape were the only thing to be called *rhusmos*, those etymologies would be plausible; as it is, however, they call every shape a *rhusmos*, so that one cannot let those who explain this etymologically have it their way. For what will they say about the cube? For it is not the case that that, too, flows. Yet if the phrase is to be explained etymologically at all, it is clear that the etymology will be through the paternal tongue, just as, for instance, Roman
10   phrases or others are explained etymologically in their own tongue, too.

The followers of Democritus have used three vernacular words, which are *rhusmos*, *tropê*, and *diathigê*.[449] *Rhusmos* means shape, *tropê* means position, and *diathigê* means arrangement. Now Democritus, he says, used to say that since spherical objects are easily moved, the soul consists of these; for they can penetrate more easily
15   than others and, when moved, they move the whole living being. And yet pyramid-shaped atoms should be able to penetrate better since

they have sharp angles and cut more sharply, unless someone were to say that their bases pose an obstacle, whereas the spherical ones slip away because they are without angles.

404a9 This is also why respiration is a determining principle of life, <he says>. [For when the surrounding air compresses the bodies <of living beings> and extrudes those shapes that provide movement to living beings – because they are never at rest themselves – they <i.e. the living beings> receive help from outside by the inflow of other such shapes in the process of respiration.]

The followers of Democritus tried to show that all attributes of a living being are consonant with their own doctrine. They said that what surrounds the body is cold, and therefore makes bodies compact, and when made compact their spherical atoms are squeezed out – these atoms being that from which the living being derives soul and life. Now since, when the spherical atoms are squeezed out, the living being is in danger of passing away, respiration has come to the rescue; for by inhaling other spherical atoms from outside that take the place of those squeezed out, it lives. This is why we live only as long as we breathe; when we stop breathing, we also cease to live.[450] The fact that we live happens[451] not only by our taking in the spherical atoms through respiration and by the fact that they are assimilated to us and take the place of those that go out; it is also by the fact that those that come in through respiration by their greater force prevent those that are about to be excreted <from doing so>, and thus, becoming more numerous and, by the ease with which they move, heating their substrate, they extrude the cooling which comes from outside and which is the cause of their being squeezed out.

Now if someone were to ask: 'Now tell me, do we inhale spherical atoms only?', they would reply that even though it is not spherical atoms alone, yet they constitute the majority, as they move more easily, just as, as a result of the cooling, they are more likely to be squeezed out in the process of condensation, because they easily slip out on account of the fact that they are without angles and of the fact that as a result of this they naturally move more easily. The word 'respiration' is used here both for inhaling and exhaling; for the moment, however, we have understood it to refer to inhaling <only>.

404a12 ... because they are never at rest themselves.

He <i.e. Democritus> now solves an objection that might seem to arise from these things. For someone might say to him: 'Now tell me, are the atoms that are present from the beginning not sufficient to cause the living being to live? Tell me, are these the only ones to be extruded by the condensation?' Yes, he says, since even if nothing extrudes them they can still move easily on their own and are scattered because they are never at rest; this is why they require help from outside.

> **404a14** For they prevent even the atoms present within living beings from being extruded [by assisting in resisting what is compressing and solidifying; and life, they say, continues as long as they are able to do this].

These <atoms>, he says, that enter through respiration are not only themselves causes of living, but they also prevent those that are about to be excreted <from doing so> by keeping off the cold of the external surroundings by means of the heat of their movement. And they also pull in along with themselves those that are going out by virtue of their greater movement; for when there are two opposite movements going on, and if the one is more powerful than the other, the stronger one pulls the weaker one along with itself. In this way, then, with some <atoms> being inhaled and others exhaled, those that are being inhaled are more numerous and pull in the others together with themselves.

> **404a16** It seems that what is said by the Pythagoreans[452] contains the same idea: some of them said that motes in the air are soul, while others said it was what causes movement to these.

The second doctrine he enumerates about the soul is that of the Pythagoreans; some of these said that it was the dusty shavings that become manifest in sun beams shining through windows, while others said it was what causes these to move. This is not to suggest that they called these things themselves soul (that would be ridiculous), but we know that the teaching of the Pythagoreans was cast in symbolic language, keeping their doctrines secret, so that, as Plato says,[453] they would not make their own wisdom clear to cobblers. Just as with the myths of poetry, as again Plato himself says,[454] if one sticks to their outward appearance, one will regard them as ridiculous, yet if one seeks the thought hidden within them one will need an inspired soul, the same applies also to the teaching of the Pythagoreans; for if we listen only to what is apparent, it will be ridiculous babble not of wise people but of old wives; yet if these people are wise men, one needs to search for something more profound than the superficial meaning. Just as by speaking of the soul as a harmony[455] they do not mean the kind of harmony that is constituted by the strings (this would be ridiculous), but that it is like a harmony – as the Pythagoreans themselves define the soul as 'a union of things that are heterogeneous[456] and that think in two opposite directions' (for harmony is achieved by mixing the bass tone and the treble one, which are opposite, thus producing one skilful tune) – likewise our soul, too, is a cause of harmony in the universe. (For there are the things that are always high up, by which I mean[457] the intelligible objects and those completely separated from matter, but there are also the things that are always low and unseparated from matter, and these do not have anything in common and really 'think in two opposite directions'; yet the soul binds these together by being itself the intermediary, it unites them and produces one harmony out of them; for although it belongs to the higher beings as far as its essence is concerned, it becomes part of the lower ones and is as it were mixed with them, mixing the unmixed through itself and letting the lower share in what is higher.) Just, then, as they said that the soul is a harmony, likewise now, too, they say that the motes in the air are the soul, thereby alluding to something different. For just as those only become apparent in the light of the sunbeams, and if there is no light they will not be known to exist, likewise the soul, too, when it appears in its own light shows what mode of being it has, i.e. a divine, incorporeal, and impassive mode of being; yet if it appears in the dark, i.e. in the body and in the affections,[458] we shall see it, as Plato says, just as those observing Glaucus the sea-god,[459] observing not his true being as such but seeing the seaweed that surrounds him as if it were he himself, I mean the affections or the body, and we will believe that it is some of those.

Some of the Pythagoreans used to say that the soul is such things, just as the Democriteans said that the soul is the atoms, whereas others said that 'it is what causes movement to these'. And they would say that the soul in general uses these <atoms> as instruments. Either, then, one should take this to mean that they talk about one universal soul using these <atoms> as instruments and causing movement to living beings through the intermediary of these things, or <one should take this to mean that it is> the individual soul in each living being that is causing movement to the body through these as its instruments.

404a19 Concerning these, it has been said that they evidently move continuously, even if there is complete absence of wind.

He now adds the cause why the Pythagoreans conceived of the soul as the motes in the air. It has been said, he says, concerning these that they are seen to be always in motion, even if there is absence of wind, which suggests that the movement they possess comes from within, not from the wind. Now since they, too, believed that movement was most peculiar to the soul, and since what causes motion must under any circumstances itself also be in motion, they have spoken of these things being the soul because of their being always in motion.

404a20 All those who say that the soul is that which moves itself tend in the same direction. [It seems that they consider movement the most proper characteristic of the soul, and they think that all other things are moved by the soul and the soul by itself, because they never see anything causing movement which is not itself also in motion.]

He alludes to Plato, Xenocrates,[460] and Alcmaeon[461] here. These, too, he says, held that what is most peculiar to the soul is its capacity to cause movement. Yet, since they thought that it cannot cause movement unless it is moved, they have said that the soul is self-moving. That Plato, by saying that the soul is self-moving, did not mean movement in the spatial sense he himself makes clear in the *Laws*: 'It leads', he says, 'the things in heaven and earth and sea by its own movements, which we call wish, thinking, and opinion, both of things that are correct and of things that are not correct'.[462] Xenocrates,[463] too, says that the soul is a number moving itself and thereby that it is self-moving.

404a25 Likewise, Anaxagoras,[464] too, says that the soul is the moving agent, as indeed anybody else did who said that the intellect has set the universe in motion [, yet not in completely the same way as Democritus[465] thought; for the latter regarded the soul simply as identical with the intellect, saying that what is apparent to the senses is the truth].

All those, he says, who have said that the universe has been set in motion by the intellect, these also seem to be among the people who say that motion is peculiar to the soul; one of these is Archelaus.[466] What does this mean?[467] If they said that it was the intellect that moves everything, how then does it follow that they also say that movement is peculiar to the soul? Yes <it does follow>, he says; for they held that soul and intellect were the same thing, as Democritus held, too. Now we possess by no means a clear statement[468] of this from these <thinkers> to the effect that intellect and soul are the same thing, yet he proves this through a syllogism. It is very clear, he says, that this is what Democritus intends; for he has said openly that what is true and what is apparent are the same thing, and that there is no difference between truth and what is apparent to sense perception, rather what is apparent to each <person> is also what is judged to be that and to be true, as Protagoras also said,[469] though according to correct reasoning they are different, with perception and imagination being concerned with the apparent, the intellect, however, with truth. Now if the intellect is concerned with truth, and the soul with what is apparent, and truth is the same as what is apparent, as Democritus thinks, then the intellect is the same thing as the soul. For just as the intellect is concerned with the truth, likewise the soul is concerned with the apparent; thus, crosswise, just as the apparent is related to truth, likewise the intellect is related to soul. Now if the apparent and the truth are identical, the intellect and the soul will be identical too.

404a29 For this reason he <i.e. Democritus> says that Homer was right when writing that Hector lay there with other thoughts. [Thus Democritus does not use the term 'intellect' as a faculty concerned with truth, but says that the intellect is identical with soul. Anaxagoras[470] is less clear on these things; for in many places he calls the intellect the cause of what is right and correct, but elsewhere he says that it is the soul, for he says that it is present in all living beings, both the large ones and the small ones and both in the higher ones and in the lower ones. Yet intellect in the sense of rational thought does not seem to be present in a similar way in all living beings, nor even in all humans.]

When Hector was lying there unconscious after the blow or deranged, the poet, he says, said that he 'lay there with other thoughts',[471] reducing perception to the same thing as thought, as though there was no sort of intellectual faculty concerned with reality apart from the faculty that was concerned with what appeared and perceived; this is why Homer called the absence of perceiving or ill-perceiving 'being with other thoughts'. Now, Democritus says openly that the intellect and the soul are identical, whereas Anaxagoras sometimes seems to differentiate between the intellect and the soul, but sometimes also seems to treat them as one and the same thing. For when he says that the intellect is the faculty and the cause of things that are right and good, he distinguishes it from the soul. As though taking it that there are also things that are not right and good and that there is obviously a different faculty of the soul that is concerned with those, he then says that the intellect is the cause of things that are right and good, as if the intellect is something more divine compared to the soul. Yet, again, in other places he seems to confuse the two and to treat the intellect and the soul as if they are one and the same thing, e.g. where he says that the intellect is in all living beings, both small and large and both those of higher value and those of lower value. The intellect in the strictest sense of the word, i.e. in the sense of intelligence,[472] is evidently not present in all living beings – indeed, why did I say 'living beings'? It is not even present in all humans.

20   Consequently, when he says that the intellect is present in all living beings, he is talking about the soul.

All these thinkers, then, held that movement was something peculiar to the soul, 'yet not in completely the same way as Democritus thought' (404a27). For contrary to Democritus, who says this clearly and always, viz. that the intellect and the soul are identical, Anaxagoras in a way says that they are identical, though in another way he says they are different, as we have just said.

'He does not use the term 'intellect' as a faculty concerned with
25 truth' (404a30): for this is also the correct definition, that the intellect is a faculty of the soul by which it knows the truth; yet Democritus and Anaxagoras said that the intellect is the soul.

404b7 All those who concentrated on the movement of ensouled beings conceived of the soul as being[473] particularly capable of causing movement, whereas all those who concentrated on its
30 knowing and perceiving things say that the soul is the principles, with some making these plural, others saying there is just one [, as does Empedocles, who held that the soul consists of all elements, and that each of these is soul, too].

He has said that especially movement and perception are peculiar to the soul, because it is in these respects that ensouled and unensouled beings differ from each other. Among those who have expressed views
73,1 on the soul, some concentrated on the aspect of movement, and hence they say that its essence is constituted from those things that, according to them, have most to do with movement, whereas others concentrated on the cognitive faculties. Having now enumerated the opinions of those who concentrated on the soul's movement and who
5   expressed views accordingly, he now wishes to enumerate those who have concentrated on its cognitive aspect. They say that what knows, desires to become similar to what is known; for like is known by like. Indeed, what knows wants to suit what is known, and likewise like wants to suit like. If, then, the soul knows all things, it must therefore
10   be composed of all things. Yet, since this is impossible, I mean that the soul is all things, it has to be composed of the principles of all things, so that by having the same principles as all things it knows them through these principles. Hence all these thinkers posit that the soul is composed of these principles, with each of them saying it is composed of the principles he happens to entertain; and whereas some say that there is a plurality of principles and accordingly posit the soul as being composed of a plurality of principles, others who say that there is just one principle posit that the soul is constituted of this
15   one principle. He begins by giving a report of the doctrine of Empedocles, who supposed that there were four material principles of things, the well-known four elements, and two creative principles, Strife and

Love. He said that the soul, too, consists of these and that it knows things also by virtue of consisting of these.

404b13 For by earth, he says, we see earth, by water water, by aether awesome aether, by fire destructive fire, [Love by Love, and Strife by gruesome Strife].[474]

It is evident that, since Empedocles was a Pythagorean and the teaching of the Pythagoreans proceeded in symbolic language, he, too, spoke about these things in a symbolic way; and by saying that the soul was composed of the four elements he meant this obviously not in the sense that it is made up of fire and water and the other elements. For <if that were the case>, why would it know the external elements rather than them knowing it? So he did not simply mean that the soul was these elements, but that it has the formulae of these things within itself. He further said that it is composed of Strife and Love, because he saw that it holds both a synthetic and an analytic faculty: he called the synthetic faculty Love and the analytic Strife. For Love is the cause of unification; and intelligible objects are more easily unified, in as much as they are closer to the one single principle of everything. But Strife rules in the perceptible objects, that is analysis.[475] Hence he also said: 'Likewise am I, too, an exile here sent from the gods and a wanderer, relying on maddened Strife'.[476]

Plato says the same thing in the *Timaeus*. For he says that the soul consists of the circles of Sameness and Difference.[477] Again, in the *Phaedrus* he says that the soul has a superior horse and an inferior one, thereby alluding to its synthetic and analytical faculties.[478] For sometimes the soul is activated intellectually and stretches itself towards the divine objects, whereas sometimes it is pulled down to matter. For this reason, then, Empedocles said that the soul is composed of Love and Strife, since he supposed that these two were the creative principles of all things, since he had perceived in all things both sameness and difference, union and disintegration. Yet in the area of the intelligible objects, Love rules, whereas in the perceptible domain it is the reverse, since as we said[479] the former are closer to the one and only principle of everything and are therefore ruled rather by union. It is evident that Empedocles made these distinctions in a symbolic way, and by saying that the soul is composed of the four elements he was not saying that the soul is the elements, but rather that their formulae are in it. Indeed, we could say to Aristotle when he refutes the apparent <meaning of what Empedocles says>: 'just as when you say that the soul is a location of ideas,[480] no one, I think, will say that there is a horse in the soul or a man, but rather when you say 'ideas' you mean the formulae of these ideas, likewise it is reasonable to think that Empedocles spoke, if indeed he was a wise man, and perhaps it is reasonable to suppose this about the other thinkers, too. For if, as the appearances suggest, they really said that the soul was perceptible fire or water or something like that and they did not assume this by way of analogy, they were far inferior even to the uneducated masses.'

'As does Empedocles, who held that the soul consists of all elements, and that each of these is soul, too' (404b11-12). The whole soul, he said, is composed of the elements, so that it differs according to each of these; and he says that he said that each of them is soul, and in addition Strife and Love; for it knows each thing through each of these, since like is known by like. In this way, <according to Empedocles,> we would have six souls. It is possible to understand the words 'and that each of these is soul' as if it referred to a part and faculty of the soul; for we, too, speak of the spirited soul and the nutritive soul,[481] and in this case we obviously give the name 'soul' to faculties of the soul.

404b16 In the same way Plato, too, in the *Timaeus* postulates that the soul consists of the elements, [saying that like is known by like ...]

Plato, too, he says, claimed that the soul,[482] too, is composed of the principles which he adopts and from which he said everything else derives its existence, in order that the soul, being composed of all the same principles, knows everything.[483] He said that there are five genera which are the principles of all things, being, sameness, difference, movement, and stability.[484] He called these 'genera',[485] not as if they are genera in the manner of the Peripatetics, where the genera are divided from each other and where from each genus a kind of line is produced of the subordinated genera and species; rather, he called them genera because they permeate all things. For in all things there is being, in virtue of which each thing has its being, as there is sameness, in virtue of which we exist as a result of the one principle of what exists; we further have difference, since the things are also plurality, and where there is plurality, there is difference. There is also movement in all things; by movement I do not mean incomplete activity, as Aristotle does,[486] but the activity of each individual thing; for all things have their own activity, even, indeed, unensouled objects; for they cause heat, cold, moisture, or dryness or some other effect to the things surrounding them. Stability, too, is perceived in all things; indeed, even things that are always in motion take part in stability, not only by the fact that their main mass is stable, but also in that the very fact of always being in motion is a form of stability.[487] In as much, then, as moving objects remain in motion either permanently or for a certain time, to that extent they partake in stability. It is of these genera, then, that Plato postulates the soul is composed. He says that the soul consists of being, sameness, and difference, not just any chance being, but the undivided being and the being that is divided over bodies.[488] He says that the essence of the soul is made up of both, in order that it can know both.[489] Yet, since knowledge of everything comes about either through some kind of similarity and sameness or through some kind of dissimilarity and difference (for we know a white object both through the juxtaposition of white – for what is similar to white is white – and through that of black – for white is the opposite of black), these <i.e. sameness and difference>, too, he says, are mixed in the soul's substance, when he speaks of the nature of sameness and that of difference. As to the fact that he also says it is self-moved,[490] this is obvious; and in this it would also have its stability.

404b18 ... and that things are made up of principles.[491]

That is, the things that exist, and of which the soul has knowledge. Because of this, then, since it is made up of the same principles as things that exist, and since like is capable of knowing like, it knows everything. Since he postulated that the soul is from the same elements as the things that exist, in order that it would know like by like, it is clear that he, too, considered knowing to be most characteristic of the soul.

404b18 Similar specifications have been given in the discussions *On Philosophy* ...

He refers to the work entitled *On the Good* here as *On Philosophy*.[492] In this work Aristotle gives a report of Plato's unwritten conversations.[493] It is a genuine work of his <i.e. Aristotle's>.[494] He gives a report there of the doctrine of Plato and the Pythagoreans about beings and their principles.[495] He says that they claim that the forms are numbers, and that these numbers are decads;[496] they said that each of the forms is a decad. They called the forms numbers either because, just as numbers measure and determine the objects they relate to, likewise the forms are capable of measuring and determining matter (for the forms define and describe matter, which in itself is indefinite, when they are instantiated in it), or because, just as all numbers are derived from one starting point, viz. the monad,[497] likewise the forms are derived from the one principle of all. This, then, is why they are numbers; they are decads because of the perfection of the forms, for ten is a perfect number, since it encompasses every number within itself; for after the decad, all numbers start again from one. This is why the decad was given its name, as if it was a kind of receptacle.[498]

The principles of these forms, he said, are the monad, the dyad, the triad, and the tetrad,[499] since combining these from one to four yields ten: one plus two plus three plus four makes ten. These tetradic principles, then, he said, are present in all things and both common and peculiar to them, both in intelligible objects and in natural objects and in perceptible objects. The monad is common to all things as the objects of intellect (for not only is their being undivided, but also their activity, which is viewed in a state of stability and absence of movement), the dyad as scientific knowledge or as the things that have scientific knowledge; for it has the property of proceeding from something to something in a determinate way. For <scientific> knowledge is a passage from some determinate things to other determinate things; it is not indefinite; indeed, this is where it has got its name from, since it leads us to a state of stability.[500] The triad is present in natural objects and those that are objects of opinion; by natural I mean universals in natural things, with which opinion is concerned,[501] as also Plato says in the *Timaeus*: 'What is it that always has being and does not have coming to be',[502] by which he means the intelligible, 'and what is it that is always in a state of coming to be, but never is',[503] by which he means what is universally present in natural things. For if he says that it is always coming into being, and natural things come into being, yet among them the particulars exist for a certain period of time and hence could not be said to be always in a state of coming to be, it is clear that this statement is about universals, with which he also says the activity of opinion is concerned.[504] 'For the one', he says, 'is grasped by intellect with reason', which evidently means the intelligible, 'the other is judged by opinion together with non-rational perception'.[505] This, then, is the triad, because it is an object of opinion, for opinion is a triad because it urges away from something, yet not in the sense that it urges to move in a determinate way towards something, but just this way or that way.[506] Such, too, are the natural objects whose being is in a state of flux and which are not in every way free from movement or change: they stand firm in the forms, but they change in this way and that way by alterations according to changes to the opposite. In this way, then, the triad is present also in these things. Indeed, one might even say that the celestial objects change place, some of them from the place where they rise to the place where they set, others in the opposite direction, and some from the south to the north, and others from the latter to the former.

In the perceptible objects, I mean the particular and individual things, the tetrad is present. In what manner the tetrad is present in these, we will show as we proceed. This, then, is the way in which the tetradic principle is viewed as being present in a way that is common to all things that exist. He <i.e. Plato> says that it is also viewed individually in the intelligible objects, and individually in the natural objects, and individually in the perceptible and individual objects. For these reasons he said that the living being as such, which in Plato is the Form of the living being and its model,[507] is itself, too, a decad consisting of the first monad, dyad, triad, and tetrad, i.e. of the one as such, the dyad as such, the triad as such, and the tetrad as such; and analogously to this, these principles are also present in the living beings that come after the living being as such, I mean those that are immortal[508] and those that are mortal. For just as all are decadic numbers, likewise they are also made up of the monad, the dyad, the triad, and the tetrad; yet the living being as such[509] is made up of the first monad, dyad, triad <and tetrad>,[510] while the others that are posterior to the living being as such are at a distance from these principles analogously to the distance that separates them from the living being as such. For the divine and immortal living beings do not stand so far away from the living being as such as the mortal living beings do. Thus the divine beings themselves, too, are made up from the second monad and the second dyad, and likewise for the triad and the tetrad, and in this way the distance from the principles gets ever greater analogously to their distance from the living being as such. He said that these tetradic principles are principles both in the intelligible objects and in the natural objects and in the perceptible objects; and for this reason, since the soul knows all these things, it, too, consists of the same principles, the monad, the dyad, the triad and the tetrad.

Now what kind of monad, dyad, triad, and tetrad he said was present in the intelligible objects, would be a subject of theology; but even for natural objects we could not easily say this. One might say that even in these there is a tetrad, because there are four kinds of living beings to be perceived in the universe: the celestial ones, the ones that live in the air, the terrestrial ones, and those that live in water.[511] In the perceptible objects he adopts the point as monad, the line as dyad, the plane as triad, and the solid as such as tetrad; for these are the principles of the body. He adopts as monad the point because it is undivided; as dyad the line, since when a point is moving it generates a line, which is terminated by two points and is a length without width; as triad the plane, either because the triangle is the first of figures or, perhaps more likely, because, just as when the point is moved it generates another point over the relevant distance in length, that same point, if it is moved in width, will generate yet another point, so that there will be three points, one being the terminus of the length, the other the terminus of the width, and a third the common point to both. The tetrad is the solid as such, either, again, because the pyramid, which results from four triangles, is the first of the solid figures, or, again, according to the same analogy: as a point when it moves lengthwise generates another point, and again when it moves in width generates another, likewise, when it moves in depth, it will generate another, so that there are four points. Think of the rising straight line which creates depth.[512] In this way, then, monad, dyad, triad, and tetrad are present in the perceptible objects.

Now since the soul knows all things, he said that it is likely for it, too, to consist of these principles, in order that it should know them all.[513] He said that in it, the monad is the intellect, through which it makes its apprehensions of the intelligible objects; for the intellect, being undivided, knows things by straightforward intuition. The dyad is discursive thinking; for this has the 'from where to what'; for it proceeds along a certain way and proceeds from certain premises to conclusions.[514] The triad is opinion, since this, once having urged to make a judgement, is in doubt and as it were makes for itself a twofold way, whether it should turn this way or that way, just as a traveller who has gone a certain way, and then meets a cross-roads and is in doubt as to whether he should turn this way or that way, likewise opinion, too, uses a kind of hypothesis, then wishing to make a judgement about this in either direction, it is in a state of doubt as to where it should turn, and whether negation or affirmation is true; for it wishes to possess some kind of insight about the soul and at once it urges towards this and makes an assumption about what soul is, it is in doubt and divided as to whether it should think of it as mortal or immortal, or again as corporeal or incorporeal; and it goes like this in all cases. The tetrad is perception, since the tetrad in the perceptible objects signifies the body, and perception is the most corporeal of all forms of cognition of the soul; for it grasps the individual; without body it does not know anything. One should not be in doubt about the question whether we have left out imagination;[515] for it is subsumed under sense perception, since it derives its starting points from there.[516]

404b19 ... that the living being as such is composed of the form of the one as such ...

That is, the one as such and what is one primarily.[517]

404b19-20 ... and of the primary length and width and depth ...[518]

We have already said that the living being as such is composed of the first monad and dyad and the rest, and those after this proportionally from the second and the third. The dyad and the triad etc. are applied both to a discrete quantity, as when they are applied to the numbers themselves, but they are also applied to the continuous, as when we view them in the case of a line or a plane. Here, then, his account is concerned with continua. One should take note here, since he named each of these magnitudes by that in which it exceeds what is prior to it, the line 'length', for it exceeds the point by its length, and plane 'width', since this exceeds the line in this respect, and the three-dimensional body 'depth'; for in this respect, it differs from plane. For plane also has length and the solid has length and width. Not only does continuous quantity consist of the tetrad, but discrete quantity does so at a much earlier stage; for if each number that comes after the number ten is broken down into decads and the principle of the number ten is one, two, three, and four, the tetrad is the principle both of the continuous and the discrete.

404b21 ... and the others in a similar way.

By 'the others' he either means those that come after the living being as such; and by 'in a similar way', he means according to the same analogy, composed of a monad, dyad, triad, and tetrad, as I already said, but not of the first, from which the living being as such is composed. Alternatively, he means the other models, for example, beauty as such, man as such, and similarly for other things. It is also written <in other copies> 'the others[519] in a similar way', and that would be in accordance with the second interpretation: the other forms, that of man, or that of angel.

404b21 And also in another way, the intellect being one, scientific knowledge two; for it proceeds in a single line to one conclusion; the number of the plane is opinion, whereas that of the solid is perception.

That is to say, by means of a different intuitive apprehension, too, he posits that the soul consists of these very same numbers. For believing that among the things that are, some are intelligible, others objects of knowledge, yet others objects of opinion and again others objects of perception, he has attributed the number one to the intellect, which has the capacity to grasp the intelligibles; for this is indivisible and similar to itself in all respects, knowing the things simultaneously by primary intuition and without lapse of time. The 'two' he has attributed to scientific knowledge; for scientific knowledge is composite, since it is in the form of a syllogism, yet it is in a single way only and not manifold, i.e., it is not this at one time and that at another, but always true and the same, leading through one way, the premises, to one end, the conclusion. The 'three' he has assigned to opinion; for opinion is not in a single way only, as is scientific knowledge; for opinion can be true and false, whereas all scientific knowledge is true. In what way the 'three' is appropriate to opinion, we have already said;[520] and the 'four' he has associated with perception for the reason mentioned.[521] This, then, is why he has said that the soul is composed of these, the monad, the dyad, the triad, and the tetrad, and thus knows everything because of its appropriateness to these.

100 Translation

80,1 But why does he <i.e. Aristotle> say that he <i.e. Plato> has called the intellect one, and scientific knowledge two, yet has not also called opinion three but said 'the number of plane'? Our reply is that one and two are not numbers. Indeed, according to the definition of number, which says that number is the plurality that is arrived at by monads, it would seem that the dyad is a number, too, yet in reality this is not the case; for it is not a plurality of monads; the first plurality is in fact that of three. Besides, each number when multiplied produces a larger number than when it is added, e.g. three plus three makes six, whereas three times three makes nine, and this applies to all numbers; yet with one it is the other way round: when it is multiplied, the result is less than when it is added; for one plus one makes two, whereas one times one makes one; and in the case of two, the same result follows when it is multiplied and when it is added. For two plus two and two times two produce in both cases four. Therefore, neither one nor two are numbers. Consequently, the first numbers are three and four, the one being the first odd number, the other the first even. One and two are principles of numbers.

404b24 For the numbers were said to be the forms and principles of things,[522] and they are composed of the elements.

One should slightly transpose the words here in order for its meaning to become clearer: 'For the forms were said to be numbers and principles of things, and they are composed of the elements.' For it is the forms that were called numbers and principles of things; for it is clear that they did not call these numbers that we have the forms of things; rather, they called the forms numbers. By means of these words he proves what has been said, I mean why the soul is made up of the monad, the dyad, the triad, and the tetrad. He says that they called the forms of things and their models numbers. These numbers are composed of elements, the monad, the dyad, the triad, and the tetrad. Indeed, we have already said[523] that they called the forms decadic numbers, the decad consisting of these; and that the forms belong to the intelligibles, the objects of scientific knowledge, opinion, and perception. He makes this clear by saying 'it judges some things by means of the intellect, others by means of scientific knowledge, yet others by opinion, and again others by perception'; for like is judged by like. Consequently, if the forms of things are composed of the monad, the dyad, the triad, and the tetrad (these being the elements of the forms) and if the soul knows everything, they plausibly postulated it as being composed of the elements of things so that like could be known by like. It is clear to us from what has been said that those who introduced the forms and said that they are the principles of things again posited as other principles of these the monad, the dyad, the triad, and the tetrad. This is why, when saying 'the numbers were called forms of things' he added 'they are composed of the elements'. Indeed, earlier on he says: 'the living being as such is composed of the form of the one as such' etc.; for the living being as such is a form and a model.

'These numbers are forms of things' (404b24). Since above he said that the numbers are forms, so that you would not think that what he means by ordinary numbers are those that occur in the bending of the fingers, when he says subsequently that 'it judges some things by means of the intellect, others by means of scientific knowledge, yet others by means of opinion, and again others by means of perception', he has added 'these numbers are forms of things'. He says 'these', meaning that the numbers that are forms are intellect, scientific knowledge, opinion, and perception. For just as there is the living being as such, likewise there is the intellect itself, scientific knowledge itself, and similarly also opinion and perception, and these are forms of intelligible objects, and of objects of scientific knowledge, of objects of opinion, and of objects of perception. The soul also, then, having in itself these forms is capable of grasping the objects in return; for it clearly judges and knows each thing in virtue of its form.

404b27 Since the soul is generally believed to be capable of causing movement and of knowing, some people have constructed an account of it on the basis of both, by saying that the soul is a number setting itself in motion.

We have said that among those who have spoken about the soul, there are those who have concentrated on its kinetic aspect, others on its cognitive aspect. Indeed, Plato sometimes defines it on the basis of its kinetic aspect, as in the passages where he shows that it sets itself in motion. Indeed, in the *Phaedrus* he says: 'Since what is moved by itself has been declared immortal, one would not be embarrassed to say that this is what the essence of the soul and its definition are all about.'[524] Consequently, he says that the definition of the soul is that which sets itself in motion. But sometimes he defines it on the basis of its cognitive aspect, as in the *Timaeus* in the passages where he says it is composed of the principles of things that exist.[525] Thus Plato sometimes looks at its capacity to cause movement, sometimes at its capacity to know. Xenocrates, who succeeded him, defines the soul on the basis of both when he says that it is a number that sets itself in motion;[526] he says that it is a number, as if he were a Pythagorean, on the basis of its capacity to know things (for according to the Pythagoreans, the number is the principle of all things); but because of its capacity to cause movement, he attributes self-movement to it; for according to them, what sets itself in motion is the principle and source of all movement. And the others, whom he is going to mention in the sequel, defined the soul on the basis of both, as he is about to show; this is why he has said 'some people'.

404b30 They disagree about the principles, about what they are as well as how many there are [, especially in that some posit the principles to be corporeal, others incorporeal; and again disagreeing with these are those who combine the two and say that the principles derive from both. They also disagree about their number, some assuming that there is just one, others assuming a plurality].

Having expounded, in the previous passages, the doctrines of his predecessors about the soul, both those who have concentrated on its capacity to cause movement and those who have looked at its capacity to know, he accordingly analyses in the present passage their disagreement about the principles. For their disagreement about the principles is also the cause of their disagreement about the essence of the soul. This is at least why some said the soul is this, others that, yet all say it consists of the principles which they supposed to be the principles of things; and in particular those who concentrated on the soul's capacity to know said it was composed of the principles, with the exception of Anaxagoras, as he is going to explain in what follows.

Now in the *Lectures on Physics* he has given an accurate account of the disagreements among the natural philosophers about the principles; but he is about to mention these now, too. It would seem that he is repeating himself, since earlier on he has mentioned their doctrines and he sums them up here again. Yet it is not mere repetition. For earlier on his intention was to expound their doctrines about the soul, but here he expounds how they disagree among themselves about the principles; and with this he connects their doctrines about the soul, which he has already summed up. He divides their disagreement on the basis of the essence, quality, and quantity <of the principles>: on the basis of their essence and quality, in that some make them corporeal, others incorporeal; on the basis of quantity, in that some say there is one, others more. Those who posited that the principles are corporeal are the natural philosophers, Thales, Democritus, Anaximenes, Anaximander, Heraclitus; those who said they are incorporeal are those who say they are numbers, such as the Pythagoreans and Xenocrates, as well as, apparently, Plato. Those who said they are mixed are Empedocles, who along with the four elements introduced Strife and Love as incorporeal natural entities, and Anaxagoras, who along with the homoeomerous parts introduced the intellect; for this, he said, is incorporeal. Among these one might also count Democritus, who together with the indivisible bodies introduced void. They disagree, he says, all among each other both concerning the quantity and about the <nature of the> principles, both those who defend corporeal principles against the incorporeal ones, and against both of these those who say that the principles are mixed.

405a3 And their account of the soul corresponded with these views.

That is, consequent upon their doctrine about the principles, they held corresponding views about the soul. For each of them posited that the soul is composed of the principles he recognised. He <i.e. Aristotle> indicates by these words that not only those who concentrated on the soul's capacity to know, but also those who concentrated on the soul's capacity to cause movement spoke plausibly in claiming that the soul is composed of the principles. This is why he adds:

405a4 They supposed that, to have a nature such as to cause movement belongs to things that are primary,[527] and not unreasonably.

Not unreasonably, he says, did they include the soul's natural capacity to cause movement in their account of a principle, for that producing <effects> and movement belong to a principle is a reasonable thing to say. This is why some said fire is the principle of all things, for it is most easily moved of all things and holds within itself the starting point of its own movement, and then, when it is itself moved, it causes other things to move. This is why it is primarily through the movement of innate heat that the living being moves, since innate heat is not set in motion by any other body but holds in itself the cause of movement, viz. nature.[528] Consequently, if the capacity to cause movement belongs to the principles, it is plausible for those who suppose that the soul causes movement most easily to postulate that it consists of the principles. This is why some supposed it to be fire, as he himself adds when he says:

405a5 Which is why some thought it is fire; for this is composed of the finest particles and is the most incorporeal of the elements [; furthermore, it primarily is <an element that> is moved and moves the others].

Having said that for those, too, who suppose the soul to be that which is most capable of causing movement, too, it was plausible to say that it is composed of the principles, because the natural capacity to cause movement belongs to the first things and to the principles (for it is characteristic of a principle to be active and to cause movement), and since the soul belongs to the things that are capable of causing movement, he has added accordingly that this is why some people thought the soul is fire, which they said is a principle of things that exist, since it consists of the finest particles and is most incorporeal and therefore most easily set in motion and the cause of its own movement and the primary cause of other things' movement. By fire they do not mean the flame (for this is an excess of fire), but the dry vapour which Aristotle says in the *Meteorology* causes earthquakes and winds and all other intense kinds of movement.[529] One could include Heraclitus[530] and Hippasus[531] among those who supposed that the principle is fire and that the soul is made of fire. However, he is going to mention Heraclitus and his doctrine a little later; now he will first set out the doctrine of Democritus, since even though the latter posited a plurality, indeed an infinite number of principles, he also posits that the soul consists of what for him are things that are most easily set in motion, I mean the spherical atoms, of which fire is also made. He <Democritus> has called fire incorporeal, but not incorporeal in the most literal sense (none of them said that), but as something incorporeal compared to other corporeal things because of the fact that it consists of delicate particles.[532]

Now one might raise a query against their saying that the soul is composed of the principles, to the effect that they even attributed to it something more than the rest; for each of them said that it is all the other things as well, since it is common to all things that consist of the principles. In response to that they could say the following: 'We have said this first to prevent one from suspecting that the soul consists of certain other principles and not of the common ones; and, subsequently, the other things have as a result of the combination of the principles become something else, either naturally, according to those who affirm that the principles are impassive, or by appearance, according to those who say that the principles are impassive and unchangeable. However, the soul really is a part of the principles, and it is different compared to the principles in virtue of the position it has adopted in relation to the things that are derived from the principles, I mean the living beings. This is why Democritus said that fire and soul are the same,[533] the difference lying, of course, in their relation, as I said; this is also why some of the others said that the soul is water, some air, even though they did not give that name to the things that are derived from these, such as bricks, wood, etc.

405a8 Democritus[534] gave a more ingenious account as to why it would be each of these [; according to him, the soul is identical with the intellect, and this consists of primary and indivisible particles, and it causes movement because of the delicacy of its particles and their shape; he says that the spherical shape is most easily moved, and of this nature are the intellect and fire].

He praises Democritus for plausibly stating the reasons for what has been said before, i.e. causing motion and being moved; for he has said that some say that fire, of which the soul, too, is composed, is what is primarily moved and causes motion to other things. Democritus has given a plausible account of the causes of these <, in answer to the question> through what fire and soul are both moved and cause movement: for both of these are composed of the same principles, I mean the spherical atoms. For he <i.e. Democritus>, he <i.e. Aristotle> says, has posited that the intellect or the soul (for these are the same for him) are composed of the first bodies, i.e. the atoms, and not just any atoms but the spherical ones, which are the most kinetic for two reasons, because they are finest and for that reason penetrate everything easily because of their fine particles, and thus, when themselves moved, they cause movement; furthermore, because of their spherical shape they are easily moved. Consequently, he has stated the reason why they are being moved as well as the reason why they cause other things to move.

It is worth raising the question for what reason Democritus said that the spherical atoms consist of the smallest parts, so that because of that they would be easily moved. That what is spherical is easy to set in motion, is obvious: he demonstrates <this by the fact> that a sphere touches a plane at one point only; since it touches a plane at one point, it moves easily because it slips easily; but why do the spherical atoms consist of small parts, so that by that fact the cause for their causing movement is yielded? This reasoning seems to be very arbitrary: for it would be possible just as much for pyramidal, or barbed shapes, or simply any other shape, to consist of very small particles. Our reply is that in geometry it is shown that of figures that have straight lines and equal circumference the ones that have more angles have a greater surface than those that have fewer angles. Let us assume, for instance, a quadrangle, each of whose sides has a length of two cubits so that its circumference is eight cubits; and let us assume another figure of six angles, each of whose sides has a length of one and a third cubit, so that its circumference, too, is eight cubits. And let us assume yet another octagonal figure, each of whose sides has a length of one cubit, so that its circumference, too, is eight cubits. Now all these figures, the quadrangle, the figure with six angles and the figure with eight angles, have the same circumference (each of these is eight cubits), but the one with eight angles has a larger surface, the one with six angles a smaller, and the quadrangle again a smaller one than that. Now if what has more angles also has a larger surface, the circle will have the largest surface of all figures with equal circumference, because the more angles a figure has, the more it approximates the circle; for in as much they have more angles, they are closer to being without angle, and the circle is without angle. The same argument also applies to solid figures; therefore a sphere will be more spacious than solid figures with straight lines and with equal circumference. Now if this is the case, and if among figures that have equal circumference those that have more angles have a larger surface, then crosswise among figures that have the same surface, those that have more angles will have a smaller circumference. Therefore spheres will have a smaller circumference than everything <else>. Democritus was therefore right in positing that of atoms that are equal in mass the spherical ones had the smallest parts, and that for this reason they can penetrate everything, and since they move very easily because they touch a plane at one point, they cause the others to move.

405a13 Anaxagoras[535] seems to say that soul and intellect are different, as we said before,[536] but he uses both terms as if they referred to one natural entity ...

By saying that the intellect is cause of what is just and good, as if there were something different that was cause of things that are not <just and good>, which is in fact the soul, he seems to distinguish the intellect and the soul from each other. For since the soul knows the nature of things on the basis of syllogisms, it is capable of error when in the premises it assumes what is not the case as if it were the case. However, the intellect grasps things by straightforward apprehensions, as he says himself,[537] and it either knows or it does not, and for this reason it is infallible; for if it erred, it would follow that the intellect is without intelligence, which is contrary to reason. In these statements Anaxagoras seems to distinguish intellect from soul; yet in those passages where he says that the intellect moves everything, and <where he says> that it can be seen in all living beings, both those that are big and those that are small, and both in those that are valuable and those of lower value, he has spoken of the intellect as if it were identical with the soul. For it is characteristic of the soul, not of the intellect, to cause movement and to be observable in all living beings.

404a15 ... except that he posits the intellect in particular as a principle of all things [; for he says that this alone of the things that exist is simple and unmixed and pure].[538]

Indeed, for even though Democritus uses the word intellect, he does not include it in his account of principles; yet Anaxagoras says that the intellect is most of all a principle, obviously in the sense of productive principle. Indeed, <Aristotle> praises him for this and for the fact that he supposes it to be a simple and unmixed body, and for not saying that just as the homoeomerous parts have all things mixed in them, likewise the intellect has, but for saying that it is unmixed and pure and simple. Which is why Aristotle himself, too, says the same things about the intellect,[539] and he does what he has promised,[540] I mean accepting the things that have been said rightly. At any rate he states about him <i.e. Anaxagoras> that he 'attributes to the same principle both knowing and moving, when he says that the intellect moves everything'; for by means of saying 'intellect', he has attributed the cognitive faculty to this principle, and he clearly says that the same principle also moves everything.

405a19 From what people report, it seems that Thales,[541] too, supposed the soul to be something that is capable of causing movement [when he said that the stone possesses soul because it attracts iron].

It seems not suitable that he mentions the doctrine of Thales here; for it being his present <concern> to show that those who concentrated on the cognitive aspect of the soul said that it is composed of the principles from which they posited things were made, because like is known by like, he now reports the doctrine of Thales without saying something similar to what he said about the others, but rather that Thales called the stone that attracts iron ensouled, thereby saying that movement was peculiar to the soul. Yet, while reporting the doctrines of those that concentrate on the soul's kinetic aspect, he has said that each of them said that what he felt was the most kinetic of all was the element of the soul, with Democritus adducing spherical atoms, the Pythagoreans the motes in the air, another fire, and yet another air; however, in the case of the doctrine of Thales, who posited water as the principle of things, he does not say something like that. For example, he does not say that Thales posits the soul to be water and says that for this reason the stone attracts iron, because it is something ensouled and therefore consisting of water. He does not say this, but solely that he called the stone ensouled. For what purpose? Either because no writings of Thales have been handed down but only his sayings, and for this reason he <i.e. Aristotle> shied away from criticising the vulgarity of what he <i.e. Thales> had said without writing it down, or because he <i.e. Aristotle> has a certain respect for him <i.e. Thales>, because many valuable doctrines of his are being reported. They say that he said that Providence extends to the extremes and nothing escapes it, not even the slightest thing.[542] For this reason, therefore, he does not say that this doctrine of the soul being from water was his, but only that he, too, attributed movement to the soul. In what comes next,[543] he says that Hippo was of this opinion, i.e. that the soul was made of water; for he, too, said that water was the principle of everything.

405a21 Diogenes,[544] as well as some others, thought it was air, [thinking that this is the most delicate of all and a principle, and that for this reason the soul knows <things> and causes movement, and in so far as it is primary and all things derive from it, it knows, while in so far as it is most delicate, it causes movement].

Diogenes of Apollonia and Anaximenes[545] said that air was the principle of things and that the soul, too, consisted of this, and that the soul knew everything because it had the principle of everything in it, and that the soul was moved most easily because of the delicacy of its parts. We have already said that what causes movement must consist of the finest particles, so that it can penetrate the whole of what is being moved, so that it indeed moves the whole; and air does consist of fine particles.

405a25 Heraclitus,[546] too, says that the principle is soul, or at any rate the vapour, from which the other things are held together [; it is most incorporeal and always in flux].

It has often been said that he <i.e. Heraclitus> said that fire was the principle of things, indeed fire, not flame; for as Aristotle himself says, the flame is an excess of fire.[547] It is rather that by fire he meant the dry vapour; of this, then, the soul is composed, too, since it moves easily and consists of very fine particles. Since he said that things are in constant movement and since he abolished stability from things, as did Protagoras[548] and many others, and since he said that knowing and causing movement is peculiar to the soul, this is the reason why he said the soul is composed of vapour; for since objects are in motion, what knows these objects must also be in motion, so that it runs parallel to them and touches upon them and suits them; for how would what is stable know what is in a state of motion? This is why he attributed the knowledge of the soul both to the fact that it is composed of the starting point of all things, I mean the vapour, and to the fact that it is composed of what is most easily set in motion; for what is being moved is known by what is being moved. He also said that it moves because of the delicacy of its particles of the vapour and because compared to bodies it is incorporeal. For what causes movement, as we have said many times, must consist of fine particles, so that it penetrates the whole of what is being moved; and the vapour consists of fine particles and it is always in motion and the cause of other movement, which is why, as Aristotle has shown,[549] earthquakes and other motions arise from it, too.

405a27 What is being moved is known by what is being moved; and he, as well as the majority of people, thought that things were in motion.

We should transpose the words here, so that its meaning becomes clearer, in the following way: he, as well as the majority of people, thought that things are in motion, and that what is moved is known by what is moved. Since they supposed that things are in motion, they said that this is why the soul is made up of what is most easily moved; for what is being moved must be known by what is being moved; for like is known by like. Yet he did not abolish stability from the realm of things that exist, as they supposed, and this is shown both by Plato in the *Theaetetus*[550] and in many other places and by Aristotle in *On the Heavens* and in the *Metaphysics*.[551] They say that if there were no stability in the universe, it would be impossible for there to be always movement; for the very fact of there being always movement is a kind of constancy and stability;[552] and if stability were abolished, movement would be abolished as well; for if what is moved does not have stability in its movement, it will obviously not be moved.

405a29 Alcmaeon seems to have held a view about the soul very similar to these.[553] [He says that it is immortal because it resembles the immortal beings; and this characteristic belongs to the soul because it is in permanent movement; for he says that all divine things are always in continuous movement, the moon, the sun, the stars, and the whole of the heaven.]

He, too, being a Pythagorean, concentrated on the fact that the soul is most apt to move, and said that it was composed of the heavenly body and for that reason immortal (for it is always in motion, as those bodies are), assuming without argument that the heavenly bodies are immortal. What his basis was for attributing to the soul its cognitive aspect, if indeed he stated other causes of some sort for its ability to know, I cannot tell; the writings of these men are not available to us, nor does Aristotle provide more information about them. What I am saying, then, is not that all of them in all respects gave an account of the soul's movement and knowledge, but rather that some gave an account of both, others of one or the other; hence there is no need for us to look for both in all.

405b1 Some of the more vulgar said that it was water, as did Hippo.[554] [They seem to have arrived at this conviction on the basis of the seed, which in all cases is moist; indeed, he refutes those who argue that the soul is blood, on the ground that seed is not blood, and seed is the primary soul.]

He <i.e. Hippo> was called the atheist for this very reason, viz. that he attributed the cause of all things to nothing else than water.[555] <Aristotle> has called his doctrine 'vulgar', especially because it is merely bombastic to the audience, and also because it drags the soul down to something material and low in matter, and because water is neither easily moved nor is it similarly apt to move, and it is passive rather than active (for the moisture in which water's being consists is passive), whereas it is more appropriate for the soul to be active rather than passive. He says that <Hippo> thought that the soul was water on the ground that the seed of everything is moist; indeed, the seeds of fruits are moist to start with. And against those who said that the soul is blood he argued that the seed, which for living beings is the source of being and life, is water and not blood. Yet if moisture in the straightforward sense were soul, all moisture ought to be soul. Moreover, the seed is not ensouled in so far as it is moist; obviously, if it evaporates, it will still be moist, yet also lifeless and dead. And not just that; for there are many things that have a moist natural heat yet are not ensouled; they also require natural formulae.[556] He says that the seed is the first soul, as if it is the seed of the soul and the principle of the soul. For just as it is the principle of the human body, likewise, he believes, it is the principle of soul.

405b5 Others said it was blood, as did Critias,[557] supposing that perception is most characteristic of the soul [, and that this belongs to it because of the nature of the blood].

Whether by Critias he means one of the Thirty who also attended Socrates' teaching, or someone else, does not make any difference for us.[558] They say that there was yet another Critias, a sophist, to whom the writings that have been handed down belong, as Alexander says;[559] for the member of the Thirty is said to have written nothing beyond political works in verse. However this may be, Critias said that the soul is blood: 'for thought is blood in the region of the human heart'.[560] This is because he said the soul was characterised by perception, and those bodily parts that are bloodless lack perception, such as hair, bone, nails, etc.; therefore blood is the cause of perception. Perception is peculiar to the soul; therefore the blood is soul. Yet medical theory shows that nerves are either the only parts to be sensitive or to the highest degree, and not just all nerves but only some.[561] Furthermore, if the soul is blood, bloodless animals will be unensouled; and all insects, flies, ants and the like are bloodless, yet it is evident that they share in perception. Therefore the blood is not the cause of perception, and therefore the soul is not blood, since bloodless animals, too, are ensouled and sensitive.[562]

405b8 All elements have received their judge, except earth.[563] [No one has said that that is the soul.]

He uses the word 'judge' instead of 'champion' for the person who judges and posits each of them as being a principle. No one said that the soul is earth only, because no one supposed earth alone to be the principle of things either, except, he says, those who have said that all the elements are the principle, as Empedocles did; he said that the element earth, too, is soul.[564] Or rather it is more plausible to say that he gave the name soul to the combination of the elements. But against this we are faced with what was said earlier on, that he said that each of them individually, too, is soul, unless by soul we will understand the faculty of soul, since we, too, often call the faculties of the soul souls; for we say that man also has a vegetative and non-rational soul.[565] Against nearly all doctrines that have been enumerated, which say that the soul is composed of more than one thing, the objection can be raised that they say that the soul and the body are identical, since both are composed of the same principles. Why, then, is the soul a body rather than that the body is soul? One could say in defence of the majority that, even if they said that the soul and the body are composed of the same principles, these are not in a similar state; for it is by such and such a mixture and separation of the principles that there come into being souls and the different kinds of bodies, just as we, too, are different in body through the different mixture of elements, and also the different kinds of metals come from the different mixture of evaporations. However, in *On Coming-to-Be and Perishing* Aristotle has refuted this doctrine which says that the coming into being and passing away occurs through mixture and separation of the elements.[566]

405b9 Except that some said it is composed of all the elements or is all the elements.

Since the phrase 'composed of all' also refers to processes of mixture, in which some sort of external form supervenes on the mixture, as the form of flesh supervenes on the mixture of the four elements, and since those who say that it is composed of all did not mean this in the way in which we do now, but referred just to the bare combination of elements as being the soul, for this reason, after saying 'composed of all', he has added 'or is all'.

405b11 All define the soul, so to speak, by three aspects, movement, perception, and being incorporeal [; and each of these is referred to the principles].

This is, as it were, a summing up of what has been said. 'Define' is meant in the sense of 'describe' and 'characterise'. Earlier he had said that the soul is recognised by movement and perception, and now he has added 'being incorporeal', as this, too, had emerged and had been discovered on the basis of the doctrines enumerated before. For moving easily and being always in movement is followed by being incorporeal; here he does not mean incorporeal in the proper sense, but in the sense of 'consisting of small particles'. All these, he says, movement, perception, and incorporeality are referred back to the principles, i.e. they say that the soul is of this nature as it comes from principles that are of this nature. And the phrase 'all define' is not meant in the sense that all determine these three as aspects of the soul but (and this is why he has added 'so to speak') some have attributed all to it, others some, as can be found to be the case on the basis of what has been said about their doctrines.

405b13 This is why those who defined the soul by its cognitive aspect made it into an element or something composed of the elements, speaking in very similar terms,[567] except one of them. [They say that like is known by like, and since the soul knows everything, they say that it is made up of all principles. Those who say that there is just one principle and one element, also posit that the soul is one, for example, fire or air; those who say that there are more principles, also posit that the soul consists of more. Anaxagoras is the only one to say that the intellect cannot be acted upon and has nothing in common with any other thing. But how the intellect, being like this, will know things and through what cause he has not told us ...]

That is, all refer these three things, which they say are attributes of the soul, back to the principles. At least among those who concentrated on its cognitive aspect, since like is known by like, each of them said that the soul is composed of the principles he recognises, with those saying that the soul is many, saying it is composed out of many, and those saying that it is one, saying that it is composed out of one. Since it is capable of knowing everything, they thought it had to contain everything in itself. The only one, he says, not to go down the same road as they did is Anaxagoras; for while all have attributed corporeal principles to the soul because of its knowledge, he said that the intellect was soul, since one of the activities of the soul is movement, and since he said that the intellect moves everything; consequently, he said that the intellect was soul, and this intellect he said is pure, unmixed, and impassive, that is, incorporeal. He mentioned the homoeomerous parts as the principles of things, and said that these are in a state of mixture among each other, but the intellect, he said, is unmixed with them and pure, as if he meant to say that it were different from the principles from which all things are made, thus going in the opposite way to all. Hence Aristotle accepts him as someone who has said the soul is incorporeal, yet he says his account of the soul was not correct; for he left it unclear how it, being unmixed and unsharing and having no relationship to the principles from which all things are made, will be able to know all things. For neither does Anaxagoras himself help us in this respect, nor is it possible to infer this from his words. All, then, have posited principles of the soul, some corporeal, some incorporeal only, yet no account was correct, but each has said part of the truth. For the essence of the soul must be incorporeal, since what knows must be superior to what does not know, yet the principles of bodies must be in this incorporeal mode of being, not the material principles but their formulae.

405b22 ... nor is it clear from what he has said.[568]

In many cases something has often not been said explicitly by the ancients, but it can be inferred from what they have said, as he has inferred that Democritus and Anaxagoras said that the intellect is the same as the soul.

405b23 All those who posit oppositions within the principles also suppose the soul is composed of opposites.

Such a person was Empedocles. The four elements, from which he says the soul is made up, consist of opposite qualities, and so do Strife and Love.

405b23 Those, on the other hand, who posit one or the other of the opposites, e.g. hot or cold or something else of the sort, similarly posit that the soul is one of these. [This is why they are guided by names: some say <the soul> is heat, and that this is also why life is so called, whereas others who say that it is cold say that the soul is so called because of respiration and cooling.][569]

One of the opposites is posited by Hippo and Heraclitus.[570] One of them posits the hot; for he says that the principle is fire; the other the cold, positing that water is the principle. Each of these, then, he says, tries to provide an etymological basis about the word soul for his own doctrine, the one saying that living things are said to be alive (*zên*) because of the boiling (*zein*), i.e. the hot, the other saying that the name soul (*psukhê*) is given because of the cold (*psukhos*), from which it derives its mode of being, since it is the cause of our being cooled through respiration.[571] For since life is present as a result of soul, and the soul as a result of cold (for it is made of water), this is why it requires respiration, which by its cooling effect tempers the heat in the region of the heart and does not allow it to become superior to the power of the soul, I mean the cold.

Notes

1. On the interpretation of this phrase, and on the relationship between Ammonius' commentaries and those by Philoponus in general see Blumenthal (1996) 49 and 58-60, and see Introduction above, p. 1.

2. On the relationship between the Prooemium and the Commentary, and the unusual range and agenda of this Prooemium compared to other Neoplatonist introductions to commentaries on Aristotle's works see Verbeke (1985) 454: 'instead of dealing with methodological questions, it [i.e. the Prooemium, PJvdE] presents a comprehensive justification of the interpretation which is given of the Aristotelian text. In this prologue a coherent doctrine regarding the nature of the human soul and its various powers is developed: in the commentary itself the author endeavours to show that this psychological doctrine corresponds to the text of Aristotle.'

3. i.e. to mention all those in which they are divided; the point is not to find an answer to the question 'how many', but to ensure that all faculties are comprised in the answer. This will be discussed in 1,9-9,2.

4. i.e. to state all the doctrines of the ancients. Again, the point is not to find an answer to the question 'how many doctrines were there?', but to ensure that all those doctrines are dealt with (see previous note). This will be discussed below at 9,3-12,9.

5. *diairesis*: this starts at 12,12, where the discussion about the incorporeality of the soul is arranged according to the various faculties of the soul distinguished in the preceding sections.

6. *logikai ... alogoi*: this division is not found in Aristotle's *DA* but reflects Philoponus' Neoplatonic background; below in 20,28ff., Philoponus applies this division to Aristotle's practice in *DA*. A division between a 'rational' and a 'non-rational' part of the soul is found in Aristotle's *Nicomachean Ethics* (1102a23-8), though with different subdivisions from what we find here. See Blumenthal (1996) 28 and (1986) 332, referring to the parallel division in Simplicius *in Phys.*, Prooemium, 1,6-11.

7. *zôtikai kai orektikai*: on these see below, 5,24ff. (with n. ad loc.).

8. These will be discussed below in 5,34ff.

9. This is in accordance with Aristotelian usage of *doxa*: cf. *DA* 428a27; *EN* 1147a26, 1147b17-18; *Insom.* 458b10-13; see also Verbeke (1966) li-lii, and Blumenthal (1986) 332, who refers to parallels in Proclus, (Ps?-)Simplicius *in DA* 2, 237,8-9 (on which see Blumenthal (2000) 145 n. 410) and (Ps?-)Philoponus *in DA* 3, 501-4 *passim*.

10. For *diakritikon* cf. Plato *Tim.* 67E5 and Aristotle *Metaph.* 1057b8. The example shows the close relationship between 'opinion' (*doxa*) and sensible objects.

11. *dianoêta*, objects of *dianoia*, 'discursive thinking', which is closely associated with *logos*, 'giving account'; cf. Aristotle, *DA* 428a13-14 and see n. 16 below.

12. After this, t (see Introduction, p. 7) has an addition: 'Therefore, opinion is that which knows the universal in the perceptible objects and the conclusions of objects of discursive thinking.'

13. Plato *Soph*. 264A10: *doxa de dianoias apoteleutêsis*.

14. A pun on *dianoia* ('discursive thinking') and *dianuein* ('complete', 'accomplish').

15. i.e. clearer than the subject under investigation.

16. cf. Plato *Phdr*. 245C5-246A2.

17. *nous*, the highest cognitive faculty, which apprehends by direct mental intuition, as opposed to *dianoia*, which understands intelligible objects by means of reasoning (*logos*) and argumentation. Philoponus also distinguishes the two in *in DA* 1.4, 155,4-35, where he points out that whereas *nous* is separable from the *sunamphoteron*, the combination of soul and body, *dianoia* is not; see also *in DA* 2.2, 229,29-32, *On the Intellect* 4, 20,71-88 and, in relation to the rational activities of the heavenly bodies, *in DA* 2.3, 258,36-259,2 and 260,18-25. For the distinction see also Plotinus 5.3.3,23-9 (and on *dianoia* itself see Plotinus 3.7.11,35-6); see also Blumenthal (1988) 110. The distinction between *nous* and *dianoia* has some basis in Aristotle's works (cf. *An. Post.* 89b7), although it is never fully or consistently articulated there (cf. *EN* 1142a25-6 and 1143a35-6, where, however, the distinction is between *nous* on the one hand and *phronêsis* and *logos* on the other); and in the *DA*, *dianoia* and cognate terms are mostly used to refer to activity of the intellectual part of the soul as a whole and as distinct from the sensitive part of the soul (e.g. 431a14; 427b15; 429a23) rather than distinct from the activity of *nous*. A distinction between *noêsis* and *dianoia* is made in Plato *Rep.* 511D6-E2.

18. This renders the verb *epiballein* and the noun *epibolê*, which refer to immediate mental viewing or intuition, as opposed to discursive, argumentative reasoning.

19. cf. Philoponus, *On the Intellect* 7, 91,62-5.

20. cf. Philoponus, *On the Intellect* 6, 89,96-9: 'They say, however, that such functioning (i.e. thinking about the transcendent forms) comes only to those who have reached the summit of a good life and of knowledge, and rarely even to them. Hence Plotinus (5.8.1) says in this connection that whoever shall have functioned in this way will know what he means' (tr. Charlton [1991] 103); see also the comments by Verbeke (1985) 469.

21. For the idea of virtue (*aretê*) as 'purification' (*katharsis*) see Plato *Phaed*. 69C, quoted by Plotinus in 1.2.3,8-10 and 1.2.4. For such purification see also below, 18,16-24; 58,19-21; and 52,2ff.

22. i.e. without having to use *phantasmata*, appearances in which the intelligible object is presented as having particular material properties (such as size, shape, etc.; cf. Aristotle *Mem*. 450a1-10). Cf. below 58,19-21.

23. As Hayduck notes, no passage can be found that exactly matches this reference (he refers to Plotinus 5.3.14 and 17, and 6.7.35-6). One may also think of Plotinus 6.7.30,23-7 and 6.7.39,3, or of 5.8.1,1-6. The One's incapability of being communicated in words is referred to by Plotinus in 6.9.11,26 and 5.3.14,129.

24. *noêsis*, the noun indicating the activity of exercising *nous*.

25. *Tim*. 28A1-2; 'reason' renders *logos* here, 'rational account'.

26. *Tim*. 28A2-3.

27. On this typically Neoplatonic analogy between the hierachy of cognitive faculties and the hierarchy within the universe see Blumenthal (1996) 86, 168.

28. On contemplation of the intelligible objects as the highest activity of the soul see Festugière (1950).

29. *Phaed.* 66D2-7.

30. *phantasia*; however, for a more positive valuation of *phantasia* by Philoponus see below 5,36ff. In the Platonic passage, *phantasia* is not mentioned: the confusing agent there is the body itself. See Verbeke (1966) xlvi-xlvii. For a discussion of the notion of *phantasia* in Philoponus see Lautner (1993).

31. i.e. intermediate between perceptible and intelligible objects; cf. Blumenthal (1996) 168: 'soul on its way upwards must operate in accordance with reason, which is directed to the intermediate kind of objects, *ta dianoêta*'.

32. i.e. the essence of mathematical objects does not involve matter, but they do not exist separate from material objects in which they are instantiated.

33. i.e. in the domain of objects of reason, mathematics, etc.

34. Loosely resembling Plotinus 1.3.3,5-10, though the quotation is not very accurate; Philoponus has *phuseôs* for Plotinus' *pisteôs* ('belief', 'proof'). Cf. also Ammonius, *in Isag.* 12,20-33 and Olympiodorus *Prolegomena* 8,29-9,13.

35. For this 'intertwining' cf. (Ps.?-)Philoponus *in DA* 3.3, 491,21-7. On the ambivalent state of *dianoia* in between *phantasia* and *nous* see also Philoponus *in DA* 1.4, 155,4-35.

36. Adopting the reading *peri* (with Pal. and t) instead of D's *epi* (preferred by Hayduck).

37. *indalmata*, a frequent word in Neoplatonic texts (e.g. Plotinus 5.3.8,47; 6.8.18,27) for traces or images of transcendent beings.

38. *koinai ennoiai*, universally accepted ideas; cf. Aristotle *An. Post.* 76a37-b2 and Euclid *Elements* 1.3, and von Fritz (1955). Philoponus returns to these ideas below in 5,17 and 19,2.

39. For a discussion of these examples see Wolff (1971) 75 n. 77, who points out that these are all propositions (as opposed to Stoic *phantasiai*).

40. Several textual witnesses (Pal., Suid., t) add here: 'This is why the intellect is called the starting point of knowledge, by which we know the intelligible objects'.

41. *An. Post.* 72b23; 'determining principle' renders *horos*, which means 'limit', 'boundary'; it is often used in the sense of 'definition', but here a more general meaning of what can be called a 'definition' seems envisaged.

42. Above, 3,16-17.

43. See n. 41 on the meaning of *horos*; 'limit' here renders Philoponus' *peras*.

44. See n. 41 on the meaning of *horos*.

45. cf. Euclid *Elements* 1, def. 13.

46. Above, 2,2.

47. The two horses of Achilles (*Iliad* 16.149).

48. Below, 5,35ff.

49. *Cael.* 291b17ff., also quoted below in 30,20-2; see also *An. Post.* 88a12-17 and 90a26 and the discussion of this by Richard Sorabji (see Preface above, p. vii). In ancient astronomical thought, the moon counts as an *astron*, a 'star', as much as the sun and other celestial bodies.

50. Above, 4,20-1.

51. Or 'individual things' (*merikôn*, the reading of t).

52. As the wording suggests, Philoponus adds a thought here which is not in Aristotle, i.e. the notion of innate knowledge of the formal principles of things, which is evoked by sense perception through opinion; cf. further down, 51,16ff., and Philoponus *On the Intellect* 6, 83,42-4.

53. Adopting Hayduck's emendation *hoion enkatekhôsthêsan*.

54. For this comparison see also Philoponus, *On the Intellect* 4, 20,71-88, where a distinction is made between 'discursive thinking' (*dianoia*) and 'intellect' (*nous*), with the former being 'intellect impeded by the body': 'for the body does not cooperate with the intellect, but rather hinders its natural operations, as ash does those of a burning coal ... Just as if a burning coal is not functioning in accordance with its nature because it is buried in ash, and someone says that it is a burning coal in potentiality, that is, dispositionally, and that such a thing does not exist without ash, he says this not because such a burning coal is composed of burning coal and ash, but because it is only by ash that it is hindered from functioning perfectly; in the same way, if *dianoia* should be said to be not without body, this is how we will interpret the saying' (tr. Charlton (1991) 44). On *dianoia*'s susceptibility to influence and disturbance from the body see also Philoponus *in DA* 1.4, 155,4-35 (and n. 17 above).

55. On this passage, esp. the notion of 'projection' (*proballein*) see Sorabji's Preface above, p. vii, with references to Proclus *in Tim.* 1, 251,4-9; *in Euclid. Elem.* 1, 121,1-7 and 1, 141,2-19.

56. This is, of course, strongly reminiscent of the theory of knowledge as recollection in Plato's *Meno*. See Sorabji's Preface above, p. vii, and cf. Philoponus *On the Intellect* 4, 40,36; cf. also Wolff (1971) 76-7.

57. Following Hayduck's preference for D's reading *sunaisthometha* over t's *sunesometha* cf. Philop. *in DA* 293,22 and Lampe (1986) s.v.

58. cf. Blumenthal (1996) 167; Verbeke (1966) lii.

59. Greek *aposkiasmata*.

60. Reading *panta gar haper* (with t) instead of *pan gar hoper* (D Pal.) adopted by Hayduck.

61. There is divergence between the manuscripts regarding the place of this paragraph, which is located after *alogoi dunameis* at 6,25 in D and t. But this clearly cannot be correct. Pal. has it here, and rightly so. It seems that this paragraph constitutes the fulfilment of what Philoponus had announced at 1,12, the 'rational faculties concerned with life and appetite', although the terminology is slightly different here; nor do we find an explicit reference to 'faculties concerned with life' in this paragraph. The unclarity seems to be due to the ambivalent position of deliberate choice (*proairesis*), which is here said to be 'intertwined' with non-rationality (27-8) and hence to fit in somewhat awkwardly with the division into 'rational' and 'non-rational' faculties (cf. the use of *proairesis* in (Ps.?-)Philoponus, *in DA* 3.9, 578,12-13, where it is said to be the cause of locomotion).

62. *boulêsis* and *proairesis*.

63. cf. Philoponus, *in DA* 2.3, 249,15; see Verbeke (1966) liii, and Sorabji, Preface (above, p. viii), who refers for the 'wavering' nature of *proairesis* to Iamblichus, *On the Mysteries* 1.10, 36,1-5, and for the superiority of wish over choice to 1.12, 41,3-4.

64. cf. Charlton (1991) 22, who compares *in DA* 2.2, 241,7-9, where Philoponus says that the intellect is practical only 'from its relation to the body, which is why, after its release from the body, it is exclusively contemplative', and *On the Intellect* 7, 107,51-5: 'True and false are good and bad apart from action; but the good which is truth differs from the practically good, and the bad which is falsity from the practically bad, in that the true is absolutely and more universally and by nature good, and the false is bad in the same way. What is good and bad in things to be done, by contrast, is good or bad not absolutely but at certain times and for certain agents' (Charlton [1991] 121).

65. A clear indication of the belief in the soul's pre-existence before its union with the body; cf. Blumenthal (1982) 60.

66. Below, 6,20-6.

67. For this notion of being 'interwoven' (*epiplokê*) see Wolff (1971) 74, who suspects influence of Hierocles here.

Notes to pages 19-20

68. cf. Verbeke (1966) xxviii and xliii: 'L'âme rationnelle, au cours de son existence transcendante, est fixée dans le bien; son dynamisme volitif est orienté vers le bien véritable dont elle ne s'écarte pas. La possibilité d'option surgit quand l'âme rationnelle s'engage dans le devenir et quand les puissances irrationnelles lui sont attachées. C'est à partir de ce moment que l'homme est en état de choisir ce qui est conforme à la raison ou ce que lui est contraire. Alors que le vouloir (*boulêsis*) appartient à l'âme rationnelle par elle-même, en dehors de tout autre contexte, le choix (*proairesis*) n'est pour elle que le résultat de son "entrelacement" avec les puissances irrationnelles.'

69. *phantasia*; see n. 30 above.

70. *tupoi*, a term used sparingly in Aristotle and only for non-standard perception (cf. *Mem*. 450a31, 450b5) but widely used in Hellenistic and Imperial theories of sense perception: see Verbeke (1966) liii-liv; Charlton (1991) 14; Lautner (1993) 165. For its use by (Ps.?-)Simplicius and (Ps.?-)Philoponus (*in DA* 3) in relation to 'imagination' (*phantasia*) see Sheppard (1991) 170-3.

71. Actually there is no such statement in *DA*: *phantasia* is closely related to, but still separated from *nous* by Aristotle. For Philoponus' interpretation of *phantasia* see also further down, 11,5-11, and *On the Intellect* 4, 13,1-4: 'For imagination is not strictly speaking intellect; it is not intellect without an added qualification; with an added qualification it is called "passive intellect" – which is as much as to say that it is not intellect at all' (tr. Charlton [1991] 38). See Blumenthal (1991) 202-5; Blumenthal (1996) 87 and esp. 159-60; Verbeke (1966) liv-lv; and Lautner (1993). The view that *phantasia* and *nous pathêtikos* are identical is alluded to (but not endorsed) by (Ps.?-)Simplicius *in DA* 1.2, 27,20; see Urmson and Lautner (1995) 164 n. 81 and 167 n. 127. On the question how *phantasia*, being 'non-rational', 'concerned with particulars' and 'perishable' (see 11,5-11 below), can be passive *intellect*, see Sorabji, Preface (above, pp. vii-viii); see also Proclus *in Euclid. Elem.* 1, 51,10-52,20 and Ammonius *in Int.* 6,4-22.

72. i.e. in the activity of imagination, things are imagined with size, shape etc.; cf. n. 22 above and Aristotle *Mem*. 450a1-10.

73. A pun on *phantasia* and *phaostasia*, the latter consisting of *phaos* ('light') and *stasis* ('stand still', 'coming to a halt'). Cf. Sophonias *Paraphrase of DA* (121,19-20): *phaostasia tis ousa kai tôn phanentôn stasis kai hupêremêsis*.

74. i.e. colour for sight, sound for hearing, odour for smell, etc. Cf. Aristotle *DA* 418a10ff.; *Insomn*. 458b4-6. For imagination's close connection to the controlling common sense faculty cf. Aristotle *Mem*. 450a10-11.

75. Or: 'anger' (*thumos*).

76. *epithumia*. The distinction between *thumos* and *epithumia* is, of course, already present in Plato's tripartition of the soul in the *Republic*.

77. cf. the 'formal' description of anger in Aristotle *DA* 403a30-1, commented upon by Philoponus below at 44,3-4; 55,3-5; 57,16-17; 58,24-5; 59,8. The point of these imaginary questions is that 'desire' (*epithumia*) is also inherent in 'anger' and 'reason' and thus not to be treated as a separate faculty.

78. *diathesis*, here confronted with *hexis* ('state'); cf. Philoponus *in DA* 1.3, 95,27; *in DA* 2.3, 249,16-18 and 251,12-13; *in DA* 2.5, 296,30-2. Cf. Aristotle *Cat.* 8b27; *DA* 417b15-16.

79. For this idea see Aujoulat (1998) 9-10, referring to Plato *Tim*. 30B; 39E-40A; Plotinus 4.8.1,41; and Wolff (1971) 74, who suspects influence of Hierocles here. See also Festugière (1953) 73ff. For the role of Providence see also below, 17,29 and 20,17. For the expression 'things here' see below, 23,26 (with note).

80. i.e. the body; see below, 52,3-4.

81. cf. Plato *Phaed.* 87D-E.
82. Or 'plant-like', *phutikos*.
83. cf. Philoponus *On the Intellect* 5, 48,42.
84. cf. Blumenthal (1996) 117: 'He now divides them into the powers of nourishment, growth and reproduction, thus maintaining the Aristotelian division which we find in the *De anima*, but doing so in such a way as to prepare the ground for seeing the operations of this part of the soul as separate functions, each corresponding to an activity of what might otherwise be seen as a unitary area of the soul.'
85. cf. Aristotle *DA* 415a1ff.
86. Philoponus here posits a hierarchy of the senses: sight, hearing, smell, taste, touch. In Aristotle, sight is often treated as the most important sense (cf. Stigen [1961]; cf. *Metaph.* 980a22-3; *Sens.* 437a3; *Insomn.* 460b21-2), while touch is said to be the most fundamental (*DA* 413b5-7; 414a2-3; 414b3; 415a3-5; 434a1; 435a12-14), but no strict hierarchy of the other three senses is found.
87. The same notion of *eidos* underlies the translations 'form' and 'species'.
88. i.e. mortal beings subject to decay.
89. cf. Aristotle *Metaph.* 1072b1-14.
90. i.e. individually.
91. Adopting the reading of t: *homoion hautôi auto* (deviation from Hayduck). For the idea cf. Aristotle *GA* 2.1 *passim* (esp. 731b25-35) and *DA* 415a25-b7.
92. Adopting the reading of t: *homoion hautôi* (deviation from Hayduck).
93. Plotinus 3.4.2.
94. cf. Blumenthal (1996) 118.
95. Adopting Hayduck's conjecture *trophês* for *truphês* ('enjoyment').
96. 6,21-2.
97. i.e. the body.
98. i.e. the rational soul.
99. Omitting (with t) the first *kai* in line 19 (deviation from Hayduck).
100. *sumpatheia*, an originally Stoic notion but freely incorporated in Neoplatonic thought; see Aujoulat (1998) 7 (referring to Plotinus 6.4.3,17-23) and 11.
101. Cf. Aristotle, *EN* 1102b25-1103a10.
102. *Odyssey* 20.17.
103. *Odyssey* 20.18.
104. Provenance unknown.
105. cf. *DA* 405a5 ff., discussed by Philoponus below at 83,10 and 90,10. Some of the thinkers mentioned here, and the characterisations of their positions, recur in Philoponus' discussion of Aristotle's doxography in *DA* 1.2.
106. Fr. 99 Wehrli.
107. See also below, 83,22.
108. DK 13 A 23; see also Wöhrle (1993) fr. 48, with his comments on pp. 80-1.
109. See also below 82,18.
110. See also below at 86,34 and 88,23.
111. cf. *DA* 405b8, discussed by Philoponus below at 89,24ff.
112. cf. *DA* 403b31, discussed by Philoponus below at 67,11ff. and *DA* 405a8, discussed by Philoponus below at 84,9ff.
113. i.e. one of the 'Thirty', the oligarchs taking control of Athens in 404, also discussed below in 89,8ff.
114. DK 88 A 23, also quoted below in 89,12-13.
115. *logos tês kraseôs*, a view attributed by Alexander of Aphrodisias to the Stoics (*DA* 25,2-9; see Todd [1977] 133 n. 62). See also below, 35,25-6 and

50,31ff., where Philoponus refers to a medical view which attributes the movements of the soul to the variations in the 'mixture' (*krasis*) of the body. Cf. also the discussion of the *harmonia* theory of the soul in Philoponus *in DA* 1.4, 149,19ff.

116. See below, 26,22-4; 33,1-5, where this view is attributed to 'the doctors'; and Philoponus *in DA* 1.4, 150,3ff., where the view is attributed to Empedocles.

117. *entelekheia*, the term coined by Aristotle to express his idea of the soul as the form of the body that makes the body capable of exercising its functions and thus brings it to completion and perfection (*DA* 412a10.21.27). Below in 33,4, Philoponus identifies Aristotle as the holder of this theory.

118. Fr. 47 des Places; cf. also Damascius *in Phaed.* 1.177. The view that the whole soul is immortal is also referred to by Philoponus later on in *in DA* 2.2, 237,11.

119. *Phdr.* 245C5: *psukhê pasa athanatos*.

120. Below, 11,29ff. I read *rhêseis* here (with t), contrary to Hayduck's preferred variant *khrêseis* (see his addenda).

121. Alexander's commentary on *DA* has not been preserved; for a similarly critical assessment of it by Philoponus see below, 21,22-3, and *On the Intellect* 4,70-2, on which see Blumenthal (1987b) 97-8; see also Philoponus *in DA* 1.4, 159,5 for more extensive polemics against Alexander. Alexander's own treatise *On the Soul* is extant (ed. Bruns, *Supplementum Aristotelicum* 2.1 [1887]; for translations with commentary see Fotinis [1979] and Accattino and Donini [1996]); see also his *Mantissa* (ed. Bruns, *Supplementum Aristotelicum* 2.1, 1887; tr. Sharples [2004]). For his views on the soul see Sharples (1987) 1202-14, who points out that, although Alexander's views on the intellect and the question of its immortality are notoriously elusive and problematic, the intellect is for Alexander not, strictly speaking, immortal in the sense in which it is for Aristotle; see also Huby (1991) 138-40. For a discussion of some of the fragments from Alexander's commentary on *DA* as preserved by Philoponus see Moraux (2001) 317-53.

122. i.e. the physical body, as distinct from the pneumatic body that serves as the vehicle for the soul, which is mentioned a few lines further down and which will be discussed more elaborately below in 12,20ff. On this distinction cf. (Ps.?-)Simplicius *in DA* 3.3, 214,1-2 with Blumenthal (2000) 136-7 n. 278.

123. On this see below, 12,19ff., 15,11 and 17,17ff. (with note); see also Karamanolis (2002) 278.

124. For an analysis of Philoponus' claim that Aristotle believes that the rational soul is separable and immortal, see Verrycken (1994) 220 n. 195 and 222-4. Cf. Philoponus *On the Intellect* 4, 39,21-7, and 5, 49,55-50,77.

125. In fact, this is in Book 1 of *PA*, 641a17ff.

126. That *DA* was considered to follow on *PA* 1 is understandable in the light of what Aristotle says towards the end of *PA* 1 about the priority of the 'functions' over the parts (645b20-646a3). On the arrangement of Aristotle's works in the Alexandrian curriculum in general see Hadot (1987a).

127. cf. 26,9 below. By 'width' (*platos*), Philoponus means variety across a wide number of animal species, by 'depth' (*bathos*) different levels of 'psychic' organisation; cf. Urmson and Lautner (1995) 157 n. 10.

128. *PA* 641a33ff., a passage which is also quoted by Philoponus, at *in DA* 2.3, 261,28, and discussed at some length by (Ps.?-)Simplicius *in DA* 1,25-3,2.

129. cf. below 25,10ff.

130. On this argument in Aristotle, the so-called 'correlative argument', see Lennox (2001) 142-4; Broadie (1997); and Charlton (1987) 410-11.

131. In fact, the quotation is from *GA* 736b27ff. (t reads *geneseôs* here instead

of *moriôn*, obviously a scribal correction). On any MS reading, Philoponus' quotation is not entirely accurate; I suggest reading *tais tou sômatos energeiais* (with Pal.); there is no need to adopt Hayduck's conjecture *sômatikêi energeiai*.
132. *DA* 403a27.
133. *DA* 413b24.
134. *DA* 429a13.
135. *DA* 430a22; *khôriston de esti* D^1R ; *khôrizetai* t : *khôristheis d'esti* D^2 et Arist.
136. cf. above 6,1-2 with note.
137. *DA* 429a22.
138. *DA* 429a31-b4.
139. *DA* 429b4-5.
140. *DA* 430a17.
141. *DA* 408b18.
142. *DA* 411b18.
143. *DA* 413b24, also quoted earlier (10,31-11,3).
144. For the immortality of the rational soul see also Philoponus *in DA* 2.2, 241,27-8 and 242,18 and Philoponus *On the Intellect* 5, 49,56.
145. *Tim.* 41Bff.
146. i.e. the lower gods created by the Craftsman.
147. *touto deontôs* Philoponus: *tode ontôs* ('this truly') Plato.
148. *thnêtôn* Philoponus: non habet Plato.
149. Omitting Plato's words *tôn aei dikêi kai humin ethelontôn hepesthai* ('in those that are prepared always to follow justice and you').
150. A German translation of the section that now follows (12,10-15,8, with some excisions) can be found in Böhm (1967) 233-6.
151. For this justification of the study of soul in the philosophical curriculum see Blumenthal (1996) 3.
152. See also Philoponus *in DA* 2.3, 261,1-262,4.
153. On this pneumatic body (mentioned briefly above at 10,7), a fine-textured material substrate for the soul interpenetrating the solid, mortal body but also outlasting it, see below 17,17ff. (with note).
154. What follows is not an actual quotation, but a rather free paraphrase of *DA* 3.2, esp. 426b30ff.
155. cf. *DA* 426b29ff.
156. i.e. 'be'.
157. *DA* 426b19.
158. I prefer the reading *phutikoi* (with t) for *phusikoi* (D R Pal., preferred by Hayduck), also in 26 and 30; Philoponus is still working with (his version of) the Aristotelian framework set out in the beginning (6,25). (See, however, the reference to *phusikoi logoi* later on in 89,3.)
159. On the notion of *epitêdeiotês*, matter's suitability or predisposition for receiving the form, i.e. its capability of being 'informed', see Todd (1972) and (1980) 162-3 nn. 50 and 53.
160. Because it needs a certain extension to exist.
161. i.e. in the Neoplatonic sense of *epistrophê*, re-orientation towards the One, which is impossible for corporeal things; see Proclus *ET* 83 and 171, and Porphyry *Sentences* 41, 52,7-53,5 Lamberz.
162. cf. Blumenthal (1996) 149: 'According to Philoponus (162,17-24) only the intellect can turn to itself, just because it is entirely separate from the body, and therefore has no conflict either with itself or with the body and the affections and emotions that beset it.'
163. For a very similar argument see below, 51,35-52,4.

164. See above, 10,8 and 12,18.
165. t adds 'i.e. in the solid' <i.e. body>, which is no doubt what is intended.
166. *DA* 402b21-403a12.
167. See the discussion of this passage by Verrycken (1994) 221. Philoponus refers back to the present passage in *On the Intellect* 4, 35,21-7.
168. i.e. what something is.
169. cf. *Cael.* 271a33.
170. See also below, 24,12; 39,3ff.; 46,20-49,14.
171. I have kept the words *kreitton de to têi phusei proteron* in the text; Hayduck in the apparatus suggests that they be deleted.
172. Or 'potentiality' (*dunamis*).
173. Adopting Hayduck's conjecture *to akhôristou to khôriston*.
174. cf. Aristotle *Poet.* 1451b18-19.
175. See also below, 46,28ff.
176. 'Harmony' (*harmonia*) refers to the 'attunement' or correct interrelation between the constituents of a whole, e.g. the tones in a musical scale. Cf. below, 52,8-11.
177. See also *in DA* 2.2, 241,27-8 and 242,16-19.
178. cf. *DA* 403a30-1, often quoted as an example by Philoponus in his commentary on Chapter 1, e.g. in 44,7-8, 50,19, etc.
179. cf. Plato *Tim.* 71B.
180. This is because the *pneuma* is linked to perception and emotion, which plants do not have.
181. The MSS here read 'where does this unsound and easily refutable doctrine come from?' I follow Hayduck in deleting this, as it obviously seems to be a gloss. See also the next note.
182. At this point, Pal. adds: 'But perhaps this theory is not true; for they say that these <parts> do not grow but rather that, when the flesh around these <parts> is decaying and waning, they are exposed and this is the reason why they appear larger and to have grown; but these matters must be studied separately.'
183. The doctrine of soul 'vehicles' (*okhêmata*) or 'envelopes', and of *pneuma* as the material constituent of these, has a long and complicated history, which has been well described by Dodds (1933) 313-21. Elements of the theory go back as far as Plato (e.g. *Phaedrus* 247B; *Phaedo* 113D and *Timaeus* 41D-E, 69C; *Laws* 898E) and, as far as the specific role of *pneuma* is concerned, to Aristotle (*Generation of Animals* 736b27ff.; *On Sleep* 456a7 and 456a13-18; see below, n. 209); thus Galen attributes a variant of the theory to Aristotle and 'the Stoics' (*On the Doctrines of Hippocrates and Plato* 7.7.20-6 [5.643-4 K] = *SVF* 2.774, 885); and in a Christian context, we find Origen developing the notion of the 'radiant' or 'luminous' body (*augoeides sôma*) as a special, ethereal body with which the soul is joined at the resurrection (cf. Philoponus below in 18,27-8, and see Crouzel [1977] for references and discussion of passages in Origen). In Neoplatonic thought, the concept of soul vehicles finds a more developed articulation in Plotinus, Porphyry and Iamblichus (for references see Dodds [1933] 318-19; see also Finamore and Dillon [2002] 103-4 and 183-6). Philoponus' ideas represent a later stage in the theory, strongly influenced by Proclus (see Blumenthal [1996] 112), in which three bodies are distinguished: first, the pneumatic body is distinguished from the 'solid' body as the material vehicle for psychic activity (cf. *in DA* 1.4, 158,16-17 and 164,8-13; *in DA* 2.1, 222,15 and 2.2, 239,3ff.); but there is a further distinction between a pneumatic and a 'luminous' or 'astral' body, referred to by Philoponus below in 18,27-8 (see also below, 49,5), with the former representing the lower, perishable vehicle associ-

ated with the non-rational soul and indeed open to the influence of demons (see below, 20,12). Especially this latter distinction represents a later development in the theory first expressed by Porphyry, Synesius and Hierocles and subsequently developed by Proclus, who refers to the pneumatic body as 'the second vehicle' (*to deuteron okhêma*) (*in Tim*. 3, 236,31ff.; 238,18-21; 298,12ff.; *ET* 196, 207-9; *TP* 3.5, 18,24-19,15). For discussions see also Blumenthal (1996) 28, 84-5 and 98; Blumenthal (1992); Bidez (1913) 88-92; Kissling (1922) 322-3; Finamore (1985); Verrycken (1994) 225-31; Urmson and Lautner (1995) 162 n. 57 (on (Ps.?-)Simplicius *in DA* 1.1, 17,17) and 164 n. 83; Trouillard (1957); Aujoulat (1986) 228-85 and (1998) and Sorabji (2004a), vol. 1, ch. 8.

184. cf. Plato *Rep*. 615A-616B; *Gorg*. 525B-C; *Phdr*. 249A.

185. A well-known principle, derived from Hippocratic medicine (cf. *On Breaths* 1.5, 6.92 L) but widely known in antiquity (cf. Plato *Phileb*. 31C; Aristotle *EN* 1104b17); also cited by Philoponus below in *in DA* 2.3, 250,17 and 254,10.

186. The terminology (expansion and contraction of the *pneuma* under the influence of heating and cooling as pleasant or painful) is probably Stoic (see Sorabji [2000] 37-41), but may also be an echo of Plato *Phaed*. 86B-C.

187. On *sumpatheia*, see n. 100 above.

188. On this notion, and its possible sources, see n. 183 above.

189. See above 4,31; 6,20-6; 12,6-9.

190. See above 6,20-6 and 12,6-9.

191. The use of 'they say' (*phasin*) here and throughout this passage is striking, although Philoponus seems to adopt this view without reservation (contrary to Évrard [1953] 350 n. 7, who claims that Philoponus does not endorse the views reported here). He may be referring to Proclus, Porphyry and Hierocles (see Aujoulat [1998] 13-15).

192. This might appear to be a reference to some sort of transmigration of souls, but presumably what Philoponus means here is a return of the soul not to the solid but to the pneumatic body, leading the kind of shadowy existence referred to further down (19,20ff.). See Verbeke (1966) xxxiii and (1985) 459; Verrycken (1994) 225; Aujoulat (1998) 13.

193. This is also referred to below in 49,5-6 (where it is similarly referred to as something 'they say'); *in DA* 1.3, 138,9; *in DA* 1.4, 162,2-27; and *On the Intellect* 4, 24,60-5. Cf. also Themistius, *in DA* 1.1, 19,33 with Todd (1996) 161 nn. 26-7. On this 'luminous' body and its various versions in Neoplatonic thought see n. 183 above; see also Dodds (1963) 315-16; Kissling (1922) 324 with n. 62; Todd (1984) 108 n. 54; Verrycken (1994) 225-31; Aujoulat (1998) 14.

194. On this explanation see Verbeke (1966) xxxiii-iv: 'L'idée qui semble inspirer ces réflexions de Philopon est sans doute que l'âme, *psukhê*, doit "animer" une certaine partie du cosmos ... il faut qu'on lui (i.e. l'âme rationnelle) assigne une fonction à remplir dans l'ensemble de l'univers et celle-ci ne peut être que le gouvernement d'une portion du monde.' Verbeke points out that this means that the luminous body is not necessary for the rational soul's existence in the way the pneumatic body is for the non-rational soul's existence. See also Aujoulat (1998) 14.

195. cf. Blumenthal (1986) 332, who compares Proclus *in Tim*. 3,237,24-7.

196. On this penetration to lower soul levels see Hadot (1978) 174-5 and Aujoulat (1998) 16 n. 96.

197. See 3,17 above.

198. cf. Plato *Tim*. 70B-D and 71B.

199. This was the by then accepted Galenic view on the physiology of sense perception; see Siegel (1970). Aujoulat (1998) 17 n. 103 refers to Synesius *On Dreams* 5,564,17-18 Garzya. See also Hadot (1978) 184-6.

200. Philoponus is probably thinking particularly of Galen here, as seems often the case when he mentions 'doctors'; see the experiments mentioned in the latter's *On the Doctrines of Hippocrates and Plato* quoted in the next note; see also 89,16-17 for a reference to 'medical theory' about sensory nerves. For Philoponus' use of medical ideas in general see below, n. 371 on 50,31.

201. On this see Todd (1984) 106 n. 30, who refers to Galen, *On the Doctrines of Hippocrates and Plato* 1.6 (78,33-80,3 De Lacy; 5.186 K): 'If even before inflicting a wound you apply pressure on any one of the ventricles the animal will immediately lose voice and sensation, breath and voice. And the same results are seen in the case of human beings themselves who have undergone trepanning. When we excise the broken fragments of bone we are compelled for safety to insert underneath the instruments called protectors of the dura mater, and if you press the brain with them a little too heavily, the patient is rendered incapable of sensation and all voluntary movements'; further references are given by De Lacy in his note (vol. 3, 618); cf. also *On the Affected Parts* 2.10 (8.128 K) and 4.3 (8.232 K). For a discussion of Galen's anatomical experiments and of the use of this instrument see Rocca (2003) 183-4 and Debru (1994) 1734; on the philosophical significance attributed to it by Galen see Tieleman (1996). See also the interesting passage in Nemesius, *On the Nature of Man* 13, 69,17-71,4 Morani, on the disturbance suffered by several mental functions as a result of different parts of the brain being damaged, and ibid. 8, 64,1-15 Morani, on the connection between the brain and the nerves in sense perception.

202. For these vivisectory experiments see Galen *Anatomical Procedures* 9.11-13; see also *On the Doctrines of Hippocrates and Plato* 1.6.4-6 (5.185-6 K); *On the Affected Parts* 2.5 and 4.3 (8.128 and 8.230-3 K); *On the Organ of Smell* 6 (2.886 K), and the discussion by Debru (1994) 1731-6.

203. For this belief in shadowy phantasms of the soul hanging around tombs cf. Plato *Phaedo* 81C-D, where it is said of the human soul that has been polluted by physical desires and pleasures that after its departure from the body it continues to be permeated by and associated with the material world: '... this bodily element is heavy, ponderous, earthy and visible. Through it, such a soul has become heavy and is dragged back to the visible region in fear of the unseen and of Hades. It wanders, as we are told, around graves and monuments, where shadowy phantasms, images that such souls produce, have been seen, souls that have not been freed and purified but share in the visible, and are therefore seen' (81C8-D4, tr. Grube). It is also alluded to by Origen (*Against Celsus* 2.60, 1,183,5 Koetschau = 425,10 Crouzel-Simonetti), by Porphyry (*Cave of the Nymphs* 11, 64,15-21 Nauck; *Sentences* 29, 17,11-18,13 Lamberz), and by Proclus (*in Remp.* 2, 156,25-157,8 and 164,19-27 Kroll; cf. also *in Tim.* 3, 331,6-9 Diehl and *in Remp.* 1, 119,11-122,20 Kroll). For discussions see Crouzel (1977) 228; Blumenthal (1996) 200 n. 20; Kissling (1922) 329-30; Todd (1984) 109 with nn. 65-6. Philoponus seems to refer to this same theory further down in *in DA* 2.2, 239,8-12, where he cites people (presumably he has Porphyry and Proclus particularly in mind here) who argue that the sense faculties are based in *pneuma* and who refer for support of this claim to the ghost-like phantasms seen around tombs, which are alleged to arise from the thickening of the *pneuma* by vapours as a result of a vicious mode of life: 'For the *pneuma* is not equipped with organs, but just as water or anything else like that when thickened in a pot becomes shaped along with the container, so also the *pneuma*, as a result of a vicious mode of life in this body, is thickened by its vapours, which is why phantasms are seen in tombs shaped like the body here, because it is easily moulded and is changed to other shapes when it is moulded along with imagination. That, they say, is why the more serious people use purgatives to thin the vapours that arise in it and cultivate a delicate mode of life, and abstain from many foods, which make it thicker; for it too is nourished by vapours' (tr. Charlton [2005a] 41, slightly modified). The resemblance in wording between the two passages is very close indeed. Yet whereas in 239,15ff. Philoponus criticises this view, or at least aspects of it (especially the claim that *pneuma* is not 'equipped with organs'), in the present passage he seems more sympathetic to the theory (or at least some aspects of it; cf. Aujoulat [1998] 18), for he introduces it in 19,18 as 'even clearer evidence of the facts themselves', i.e. evidence for the existence of the pneumatic body and of spirit's and desire's being inseparable from it. And although he is careful to present the theory throughout as something which is 'said' (*phasin*) by others, he does not explicitly distance himself from it; at 20,10 he does raise some problems, yet without coming to a clear conclusion, and the objection raised there is put in the mouth of 'someone', *tis erei aporôn*, as opposed to 'I would say', *eipoimi an* in 239,15, and it perhaps applies more specifically to that part of the theory concerned with demons (from 20,7 onwards).

204. cf. Philoponus, *in DA* 2.2, 239,8-9.

205. i.e. less compact.

206. *katharmoi*, medicinal purgatives, as suggested by the parallel passage in 239,12.

207. On this passage see Aujoulat (1998) 18-19, who refers to Porphyry *On Abstinence* 2.42, 172,2-6 Nauck and *Cave of the Nymphs* 11, 64,13-22 Nauck.

208. Aujoulat (1998) 20 compares Synesius *On Dreams* 5, 564,14 Garzya.

209. No such statement can be found in the *Metaphysics* as we have them; see, however, *On Sleep* 455a20 (*kuriôs*), which fits the quotation very well; moreoever, in the same work, at 455a23-6, Aristotle explains the simultaneous loss and recovery of all sensory function; and further on in *On Sleep*, we also find the doctrine of the 'connate *pneuma*', and the body's expansion and contraction under its influence (456a7 and 456a13-18).

210. cf. Plato *Phaed.* 81E; *Rep.* 620A-D; *Tim.* 90E-92C.

211. cf. the very similar wording in Philoponus, *in DA* 2.2, 239,7-9 (quoted above in n. 203).

212. Philoponus seems to allude to the same theory at *in DA* 2.3, 255,6-15 where, as here, he refers to something 'they say' in relation to Aristotle's words at *DA* 414b19 'anything else there may be similar and superior <sc. to humans>': 'they say he says <this> with reference to certain supernatural beings (*daimonôn tinôn ... sustoikhôn anthrôpeiai phusei*) that are ranged along with human nature. For the descent and the journey down, they say, from those that are always above us ought not to be immediate, nor should the fall of rational substance come straight to the last things, but there should be a sort of mean, which is neither as involved in non-rationality as we nor yet unrelated to it. And they say that the soul does not fall straight to this, but first becomes airy and lives for a certain time a life less affected than this one, yet not totally unrelated to the non-rational powers; which perhaps he hints at in these <words>' (tr. Charlton [2005a], 58). Cf. also (Ps?-)Simplicius *in DA* 2.3, 106,24-30. The holders of this theory presumably include Iamblichus and Porphyry (cf. *On Abstinence* 2.39; *Cave of the Nymphs* 11; *To Gaurus* 6.1, 42,6-11 Kalbfleisch).

213. It seems that in this paragraph (from 20,10 onwards) Philoponus raises some questions about the theory of shapes surrounding graves being pneumatised human souls, which he had apparently accepted in 19,17-8 (where he presented it as 'evidence of the facts themselves'). There is no inconsistency as long as we take it that his criticism here is particularly directed to the view that demons may be involved in the production of these phantasms too (20,7-8), an assumption made by the spokesmen but which Philoponus thinks confusing (cf. Aujoulat [1998] 21). Philoponus wonders whether, on this assumption, the shapes seen around tombs are actually to be regarded as human souls, and whether it is not more likely that these shapes are actually demons rather than humans (20,14). He argues that if the human soul is forced by Providence to remain where it is rather than ascend to the higher world, how can it do even worse things than demons do, whereas one would expect it to be aware of its faults and of the proximity of the places of punishment under the earth and hence be more moderate. On the tentative nature of the passage see Verbeke (1966) xxxv-vi ('Il s'agit ici d'un essai d'interprétation, qui ne manque pas de susciter dans l'esprit de Philopon toute une série de questions laissées sans réponse') and Aujoulat (1998) 21-2.

214. On this division see n. 6 above.
215. *Phys.* 8.6.
216. *Metaph.* 1072b13, also referred to in 55,17.
217. *GC* 2.9-11.
218. The Greek word is *eidêsis*, a noun derived from the verb *eidenai*, lit. 'to have seen' and therefore 'to know'; it is rarely used in Aristotle (see Hicks ad loc.). In this section Philoponus associates the word with *epistêmê* (and the verb *epistasthai*), which is mostly used in the sense of 'understanding', 'scientific knowledge', i.e. knowing why a thing is as it is (see below 22,11). A third term used in this context (e.g. 21,10; 22,9; 22,12) is *gnôsis* (verbs *gignôskein*, *gnôrizein*), which is not explained by Philoponus, but which is the least qualified of the three; it often refers to the act of getting to know and to perceptual knowledge.
219. The discouragement is expressed by Aristotle ten lines later on (402a10-11); this is quoted by Philoponus in 21,16.
220. Plutarch of Athens, the fourth-century Neoplatonist commentator, mentioned only once in Philoponus' commentary on Books 1 and 2, but very frequently in Book 3, and by (Ps?-)Simplicius *in DA*; on him see Blumenthal (1996) 56-7; the fragments have been collected and discussed by Taormina (1989); the present passage is fr. 18 Taormina (with comments on pp. 183-4).
221. For a similarly sarcastic remark by Philoponus on Alexander's distorting interpretation of Aristotle's psychology see above, Prooemium, 10,12-13 with note; on Alexander's reputation among Neoplatonist commentators in general see Blumenthal (1987). Alexander's commentary on *DA* is not extant; the references to it are discussed by Moraux (2001) 317-53 (present passage on pp. 324-5).
222. i.e. 'on these introductory words', i.e. of Aristotle's; this interpretation is also favoured by Taormina (1989) 115: 'Egli dunque, ha mostrato la sua propria perversa concezione ricavandola da queste parole del proemio, e ha interpretato lo stesso proemio in modo distorto', although the absence of a definite article is somewhat problematic. Blumenthal (1987) 98 renders *ek prooimiôn* as 'from the start'.
223. Alexander took the words *tôn kalôn kai timiôn* not as a partitive but as an objective genitive with *eidêsin*: 'considering that knowing the things that are fine and valuable' and then supplied 'is <itself> fine and valuable'.
224. These are also mentioned below in 46,18 and 51,15, and at *in DA* 2.2, 232,5 (cf. also Olympiodorus *in Cat.* 8, 120,33; *in Phaed.* 83,31 and 94,12); on the expression see Immisch (1904) 31. Philoponus may be referring to Plutarch of Athens (see n. 220 above), and perhaps also Proclus and Damascius.

225. *Metaph.* 980a22, where the infinitive *eidenai* is used.
226. Here the word *gnôsis* is used.
227. Hayduck compares Plato *Prot.* 357Dff.
228. On the word *epistêmê* see n. 218 above.
229. *Phaedo* 75D8-10; Plato's text has *apolôlekenai* ('having lost') instead of *apobeblêsthai*.
230. Hayduck compares *Gorgias* 454E3-9, where *eidenai* is used.
231. *Phys.* 184a10; Aristotle's text has at *methodous* instead of *epistêmas*.
232. For this hierarchy of sciences according to criteria such as exactness and nature of the subject-matter cf. Aristotle *An. Post.* 1.9; see also 1.13, esp. 78b37-79a2 and 79a14; on 'exactness' (*akribeia*) in the sciences in general see also *An. Post.* 1.27, 87a31-5 and *Metaph.* 982a25-8. Cf. also Themistius *in DA* 1.1, 1,11-23, and (Ps.?-)Simplicius *in DA* 1.1, 7,1-14, where the same examples (geometry, medicine, etc.) are found.
233. cf. Aristotle *An. Post.* 76a24; 78b37.
234. cf. Aristotle *An. Post.* 75b16; 76a10; 76a24; 78b38; 87a34.
235. *teîde*, i.e. in mortal life in the natural world, as opposed to *ekei*, 'yonder', i.e. the transcendent spiritual world; for these expressions see Urmson and Lautner (1995) 157 n. 8; Verrycken (1994) 208 n. 127.
236. *An. Post.* 78b35, loosely paraphrased; see Lautner (2002) 89.
237. cf. Aristotle *Sens.* 436a18-b2 and *Respir.* 480b22-31, where Aristotle says that the more distinguished and philosophically-minded doctors derive their principles from physics; for a discussion of these passages see van der Eijk (1995); see also Todd (1984) 105 n. 21, who refers to parallels in Philoponus' *in An. Post.* 34,24-35,1, 146,17-25, and 100,25-31 (Wallies), and to Themistius *in An. Post.* 25,25.
238. *An. Post.* 87a31-7.
239. *Metaph.* 993a30ff.
240. As distinct from the soul, which does change in actuality, as pointed out below in 24,26.
241. *Metaph.* 993b9-11.
242. cf. above, Prooemium, 15,15-22.
243. Alexander's views on the inseparability and the mortality of the soul are also referred to by Philoponus above, Prooemium, 10,1-3. On the present passage see Moraux (2001) 325.
244. The words translated as 'inquiry' and 'inquirer' are *historia* and *epiïstôr*, which connote 'expertise' as against unprepared knowing (*gnôsis*).
245. The Greek has *prôton* and *prôtiston* respectively.
246. Or 'activity' (*energeia*). It is possible that what lies behind this is the view, taken by Proclus (*in Tim.* 3, 335,23-336,2; 338,6-13; 340,14-17; *On the Subsistence of Evils* 21,22-8 Boese) and earlier by Iamblichus (*On the Mysteries of the Egyptians* 1.10, 36,1-5), Plotinus (3.6.3,27-34) and Porphyry (*On Abstinence* 3.8.6) that the activities of the soul are subject to change, but not its substance or essence (I am indebted to Richard Sorabji for these references).
247. *Tim.* 41C6ff.
248. *Metaph.* 1072b5-7.
249. *EN* 1102a18ff.
250. This question is discussed in the Prooemium, 10,9-11,29 and in *On the Intellect* 4, 39,21-7, and 5, 49,55-50,77.
251. Or 'intellection': in Greek, the word *nous* can refer both to the faculty and its activity.
252. *PA* 641a33ff., also discussed above in the Prooemium, 10,11ff.

253. 'Contribute' is taken up from Aristotle's usage of *sumballesthai* in 402a5, quoted above in 24,32; see the discussion by Lautner (2002) 91.

254. This reflects standard Neoplatonist doctrine; cf. Verrycken (1994) 204.

255. cf. above, Prooemium, 10,11ff.; On the relationship between the study of the soul and the study of nature see Aristotle *PA* 641a18-b10, esp. 641b8-10.

256. e.g. *PA* 1.1, 640b28-9 and 641a18ff.; *DA* 2.1, 412a15ff.

257. *diorganôsis*, i.e. its 'organisation' in parts, as described by Aristotle in *PA* 2-4.

258. i.e. a hierarchy of different levels of psychological organisation and activity; for this use of *bathos* cf. above, Prooemium, 10,16 with note.

259. *theôrêsai*, usually used for theoretical study, can also refer to initial observation or consideration of a topic to be explored in greater depth.

260. *gnônai*; see n. 218 above.

261. *phusis kai ousia*. The latter term is used here (and below in lines 21, 25 and 28) to refer to the 'what-it-is', the essence of something; in lines 21-2 it is used in the sense of 'substance', i.e. an entity.

262. For the view that the soul is a mixture, or a proportion of a mixture, see above, Prooemium, 9,23-6 and n. 115 with further references; see also further down, 33,1-6. The view will be further discussed in Philoponus' comments on *DA* 1.4.

263. Aristotle here uses *sumbebêke*, which Philoponus points out is not to be taken in the sense of *kata sumbebêkos*, 'accidentally', in the way in which whiteness belongs accidentally to a stone, but in the sense of belonging to something necessarily (in the way in which 'having interior angles equal to two right angles' is a necessary feature of the triangle), though not necessarily constituting the definition. See, however, below, 29,4 (with note) for a slightly different sense of the expression *kata sumbebêkos*.

264. *An. Pr.* 24b18.

265. *koina kai tois zôiois di' ekeinên* Philoponus: *di' ekeinên kai tois zôiois* Aristotle vulg.

266. Here and in what follows, *pathos* is used; the Greek term covers anything that may happen to, occur to, be experienced by, or be a property of, something else.

267. The complex of soul and body, *to sunamphoteron*.

268. cf. *DA* 417b2-7; 431a4-7.

269. *Sophist* 244Dff.

270. The first-century BC 'editor' of the Aristotelian corpus; on his activities see Moraux (1984) 45-142; he is also mentioned by Philoponus below, 45,8ff.

271. cf. Ammonius *in Int.* 5,24-7,14.

272. In the sequel: 402a13.

273. On 'description' (*hupographê*) see Urmson and Lautner (1995) 162 n. 62.

274. *sustatikos*.

275. *huparxis*.

276. *apodeixin* Philoponus: *apodeixis* Aristotle.

277. Aristotle had written *tôn kata sumbebêkos idiôn*, 'the proper attributes'. Philoponus here attributes to Aristotle a distinction between *sumbebêkos*, 'accidental', and *kata sumbebêkos* (rendered 'attribute'). The former is 'accidental in the proper sense' (29,12) and added 'from outside' (29,6), in the way whiteness is accidental to a stone; the latter refers to features that accompany or are 'added to' (*episumbainei*, 29,11) others even if they necessarily follow from them. While the distinction is entirely Aristotelian, the terminology is not: for while in Aristotle *sumbainein* can be used to express both accidental and essential connections (the latter usually in combination with expressions like *kath' hauto*), Aristotle uses *kata sumbebêkos* almost invariably in contrast to *kath' hauto* or *phusei* (see Bonitz [1870] 714b5-43). Philoponus' distinction here is also slightly different from what he says about Aristotle's use of *sumbebêke* in 26,27ff. above, which does refer to necessary attributes expressed in syllogistic reasoning.

278. This is easier in Greek, where the verb *sumbainein* can be connected with a noun in the sense of 'belong to', 'is peculiar to'.

279. In Greek *kata sumbebêkos idia*.

280. *An. Post.* 75a28ff.

281. *Cael.* 291b18. See also above, Prooemium, 4,22.

282. 'Indication' renders *tekmêrion*, 'sign' *sêmeion*.

283. *phêsi* is not in Aristotle's text.

284. cf. Aristotle *Cat.* 1.4.

285. cf. Simplicius *in Phys.* 722,30.

286. Xenocrates of Chalcedon, head of the Academy, contemporary with Aristotle (fr. 180 Isnardi Parente). His theory is discussed by Aristotle in *DA* 408b32 and commented upon by Philoponus at *in DA* 1.4, 165,18ff. It is also referred to below in 44,11, 71,13, 81,25 and 82,30.

287. For the view that the soul is a mixture, or a proportion of a mixture, see above, Prooemium, 9,23-6 and 1.1, 26,22-3 with n. 262; see also below, 50,31ff.

288. 'Actuality' renders *entelekheia*.

289. This has not yet been established in the commentary (though it has been taken for granted in the Prooemium, at least for the rational soul, in 16,3ff.) and is therefore to be regarded as *ex hypothesi*. See below, 34,5.

290. Porphyry *Isagoge* 2,16.

291. i.e. the essence.

292. *Phaedrus* 237B7. *Phaidrôi* is Hayduck's conjecture for the MSS reading *Phaidôni*, since no corresponding statement is found in the *Phaedo*.

293. *Phys.* 184a1-2.

294. i.e. it has the potentiality to become something it not yet is.

295. This is the Aristotelian view in *GA*, also referred to by Philoponus in *On the Intellect* 5, 52,35; whether Philoponus himself adheres to this, considering the Galenic view that the female contributes seed, is another matter (see Todd [1980] 163).

296. i.e. why not 'in actuality' (*entelekheiai*) instead of 'actuality' (*entelekheia*)? In the translation the dative expressions are rendered by the adverbs 'actually' and 'potentially' (*dunamei*).

297. In Greek *dunamis* and *en dunamei*.

298. This is difficult to convey in English; the Greek has datives *dunamei* and *energeiâi*.

299. Or 'pure actualities'; cf. Philoponus *On the Intellect* 84,24. See Verrycken (1994) 116 with n. 65.

300. *Int.* 23a23.

301. See above, n. 121.

302. cf. DK 68 A 105 (= fr. 110d Taylor). For a more extensive discussion of Democritus' position see below, 71,22ff.

303. On *sumpatheia* see n. 100 above.

304. For this typically Neoplatonist element see above, Prooemium, 13,24-14,1.

305. The view that the soul is a mixture, or a proportion of a mixture, is also referred to by Philoponus in the Prooemium, 9,23-6, and above in 26,22-3, and 33,1-6, where it is attributed to 'doctors', and below, 50,31ff.

306. See n. 121 above, and Moraux (2001) 325-7.

Notes to pages 52-60

307. cf. *Tim.* 91D6-92C9 (animals) and 76E-77C5 (plants).

308. i.e. the non-existence (or rejection) of A would involve the non-existence (or rejection) of B, but not the other way round.

309. What is presupposed is prior by nature to the presupposing (at least in cases where the relation is not mutual).

310. For this division of the soul see above, Prooemium, 5,34 and 6,26.

311. For the idea that the presence of the higher souls automatically implies that of the lower ones see Aristotle *DA* 2.3, 414b28-415a11.

312. cf. the example of 'health' in *Metaph.* 4.1.

313. On Aristotle's various attempts to give a definition of the soul in *DA* 2.1-2 see Ackrill (1972-73).

314. i.e. by using the expression 'the living being in general' (*to de zôion to katholou*). Cf. Moraux (2001) 325-7, who refers to Alexander's *Quaestiones* 1.11b.

315. *Metaph.* 1075a13-15.

316. *Metaph.* 4.1, 1003a34-b3; 1060b36-1061a6.

317. *DA* 430a14-15; 431a1.

318. *DA* 429a27.

319. *Metaph.* 1074b33ff.

320. See Moraux (2001) 327-8.

321. This is a free paraphrase of *DA* 402b5.

322. On these 'creative formal principles' see below, 52,15-16.

323. *ennoêmatikos*.

324. Omitting *ekeina* (with R, t) (deviation from Hayduck).

325. This is one of the Aristotelian 'rules' which Philoponus refers to above in the Prooemium, 15,15-22. See also above, 24,12.

326. This is true up to a point: cf. *DA* 3.4-5, which are primarily concerned with the intellect before in 3.6 attention is focused on the objects of thought, although in reality the distinction is not kept that sharp.

327. Here and in what follows, Philoponus is quoting Aristotle and interspersing it with comments of his own; *epi* is not in Aristotle's text.

328. At this point, the MSS have the phrase *tou nou kai tou noêtou, doxês kai doxastou, kai tôn loipôn* ('both the intellect and the intelligible object, opinion and the objects of opinion, etc.'). Hayduck has deleted this.

329. Plato *Phdr.* 245C.

330. Above, 29,14.

331. For these 'common insights' (*koinai ennoiai*) see above, Prooemium, 3,17.

332. *Phys.* 210b32 (freely paraphrased).

333. cf. *Phys.* 203b15ff.; 213a19; 217b30.

334. *Meteor.* 347b34.

335. *to te* Philoponus: *ti to* Aristotle.

336. On the interpretation of Aristotle's phrase *kata tên phantasian* here see Ross (1961) ad loc.

337. See Moraux (2001) 328.

338. Plato *Phdr.* 237B.

339. *An. Post.* 2.1, 89b23-5. See also Philoponus *in DA* 2.2, 226,1-3.

340. This is Aristotle's example given in *DA* 403a30-31, commented upon extensively by Philoponus below at 44,3-4; 55,3-5; 57,16-17; 58,24-5; 59,8; see also above, Prooemium, 6,13-14.

341. As of now, *thumos* is used more or less interchangeably with *orgê* in the sense of 'anger'. Its use in the wider sense of 'spirit', 'spirited part', is found predominantly in the Prooemium, e.g. 6,11; see also 38,27 above.

342. See above, 32,33, with note and further references.
343. Above, 44,3.
344. *noein*, 'thinking' or 'intellection', the activity of *nous*, 'intellect'.
345. cf. above, 27,21ff.
346. *Int.* 16a6.
347. i.e. hypothetically; cf. (Ps.?-)Simplicius *in DA* 1.1, 17,3-5.
348. *DA* 432a12.
349. For a slightly different listing of different usages of the expression 'not without' (*ouk aneu*) see Philoponus *On the Intellect* 8, 119,42-9 (with Charlton [1991] 132 n. 41).
350. i.e. these exegetes claim that Aristotle argued that *if p, then q* entailed *if not-p, then not-q* instead of *if not-q, then not-p*.
351. See above, 21,28, with n. 224.
352. See above, Prooemium, 15,12-35 (and 24,12). For the slight discrepancy between these two passages see Verrycken (1994) 221 n. 197.
353. See above, Prooemium, 16,19-21 and below, 52,8-11.
354. See above, Prooemium, 15,20-1.
355. A mixture of wine and honey widely used in ancient medicine.
356. For Philoponus' views on the anatomy and physiology of visual perception see *in DA* 2.7, 336,29ff. and the discussion by Kupreeva (forthcoming).
357. Instead of 'for it requires wholeness for its existence', the MS A has the following textual addition, which Hayduck prints at the bottom of the page: 'The old solution seems to resolve the objection by means of homonymy. But whether it is rightly targeted and to the point, is another story. It would come closer to a solution, I think, to say that seeing is the activity of the eye, but not in the sense of the activity of the essence, but of the instrument, yet many instruments do not allow separation nor a unity of such kind. And the activity of the soul was taken in the sense of the activity of the essence and not of the instrument. Furthermore, the eye is not in the body as something that is alien to it, for both <the eye and the body> belong to the same corporeal substance. The soul is something different from the body but is connected to it, which is why it is shown to have its own activity and is seen and spoken of separately from the body. More such things can be said, which the survey has to leave out.'
358. The analogy of the steersman is given by Aristotle himself: see *DA* 413a8-9, with Philoponus' comments at *in DA* 2.1, 224,12ff.
359. The MS A has the following textual addition, which Hayduck prints at the bottom of the page: 'Perhaps there is also another solution which is not inferior, viz. that in this case <of soul and body> the joint nature is one, even though it is naturally joined from two different essences; but in this case, what is the joint nature of the steersman and the ship? Or in what way is the ship related to the body and will the steersman preserve the kinship to the soul, etc.?'
360. *skhesis*, 'relation' or 'interrelation' (cf. Prooemium, 9,29-30), refers to the soul in its relationship to the body, i.e. as part of the 'joint combination' (*sunamphoteron*) of the two, as opposed to the soul 'on its own' (*autê kath' hautên*); see also the discussion in *in DA* 1.4, 155,11-12.
361. On the 'solid body' (*pakhu sôma*), as distinct from the pneumatic and the luminous bodies, see above, Prooemium, 18,11ff. On the present passage, and on its interpretation as a cautious reference by Philoponus to the possibility of transmigration of souls, see Verrycken (1994) 225.
362. *augoeidous* is Hayduck's conjecture for the MSS reading *autoeidous* (but see Finamore and Dillon (2002) 131 n. 57 for references to occurrences of *autoeidês* in Iamblichus and (Ps.?-)Simplicius). For the 'luminous' body see

above, Prooemium, 18,27ff. and the discussion by Blumenthal (1996) 84-5 and 112-13. On the present passage see Verrycken (1994) 229.

363. cf. *An. Pr.* 32a18.

364. *An. Pr.* 25a38.

365. i.e. that it is an attribute or characteristic of a straight line that it touches a sphere at a point. On the meaning of *pathos* see n. 266 above.

366. For the purpose of consistency the word *pathos* has been translated throughout as 'affection', although in several places 'emotion' would be preferable for being clearer and more specific. In this section the Greek term covers everything the soul experiences, including perception, imagination, and thought. See also n. 266 above.

367. i.e. the complex of soul and body (*to sunamphoteron*).

368. The first ground follows immediately; the second one follows in line 24.

369. The Greek words rendered as 'mixed' and 'mixture' are *kekramenoi* and *krasis*. In Greek medical thought the terms primarily denote a physiological state determined by a blend, or rather a proportion, of different primary physical qualities such as warm, cold, dry, and wet (as illustrated by the use of the term in 51,5: 'a dryer mixture') or bodily fluids (such as black bile, yellow bile, blood, and phlegm). Such a mixture can be present from birth, in which case it 'constitutes' a person's 'nature' (*phusis*), but it can also be acquired as a result of a particular regimen (see 51,7-8: 'the effect produced by the original mixture may also be produced by the regimen which leads to this mixture'). This 'mixture' or 'constitution' is particularly defined in terms of inclinations towards particular affections or diseases ('constitution types' such as bilious, phlegmatic, splenetic, melancholic, etc.). But because of their relevance to emotional and cognitive performance, the word *krasis* (and its Latin equivalent *temperamentum*) gradually also came to be used to refer to the 'temperament' (in the psychological sense) which was thought to correspond with this physiological state. However, the translation 'temperament' would obscure the fundamentally physical nature of the term, which is clearly present here in 51,5 and which has been alluded to several times in the preceding pages (e.g. 9,26; 35,25-6). In the present context, it is said that when the way people respond to certain emotive stimuli shows a certain pattern, this is due to their *krasis*, i.e. their natural, physiologically determined inclination to certain affections. (Ps.?-)Simplicius, in his comments on the same passage (*in DA* 1.1, 19,34 and 20,4) uses in addition to *krasis* also *diathesis* ('disposition', 'inclination', cf. *diakeimenoi* in Philoponus *in DA* 1.1, 53,18).

370. On the term *epitêdeios*, also used above in 14,6 and 14,18 (with n. 159), see Todd (1972) and (1980) 162.

371. This is probably a reference to Galen's treatise *That the Faculties of the Soul Follow the Mixtures of the Body*, in which Galen quotes a number of passages from Plato, Aristotle, and Hippocrates in support of his view of the dependence of the soul on the body (for a translation of this Galenic work see Singer [1997] 150-76; for a discussion of Galen's method in this work see Lloyd [1986]). Philoponus refers to the same view at *in DA* 1.4, 155,33-4 (where he accepts that even *dianoia*, 'discursive thinking', is susceptible to the influence of the bodily mixture), and at *in DA* 1.3, 138,5, where, however, he claims that when the soul is in control of the body, it does not follow the body's movements. He does not mention Galen by name in either of these passages, or indeed anywhere else in this commentary (but see p. 407 Hayduck in app., where in the commentary on *DA* 422b15 there is a discrepancy between the MSS, with MS A having a longer version in which there is an explicit reference to Galen's work on *Simple Medicines*; and in his *Corollaries on Place* 576,13-21, Philoponus refers to Themistius' criticism of Galen; furthermore, Proclus *in Tim.* 3, 349,22 Diehl, attributes the same view as that quoted here by Philoponus explicitly to Galen). For a discussion of the present passage, also in relation to earlier commentators, and for Philoponus' knowledge and use of medical ideas in general, and Galenic ideas in particular, see Todd (1977), (1980) 168-9, and (1984), who cites Philoponus' references at *in DA* 2.4, 274,8-10 to 'the treatises of doctors on the usefulness of the parts' (*hai peri khreias moriôn tôn iatrôn pragmateiai*), which could be a reference to, *inter alia*, Galen's work with that title, especially considering the teleological context and the fact that fragments of an Arabic version of a commentary by John Philoponus on Galen's *On the Usefulness of the Parts* have been preserved in a Gotha manuscript; see Strohmaier (2003); Todd also refers to Philoponus' *On the Eternity of the World against Proclus* 319,5-8 and 600,2 Rabe, where Philoponus refers to Galen's works *On the Affected Parts* and *On Demonstration*. See also Introduction, p. 2.

It should be noted, however, that the idea of the soul's dependence on the body is not restricted to medicine: indeed, the present passage also strongly echoes the beginning of the pseudo-Aristotelian treatise *Physiognomonica* (805a1): 'That mental states follow the bodies (in which they occur) and do not exist on their own being unaffected by the movements of the body' (*hoti hai dianoiai hepontai tois sômasi kai ouk eisin autai kath' heautas apatheis ousai tôn tou sômatos kinêseôn*); and the use of the word *dianoia* is particularly striking here in connection to what Philoponus has to say about the susceptibility of *dianoia*, 'discursive thinking', to bodily influence and suitability, *epitêdeiotês*, in *in DA* 1.4, 155,4-35; in this context, Philoponus explicitly refers to 'physiognomonists' at *in DA* 1.4, 155,22-3, a few lines before again quoting the principle that 'the faculties of the soul follow the mixtures of the body' in 155,33-4. The idea is indeed fundamental to ancient physiognomical thought; see Barton (1994) ch. 2; see also Sorabji (2003) 157-8.

372. On Aristotle's notion of 'the melancholics' and the medical background of his views, see van der Eijk (1990). Melancholics are people whose bodily constitution is characterised by a predominance of black bile, or by the presence of black bile in particular parts of the body; this affects their behaviour and their cognitive performance. The melancholics are Aristotle's standard example for people whose mental abilities and activities are influenced by the natural state of their bodies; see especially *EN* 1154b11; 1150b25.27; 1152a19.28; *Mem.* 453a19; *Insomn.* 461a22; *Somn.* 457a27; *Div.* 463b17; 464a32; *EE* 1248a39. Cf. also (Ps.?-)Simplicius, *in DA* 1.1, 19,39.

373. cf. Aristotle, *Mem.* 449b7-8 and 450a31. That Philoponus was aware of Aristotle's work *On Memory and Recollection* is argued for by Lautner (1993). For Philoponus' views on the location of memory in the brain and in the *pneuma* see *in DA* 1.4, 155,28-9, 158,8-22 and 164,8-28 and Blumenthal (1996) 148-9.

374. For the idea that regimen may lead to better intellectual and moral development see Galen, *That the Faculties of the Soul Follow the Mixtures of the Body* (see n. 371 above), ch. 11 (p. 79,2-4 Müller, 4.821 K). As pointed out by Todd (1977) 132 n. 54, the quotation 'a fat belly does not produce a subtle mind' occurs in Galen's *Thrasybulus* 38 (p. 85,8-9 Helmreich; 5.878 K), but Galen himself says that it is a widely used proverb; it is also quoted by Anonymus Londiniensis 16.3 in his report of Plato's views in *Timaeus* 74A-75C.

375. Or 'more intelligent', 'brilliant': as in Aristotle, *euphuês* often denotes a kind of natural cleverness or genius (cf. *Poet.* 1455a32; *Probl.* 954a32; *MM* 1203b1).

376. See above, 21,28. Cf. (Ps.?-)Simplicius, *in DA* 1.1, 19,4-11: '… in the uneducated the bodily mixture is evident and becomes the cause of these affections, while in the educated this is the initiating activity of the soul, which does so either without exciting the body, or controls the change if the body is excited. But Aristotle omitted to mention that the rational soul controls the arousal and domination of these affections, as being obvious from moral philosophy. That is why towards the end of this book it is confirmed that the intellect also rules and controls the body' (Urmson and Lautner [1995] 34). For a translation and discussion of this passage see Sorabji (2000) 267-8.

377. Here, and also in lines 21, 28 and 33, *hormê* ('impulse', 'drive') is used instead of *dunamis* ('faculty', 'power') or *pathos* ('affection', 'experience'). It refers particularly to what initiates and motivates action; see above, Prooemium, 18,21, and below, ch. 2, 65,31. Cf. also Todd (1977) 132 n. 50 and (1984) 105 n. 18.

378. *apotelesma kraseôs*, an expression attributed by Philoponus to doctors also in his commentary on *On Coming-to-Be and Perishing* 169,5-6, as pointed out by Todd (1977) 133 n. 63; see also Berryman (2002) 68-9. *Apotelesma* is also used above in 8,8; on its philosophical significance see Sorabji (2003) 156-8. It was also used as a technical term in medical thought referring to the long term effect or outcome of a disease or condition, which was believed to be difficult to cure; see Caelius Aurelianus, *Chronic Affections* 2.12.137.

379. There is no explicit statement to this effect in Galen's *That the Faculties of the Soul follow the Mixtures of the Bodies* (*pace* Todd [1984] 110). But the idea corresponds roughly with the tenor of Galen's other psychological work *On the Affections and Errors of the Soul*; see Hankinson (1991b).

380. i.e. if the body were the soul's subject, the existence of the body would be necessary for the preservation of the soul. Consequently, fighting against the body would imply a struggle for death, which is absurd. Cf. above, Prooemium, 15,5, and *in DA* 1.4, 162,20; see also Proclus *in Tim.* 3, 349,21-350,8 Diehl.

381. i.e. the cause of its existence.

382. See also *in DA* 1.4, 155,4ff., where Philoponus considers this question in relation to *dianoia*, 'discursive thinking'.

383. i.e. if the body were the soul's substrate, *quod non*.

384. I take it that Philoponus' report on what 'the Attic interpreters' had to say on this passage ends here, and that what follows in the next paragraph is his own additional comment, as is suggested by the references he inserts to earlier passages in his commentary; moreover, the next section picks up a number of points made in the Prooemium.

385. See above, Prooemium, 17,26-18,16.

386. i.e. the material vehicle of the soul; see above, Prooemium, 12,18; 18,26.

387. See above, Prooemium, 18,11.

388. See above, Prooemium, 16,20-21.

389. On the expression *apotelesma kraseôs*, see n. 378 above.

390. For this phrase see also Philoponus *in DA* 2.4, 268,33, and *in GC* 169,7, with the discussion by Todd (1980) 163 n. 54, who refers to Proclus, *in Tim.* 3, 53,6-9 Diehl; 1,446,1-7 Diehl, and Damascius *in Phaed.* 1.3 Westerink.

391. See above, 38,14-15.

392. *axia*, a term referring to a thing's status in a hierarchy, also used above in 37,7.

393. Here, in Greek the word *mixis* is used.

394. The Greek text, as it stands, produces an anacoluthon, and there seems to be a lacuna after *dêmiourgousi*, but the meaning is clear.

395. From 51,18 onwards. Cf. also above, Prooemium 15,22-34.

396. This is, of course, Aristotle's own hylomorphic position, which Philoponus himself adopts only for the non-rational soul. The difference between the 'mixture' theory, which is essentially 'bottom-up' and determinist, and the hylomorphic theory, which is essentially 'top-down', is clearly expressed here. Philoponus argues that the view that the soul is related to the body as to its substrate clearly gets the priority wrong and reduces the soul to a mere attribute of the body.

397. *sumbainontôn* Aristotle: om. Philoponus.

398. i.e., when their natural bodily mixture is of the same kind as the bodily mixture *any* man may *incidentally* get when being frightened.

399. Homer *Iliad* 3.35.

400. i.e. not similarly to the states of the body, but similarly to itself: the pattern of reactions to affections should be constant, irrespective of bodily changes.

401. In Greek *logoi enuloi*. Both words are difficult to interpret, and the phrase has extensively been discussed (see Hicks [1907] ad loc.). *Logos* is usually translated as 'form' or 'formula', which suits Philoponus' context rather well, although from an Aristotelian view, something may be said for 'proportion' (just as perception is, in Aristotle's view, a kind of proportion: see e.g. *DA* 424b27). *enulos* is rare in Aristotle, but very frequent in Neoplatonist thinking to express the immanent status of the forms.

402. 'Expert' and 'expertise' render *tekhnitês* and *tekhnê* respectively; the latter can also be translated 'skill', 'craft', 'art', or 'science'.

403. *Gorgias* 465A5-6.

404. *PA* 641a32, quoted above in 25,13 and in the Prooemium, 10,11ff.

405. Above, Prooemium, 21,4-6.

406. cf. above, Prooemium, 21,4; as stated there in n. 216, the reference is in fact to *Metaph.* 1072b13 (*kosmos* Philoponus: *phusis* Aristotle); cf. also *Phys.* 8.6.

407. *GC* 2.10.

408. *Tim.* 33B.

409. *Cael.* 286b10ff.

410. Plotinus 2.2.1.

411. See above, Prooemium, 14,35-8, and *in Meteor.* 12,25-6.

412. Greek: *plêrôma*; cf. Philoponus *in DA* 1.3, 126,32 and *On the Intellect* 8, 111-112,67-8; cf. Proclus *ET* 177 (156,1 Dodds) with Beierwaltes (1979) 39-41.

413. For this expression cf. Aristotle *DA* 432a2.

414. *Gorgias* 465A5-6. See above, 54,26 and below 61,33.

415. This is in accordance with Aristotle's views on common sense-objects: see *DA* 418a10ff.; 425a14ff.; 428b22; *Sens.* 437a8-9 and 442b4ff.; *Mem.* 450a9; *Somn.* 455a14ff.; *Insom.* 458b4-6. On Aristotle's notion of 'common sensibles' see Block (1964), (1965), and (1988); Graeser (1978); Hamlyn (1959) and (1968); Kahn (1966); Kosman (1975); Owens (1982); Welsch (1987).

416. On this passage see the comments by Sheppard (1997) 117-18: 'Philoponus ... combines the distinction between extended and unextended Forms with an "Aristotelian" abstractionist account of how the mathematician grasps figures such as the triangle and the circle ... It is interesting that Philoponus, like Syrianus, mentions the *abakion*, a board for drawing diagrams ... Philoponus, or the tradition on which he is drawing, has transferred the board from the level of perceptibles to the level of *phantasia*.'

417. *arkhetupos*, a term used by Philoponus in this commentary only here; cf. *in Phys.* 2.8, 316,25, and *in Nicom.* 1, λσ, 4. For a discussion of this passage see Verrycken (1994) 219.

418. *eidê dêmiourgika*, also referred to above as 'formulae', or 'formal principles' (*logoi*) in 38,14-15 and 52,20.

Notes to pages 76-85

419. This, of course, reminds us of the doctrine on Plato's *Meno* 81C9-D5. See the discussion of this passage by Lautner (1993) 164.

420. *ho de tou pragmatos* Philoponus: *eidos tou pragmatos* Aristotle.

421. The words in round brackets are not in Aristotle, but clearly explicative expansion by Philoponus.

422. *Gorgias* 465A5-6, also quoted above at 54,25 and 57,12; the Greek word *tekhnê* conveys systematic skill and expertise with practical application, which is capable of being taught to others; translations vary between 'skill', 'expertise', 'discipline' or 'science'.

423. On Alexander's (lost) commentary on *DA* see above, n. 121. Moraux (2001) does not discuss the present passage.

424. i.e. to acknowledge.

425. *Metaph.* 1075a11, also quoted above in 37,21-2.

426. *Int.* 23a23; see also above, 35,2.

427. On *pneuma* as the material substrate for emotions see above, Prooemium, 10,7-8; 15,11; 18,9; 18,26.32.33; 52,6.

428. On this passage see Todd (1984) 109 n. 58: 'The discussion turns on the relation between *thumos* and the body; *thumos* is said to be in reason and *to pneuma*, but reason moves desire by means of *pneuma*, while *pneuma* moves the blood around by means of desire. The basic physiology here may be Aristotelian rather than Galenic, but there is also a dual role assigned to the *pneuma*, as the substrate of a psychic faculty (cf. 64,14-15, where it is said to be separable from the physical body) and also as an agent in the operation of that faculty.'

429. cf. *Metaph.* 1075a11ff., also quoted above in 37,21-2.

430. e.g. in *Metaph.* 995a27-b4, with the same pun on *euporia* and *aporia* as Philoponus uses here.

431. See above, 44,21ff.

432. See above, 40,17-22.

433. See *DA* 2.1, esp. 412a13ff.

434. For a German translation of the next section see Scholten (1996) 208-9. See also the discussion by Wolff (1971) 69-81.

435. So far from earth having a natural tendency to move downwards, Philoponus says, the natural state of any element is to be at rest in the main mass (*holotês*) of that element. It is only if it gets unnaturally trapped away from its natural place that it moves and it does so in order to reach its natural place and rest there. In the next sentence, Philoponus considers the possibility that there might be an exception for the fiery sphere just below the fifth element, since the fifth element moves in a circle according to Aristotle (not that Philoponus believes in this; see next note). But in fact, Philoponus argues, rotation is a kind of rest, for it is only the parts of the spinning top that move; it does not move as a whole.

436. The highest sphere in the sublunary world, according to Aristotle, see *Cael.* 311b21ff. and *Meteor.* 340b21ff. For the reception of this theory, and of the question about its movement, in late antique cosmology, see the discussion by Wildberg (1988) 125-34 and Scholten (1996) 208ff.

437. i.e., if one wants to know what is natural for air, water, etc. one should look for it in their 'main mass'; see n. 435 above, and Proclus *ET* 209.

438. *hodoi*, 'ways'; for the expression cf. Aristotle *Phys.* 193b13.

439. Aristotle *Metaph.* 12.7, esp. 1072b3.

440. DK 67 A 28 (= fr. 106a Taylor).

441. The atoms.

442. *Phys.* 188b22-6. Philoponus is freely paraphrasing Aristotle, but preserving elements of direct speech.

443. If this conditional clause represents an observation by Philoponus, it could be a reference to Galen, esp. his work *On the Elements according to Hippocrates*, although the view was more widely accepted and could even be said to go back to fifth- and fourth-century BC medical theory roughly contemporary with Democritus, such as Empedocles, Philistion of Locri (Anon. Lond. 20.25ff.), and of course Plato's *Timaeus*. (The Hippocratic work *On the Nature of Man* has a theory of four elementary qualities, but not of the four elements themselves.)

444. *stoikheion* Philoponus: *stoikheia* Aristotle.

445. DK 67 A 28.

446. *panspermia*, a word referring to a chaotic mixture of different items; for parallels see Hicks (1907) ad loc.; see also Morel (1996) 140 n. 30.

447. cf. Aristotle *Metaph.* 985b16; 1042b14; see DK 67 A 6.

448. Suggesting a connection between *rhusmos* and the verb *rhein*, 'flow'.

449. *rhusmos* (see above), *tropê* and *diathigê*; cf. Aristotle *Metaph.* 985b16-17: 'They say that being is differentiated by *rhusmos*, *diathigê* and *tropê* only; of these, *rhusmos* is shape (*skhêma*), *diathigê* arrangement (*taxis*), and *tropê* position (*thesis*)'; cf. also *Metaph.* 1042b14; cf. Plotinus 4.5.2; 4.5.6.

450. For a more extensive account of Democritus' theory of respiration see Aristotle *Respir.* 471b30-472b5.

451. I suggest emending *sumbainein* to *sumbainei* (deviation from Hayduck), although the infinitive may also be related to the use of reported speech in lines 21-3.

452. DK 58 B 40.

453. Hayduck refers to *Theaet.* 180D, but concedes that no really matching passage can be found.

454. Hayduck refers to *Epist.* 2, 314A, but concedes that no really matching passage can be found.

455. This will be discussed in Chapter 4; on the meaning of *harmonia* see above, n. 176.

456. cf. Philolaus DK 44 B 10.

457. Reading *phêmi* instead of *phêsi*, an emendation suggested by Hayduck in app., as there is no satisfactory referent for 'he says'. I regard this whole parenthesis (70,10-16) as Philoponus' comment, not a rendering of the Pythagorean doctrine.

458. *pathê*; see above, 52,4-5 and Prooemium, 17,26-18,16.

459. *Rep.* 611D, also quoted by Philoponus in *On the Intellect* 5, 53,64 and by Plotinus 1.1.12.

460. Plato's successor as head of the Academy; his view that the soul is a self-moving number is referred to by Aristotle in *DA* 408b32ff. (with Philoponus' comments at *in DA* 1.5, 172,22ff.); Philoponus has already referred to it several times in the previous chapter (see above 32,33 and 44,1, with note); see also below in 81,25 and 82,20.

461. The sixth/fifth-century Pythagorean philosopher and medical writer from Croton, quoted by Aristotle in *DA* 405a29 (DK 24 A 12) and by Philoponus in 88,9-12.

462. A strongly edited and abbreviated version of Plato *Laws* 10, 896E8-897A2.

463. This is Hayduck's emendation for the MS reading *Anaxagoras*. See above, n. 460.

464. DK 59 A 99.

465. DK 68 A 101.

466. Pupil of Anaxagoras; see DK 60 A 18. Hicks (1907) ad loc. suspects that Aristotle alludes to Hermotimus of Clazomenae here.
467. The following passage is printed by DK as 68 A 113; see also Taylor (1996) fr. 183a, and Morel (1996) 178.
468. I take it that *oudamôs* is to be construed with *ekhomen*, not with *hoti tauton nous kai psukhê*. Philoponus is not saying that he has a clear statement from these thinkers saying that intellect and soul are not by any means the same thing; rather he is saying that whereas he has not by any means a clear statement from these thinkers saying that intellect and soul are identical, he can prove that this is what they thought. 'They' must be Anaxagoras and his followers; as for Democritus, in 72,8-9 we read 'Now Democritus says openly (*antikrus*) that the intellect and the soul are identical'.
469. cf. DK 80 B 1.
470. DK 59 A 100.
471. *Iliad* 23.698: *allophroneôn*, though said of Euryalus, not Hector; see Hicks (1907) ad loc., who compares *Metaph.* 1009b28, and Mansfeld (1986) 39-40.
472. *nous kata tên phronêsin*.
473. *einai* Philoponus: om. Aristotle.
474. DK 31 B 109.
475. Or 'dissolution'.
476. DK 31 B 115,13-14 (= fr. 107,13-14 Wright [1995]).
477. *Tim.* 35A4ff. and 37A-C. See also further below, 74,30ff., where Philoponus discusses Plato's position at greater length.
478. *Phdr.* 246Bff.
479. Above, 70,10-17.
480. *DA* 429a27-8.
481. For this division of the soul see above, Prooemium, 6,11 and 6,26.
482. i.e. the world-soul.
483. Plato *Tim.* 34Cff., 37A-C ('like by like') and 41D4ff. (other souls).
484. cf. Plato *Tim.* 35A, which distinguishes between indivisible being, divisible becoming, being, sameness, and difference; see also *Soph.* 251A-259B.
485. Actually, in the *Timaeus* they are called *eidê*, or *ideai*. The term *genos* is used in the *Sophist*, e.g. 254D4.
486. *Phys.* 201b31.
487. See above, 65,36-8.
488. *Tim.* 34C3-35A8.
489. *Tim.* 37A3-C5.
490. *Tim.* 37A7-8; cf. *Phdr.* 245C5ff.
491. Printed by Hayduck as a quotation, not as a lemma.
492. There has been considerable controversy over the question whether by the phrase *en tois peri philosophias legomenois* Aristotle refers here to lectures by Plato or to his own (lost) dialogue *On Philosophy* (*Peri philosophias*), a work to which he sometimes refers himself (see Bonitz [1870] 104b28-37, though not all references are equally secure, cf. Gigon [1983], p. 270) and which is attested in the indirect tradition. There is also discussion as to where exactly in Aristotle's text the report of Plato's doctrines ends and at what point Xenocrates (referred to at 404b28 without his name being mentioned) comes into the picture. For an account of the discussion see Ross (1961) 177-8. Philoponus here clearly takes the passage as a reference to a work by Aristotle (which Philoponus also refers to at *in DA* 1.5, 186,25). But the exact basis of this interpretation, and in particular of his (and (Ps?-)Simplicius') more specific claim that this is in fact the same work as Aristotle's *On the Good*, is less clear. Aristotle is reported

also by other sources to have written a work *On the Good* (see fr. 84-97 Gigon), but apart from the present passage in Philoponus (and the corresponding one in (Ps?-)Simplicius) there is no other evidence to suggest that this was the same work as *On Philosophy*, and it does not seem *prima facie* very likely (see Stenzel [1924] 94-5, n. 2). Whether Philoponus had actually seen the work is doubtful, and several interpreters think that he, and (Ps.?-)Simplicius in his discussion of the same passage (*in DA* 1.2, 28,7-9), were relying on an intermediate source such as the report (supposedly) given by Alexander in his (lost) commentary *in DA*; cf. Gaiser (1963) 486; Moraux (1951) 39 n. 64; Stenzel (1924) 95ff.; Saffrey (1971) 11-12, 19 n. 1, and 45; Cherniss (1944) 119 n. 77 and 566; Cherniss (1959) 39 (comparing Philoponus *in GC* 226,17-30); Gourinat (1996) 90-5.

493. See Isnardi Parente (1997) 479-84; other discussions in Aristotle's works relating to this topic which provide parallels to Philoponus' report can be found in *Metaph.* 992a10ff.; 992b13ff.; 1036b13; 1085a7ff.; 1090b21ff. See also Themistius *in DA* 1.2, 11,30, with the comments by Todd (1996), and Sextus Empiricus *Adv. Math.* 10.281 (on which see Wilpert [1941] and de Vogel [1949] 209-16).

494. On this phrase see Saffrey (1971) 11 n. 2, who suggests that this phrase points to research into the authenticity of the *Peri tagathou*, perhaps prompted by a comparison between fragments of the work preserved by Alexander and a 'Neopythagorean' version of Plato's unwritten doctrines as testified by Sextus Empiricus (see previous note). A critical stance on Saffrey's views (first published in 1955) was taken by Cherniss (1959), reprinted in Saffrey (1971).

495. A detailed assessment of Philoponus' report as a testimony to Plato's unwritten doctrines, also in relation to the other evidence, cannot be offered here. For a discussion see Saffrey (1971) *passim*, esp. 11 n. 2 and 44-6, where he characterises Philoponus' report as 'le plus invraisemblable mélange d'éléments platoniciens et pythagoriciens'. The Platonic elements, according to Saffrey, are: (1) the Forms as determining principles of things (76,4ff.); (2) the correspondences between the objects of intellection, thinking, opinion and sense-perception with the one, the two, the three and the four (76,14-77,5), both based on *Tim.* 27D and 28A (quoted by Philoponus in 76,23-5 and 76,28-30); (3) the distinction between the 'living being as such' (*to autozôion*) and the 'divine and immortal beings' (77,10.16.17); (4) the distinction between beings that live in the heavens, in the sky, on the earth, and in water (77,26-7); and (5) the definition of a line as a 'length without width' (77,32). 'Pythagorean' elements, according to Saffrey, are the theory of decads (76,2ff.); the qualities ascribed to the number ten and the etymological connection between *dekas* and *dekhas* (76,11); the theories of the moving point (77,30-31, 33-7, 78,3-5), for which cf. Gaiser (1963) 355 n. 64; and the doctrine of the triangle as the primary plane figure (77,33) and of the pyramid as the primary three-dimensional figure. Saffrey suspects that Philoponus, just as (Ps?-)Simplicius, Themistius, and Alexander, had no immediate access to Aristotle's *On Philosophy* and that the confusion of ideas of different provenance which their reports represent may have been influenced by a 'rédaction néopythagoricienne' of the *Peri tagathou*, which is not extant but traces of which can be found in Sextus Empiricus (see n. 493). Saffrey also suspects influence of Proclus here (45). Other scholars writing on Plato's unwritten doctrines largely seem to share Saffrey's scepticism regarding the value of Philoponus' report: see van der Wielen (1941) 159-68; Kucharski (1952) 42 n. 1; Robin (1908) 481; Cherniss (1944) 565-80 and (1959) 74-5; De Vogel (1949); Wilpert (1941) and (1949).

496. Or 'companies of ten', *dekadikos*.

497. *monas*, 'monad' or 'unit'; in Greek mathematics, one and two were not regarded as numbers (see below, 80,2).

498. *dekas* is related here to *dekhas* ('receptacle'), related to the verb *dekhomai* ('receive'). Cf. (Ps.?-)Iamblichus *Theol. Arith.* 59, p. 80,8 De Falco, and Saffrey (1971) 44 n. 4 for further references.

499. Or, alternatively: 'unity, duality, the threefold, and the fourfold'.

500. A widely used pun on *epistêmê* ('knowledge') and *epistasis* ('standstill'); cf. Plato *Phaed.* 96B8; Aristotle *MA* 701a27; *An. Post.* 100a1ff. and 15; *Int.* 16b20; *DA* 407a32-3.

501. cf. Prooemium, 1,16.

502. *Tim.* 27D6.

503. *Tim.* 28A1-3.

504. cf. above, Prooemium, 1,16.

505. Plato *Tim.* 28A.

506. On the 'third rate' status of opinion cf. Prooemium, 2,22-4.

507. cf. *Tim.* 39E-40A and the discussion of Saffrey (1971) 49, who points out that Philoponus diverges here from the interpretation of this phrase as referring to the intelligible world found in Themistius and (Ps?-)Simplicius; see also van der Wielen (1941) 161.

508. i.e. the lower gods created by the Craftsman; cf. Prooemium, 11,33.

509. The *autozôion*; cf. Themistius, *in DA* 1.2, 12,1, who interprets this as the intelligible cosmos.

510. *kai tetrados* add. Hayduck.

511. For a German translation and discussion of this passage see Stenzel (1924) 97-8. See also Wilpert (1949) 175 n. 6.

512. i.e. if one takes the point as able to flow along any of three dimensions, it will create a terminal point additional to itself in each of those three directions, rendering four points altogether.

513. For the following cf. the discussion of the cognitive functions of intellect, discursive thinking, and opinion in the Prooemium, 1,13-5,23.

514. cf. Prooemium, 2,2-3.

515. *phantasia*. The present comment by Philoponus makes good sense in relation to his hierarchy of cognitive faculties as expounded in the Prooemium: after the 'rational' modes of cognition intellect, thinking, and opinion, come imagination and sense-perception (5,35-6,10). Therefore, one would expect *phantasia* also to be mentioned here; however, it is not, but subsumed under *aisthêsis*.

516. cf. Prooemium, 6,9-10, where imagination is said to receive the 'impressions' (*tupoi*) from sense perception. The close connection between the two is in accordance with Aristotle's thought; cf. *DA* 429a1-2; 428b11ff.; 432a31-b2; *Insom.* 459a16-17.

517. On this see Cherniss (1959) 75 n. 2.

518. Printed by Hayduck as a quotation, not as a lemma.

519. *tas allas* sc. *ideas* instead of *ta alla*.

520. Above, 76,22ff.

521. See above, 77,1ff.

522. *tôn ontôn* Philoponus: om. Aristotle.

523. Above, 76,2.

524. *Phdr.* 245E2-4.

525. *Tim.* 35Aff., also quoted above at 74,1.

526. See above, n. 460.

527. Aristotle's Greek is ambiguous, but the present translation follows the interpretation of the commentators (cf. Themistius *in DA* 13,7; (Ps.?-)Simplicius *in DA* 30,33ff.). See Hicks (1907) ad loc.

528. This is in accordance with Aristotelian physiological theory as expounded in the *On Youth and Old Age*; see King (2001) 95-106.
529. *Meteor.* 2.4, 2.8, 2.9.
530. cf. DK 22 B 118.
531. The Pythagorean philosopher from Croton (or Metapontus), mentioned in one breath with Heraclitus also in Aristotle *Metaph.* 984a7 (DK 18 A 7).
532. cf. DK 68 A 101.
533. Deleting *kai*, following Hayduck's suggestion in the apparatus.
534. DK 68 A 101 (cont.).
535. DK 59 A 100.
536. *DA* 404b1ff.
537. *Metaph.* 1051a22-1052a11, cf. Plotinus 1.1.9 and Philoponus *On the Intellect* 6, 88,61-3. Cf. *An. Post.* 100b10-15.
538. Printed by Hayduck as a quotation, not as a lemma. For Anaxagoras cf. DK 59 B 12.
539. *DA* 429a18-19 (where Anaxagoras is also mentioned); 430a18.
540. At the beginning of *DA* 2, 403b23.
541. DK 11 A 1 and 22.
542. Not in DK, but cf. DK 11 A 22.
543. *DA* 405b1-3.
544. DK 64 A 20.
545. cf. DK 13 A 5, 6, 7.
546. DK 22 A 15.
547. *GC* 331b25.
548. See above, 71,26.
549. See above, n. 529.
550. Hayduck says it is uncertain which passages Philoponus has in mind, and tentatively suggests *Soph.* 249Bff and *Theaet.* 180Dff. In his 'Addenda et corrigenda' he refers to *Theaet.* 181Dff.
551. *Cael.* 1.3, 1.9, and 2.6, esp. 288a27ff.; *Metaph.* 12.6, esp. 1072a9ff.
552. See above, 75,13.
553. DK 24 A 12.
554. DK 38 A 8.
555. See Hicks (1907) ad loc. Cf. Prooemium, 9,10-11.
556. *phusikoi logoi*; cf. above, 52,16.
557. DK 88 A 23.
558. cf. above, Prooemium, 9,19, and DK 88 A 22.
559. See Hicks (1907) 233.
560. See above, Prooemium, 9,19, where the same Empedoclean quotation is attributed to Critias.
561. The role of the nerves in sense perception had been discovered by means of dissection by the Alexandrian anatomist Herophilus in the third century BC, and was adopted and further explored by Galen; see Siegel (1970). See also Nemesius of Emesa, *On the Nature of Man* 8, 64,1-15 Morani on the connection between the brain and the nerves in sense perception. See also Prooemium, n. 201 above.
562. cf. the Aristotelian position as set out in *PA* 656b19ff.; 666a17ff.; 650b3ff., with the comments by van der Eijk (1994) 81-2.
563. cf. Prooemium, 9,12-13.
564. See *DA* 404b13; cf. Prooemium 9,3 and 9,16.
565. For this division of the soul, see Prooemium, 6,26-7.
566. *GC* 1.2.

567. The Aristotelian text has *allêlois* here ('to each other'), which Philoponus omits (except in t).
568. Printed by Hayduck as a quotation, not as a lemma.
569. Printed by Hayduck as a quotation, not as a lemma. The point is the etymological links between *zein* ('blaze', 'boil') and *zên* ('live'), and between *katapsuksis* ('cooling') and *psukhê* ('soul').
570. DK 38 A 10.
571. cf. Plato *Crat.* 399Dff.

Bibliography

Accattino, P. (1987), 'Ematopoiesi, malattia cardiaca e disturbi mentali in Galeno e in Alessandro di Afrodisia', *Hermes* 115, 454-73
Accattino, P., Donini, P. (1996), *Alessandro di Afrodisia. L'anima*, Rome & Bari
Ackrill, J.L. (1972-73), 'Aristotle's definitions of psuchê', *Proceedings of the Aristotelian Society* 73, 119-33 (reprinted in Barnes, Schofield and Sorabji [eds], vol. 4, 65-75)
Adnouf, D. (1995), 'Die medizinhistorische Bedeutung des Johannes Philoponos und die Gothaer handschrift Ms. Orient. A 1906', in *Ulrich Jasper Seetzen (1767-1811), Leben und Werk. Die arabischen Länder und die Nah-Ostforschung im napoleonischen Zeitalter*, Gotha, 149-54
Armstrong, A.H. (1991), 'Aristotle in Plotinus: the continuity and discontinuity of *psyche* and *nous*', in Blumenthal and Robinson (eds), 117-27
Armstrong, A.H. (ed.), (1967), *The Cambridge History of Later Greek and Early Medieval Philosophy*, Cambridge
Aujoulat, N. (1983-4), 'Les avatars de la *phantasia* dans le *Traité des Songes* de Synesius de Cyrène', *Koinonia* 7, 157-77 and 8, 33-55
Aujoulat, N. (1986), *Le Néoplatonisme Alexandrin: Hiéroclès d'Alexandrie*, Leiden
Aujoulat, N. (1988), 'De la *phantasia* et du *pneuma* stoïciens, d'après Sextus Empiricus, au corps lumineux néo-platonicien (Synésios de Cyrène et Hiéroclès d'Alexandrie)', *Pallas* 34, 123-46
Aujoulat, N. (1998), 'Le "pneuma" et le "corps lumineux" de l'âme d'après le "Prologue" du *Commentaire sur le De Anima d'Aristote* de Jean Philopon', *Byzantinoslavica* 59, 1-23
Balleriaux, O. (1989), 'Thémistius et l'exégèse de la noétique aristotélicienne', *Revue de philosophie ancienne* 7, 119-233
Baltes, M. (1976-78), *Die Weltentstehung des platonischen Timaios nach den antiken Interpreten*, I-II, Leiden
Barker, A. (1981), 'Aristotle on perception and ratios', *Phronesis* 26, 248-66
Barnes, J. (1971-72), 'Aristotle's concept of mind', *Proceedings of the Aristotelian Society* 72, 101-14 (repr. in Barnes, Schofield and Sorabji [eds], vol. 4, 32-41)
Barnes, J., Schofield, M. and Sorabji, R. (eds) (1975-9), *Articles on Aristotle*, 4 vols (1. Science; 2. Ethics and Politics; 3. Metaphysics; 4. Psychology and Aesthetics), London
Barton, T. (1994), *Power and Knowledge. Astrology, Physiognomics and Medicine under the Roman Empire*, Ann Arbor
Bäumker, C. (1877), *Des Aristoteles' Lehre von den äussern und innern Sinnesvermögen*, Leipzig
Beare, J. (1906), *Greek Theories of Elementary Cognition from Alcmaeon to Aristotle*, Oxford

Beierwaltes, W. (1979²), *Proklos. Grundzüge seiner Metaphysik*, Frankfurt am Main
Bekker, I. (1831), *Aristotelis opera*, 2 vols, Berlin
Bernard, W. (1987), 'Philoponus on self-awareness', in Sorabji (ed.) (1987b), 155-63
Berryman, S. (2002), 'The sweetness of honey: Philoponus against the doctors on supervening qualities', in C. Leijenhorst, C. Lüthy, J.M.M.H. Thijssen (eds), *The Dynamics of Aristotelian Philosophy from Antiquity to the Seventeenth Century*, Leiden, 65-79
Berti, E. (1962), *La filosofia del primo Aristotele*, Padua
Bidez, J. (1913), *Vie de Porphyre*, Paris (repr. Hildesheim 1964)
Block, I. (1960), 'Aristotle and the physical object', *Philosophy and Phenomenological Research* 21, 93-101
Block, I. (1961a), 'The order of Aristotle's psychological writings', *American Journal of Philology* 82, 50-77
Block, I. (1961b), 'Truth and error in Aristotle's theory of sense-perception', *Philosophical Quarterly* 11, 1-9
Block, I. (1964), 'Three German commentators on the individual senses and the common sense in Aristotle's psychology', *Phronesis* 9, 58-63
Block, I. (1965), 'On the commonness of the common sensibles', *Australasian Journal of Philosophy* 43, 189-95
Block, I. (1988), 'Aristotle on the common sense. A reply to Kahn and others', *Ancient Philosophy* 8, 235-50
Blumenthal, H.J. (1972), 'Plotinus' psychology: Aristotle in the service of Platonism', *International Philosophical Quarterly* 12, 340-64 (reprinted in Blumenthal [1993], ch. V)
Blumenthal, H.J. (1976a), 'Plotinus' adaptation of Aristotle's psychology: sensation, imagination and memory', in R. Baine Harris (ed.), *The Significance of Neoplatonism*, Norfolk VA, 41-58 (reprinted in Blumenthal [1993], ch. VII)
Blumenthal, H.J. (1976b), 'Neoplatonic elements in the *De anima* commentaries', *Phronesis* 21, 64-97 (repr. with addendum in Sorabji [ed.], [1980], 305-24)
Blumenthal, H.J. (1977-78), 'Neoplatonist interpretations of Aristotle on *phantasia*', *Review of Metaphysics* 31, 242-57
Blumenthal, H.J. (1982), 'John Philoponus and Stephanus of Alexandria: two Neoplatonic Christian commentaries on Aristotle?', in D.J. O'Meara (ed.), *Neoplatonism and Christian Thought*, Norfolk VA, 54-63 and 244-6 (reprinted in Blumenthal [1993], ch. XV)
Blumenthal, H.J. (1983), 'Some problems about body and soul in later pagan Neoplatonism: do they follow a pattern?', in H.D. Blume, F. Mann (eds), *Platonismus und Christentum. Festschrift für H. Dörrie* (*Jahrbuch für Antike und Christentum*, Ergänzungsband 10), Münster, 75-84 (reprinted in Blumenthal [1993], ch. VIII)
Blumenthal, H.J. (1986), 'John Philoponus: Alexandrian Platonist?', *Hermes* 114, 314-35
Blumenthal, H.J. (1987a), 'Simplicius (?) on the first book of Aristotle's *De Anima*', in I. Hadot (ed.), *Simplicius – sa vie, son œuvre, sa survie*, Berlin & New York, 91-112 (reprinted in Blumenthal [1993], ch. XVI)
Blumenthal, H.J. (1987b), 'Alexander of Aphrodisias in the later Greek commentaries on Aristotle's *De Anima*', in Wiesner (ed.), 90-106 (reprinted in Blumenthal [1993], ch. XIV)
Blumenthal, H.J. (1988), 'Simplicius and others on Aristotle's discussions of

reason', in *Gonimos. Neoplatonic and Byzantine Studies Presented to L.G. Westerink*, Buffalo, 103-19

Blumenthal, H.J. (1991), '*Nous pathêtikos* in later Greek philosophy', in Blumenthal and Robinson (eds), 191-205

Blumenthal, H.J. (1992), 'Soul vehicles in Simplicius', in S. Gersh, C. Kannengiesser (eds), *Platonism in Late Antiquity*, Indiana, 173-88 (reprinted in Blumenthal [1993], ch. XVII)

Blumenthal, H.J. (1993), *Soul and Intellect. Studies in Plotinus and Later Platonism* (Variorum Collected Studies Series), Aldershot

Blumenthal, H.J. (1996), *Aristotle and Neoplatonism in Late Antiquity. Interpretations of the De anima*, London

Blumenthal, H.J. (1997), 'Were Aristotle's intentions in writing the *De Anima* forgotten in late Antiquity?', *Documenti e studi sulla tradizione filosofica medievale* 8, 143-57

Blumenthal, H.J. (2000), '*Simplicius*': *On Aristotle On the Soul 3.1-5*, London & Ithaca, NY

Blumenthal, H.J., Lloyd, A.C. (eds) (1992), *Soul and the Structure of Being in Late Neoplatonism: Syrianus, Proclus and Simplicius*, Liverpool

Blumenthal, H.J., Robinson, H.M. (eds) (1991), *Aristotle and the Later Tradition* (Oxford Studies in Ancient Philosophy, suppl. vol.), Oxford

Bodéüs, R. (1996), 'Âme du monde ou Corps céleste? Une interrogation d'Aristote', in G. Rohmeyer Dherbey (ed.), *Corps et âme. Sur le De anima d'Aristote*, Paris, 81-8

Böhm, W. (1967), *Johannes Philoponos, Grammatikos aus Alexandrien (6. Jh. n. Chr). Christliche Naturwissenschaft im Ausklang der Antike, Vorläufer der modernen Physik, Wissenschaft und Bibel. Ausgewählte Schriften*, Munich, Paderborn and Vienna

Bollack, J. (1965-69), *Empedocle*, 4 vols, Paris

Bonitz, H. (1870), *Index Aristotelicus*, Berlin (repr. 1961)

Booth, E.G.T. (1982), 'John Philoponus, Christian and Aristotelian conversion', *Studia Patristica* 17.1, 407-11

Brentano, F. (1867), *Die Psychologie des Aristoteles*, Mainz

Brès, Y. (1968), *La psychologie de Platon*, Paris

Broadie, S. (1997), '*Nous* and nature in *De Anima* III', *Proceedings of the Boston Area Colloquium in Ancient Philosophy* 1997, 163-75

Bruins, E.M. (1951), 'La chimie du Timée', *Revue de métaphysique et de morale* 56, 269-82

Burkert, W. (1977), 'Air-imprints or eidola? Democritus' aetiology of vision', *Illinois Classical Studies* 2, 97-109

Cashdollar, S. (1973), 'Aristotle's account of incidental perception', *Phronesis* 18, 156-75

Caston, V. (1997), 'Epiphenomenalism, ancient and modern', *Philosophical Review* 106, 309-63

Charlton, W.W. (1970), *Aristotle's Physics I & II,* Oxford

Charlton, W.W. (1985), 'Aristotle and the *harmonia* theory', in A. Gotthelf (ed.), *Aristotle on Nature and Living Things*, Pittsburgh and Bristol, 131-50

Charlton, W.W. (1987), 'Aristotle on the place of mind in nature', in A. Gotthelf, J. Lennox (eds), *Philosophical Issues in Aristotle's Biology*, Cambridge, 408-23

Charlton, W.W. (1991), *Philoponus: On Aristotle On the Intellect [De Anima 3.4-8]*, London & Ithaca, NY

Charlton, W.W. (2000a), '*Philoponus*': *On Aristotle On the Soul 3.1-8*, London & Ithaca, NY

148 Bibliography

Charlton, W.W. (2000b), *'Philoponus': On Aristotle On the Soul 3.9-13, with Stephanus: On Aristotle On Interpretation*, London & Ithaca, NY
Charlton, W.W. (2005a), *Philoponus: On Aristotle On the Soul 2.1-6*, London & Ithaca, NY
Charlton, W.W. (2005b), *Philoponus: On Aristotle On the Soul 2.7-12*, London & Ithaca, NY
Cherniss, H.F. (1944), *Aristotle's Criticism of Plato and the Academy*, Baltimore
Cherniss, H.F. (1959), Review of Saffrey (1973), *Gnomon* 31, 36-51
Christensen de Groot, J. (1983), 'Philoponus on *De Anima* II.5, *Physics* III.3, and the propagation of light', *Phronesis* 28, 177-96
Clarke, E. (1963), 'Aristotelian concepts of the form and function of the brain', *Bulletin of the History of Medicine* 37, 1-14
Clarke, E., Stannard, J. (1963), 'Aristotle on the anatomy of the brain', *Journal of the History of Medicine* 18, 130-48
Cohen, S.M. (1978), 'Sensations, colors and capabilities in Aristotle', *The New Scholasticism* 52, 558-68
Cohen, S.M. (1986), 'The credibility of Aristotle's philosophy of mind', in M. Matthen (ed.), *Aristotle Today*, Alberta, 103-21
Cornford, F.M. (1937), *Plato's Cosmology*, London
Corte, M. de (1934), *Le commentaire de Jean Philopon sur le troisième livre du Traité de l'Âme d'Aristote*, Liège & Paris
Cosenza, P. (1968), *Sensibilità, percezione, esperienza secondo Aristotele*, Naples
Couloubaritsis, L. (1982), 'Le problème de l'imagination chez Aristote', in *Actes du xviiime congrès des sociétés de philosophie de langue française*, Strasbourg, 153-8
Croissant, J. (1932), *Aristote et les mystères*, Liège & Paris
Crouzel, H. (1977), 'Le thème platonicien du "vehicule de l'âme" chez Origène', *Didaskalia* 7, 225-37
Debru, A. (1994), 'L'expérimentation chez Galien', *ANRW* II 37.2, 1718-56
De Lacy, P. (1978-84), *Galen. On the Doctrines of Hippocrates and Plato*, 3 vols, Berlin
Des Places, E. (1966), *Iamblique. Les mystères d'Egypte*, Paris
Des Places, E. (1973), *Numenius, Fragments*, Paris
Diels, H. (1879), *Doxographi graeci*, Berlin (repr. 1965)
Diels, H., Krantz, W. (1961), *Die Fragmente der Vorsokratiker*, Berlin (10th edn)
Dodds, E.R. (1963²), *Proclus: The Elements of Theology*, Oxford
Dudley, J. (1974/5), 'Johannes Grammaticus Philoponus Alexandrinus, *In Aristotelis De anima*, Proemion, translated by Dudley, J.', *Bulletin de la société internationale pour l'étude de la philosophie médiévale* 16/7, 62-85
Düring, I. (1957), *Aristotle in the Ancient Biographical Tradition*, Göteborg
Düring, I. (1966), *Aristoteles. Darstellung und Interpretation seines Denkens*, Heidelberg
Düring, I. (1968), 'Aristoteles', *RE* Suppl. Bd. XI, 159-336
Ebert, Th. (1983), 'Aristotle on what is done in perceiving', *Zeitschrift für philosophische Forschung* 37, 181-98
Eijk, P.J. van der (1990), 'Aristoteles über die Melancholie', *Mnemosyne* 43, 33-72 (revised and translated into English in van der Eijk [2005], ch. 5)
Eijk, P.J. van der (1994), *Aristoteles. De insomniis. De divinatone per somnum*, Berlin
Eijk, P.J. van der (1995), 'Aristotle on "distinguished physicians" and on the medical significance of dreams', in P.J. van der Eijk, H.F.J. Horstmanshoff, P.H. Schrijvers (eds), *Ancient Medicine in its Socio-Cultural Context*, vol. 2, Amsterdam, 447-59 (revised and included in van der Eijk [2005], ch. 6)

Eijk, P.J. van der (1997), 'The matter of mind. Aristotle on the biology of 'psychic' processes and the bodily aspects of thinking', in Kullmann/Föllinger 1997, 231-58 (revised and included in van der Eijk [2005], ch. 7)

Eijk, P.J. van der (2000a), *Diocles of Carystus. A Collection of the Fragments with Translation and Commentary*, vol. 1: *Text and Translation*, Leiden

Eijk, P.J. van der (2000b), 'Aristotle's psycho-physiological account of the soul-body relationship', in J.P. Wright, P. Potter (eds), *Psyche and Soma. Physicians and Metaphysicians on the Mind-Body Problem from Antiquity to Enlightenment*, Oxford, 57-77

Eijk, P.J. van der (2001), *Diocles of Carystus. A Collection of the Fragments with Translation and Commentary*, vol. 2: *Commentary*, Leiden

Eijk, P.J. van der (2003), 'Aristotle on cognition in sleep', in T. Wiedemann, K. Dowden (eds), *Sleep* (Nottingham Classical Literature Series / Midlands Classical Series 8), 25-40 (revised and included in van der Eijk [2005], ch. 6)

Eijk, P.J. van der (2005), *Medicine and Philosophy in Classical Antiquity. Doctors and Philosophers on Nature, Soul, Health and Disease*, Cambridge

Engmann, J. (1976), 'Imagination and truth in Aristotle', *Journal of the History of Philosophy* 14, 259-65

Évrard, E. (1953), 'Les convictions réligieuses de Jean Philopon et la date de son Commentaire aux *Météorologiques*', *Bulletin de l'Académie Royale de Belgique, Classe des lettres, sciences morales at politiques*, series 5, 39, 299-357

Évrard, E. (1965), 'Jean Philopon: son commentaire sur Nicomaque et ses rapports avec Ammonius', *Revue des études grecques* 78, 592-8

Évrard, E. (1985), 'Philopon, la tenèbre originelle et la création du monde', in *Aristotelica: Mélanges offerts à M. de Corte*, Brussels & Liège, 177-88

Festugière, A.J. (1950), *Contemplation et vie contemplative selon Platon*, Paris

Festugière, A.J. (1953), *La révélation d'Hermès Trismégisthe*, vol. III: *Les doctrines de l'âme*, Paris

Finamore, J.F. (1985), *Iamblichus and the Theory of the Vehicle of the Soul*, Chico, CA

Finamore, J.F., Dillon, J. (2002), *Iamblichus. De Anima*, Leiden

Fladerer, L. (1999), *Johannes Philoponos' De opificio mundi. Spätantikes Sprachdenken und christliche Exegese*, Stuttgart

Flashar, H. (1962), *Aristoteles. Problemata physica*, Berlin & Darmstadt

Flashar, H. (1966), *Melancholie und Melancholiker in den medizinischen Theorien der Antike*, Berlin

Flashar, H. (1983), 'Aristoteles', in H. Flashar, H. (ed.), *Grundriss der Geschichte der Philosophie. Die Philosophie der Antike*, Band 3, Basel, 175-457

Fortenbaugh, W.W. (1967), 'Recent scholarship on the psychology of Aristotle', *Classical World* 60, 316-27

Fortenbaugh, W.W. (1970), 'Aristotle's *Rhetoric* on emotions', *Archiv für die Geschichte der Philosophie* 52, 40-70

Fortenbaugh, W.W. (1975), *Aristotle on Emotion*, London

Fortenbaugh, W.W., Steinmetz, P. (eds) (1989), *Cicero's Knowledge of the Peripatos*, New Brunswick & London

Fotinis, A.P. (1979), *The De Anima of Alexander of Aphrodisias: A Translation and Commentary*, Washington DC

Frede, M. (1986), 'Philosophy and medicine in Antiquity', in A. Donagan et al. (eds), *Human Nature and Natural Knowledge*, Essays Presented to Marjorie Grene on the Occasion of Her Seventy-Fifth Birthday, Dordrecht, 211-32 (repr. in Frede [1987], 225-42)

Frede, M. (1987), *Essays in Ancient Philosophy*, Oxford

Frede, M. (1992), 'On Aristotle's conception of the soul', in Nussbaum and Oksenberg-Rorty (eds), (1992), 93-108
Freeland, C. (1992), 'Aristotle on the sense of touch', in Nussbaum and Oksenberg-Rorty (eds), (1992), 227-48
Freudenthal, G. (1995), *Aristotle's Theory of Material Substance: Heat and Pneuma, Form and Soul*, Oxford
Freudenthal, J. (1863), *Über den Begriff des Wortes phantasia bei Aristoteles*, Göttingen
Fritz, K. von (1955), 'Die Archai in der griechischen Mathematik', *Archiv für Begriffsgeschichte* 1, 44ff.
Froschammer, J. (1881), *Über die Prinzipien der aristotelischen Philosophie und die Bedeutung der Phantasie in derselben*, Munich
Gaiser, K. (1963), *Platons ungeschriebene Lehre*, Stuttgart
Garofalo, I. (1999), 'La traduzione araba del commento di Ioannes Grammatikos al *De pulsibus* di Galeno', in A. Garzya (ed.), *I testi medici greci. Tradizione e ecdotica*, Naples, 185-218
Garofalo, I. (2000), 'Il Sunto di Ioannes "Grammatikos" delle Opere del Canone di Galeno', in D. Manetti (ed.), *Studi su Galeno*, Florence, 135-51
Garofalo, I. (2003), 'I *Sommari* degli Alessandrini', in I. Garofalo, A. Roselli (eds), *Galenismo e medicina tardoantica: fonti greche, latine e arabe*, Naples, 203-32
Gätje, H. (1971), *Studien zur Überlieferung der aristotelischen Psychologie im Islam*, Heidelberg
Gersh, S.E. (1973), *Kinêsis Akinêtos. A Study of Spiritual Motion in the Philosophy of Proclus*, Leiden
Gigon, O. (1983), *Aristotelis Opera III: Librorum deperditorum fragmenta*, Berlin
Gotthelf, A. (ed.), (1985), *Aristotle on Nature and Living Things*, Pittsburgh & Bristol
Gotthelf, A., Lennox, J.G. (eds), (1987), *Philosophical Issues in Aristotle's Biology*, Cambridge
Gourinat, M. (1996), 'La doctrine platonicienne de l'âme du monde d'après de *De anima* d'Aristote (I, 2, 404b16-27)', in G. Rohmeyer Dherbey (ed.), *Corps et âme. Sur le De anima d'Aristote*, Paris, 81-105
Grabmann, M. (1929), 'Mittelalterliche lateinische Übersetzungen von Schriften der Aristoteles-kommentatoren Johannes Philoponos, Alexander von Aphrodisias und Themistios', *Sitzungsberichte der Bayerischen Akademie der Wissenschaften*, Philos.-hist. Abteilung, Heft 7, Munich
Graeser, A. (1978), 'On Aristotle's framework of sensibilia', in Lloyd and Owen (eds), 69-97
Granger, H. (1990), 'Aristotle and the functionalist debate', *Apeiron* 23, 27-49
Groot, J. de (1991), *John Philoponus on Light*, New York
Gudemann, A., Kroll, W. (1916), 'Philoponos', *RE* IX,2, 1764-95
Gundert, B. (2000), 'Soma and Psyche in Hippocratic medicine', in J.P. Wright and P. Potter (eds), *Psyche and Soma. Physicians and Metaphysicians on the Mind-Body Problem from Antiquity to the Enlightenment*, Oxford, 13-36
Guthrie, W.K.C. (1962-81), *A History of Greek Philosophy*, 6 vols, Cambridge
Haas, F.A.J. de (1996), *Philoponus' New Definition of Prime Matter*, Leiden
Haas, F. de (1999), 'Mixture in Philoponus: An encounter with the third kind of potentiality', in J.M.M.H. Thijssen, H.G.M. Braakhuis (eds), *The Commentary Tradition on 'De generatione et corruptione'. Ancient, Medieval and Early Modern*, Turnhout, 21-46
Haase, W. (1965), 'Ein vermeintliches Aristoteles-Fragment bei Johannes

Bibliography 151

Philoponos', in *Synusia. Festschrift Wolfgang Schadewaldt*, Pfullingen, 323-54
Hadot, I. (1978), *Le problème du néoplatonisme alexandrin. Hiéroclès et Simplicius*, Paris
Hadot, I. (1987a), 'La division néoplatonicienne des écrits d'Aristote', in Wiesner (ed.), II, 249-85
Hadot, I. (1987b), 'Les introductions aux commentaires exégétiques chez les auteurs néoplatoniciens et les auteurs chrétiens', in M. Tardieu (ed.), *Les règles de l'interprétation*, Paris, 99-122
Hagen, H. (1961), *Die physiologische und psychologische Bedeutung der Leber in der Antike*, Bonn
Hamlyn, D.W. (1959), 'Aristotle's account of *aesthesis* in the *De Anima*', *Classical Quarterly*, n.s. 9, 6-16
Hamlyn, D.W. (1963), *Sensation and Perception. A History of the Philosophy of Perception*, London
Hamlyn, D.W. (1968a), 'Koine aisthesis', *The Monist* 52, 195-209
Hamlyn, D.W. (1968b), *Aristotle's De Anima Books II and III*, Oxford
Hammond, W.A. (1902), *Aristotle's Psychology. A Treatise on the Principles of Life (De Anima and Parva naturalia)*, London & New York
Hankinson R.J. (1991a), 'Greek medical models of mind', in S. Everson (ed.), *Psychology*, Cambridge, 194-217
Hankinson, R.J. (1991b), 'Galen's anatomy of the soul', *Phronesis* 36, 197-233
Hardie, W.F.R. (1964), 'Aristotle's treatment of the relation between the soul and the body', *Philosophical Quarterly* 14, 53-72
Hardie, W.F.R. (1976), 'Concepts of consciousness in Aristotle', *Mind* 85, 388-411
Harris, C. (1973), *The Heart and the Vascular System in Ancient Greek Medicine*, Oxford
Hartman, E. (1977), *Substance, Body and Soul*, Princeton
Heinaman, R. (1990), 'Aristotle and the mind-body problem', *Phronesis* 35, 83-102
Hett, W.S. (1957^2), *Aristotle. On the Soul. Parva Naturalia. On Breath*, Cambridge MA & London
Hicks, R.D. (1907), *Aristotle. De Anima*, Cambridge
Hoffmann, P. (1987), 'Simplicius' polemics. Some aspects of Simplicius' polemical writings against John Philoponus. From invective to a re-affirmation of the transcendency of the heavens', in Sorabji (ed.) (1987b), 57-83
Horn, H.-J. (1988), 'Aristote, *Traité de l'âme*, III, 3 et le concept aristotélicien de la *phantasia*', *Les études philosophiques* 63, 221-34
Huby, P.M. (1991), 'Stages in the development of language about Aristotle's *nous*', in Blumenthal and Robinson (eds), 129-43
Huby, P.M., Steel, C., Lautner, P. (1997), *Priscian: On Theophrastus On Sense-Perception, with 'Simplicius': On Aristotle On the Soul 2.5-12*, London & Ithaca, NY
Immisch, O. (1904), 'Attikoi exegetai', *Philologus* 63, 31-40
Isnardi Parente, M. (1982), *Senocrate – Ermodoro. Frammenti*, Naples
Isnardi Parente, M. (1997), *Testimonia Platonica. Per una raccolta delle principali testimonianze sui legomena agrapha dogmata di Platone*, vol. 1. *Le testimonianze di Aristotele* (Atti della Accademia Nazionale dei Lincei 394, Classe di Scienze Morali, Storiche a Filosofiche. Memorie, ser. IX, vol. VIII, fasc. 4), Rome
Isnardi Parente, M. (1998), *Testimonia Platonica. Per una raccolta delle principali testimonianze sui legomena agrapha dogmata di Platone*, vol. 2.

Testimonianze di età ellenistica e di età imperiale (Atti della Accademia Nazionale dei Lincei 394, Classe di Scienze Morali, Storiche a Filosofiche. Memorie, ser. IX, vol. X, fasc. 1), Rome

Jaeger, W.W. (1938), *Diokles von Karystos. Die griechische Medizin und die Schule des Aristoteles*, Berlin

Jaeger, W.W. (1948), *Aristotle. Fundamentals of the History of his Development*, 2nd edn, Oxford

Jaeger, W.W. (1959³), *Paideia*, vol. 2, Berlin

Jaeger, W.W. (1980), *The Theology of the Early Greek Philosophers*, repr. Westport (first published Oxford 1947)

Johansen, T.K. (1997), *Aristotle on the Sense-Organs*, Cambridge

Jones, W.H.S., Withington, E.T. (1923-31), *Hippocrates*, 4 vols (Loeb Classical Library), Cambridge MA & London

Jugie, M. (1930), 'George Scholarios et Saint Thomas d'Aquin', *Mélanges Mandonnet*, I, Paris, 423-40

Kahn, C. (1966), 'Sensation and consciousness in Aristotle's psychology', *Archiv für die Geschichte der Philosophie* 48, 43-81

Kahn, C. (1992), 'Aristotle on thinking', in Nussbaum and Oksenberg-Rorty (eds), 359-80

Kampe, F.F. (1870), *Die Erkenntnisstheorie des Aristoteles*, Leipzig

Karamanolis, G. (2002), 'Plethon and Scholarios on Aristotle', in K. Ierodiakonou (ed.), *Byzantine Philosophy and its Ancient Sources*, Oxford, 253-82

Kauder, E. (1960), *Physikalische Modellvorstellung und physiologische Lehre im Corpus Hippocraticum und bei Aristoteles*, Hamburg

Kenny, A.J.P. (1967), 'The argument from illusion in Aristotle's *Metaphysics*', *Mind* 76, 184-97

Kenny, A.J.P. (1992), *Aristotle on the Perfect Life*, Oxford

Kissling, R.C. (1922), 'The *okhêma-pneuma* of the Neoplatonists and the *De insomniis* of Synesius of Cyrene', *American Journal of Philology* 43, 318-30

Kollesch, J. (1997), 'Die anatomischen Untersuchungen des Aristoteles und ihr Stellenwert als Forschungsmethode in der Aristotelischen Biologie', in W. Kullmann, S. Föllinger (eds), *Aristotelische Biologie. Intentionen, Methoden, Ergebnisse* (Philosophie der Antike 6), Stuttgart, 367-73

Kosman, L. (1975), 'Perceiving that we perceive: *On the soul* III 2', *Philosophical Review* 84, 499-519

Kremer, K. (1961), *Der Metaphysikbegriff in den Aristoteles-Kommentaren der Ammonius-Schule*, Münster

Kucharski, P. (1952), *Étude sur la doctrine pythagoricienne de la tétrade*, Paris

Kucharski, P. (1954), 'Sur la théorie des couleurs et des saveurs dans le *De sensu* aristotélicien', *Revue des études grecques* 67, 355-90

Kühn, J.-H., Fleischer, U. (1986-89), *Index Hippocraticus*, 4 vols, Göttingen

Kullmann, W. (1982), 'Aristoteles' Grundgedanken zu Aufbau und Funktion der Körpergewebe', *Sudhoffs Archiv* 66, 209-38

Kupreeva, I. (forthcoming 2006), 'Anatomical knowledge and theories of sense perception in Aristotelian commentators', in R. Arnott and L. Dean-Jones (eds), *Anatomical Knowledge in the Ancient World*, Oxford

Labarrière, J.L. (1984), 'Imagination humaine et imagination animale chez Aristote', *Phronesis* 29, 17-49

Lacombe, G. (1931), 'The mediaeval Latin versions of the *Parva Naturalia*', *The New Scholasticism* 5, 289-314

Lamberz, E. (1975), *Porphyrii sententiae ad intelligibilia ducentes*, Leipzig

Lampe, G.W.H. (1982⁶), *A Patristic Greek Lexicon*, Oxford

Bibliography

Lautner, P. (1992), 'Philoponus, in de anima III. Quest for an author', *Classical Quarterly* 42, 510-22
Lautner, P. (1993), 'Philoponean accounts on *phantasia*', *Acta Antiqua Academiae Scientiarum Hungaricae* 34, 160-70
Lautner, P. (2002), 'Status and method of psychology according to the late Neoplatonists and their influence during the sixteenth century', in C. Leijenhorst, C. Lüthy, J.M.M.H. Thijssen (eds), *The Dynamics of Aristotelian Philosophy from Antiquity to the Seventeenth Century*, Leiden, 81-108
Lee, H.D.P. (1952), *Aristotle. Meteorologica*, Cambridge MA
Leemans, E.A. (1932), 'Michel Psellos et les *Doxai peri psukhês*', *L'Antiquité Classique* 1, 203-11
Lefèvre, Ch. (1972), *Sur l'évolution d'Aristote en psychologie*, Louvain
Lefèvre, Ch. (1978), 'Sur le statut de l'âme dans le *De Anima* et les *Parva Naturalia*', in Lloyd and Owen (eds), 21-68
Leisegang, H. (1919), *Der Heilige Geist. Das Wesen und Werden der mystisch-intuitiven Erkenntnis in der Philosophie und Religion der Griechen*, vol. I, Berlin
Lennox, J.G. (2001), *Aristotle. Parts of Animals*, Oxford
Lloyd, G.E.R. (1986), 'Scholarship, authority and argument in Galen's *Quod animi mores*', in P. Manuli, M. Vegetti (eds), *Le opere psicologiche di Galeno*, Naples, 11-42
Lloyd, G.E.R. (1991), *Methods and Problems in Greek Science*, Cambridge
Lloyd, G.E.R. (1992), 'Aspects of the relationship between Aristotle's psychology and his zoology', in Nussbaum and Oksenberg-Rorty (eds), 147-67
Lloyd, G.E.R. (1996), *Aristotelian Explorations*, Cambridge
Lloyd, G.E.R., Owen, G.E.L. (eds) (1978), *Aristotle on Mind and the Senses. Proceedings of the 7th Symposium Aristotelicum*, Cambridge
Lowe, M.F. (1983), 'Aristotle on kinds of thinking', *Phronesis* 28, 17-30
Lucchetta, G.A. (1978), 'Aristotelismo e cristianesimo in Giovanni Filopono', *Studia Patavina* 25, 573-93
Lycos, K. (1964), 'Aristotle and Plato on appearing', *Mind* 73, 496-514
MacCoull, L.S.B. (1995), 'A new look at the career of John Philoponus', *Journal of Early Christian Studies* 3, 47-60
MacCoull, L.S.B. (1997), 'Notes on Philoponus' theory of vision', *Byzantion* 67, 558-62
Macierowsky, E.M., Hassing, R.F. (1988), 'John Philoponus on Aristotle's definition of nature', *Ancient Philosophy* 8, 73-100
MacLeod, C.M.K. (1964), *Jean Philopon, Commentaire au De Intellectu. Traduction latine de Guillaume de Moerbeke*, Diss. Louvain
Mansfeld, J. (1986), 'Aristotle, Plato and the Pre-Platonic doxography and chronography', in G. Cambiano (ed.), *Storiografia e dossografia nella filosofia antica*, Turin, 1-59 (repr. in J. Mansfeld, *Studies in the Historiography of Greek Philosophy*, Assen 1990, 22-83)
Mansfeld, J. (1986), *Die Vorsokratiker*, 2 vols, Stuttgart
Mansion, A. (1946), *Introduction à la Physique aristotélicienne*, Louvain & Paris
Mansion, A. (1947), 'Le texte de *De intellectu* de Philopon', *Mélanges A. Pelzer*, Louvain, 325-46
Mansion, A. (1960), 'Le Dieu d'Aristote et le Dieu des chrétiens', in *La philosophie et ses problèmes, Mélanges offerts à R. Jolivet*, Lyon & Paris, 21-44
Mansion, S. (1961), 'Le rôle de l'exposé et de critique des philosophes antérieures chez Aristote', in S. Mansion (ed.), *Aristote et les problèmes de méthode*, Louvain & Paris, 35-56

Manuwald, B. (1985), 'Die Wurftheorien im Corpus Aristotelicum', in Wiesner (ed.), I, 151-67
McGuire, J.E. (1985), 'Philoponus on Physics II.1. *Phusis, dunamis* and the motion of simple bodies', *Ancient Philosophy* 5, 241-67
Mendelsohn, E. (1964), *Heat and Life. The Development of the Theory of Animal Heat*, Cambridge MA
Merlan, P. (1963), *Monopsychism, Mysticism, Metaconsciousness: Problems of the Soul in the Neo-Aristotelian and Neoplatonic Tradition*, The Hague
Meyerhof, M. (1930), 'Von Alexandrien nach Bagdad. Ein Beitrag zur Geschichte des philosophischen und medizinischen Unterrichts bei den Arabern', *Sitzungsberichte der Preussischen Akademie der Wissenschaften*, Phil.-hist. Klasse, Berlin, 389-429
Meyerhof, M. (1931), 'Joannes Grammatikos (Philoponos?) von Alexandrien und die arabische Medizin', *Mitteilungen des deutschen Instituts für Ägyptische Altertumskunde in Kairo* 2, 1-21
Modrak, D.K.W. (1981), 'Koinè aisthèsis and the discrimination of sensible differences in De Anima III 2', *Canadian Journal of Philosophy* 11, 405-23
Modrak, D.K.W. (1986), '*Phantasia* reconsidered', *Archiv für die Geschichte der Philosophie* 68, 47-69
Modrak, D.K.W. (1987), *Aristotle: The Power of Perception*, Chicago
Modrak, D.K.W. (1990), 'Aristotle the first cognitivist?', *Apeiron* 23, 65-75
Moraux, P. (1951), *Les listes anciennes des ouvrages d'Aristote*, Louvain
Moraux, P. (1973, 1984, 2001), *Der Aristotelismus bei den Griechen*, I-II-III, Berlin
Moraux, P. (1978), 'Le *De anima* dans la tradition grecque: quelques aspects de l'interprétation du traité, de Théophraste à Thémistius', in Lloyd and Owen (eds), 280-324
Morel, G. (1960-61), 'De la notion de principe chez Aristote', *Archives de philosophie* 23, 487-511 and 24, 497-516
Morel, P.-M. (1996), *Démocrite et la recherche des causes*, Paris
Morel, P.-M. (2000), *Aristote. Petits traités d'histoire naturelle. Traduction et présentation*, Paris
Morel, P.-M. (2002a), 'Démocrite dans les *Parva naturalia* d'Aristote', in A. Laks, C. Louguet (eds), *Qu'est-ce que la philosophie présocratique?*, Villeneuve d'Asq, 449-64
Morel, P.-M. (2002b), 'Les *Parva naturalia* d'Aristote et le mouvement animal', *Revue de philosophie ancienne* 20, 61-88
Morrow, G.R. (1970), *Proclus. A Commentary on the First Book of Euclid's Elements*, Princeton
Mugler, Ch. (1964), *Dictionnaire historique de la terminologie optique des Grecs*, Paris
Mugnier, R. (1953), *Aristote. Petits traités d'histoire naturelle*, Paris
Neuhäuser, J. (1878a), review of Bäumker (1877), *Philosophische Monatshefte* 14, 429-34
Neuhäuser, J. (1878b), *Aristoteles' Lehre von dem sinnlichen Erkenntnissvermögen und seinen Organen,* Leipzig
Nussbaum, M.C. (1978), *Aristotle's De motu animalium*, Princeton
Nussbaum, M.C. (1980), Review of Hartman (1977), *Journal of Philosophy* 77, 355-65
Nussbaum, M.C., Oksenberg-Rorty, A., (eds), (1992), *Essays on Aristotle's De Anima*, Oxford
Nuyens, F. (1948), *L'évolution de la psychologie d'Aristote*, Louvain

O'Meara, D.J. (1989), *Pythagoras Revived. Mathematics and Philosophy in Late Antiquity*, Oxford
Oehler, K. (1964), 'Aristotle in Byzantium', *Greek, Roman, and Byzantine Studies* 5, 133-46
Osborne, C. (1983), 'Aristotle, *De Anima* 3.2. How do we perceive that we see and hear?', *Classical Quarterly* 33, 401-11
Ostenfeld, E. (1987), *Ancient Greek Psychology and the Modern Mind-Body Problem*, Aarhus
Owen, G.E.L. (1961), '*Tithenai ta phainomena*', in S. Mansion (ed.), *Aristote et les problèmes de méthode*, Louvain & Paris, 83-103
Owens, J. (1979), 'The relations of God to the world in the Metaphysics', in P. Aubenque (ed.), *Études sur la Métaphysique d'Aristote*, Paris, 207-22
Owens, J. (1982), 'Aristotle on common sensibles and incidental perception', *Phoenix* 36, 215-36
Peck, A.L. (1937), *Aristotle. Parts of Animals*, London & Cambridge MA
Peck, A.L. (1942), *Aristotle. Generation of Animals*, London & Cambridge MA
Peck, A.L. (1953), 'The connate pneuma, an essential factor in Aristotle's solutions to the problems of reproduction and sensation', in E.A. Underwood (ed.), *Science, Medicine and History. Essays on the evolution of scientific thought and medical practice written in honour of Ch. Singer*, vol. I, Oxford, 111-21
Peck, A.L. (1965-70), *Aristotle. Historia animalium*, Books I-III and Books IV-VI, 2 vols, London & Cambridge MA
Pellegrin, P. (1988), 'L'imaginaire de la fièvre dans la médecine antique', *History and Philosophy of the Life Sciences* 10, 109-20
Pépin, J. (1964), *Théologie cosmique et théologie chrétienne*, Paris
Pépin, J. (1971), *Idées grecques sur l'homme et sur dieu*, Paris
Peters, F.E. (1968), *Aristoteles Arabus. The Oriental Translations and Commentaries on the Aristotelian Corpus*, Leiden
Philippe, M.D. (1971), '*Phantasia* in the philosophy of Aristotle', *Thomist* 35, 1-42
Pigeaud, J. (1981), *La maladie de l'âme. Étude sur la relation de l'âme et du corps dans la tradition médico-philosophique antique*, Paris
Pigeaud, J. (1988), *Aristote. L'homme de génie et la mélancolie*, Paris
Pines, S. (1974), 'The Arabic recension of *Parva Naturalia* and the philosophical doctrine concerning veridical dreams according to al-Risâla al-Manâmiyya and other sources', *Israel Oriental Studies* 4, 104-53
Pormann, P. (2003), 'Jean le grammarien et le *De sectis* de Galien dans la littérature médicale d'Alexandrie', in I. Garofalo, A. Roselli (eds), *Galenismo e medicina tardoantica: fonti greche, latine e arabe*, Naples, 233-63
Pradeau, J.F. (1998), 'L'âme et la moelle. Les conditions psychiques et physiologiques de l'anthropologie dans le *Timée* de Platon', *Archives de philosophie* 61, 489-551
Prantl, K. (1849), *Aristoteles. Über die Farben*, Munich
Preus, A. (1975), *Science and Philosophy in Aristotle's Biological Works*, Hildesheim & New York
Preus, A. (1981), *Aristotle and Michael of Ephesus on the Movement and Progression of Animals*, Hildesheim & New York
Rees, D.A. (1971), 'Aristotle's treatment of *phantasia*', in J. Anton, G. Kustas (eds), *Essays in Ancient Greek Philosophy*, Albany & New York, 491-505
Revesz, B. (1917), *Geschichte des Seelenbegriffs und der Seelenlokalisation*, Stuttgart
Richard, M. (1950), '*Apo phônes*', *Byzantion* 20, 191-222

Riet, S. van (1965), 'Fragments de l'original grec de *De intellectu* de Philopon dans une compilation de Sophonias', *Revue philosophique de Louvain* 63, 5-40
Rist, J.M. (1988), 'Pseudo-Ammonius and the soul/body problem in some Platonic texts of late antiquity', *American Journal of Philology* 109, 402-15
Robin, L. (1908), *La théorie platonicienne des idées et des nombres d'après Aristote*, Paris
Robinson, D.N. (1989), *Aristotle's Psychology*, New York
Robinson, H.M. (1978), 'Mind and body in Aristotle', *Classical Quarterly*, n.s. 28, 105-24
Robinson, H.M. (1983), 'Aristotelian dualism', *Oxford Studies in Ancient Philosophy* 1, 123-44
Robinson, T.M. (1970), *Plato's Psychology*, Toronto
Rocca, J. (2003), *Galen on the Brain*, Leiden
Rodier, G. (1900), *Aristote: Traité de l'âme*, Paris
Rolfes, E. (1924), *Aristoteles' kleine naturwissenschaftliche Schriften*, Leipzig
Rose, V. (1854), *De Aristotelis librorum ordine et auctoritate*, Berlin
Rose, V. (1863), *Aristoteles pseudepigraphus*, Leipzig
Rose, V. (1867), 'Über eine angebliche Paraphrase des Themistius', *Hermes* 2, 191-213
Rose, V. (1886), *Aristotelis qui ferebantur librorum fragmenta*, Leipzig
Rosenmeyer, Th.G. (1986), '*Phantasia* und Einbildungskraft. Zur Vorgeschichte eines Leitbegriffs der europäischen Ästhetik', *Poetica* 18, 197-248
Ross, G.R.T. (1906), *Aristotle. De sensu and De memoria*, Cambridge
Ross, W.D. (1923), *Aristotle*, London
Ross, W.D. (1924), *Aristotle's Metaphysics*, Oxford
Ross, W.D. (1936), *Aristotle's Physics*, Oxford
Ross, W.D. (1949), *Aristotle's Prior and Posterior Analytics*, Oxford
Ross, W.D. (1955), *Aristotle. Parva Naturalia*, Oxford
Ross, W.D. (1961), *Aristotle's De Anima*, Oxford
Roth, R.J. (1963), 'The Aristotelian use of *phantasia* and *phantasma*', *The New Scholasticism* 37, 491-504
Rüsche, F. (1930), *Blut, Leben, Seele*, Paderborn
Ryle, G. (1949), *The Concept of Mind*, London
Saffrey, H.D. (1954), 'Le chrétien Jean Philopon et la survivance de l'école d'Alexandrie au VIe siècle', *Revue des études grecques* 67, 396-410
Saffrey, H.D. (1968), '*Ageometrêtos mêdeis eisitô*. Une inscription légendaire', *Revue des études grecques* 81, 67-87 (repr. in Saffrey [1990], 251-71)
Saffrey, H.D. (1971), *Le 'Peri philosophias' d'Aristote et la théorie platonicienne des idées nombres*, Leiden (2nd edn)
Saffrey, H.D. (1990), *Recherches sur le Néoplatonisme après Plotin* (Historie des doctrines de l'antiquité 14), Paris
Sambursky, S. (1958), 'Philoponus' interpretation of Aristotle's theory of light', *Osiris* 13, 114-26
Sassi, M.M. (1978), *Le teorie della percezione in Democrito*, Florence
Schiano, C. (2003), 'Il trattato inedito *Sulle febbri* attribuito a Giovanni Filopono: contenuto, modelli e struttura testuale', in I. Garofalo, A. Roselli (eds), *Galenismo e medicina tardoantice. Fonti Greche, Latine e Arabe*, Naples, 75-100
Schiller, J. (1973), 'Aristotle and the concept of awareness in sense perception', *Journal of the History of Philosophy* 13, 283-96
Schissel von Fleschenberg, O. (1932), 'Kann die Expositio in libros de Anima des

S. Thomas Aquinas ein Kommentar des Joannes Philoponos zu Aristoteles "Peri psyches" sein?', *Byzantinisch-Neugriechische Jahrbücher* 9, 104-10
Schmidt, J. (1881), *Die psychologischen Lehren des Aristoteles in seinen kleinen naturwissenschaftlichen Schriften*, Prague
Schmitt, C.B. (1985), 'Aristotle among the physicians', in A. Wear, R.K. French, I.M. Lonie (eds), *The Medical Renaissance of the Sixteenth Century*, Cambridge, 1-15
Schofield, M. (1978), 'Aristotle on the imagination', in Lloyd and Owen (eds), 99-140 (repr. in Barnes, Schofield and Sorabji [eds], vol. 4, 103-32)
Scholten, C. (1996), *Antike Naturphilosophie und christliche Kosmologie in der Schrift De opificio mundi des Johannes Philoponos*, Berlin
Schroeder, F.M., Todd, R.B. (1990), *Two Greek Aristotelian Commentators on the Intellect: the De Intellectu attributed to Alexander of Aphrodias and Themistius' Paraphrase of Aristotle, De Anima 3.4-8*, Toronto
Sezgin, F. (1970), *Geschichte des arabischen Schrifttums*, vol. 3, Leiden
Sharples, R.W. (1987), 'Alexander of Aphrodisias: Scholasticism and innovation', *ANRW* II 36.2, 1176-1243
Sharples, R.W. (1995), *Theophrastus of Eresus. Sources for his Life, Writings, Thought, and Influence*, Commentary vol. 5: *Sources on Biology*, Leiden
Sharples, R.W. (2001), 'Dicaearchus on the soul and on divination', in W.W. Fortenbaugh, E. Schütrumpf (eds), *Dicaearchus of Messana. Text, Translation and Discussion*, New Brunswick & London, 143-73
Sharples, R.W. (2004), *Alexander of Aphrodisias: Supplement to On the Soul*, London & Ithaca, NY
Sheppard, A. (1991), 'Phantasia and mental images: Neoplatonist interpretations of De Anima 3.3', in Blumenthal and Robinson (eds), 165-75
Sheppard, A. (1997), '*Phantasia* and mathematical projection in Iamblichus', *Syllecta Classica* 8, 113-20
Shields, C. (1988), 'Soul and body in Aristotle', *Oxford Studies in Ancient Philosophy* 6, 103-37
Shrenk, L.P. (1990), 'John Philoponus on the immortal soul', *Proceedings of the American Catholic Philosophical Association*, 151-60
Siegel, R.E. (1970), *Galen on Sense Perception*, Basel & New York
Silverman, A. (1989), 'Color and color-perception in Aristotle's De Anima', *Ancient Philosophy* 9, 271-92
Simon, G. (1988), *Le regard, l'être et l'apparence dans l'optique de l'antiquité*, Paris
Singer, P.N. (1992), 'Some Hippocratic mind-body problems', in J.A. López Férez (ed.), *Tratádos hipocráticos*, Madrid, 131-43
Singer, P.N. (1997), *Galen. Selected Works*, Oxford
Sisko, J. (1996), 'Material alteration and cognitive activity in Aristotle's *De Anima*', *Phronesis* 41, 138-57
Siwek, P. (1930), *La psychophysique humaine d'après Aristote*, Paris
Siwek, P. (1933), *Aristotelis De Anima libri tres graece et latine*, Rome
Siwek, P. (1963), *Aristoteles. Parva Naturalia graece et latine*, Rome
Siwek, P. (1969), 'Le Dieu d'Aristote dans les dialogues', *Aquinas* 12, 11-46
Slakey, T. (1961), 'Aristotle on sense-perception', *Philosophical Review* 70, 470-84
Smith, R.B. (1976), 'The Alexandrian scientific tradition', *Akroterion* 21.2, 14-21
Solmsen, F. (1950), 'Tissues and the soul', *Philosophical Review* 59, 435-68
Solmsen, F. (1955), 'Antecedents of Aristotle's psychology and scale of beings', *American Journal of Philology* 76, 148-64

Solmsen, F. (1957), 'The vital heat, the inborn pneuma and the *aether*', *Journal of Hellenic Studies* 77, 119-23
Solmsen, F. (1960), *Aristotle's System of the Physical World*, Ithaca, NY
Solmsen, F. (1961a), '*Aisthêsis* in Aristotelian and Epicurean thought', *Mededelingen der Koninklijke Nederlandse Academie van Wetenschappen, Afd. Letterkunde*, Nieuwe reeks, 24, 241-62
Solmsen, F. (1961b), 'Greek philosophy and the discovery of the nerves', *Museum Helveticum* 18, 151-67 and 169-97
Sorabji, R.R.K. (1971), 'Aristotle on demarcating the five senses', *Philosophical Review* 80, 55-79 (repr. in Barnes, Schofield and Sorabji [eds], vol. 4, 76-92)
Sorabji, R.R.K. (1972), 'Aristotle, mathematics and colour', *Classical Quarterly*, n.s. 22, 293-308
Sorabji, R.R.K. (1974), 'Body and soul in Aristotle', *Philosophy* 49, 63-89 (repr. in Barnes, Schofield, and Sorabji [eds], vol. 4, 42-64)
Sorabji, R.R.K. (1980), *Necessity, Cause and Blame*, London
Sorabji, R.R.K. (1987a), 'Philoponus' in Sorabji (ed.) (1987b), 1-40
Sorabji, R.R.K. (ed.), (1987b), *Philoponus and the Rejection of Aristotelian Science*, London & Ithaca, NY
Sorabji, R.R.K. (ed.), (1990), *Aristotle Transformed. The Ancient Commentators and Their Influence*, London & Ithaca, NY
Sorabji, R.R.K. (1991), 'From Aristotle to Brentano: the development of the concept of intentionality', in Blumenthal and Robinson (eds), 227-59
Sorabji, R.R.K. (1992), 'Intentionality and physiological processes: Aristotle's theory of sense perception', in Nussbaum and Oksenberg-Rorty (eds), 195-225
Sorabji, R.R.K. (2000), *Emotion and Peace of Mind*, Oxford
Sorabji, R.R.K. (2003), 'The mind-body relation in the wake of Plato's *Timaeus*', in G.J. Reydam-Schils (ed.), *Plato's Timaeus as Caltural Icon*, Notre Dame, 152-62
Sorabji, R.R.K. (2004a), *The Philosophy of the Commentators, 200-600 AD. A Sourcebook*, 3 vols, London
Sorabji, R.R.K. (2004b), *Aristotle on Memory*, London (2nd rev. edn)
Steel, C. (1978), *The Changing Self. A Study on the Soul in Later Neoplatonism: Iamblichus, Damascius and Priscianus* (Verhandelingen van de Koninklijke Academie voor Wetenschappen, Letteren en Schone Kunsten van België, Klasse der Letteren 40), Brussels
Steinschneider, M. (1869), 'Johannes Philoponus bei den Arabern: Al-Farabi (Alpharabius) des arabischen Philosophen Leben und Schriften', *Mémoire de l'Académie impériale des sciences de St. Petersbourg*, ser. 7, 13,4, 152-76
Steinschneider, M. (1893), *Die arabischen Übersetzungen aus dem Griechischen*, Leipzig (repr. Graz 1960)
Steinschneider, M. (1883-91), 'Die *Parva naturalia* bei den Arabern', *Zeitschrift der deutschen morgenländischen Gesellschaft* 37, 477-92 and 45, 447-53
Stenzel, J. (1924), *Zahl und Gestalt bei Platon und Aristoteles*, Leipzig
Stigen, A. (1961), 'On the alleged primacy of sight in Aristotle', *Symbolae Osloenses* 37, 15-44
Stratton, G.M. (1917), *Theophrastus and the Greek Physiological Psychology before Aristotle*, London
Strohmaier, G. (2003), 'Der Kommentar des Johannes Grammatikos zu Galen, *De usu partium* (Buch 11), in einer unikalen Gothaer Handschrift', in G. Strohmaier, *Hellas im Islam. Beiträge zu Ikonographie, Wissenschaft und Religionsgeschichte*, Wiesbaden, 109-12
Taormina, D.P. (1989), *Plutarco di Atene: L'uno, l'anima, le forme*, Catania

Bibliography 159

Taylor, C.C.W. (1999), *The Atomists Leucippus and Democritus. Fragments*, Toronto
Temkin, O. (1962), 'Byzantine medicine: tradition and empiricism', *Dumbarton Oaks Papers* 16, 97-115
Theiler, W. (1959), *Aristoteles. Über die Seele*, Berlin
Thielscher, P. (1948), 'Die relative Chronologie der erhaltenen Schriften des Aristoteles nach den bestimmten Selbstzitaten', *Philologus* 97, 229-65
Tieleman, T.L. (1996), *Galen and Chrysippus on the Soul*, Leiden
Todd, R.B. (1972), '*Epitêdeiotês* in philosophical literature: towards an analysis', *Acta Classica* 15, 25-35
Todd, R.B. (1974), 'Lexicographical notes on Alexander of Aphrodisias' philosophical terminology', *Glotta* 52, 207-15
Todd, R.B. (1976), *Alexander of Aphrodisias on Stoic Physics*, Leiden
Todd, R.B. (1977), 'Galenic medical ideas in the Greek Aristotelian commentators', *Symbolae Osloenses* 52, 117-34
Todd, R.B. (1980), 'Some concepts in physical theory in John Philoponus' Aristotelian commentaries', *Archiv für Begriffsgeschichte* 24, 151-70
Todd, R.B. (1984), 'Philosophy and medicine in John Philoponus' commentary on Aristotle's *De anima*', *Dumbarton Oaks Papers* 38, 103-10
Todd, R.B. (1996), *Themistius: On Aristotle On the Soul*, London & Ithaca, NY
Towey, A. (2000), *Alexander of Aphrodisias: On Aristotle On Sense Perception*, London & Ithaca, NY
Tracy, T.J. (1969), *Physiological Theory and the Doctrine of the Mean in Plato and Aristotle*, The Hague & Paris
Tracy, T.J., (1983), 'Heart and Soul in Aristotle', in J. Anton, A. Preus (eds), *Essays in Ancient Greek Philosophy*, vol. 2, Albany, 321-39
Trouillard, J. (1957), 'Réflections sur l'*okhêma* dans les "Eléments de Théologie" de Proclus', *Revue des études grecques* 70, 102-7
Ullmann, M. (1970), *Die Medizin im Islam* (Handbuch der Orientalistik, 1. Abt., Ergänzungsband VI/1), Leiden
Urmson, J.O., Lautner, P. (1995), *Simplicius: On Aristotle On the Soul 1.1-2.4*, London & Ithaca, NY
Vancourt, R. (1941), *Les derniers commentateurs alexandrins d'Aristote*, Lille
Verbeke, G. (1945), *L'évolution de la doctrine du pneuma*, Paris & Louvain
Verbeke, G. (1966), *Jean Philopon. Commentaire sur le De anima d'Aristote. Traduction de Guillaume de Moerbeke*, Louvain & Paris
Verbeke, G. (1978), 'Doctrine du pneuma et entelechisme chez Aristote', in Lloyd and Owen (eds) (1978), 191-214
Verbeke, G. (1985), 'Levels of human thinking in Philoponus', in C. Laca, J.A. Munitiz, L. van Rompay (eds), *After Chalcedon. Studies in Theology and Church History offered to Professor Albert von Roey for his Seventieth Birthday*, Louvain, 451-70
Verrycken, K. (1985), *God en wereld in de wijsbegeerte van Ioannes Philoponus*, Louvain
Verrycken, K. (1990a), 'The development of Philoponus' thought and its chronology', in Sorabji (ed.) (1990), 233-74
Verrycken, K. (1990b), 'The Metaphysics of Ammonius Son of Hermeias', in Sorabji (ed.) (1990), 199-231
Verrycken, K. (1991), 'La psychogonie platonicienne dans l'œuvre de Philopon', *Revue des sciences philosophiques et théologiques* 75, 211-34
Verrycken, K. (1994), *De vroegere Philoponus. Een studie van het Alexandrijnse Neoplatonisme*, Brussels (Verhandelingen van de Koninklijke Academie voor

wetenschappen, letteren en schone kunsten van België, Klasse der Letteren, 56.153)
Verrycken, K. (1997), 'Philoponus' interpretation of Plato's cosmogony', *Documenti e studi sulla tradizione filosofica medievale* 8, 269-318
Verrycken, K. (1998), 'Johannes Philoponos', *RAC* 18, 534-53
Viano, C. (1996), 'La doxographie de *De anima* (I, 2-5) ou le contre-modèle de l'âme', in G. Rohmeyer Dherbey (ed.), *Corps et âme. Sur le De anima d'Aristote*, Paris, 51-80
Vogel, C. de (1949), 'Problems concerning later Platonism', *Mnemosyne* n.s. 2, 197-216 and 299-318
Walzer, R. (1957), 'Al-Farabi's theory of prophecy and divination', *Journal of Hellenic Studies* 77, 142-8
Waszink, J.H. (1947a), *Quinti Septimi Florentis Tertulliani De anima*, Amsterdam
Waszink, J.H. (1947b), 'Traces of Aristotle's lost dialogues in Tertullian', *Vigiliae Christianae* 1, 137-49
Watson, G. (1982), '*Phantasia* in Aristotle's *De anima* 3.3', *Classical Quarterly* 32, 100-13
Watson, G. (1988), *Phantasia in Classical Thought*, Galway
Watson, G. (1988a), 'Discovering the imagination: Platonists and Stoics on *phantasia*', in J. Dillon, A.A. Long (eds), *The Question of Eclecticism. Studies in Later Greek Philosophy*, Berkeley & Los Angeles, 208-33
Watson, G. (1988b), *Phantasia in Classical Thought*, Galway
Webb, P. (1982), 'Bodily structure and psychic faculties in Aristotle's theory of perception', *Hermes* 110, 25-50
Wedin, M.V. (1988), *Mind and Imagination in Aristotle*, London
Wedin, M.V. (1989), 'Aristotle on the mechanics of thought', *Ancient Philosophy* 9, 67-86
Wedin, M.V. (1994), 'Aristotle on the mind's self-motion', in M.L. Gill, J.G. Lennox (eds), *Self-Motion. From Aristotle to Newton*, Princeton, 81-116
Wehrli, F. (1967-69²) *Die Schule des Aristoteles. Texte und Kommentare*, 10 vols, Basel & Stuttgart
Welsch, W. (1987), *Aisthesis. Grundzüge und Perspektiven der Aristotelischen Sinneslehre*, Stuttgart
Westerink, L.G. (1962), *Anonymous Prolegomena to Platonic Philosophy*, Amsterdam
Westerink, L.G. (1964a), 'Philosophy and medicine in late antiquity', *Janus* 51, 169-77
Westerink, L.G. (1964b), 'Deux commentaires sur Nicomaque: Asclépius et Jean Philopon', *Revue des études grecques* 77, 535-62
Westerink, L.G. (1990), 'The Alexandrian commentators and the introductions to their commentaries', in Sorabji (ed.) (1990), 325-48
Wieland, W. (1962), *Die aristotelische Physik*, Göttingen
Wielen, W. van der (1941), *De ideegetallen van Plato*, Amsterdam
Wiersma, W. (1943), 'Die aristotelische Lehre vom Pneuma', *Mnemosyne* 11, 102-7
Wiesner, J. (1978), 'The unity of the treatise *De somno* and the physiological explanation of sleep in Aristotle', in Lloyd and Owen (eds), 241-80
Wiesner, J. (ed.), (1987), *Aristoteles. Werk und Wirkung*, II, Berlin & New York
Wildberg, C. (1988), *John Philoponus' Criticism of Aristotle's Theory of Aether*, Berlin & New York
Wili, W. (1955), 'Probleme der aristotelischen Seelenlehre', *Eranos-Jahrbuch* 12, 55-93

Wilpert, P. (1941), 'Neue Fragmente aus *Peri tagathou*', *Hermes* 76, 225-50
Wilpert, P. (1949), *Zwei Aristotelische Frühschriften über die Ideenlehre*, Regensburg
Wingate, S.D. (1931), *The Mediaeval Latin Versions of the Aristotelian Scientific Corpus, with Special Reference to the Biological Works*, London
Wöhrle, G. (1993), *Anaximenes aus Milet. Die Fragmente zu seiner Lehre*, Stuttgart
Wolff, M. (1971), *Fallgesetz und Massebegriff. Zwei wissenschaftshistorische Untersuchungen zur Kosmologie des Johannes Philoponos*, Berlin
Wolff, M. (1978), *Geschichte der Impetustheorie*, Frankfurt a.M.
Wolska-Conus, W. (1989), 'Stéphanos d'Athènes et Stéphanos d'Alexandrie: essai d'identification et de biographie', *Revue des études byzantines* 47, 5-89
Woollam, D.H.M. (1958), 'Concepts of the brain and its functions in classical antiquity', in F.L.N. Poynter (ed.), *The History and Philosophy of Knowledge of the Brain and its Functions*, Springfield, IL & Oxford, 5-18
Wright, J. (1920), 'The theory of the pneuma in Aristotle', *New York Medical Journal* 112, 893-900
Wright, M.R. (1995), *Empedocles. The Extant Fragments*, Bristol
Zeller, E. (1879), *Die Philosophie der Griechen, in ihrer geschichtlichen Entwicklung*, 2. Teil, 2. Abtheilung, Leipzig

English-Greek Glossary

able, be: *dunasthai*
abolish: *anairein*
absence: *apousia*
absence of movement: *akinêsia*
absence of wind: *nênemia*
abstraction: *aphairesis*
abstraction, by (means of):
   aphairesis, ex aphaireseôs
accept: *lambanein*
accept (in advance): *prolambanein*
accidental, be: *sumbainein,*
   sumbebêkenai
accidentally: *kata sumbebêkos*
accompany: *hepesthai, akolouthein,*
   parakolouthein, suntrekhein
accord, of own: *proairetôs*
accordance, in: *akolouthôs,*
   sumphônôs
accordingly: *akolouthôs*
account: *logos*
accurate: *akribês*
accustomed, being: *sunethismos*
accustomed, make: *sunethizein*
act: *poiein*
acted upon, be: *paskhein*
activate: *energein*
active: *poiêtikos*
active, be: *energein, poiein*
activity: *energeia, ergon*
actuality: *energeia, entelekheia*
actuality itself: *autoenergeia*
actually: *energeiâi (dative),*
   entelekheiâi (dative)
adapt accordingly: *metharmozein*
add: *paralambanein, suntithenai*
adduce: *sunepipherein*
adjoining: *prosekhês*
admit of: *epidekhesthai*
adopt: *paralambanein,*
   apolambanein, lambanein,
   analambanein

adorn: *katakosmein*
adornment: *kosmos*
adumbration: *aposkiasma*
aether: *aithêr*
aethereal: *aitherios*
affected, be: *paskhein*
affection: *pathêma, pathos*
affirmation: *kataphasis*
afraid, be: *phobeisthai*
age: *hêlikia*
agree on: *homologein*
aim: *skopos*
air: *aêr*
airy: *aerios*
alive, be: *zên*
allude: *ainittesthai*
alteration: *alloiôsis*
analogous account, give an: *analogein*
analogously: *analogôs, kat' analogian*
analogy: *analogia*
analogy, as an: *analogos*
analyse: *dialambanein*
analysis: *diakrisis*
analytic: *katagôgos*
ancients, the: *hoi palaioi*
angel: *angelos*
anger: *orgê, thumos*
angle: *gônia*
angles, having many: *polugônios*
angry, be: *orgizein, thumousthai*
animal: *zôion*
antecedent: *hêgoumenon*
apparent: *phainomenos, phaneros*
appearance: *dokêsis, doxa, phantasia,*
   phasma
appearances: *ta phainomena*
appetite: *orexis*
appetite, concerned with; appetitive:
   orektikos
apprehend: *antilambanesthai*
apprehending, capable of: *antilêptikos*

English-Greek Glossary

apprehension: *antilêpsis, epibolê, prosbolê*
appropriate: *oikeios, prepôdês*
appropriate, be: *prosêkein*
appropriateness: *oikeiotês*
apt to move: *kinêtikos*
archetype: *arkhetupos*
architect: *oikodomos*
argument: *logos*
arithmetic: *arithmêtikê*
arithmetical: *arithmêtikos*
arouse: *kinein*
arrangement: *diakosmêsis*
ask: *zêtein*
asleep, be: *katheudein*
assent: *suntithesthai*
assimilate: *proskrinein*
assimilation: *exomoiôsis*
assistance: *sunergia*
assume: *hupolambanein, lambanein, sullambanein*
assumed, be: *hupokeisthai*
astral: *astroeidês*
astronomy: *astronomia*
asymmetrical: *asummetros*
atheist: *atheos*
atom: *atomos*
attention: *epimeleia*
attribute: *pathos, huparkhon, parakolouthoun*
attribute (v): *anatithenai, aponemein*
attribute, be an: *sumbainein, huparkhein*
attribute, be an essential: *huparkhein kath' hauto, sumbebêkenai*
audience: *okhlos*
aware, be: *sunaisthanesthai*

back: *nôtiaios*
bad: *mokhthêros*
ball: *sphaira*
base: *basis*
bass: *barus*
battle: *makhê*
battle (v): *makhesthai*
be: *einai, huparkhein*
be as it is, to: *tôi tauta einai*
beauty as such: *autokalon*
becoming (domain of): *genesis*
beginning: *arkhê*
being: *to einai, ousia*
being, mode of: *to einai, ousia*
being, true: *ousia*

beings/things that exist: *ta onta*
beliefs, form: *hupolambanein*
believe: *nomizein*
belly: *gastêr*
belong to: *huparkhein, sumbainein*
belong to, things that: *ta huparkhonta*
belonging to the same series: *sustoikhos*
bending: *kampsis*
between, come in: *parempiptein*
birth, give: *tiktein*
blood: *haima*
bloodless: *anaimos*
blush: *eruthrainein*
bodily part: *morion*
body: *sôma*
body, of the: *sômatikos*
boil: *zein*
boiling: *zesis*
bondage: *desmos*
bone: *ostoun*
brain: *enkephalos*
break down: *analuein*
breast: *stêthos*
breathe: *anapnein*
breathing: *anapnoê*
bring to light: *ekphainein*

call: *onomazein*
capable, be: *dunasthai*
careful, be: *eulabeisthai, phrontizein*
categorise: *katêgorein*
category: *katêgoria*
causal trigger: *prophasis*
cause: *aitia, aition*
cause of: *aitios*
cause of, give as: *aitiasthai*
celestial: *ouranios*
celestial body: *ouranion (sôma)*
centre of the heavens: *mesouranêma*
cerebral membrane: *mêninx*
change: *metabolê*
change (v): *exallattein, metaballein, summetaballein*
change, free from: *ametablêtos*
character: *êthos*
characterise: *kharaktêrizein, huparkhein*
characteristic: *kharaktêristikos, oikeios*
chastise: *kolazein*
chastisement: *kolasis*
circle: *kuklos*

English-Greek Glossary

circular: *diallêlos, kuklos, peripherês*
circumference: *perimetros*
claim: *hupotithenai*
clear: *phaneros, saphês*
cognition: *gnôsis*
cognition, concerned with: *gnôstikos*
cognitive: *gnôstikos*
cognitive aspect: *to ginôskein*
coincide: *epharmozein*
cold: *psukhros*
cold, become: *psukhesthai*
combination: *sunkrisis, sunthesis*
combine: *sumplekein, suntithenai*
come into being: *ginesthai*
come into contact with: *prosballein*
coming into being: *genesis, genêtos*
coming to be: *genesis, gennêtos*
commensurate: *summetros*
comment: *hupomnêmatizein*
common: *koinos*
common, have in: *epikoinônein*
commonly: *koinôs*
communicate: *hermêneuein*
compact: *puknos*
compact, be made, become: *puknousthai*
compare: *paraballein*
complete: *pantelês, teleios*
complete (v): *sumplêroun*
completeness: *to panteles*
compose: *sunistanai*
composite: *sunamphoteron, sunthetos*
compress: *sundiatupoun*
conceive of: *hupolambanein*
concentrate on: *apoblepein*
conception: *epinoia*
conceptually: *epinoiâi (dative), kat' epinoian*
conclude: *sullogizesthai*
concluding decision: *epikrisis*
conclusion: *sumperasma*
concomitant attribute: *sumptôma*
conditional: *sunêmmenos (sunaptein)*
configuration: *sundromê*
confirmation: *kataphasis*
confuse: *sunkhein*
conjecture: *eikasia*
conjunction: *sunodos*
connect: *epharmozein, sumplekein*
connected: *prosekhês, suntetagmenos*
connecting: *sundesmos*
connection: *sunapheia*
consciousness, state of: *sunaisthêsis*

consider: *hupolambanein*
consist: *sunistasthai, sunkeisthai, huphistanai*
constancy: *monê*
constant: *sunekhês*
constitute: *sunistasthai*
constitutive: *sustatikos*
construct: *sumplekein*
contemplation: *theôria*
contemplation, of: *theôrêtikos*
contempt, holding in: *huperoptikos*
continuous: *sunekhês*
continuously: *sunekhôs*
continuum: *sunekheia*
contract: *sustellein*
contraction: *sustolê*
contraction, undergo: *sunkrinesthai*
contradistinguish: *antidiastellein*
contrast: *antidiastellein*
control: *kratein*
controversial: *amphibolos*
controversy: *amphibolia*
conversation: *sunousia*
conversion: *antistrophê*
cooling: *psuxis*
co-operate: *suntelein*
corporeal: *sôma, sômatikos, sômatoeidês*
corpse: *nekron sôma, nekros*
corresponding: *sustoikhos*
cosmic: *enkosmios*
cosmos: *kosmos*
couple with: *sunduazein*
courageous, be: *tharsein*
cowardice: *deilia*
cowardly: *deilos*
craftsman: *tekhnitês, dêmiourgos*
Craftsman, the: *dêmiourgos*
create: *dêmiourgein*
creation: *dêmiourgia*
creative: *dêmiourgikos, poiêtikos*
criterion: *kritêrion*
cross-roads: *hodos skhistê*
cube: *kubos*
cubit: *pêkhus*
curved: *kampulos*
cut: *temnein*

dark: *skotos*
dead: *nekros*
death: *thanatos*
decadic/decad: *dekadikos/dekas*
decay: *phthora*

166 English-Greek Glossary

deficient, be: *endein*
defile: *lumainesthai*
define: *diorizein, horizein*
define the form: *eidopoiein*
defined: *hôrismenon*
definite: *diôrismenon*
definition: *horismos, horos, logos*
definition, by means of: *horistikê*
definition, give a: *diorizein*
deliberate choice: *proairesis*
delicacy of parts/particles: *leptomereia*
demon: *daimôn*
demonstrate: *apodeiknunai, deiknunai*
demonstration: *apodeixis, deixis*
demonstration, based on: *apodeiktikôs*
demonstrative: *apodeiktikos*
density: *to puknon*
depth: *bathos*
descend: *kataduein*
describe: *perigraphein*
description: *hupographê*
designate: *katêgorein*
desire: *epithumia, orexis*
desire (v): *epithumein*
desire, object of: *orektos*
destroy: *aposbennunai, phtheirein*
destruction: *phthora*
destructive: *aidêlos*
determinate: *hôrismenos*
determinate way, in a: *hôrismenôs*
determine: *diorizein, horizein*
determining principle: *horos*
deviate: *existêmi*
dialectic: *hê dialektikê*
dialectical: *dialektikos*
dialectician: *ho dialektikos*
dialogue: *dialogos*
diametrical, in d. opposition: *diametros*
difference: *diaphora, heterotês*
different: *diaphoros*
differentia: *diaphora*
differentiate between: *diakrinein*
dignity: *axia*
disagreement: *diaphora*
disappear: *oikhein*
discern: *diakrinein*
discourage: *apotrepein*
discouragement: *apotropê*
discourse: *logos*
discrete: *diôrismenon*
discrete quantity: *diôrismenon poson*

discursive thinking/thought: *dianoeisthai, dianoia*
discussion: *logos*
disease: *nosos*
disintegration: *diakrisis*
dislodgement: *mokhleia*
display: *ekthesis*
disposition: *diathesis, hexis*
dispute: *amphisbêtein*
dissimilarity: *anomoiotês*
dissociated: *exeirêmenos*
dissoluble: *skedastos*
dissolution: *diastasis*
dissolve: *analuein*
distance: *diastêma, apostasis, diastasis*
distinguish: *diakrinein, diastellein, khôrizein*
distort: *sunkataspan*
distorted: *diastrophos, endiastrophos*
distraction: *periolkê*
divide: *diairein, dialambanein, merizein, temnein*
divided: *meristos*
divine: *theios*
division: *diairesis*
division, by means of: *diairetikos*
doctor: *iatros*
doctrine: *dogma, doxa*
doubt, be in: *distazein, aporein*
draw conclusion(s): *sullogizesthai, sumperainein*
draw in along with: *sunepispan*
dry: *xêros*
dryness: *xêrotês*
dull: *amauros, amudros*
dull-witted: *nôthês*
dyad: *duas*
dyad as such, the: *autoduas*

earth: *gaia, gê*
earthquake: *seismos*
earthy: *geïnos, geôdês*
element: *stoikheion*
elementary: *stoikheiôdes*
eliminate: *anairein, sunanairein*
eliminate together: *sunanairein*
embellish: *katakosmein*
embodied: *ensômatos*
emit: *ekkrinein*
emotion: *pathos*
empty: *kenos*
encapsulate: *enkatakhônnunai*

English-Greek Glossary

encompass: *periekhein, perilambanein*
encourage: *protrepein*
encouragement: *protropê*
end: *telos*
engendered in, be: *enginesthai*
enmattered: *enulos*
ensouled: *empsukhos*
ensouled being: *to empsukhon*
environment: *topos*
equal: *isos*
equipment with different organs: *diorganôsis*
equipped with different organs, be: *diorganousthai*
err: *hamartanein*
essence: *ousia*
essence, in virtue of the: *kat' ousian*
essential: *kath' hauto, ousiôdês*
essential attributes: *ta ousiôdôs huparkhonta, ta sumbebêkota kath' hauto, ta huparkhonta kat' ousian*
essentially: *kath' hauto, kat' ousian, têi ousiai*
eternal: *aidios*
eternity: *aidiotês*
ethical: *êthikos*
ethical philosopher: *ho êthikos*
ethics: *êthikê*
evaporation: *anathumiasis*
even number: *artios*
evidence: *enargeia*
evident: *dêlos, enargês, saphês*
evidently: *enargôs*
evil: *kakos*
exact: *akribês*
exactness: *akribeia*
examine: *episkopein, zêtein*
example: *paradeigma*
example, selected for: *exairetos*
excess: *huperbolê*
excess, be in: *pleonazein*
excitement: *to paroxunesthai*
exciting factors: *ta paroxunonta*
excrete: *ekkrinein*
exercise: *energein*
exercise activity: *energein*
exhale: *ekpnein*
exhaling: *ekpnoê*
exhibit: *gumnazein*
exist: *einai, huphistanai, sunistasthai*
exist before: *proüphistasthai*
exist independently: *huphistanai*

exist on own/have existence of own: *huphistanai*
existence: *huparxis, hupostasis*
existence, in a mode of existence of its own: *authupostatos*
existing in thought only: *ennoêmatikos*
expansion, undergo: *diakrinesthai*
experience: *paskhein*
expert: *tekhnitês*
expertise: *tekhnê*
explain: *exêgeisthai*
explicitly: *diarrhêdên*
extended: *diastatos*
extension: *diastatos, ekstasis*
external: *ektos*
extinction: *to aposbennusthai*
extinguish: *sbennunai*
extreme: *eskhatos*
extreme end: *akron*
extrude: *ekkrinein, ekthlibein*
eye: *omma, ophthalmos*

fact: *pragma*
fact; the fact 'that': *to hoti*
faculties, having many (different): *poludunamos*
faculty: *dunamis*
false: *pseudês*
falsehood: *pseudos*
fat: *pakhus*
fattiness: *gliskhrotês*
fear: *phobos*
feed: *trephein*
female: *thêlus*
figure: *skhêma*
final: *telikos*
final result: *apotelesma, apoteleutêsis*
fine: *kalos, leptos, leptomerês*
fine arrangement: *eutaxis*
finite: *hôrismenon (horizein)*
fire: *pur*
first things: *prôta pragmata*
fit: *epharmozein, harmozein, sunagein*
flame: *phlox*
flesh: *sarx*
flow: *rhuiskesthai*
flux: *rhuiskesthai*
flux, state of: *rhusis*
follow: *akolouthein, parakolouthein, sumbainein*
for the sake of: *heneka*
force: *bia, rhumê*

form: *eidos, idea*
form, having one: *monoeidês*
form, make up the: *eidopoiein*
formal principle: *logos*
formation, concerned with: *diaplastikos*
formative: *eidikos*
formless: *aneideos*
formula: *logos*
freedom: *skholê*
from where to what, the: *to pothen poi*
fulfilment: *teleiôsis*
fullness: *plêrôma*
function(ing): *ergon*

gain strength: *akmazein*
gain strength with: *sunakmazein*
gathering: *sunodos*
general: *genikos, haplous, katholikos, katholou, koinos*
general, in: *haplôs, holoskherês, katholou*
general kind: *katholou to*
general outline, in: *holoskherês*
generally speaking: *epipan, haplôs, katholou*
generally: *haplôs, koinôs*
generate: *gennan*
generation: *gennêsis*
generation, concerned with: *gennêtikos*
generative: *gennêtikos*
genuine: *gnêsios, ontôs*
genus: *genos*
geometrical: *grammikos*
geometrical figure: *skhêma*
geometrician: *geômetrês*
geometry: *geômetria*
germane: *prosphuês*
god: *theos*
good: *agathos, kalos*
good life: *euzôia*
grasp: *antilambanesthai, epiballein, ephaptesthai, lambanein, prosballein*
grasp, having capacity to: *antilêptikos*
grasp intuitively: *epiballein*
grasped, be: *perilêptos*
grasping: *lêpsis*
grow: *auxanein, phuein*
growth: *auxêsis*
growth, concerned with: *auxêtikos*

happen: *sumbainein*
harmonics: *harmonikê*
harmony: *harmonia*
head: *kephalê*
healing: *hugiansis, iama*
health: *hugieia, hugeia*
healthy, be: *hugiainein*
hearing: *akoê*
heart: *kardia, kradiê*
heart, in the region of the: *perikardios*
heat: *kauma, kausis, thermon, thermotês*
heat (v): *thermainein*
heat, natural: *thermotês, emphutos thermotês*
heating: *thermainesthai*
heavenly: *ouranios*
heavenly body: *ouranion (sôma)*
heavens, the: *ouranos*
hemisphere: *hêmisphairion*
heterogeneous: *heterogenês, polumigês*
hierarchical position: *taxis*
high up in the sky: *meteôros*
higher: *anô*
higher region of the atmosphere: *meteôros*
higher things: *ta hupertera*
hold: *hupolambanein*
hold together: *sunekhein, sunistanai*
homoeomerous: *homoiomerês*
homoeomerous parts: *ta homoiomereia*
homogeneous: *homogenês*
homonymous term: *homônumos phônê*
hot: *thermos*
human: *anthrôpeios, anthrôpinos, anthrôpos*
human being: *anthrôpos*
human-like shape: *andreikelon*
humour: *khumos*
hypotenuse: *diametros*
hypothesis: *hupothesis*
hypothetically, hypothetical: *ex hypothesi: en hupothesei*

idea: *dianoia, eidos*
identical in essence: *homoousios*
identical in name: *homônumos*
ignorance: *agnôsia*
ignore: *agnoein, lanthanein*
ill, be: *kamnein*
illuminate: *ellampein, phôtizein*
illumination: *ellampsis, phôtismos*
image: *eikôn, phantasma*

English-Greek Glossary

imagination: *phantasia, phantastikon*
imagine: *phantazein*
imagining: *phantasiousthai*
imitate: *mimeisthai*
imitation: *mimêma*
immaterial: *aülos*
immediately: *amesôs*
immobile: *akinêtos*
immoderate: *ametros*
immortal: *athanatos*
immortality: *athanasia*
impassive: *apathês*
impede, be an impediment:
  empodizein, parempodizein
imperishable: *aphthartos*
impression: *tupos*
impulse: *hormê*
inclination: *epitêdeiotês*
inclined, be: *diakeisthai, euemptôtôs ekhein*
inclined to: *epitêdeios*
inclined to anger: *thumikos*
inclined to get beside oneself: *manikos*
incomplete: *atelês*
incorporeal: *asômatos*
indefinite: *aoristos*
indefinitely: *eis apeira*
indicate: *mênuein, sêmainein*
indication: *tekmêrion*
indicative of: *sêmantikos*
individual: *kata meros, merikos*
individual parts, in: *meristôs*
individual thing/object: *atomos*
individually: *idiôs*
indivisible: *adiairetos*
inevitable: *anankaios, anankê*
infallible: *aptaistos*
infer: *sullogizesthai, tekmairesthai*
inferential: *tekmêriôdês*
infinite: *apeiron*
infinitum, ad: *ep' apeiron*
inform by form: *eidopoiein*
inhale: *eispnein*
inhaling: *eispnoê*
initiate: *huparkhesthai*
initiative: *hormê*
innate: *emphutos*
inquire: *epizêtein*
inquirer: *epiistôr*
inquiry: *historia, to zêtein*
insensitive: *anaisthêtos*
inseparable: *akhôristos*
insight: *ennoia*

inspired, be: *enthousiazein*
instrument: *organon*
instrument, as a kind of: *organikôs*
intellect: *noêsis, nous*
intellect (active): *nous ho kat' energeian*
intellect itself, the: *autonous*
intellect, objects of: *ta noêta*
intellection: *noêsis*
intellectual: *noeros*
intellectually: *noêtôs*
intelligence: *phronêsis*
intelligible: *noeros, noêtos*
intelligible objects (objects of thought): *ta noêta*
intermediary: *mesos*
intermediate: *mesos*
interpret: *exêgeisthai*
interpretation: *exêgêsis*
interpreter: *exêgêtês, exêgoumenos*
intertwine: *sumplekein*
interwoven with, state of being: *epiplokê*
intuition: *epibolê*
intuitive apprehension: *epibolê*
intuitive thinking: *to noein*
investigate: *episkeptein, zêtein*
invisible: *aoratos, aphanês*
irrefutable: *alutos*
itself, in itself: *kath' hauto, auto kath'hauto*

jointly: *koinôs*
journey: *hodos*
judge: *kritês*
judge (v): *krinein*
judgement: *krisis*
judgement, give: *epikrinein*
judgement, make a: *doxazein*
judging: *to krinein*
just: *orthos*
juxtaposition: *parathesis*

kind: *eidos, genos*
kind, of a: *poios*
kinetic: *kinêtikos*
kinetic aspect: *to kinêtikon*
kinship: *sumphuia*
know: *eidenai, gnôrizein, noein*
know, capacity/ability to: *gnôsis, gnostikê (dunamis), to gnôstikon*
know, get to: *gnôrizein*
knowing: *to eidenai, eidêsis, gnôsis*

knowledge: *to eidenai, eidêsis, epistêmê, gnôsis*
knowledge, have: *eidenai*
knowledge, having scientific: *epistêmonikos*
knowledge, object of: *gnôstos*

lack of internal harmony: *anarmostia*
lacking perception: *anaisthêtos*
land animal: *khersaios*
learning, objects of: *ta mathêmata*
lecture: *akroasis, logos*
length: *mêkos*
lengthwise: *kata mêkos*
let share in: *metadidonai*
life: *bios, to zên, zôê*
life (concerned with): *zôtikos*
lifeless: *azôos*
light: *phôs*
light (adj): *leptos*
lighter, become: *leptunesthai*
like: *homoios*
limit: *peras*
line: *grammê, seira*
literal sense, in the: *kuriôs*
live: *zên*
liver: *hêpar*
living: *to zên*
living being: *to empsukhon, zôion*
living being as such: *autozôion*
living in air: *aerios*
living thing: *to empsukhon*
location: *topos*
locomotion: *kinêsis kata topon, to kinêtikon*
long for: *oregesthai, zêtein*
loose: *manos*
love: *philia*
lover: *erastês*
luminous: *augoeidês*
lump of earth: *bôlos*

magnitude: *megethos*
main mass: *holotês*
make: *poiein*
make manifest: *emphainein*
man: *anthrôpos*
man as such: *autoanthrôpos*
manifest: *enargês*
manifestation: *indalma*
manifestly visible: *enargês*
manifold: *poikilos*
mark out: *aphorizein*

mass: *onkos*
master (v): *epikratein*
material: *hulê, hulikos, hulôdês*
mathematical figure: *skhêma*
mathematical form: *mathêmatikon*
mathematical object: *mathêmatikon, mathêma*
mathematician: *ho mathêmatikos*
mathematics: *ta mathêmata*
matter: *hulê*
mean: *sêmainein*
measure: *anametrein, metrein*
mechanics: *hê mêkhanikê*
mechanism: *mêkhanê*
medical: *iatrikos*
medicine: *hê iatrikê*
meet: *emballein*
melancholic, having a tendency to m. affections: *melankholikos*
membrane-protector: *mêningophulax*
memory, having a good: *mnêmonikos*
menstrual blood: *ta katamênia*
method: *methodos, tropos*
middle: *mesos*
mind: *nous*
mix: *kerannunai, kirnan, meignunai*
mixed: *miktos*
mixture: *krasis, mixis, sunkrisis*
mixture, having a particular: *kekramenos*
model: *paradeigma*
moderately: *summetrôs*
moderation: *summetria*
moist: *hugros*
moisture: *hugron*
monad: *monas*
monstrosity: *teras*
mortal: *thnêtos*
mortar: *plinthos*
mote: *xusma*
motion: *to kinein, kinêsis*
motion, set in: *kinein*
mould: *plassein, suntupoun*
move: *kinein, methistanai, rhein*
move together: *sunkinein*
move, difficult to: *duskinêtôs, akinêtos*
moved, easily: *eukinêtos*
movement: *to kinein, to kinêisthai, kinêma, kinêsis, to kinêtikon*
movement, free from: *akinêtos*
movement in the local sense: *kinêsis kata topon*

English-Greek Glossary

movement, that which causes: *to kinoun*
mover, the first: *to prôtôs kinoun*
moves, that which: *to kinoun*
moving: *to kinein*
musician: *mousikos*
myth: *muthos*

name: *onoma, onomasia*
name, called by the same: *homônumos*
natural: *kata phusin, phusikos*
natural being: *phusis tis*
natural capacity: *phusis*
natural entity: *phusis*
natural kinds: *ta phusika*
natural objects: *ta phusika*
natural philosopher: *phusikos*
natural things: *ta phusika*
naturally: *phusei*
nature: *phusis*
nature, in accordance with: *phusikos*
nature, of: *phusikos*
nature, of a certain: *poios*
nature, of the same: *homophuês*
necessarily: *anankê*
necessary: *anankaios, anankê*
necessary, absolutely: *pasa anankê*
necessity: *anankê*
necessity, of: *anankaiôs*
negation: *apophasis*
nerve: *neuron*
non-rational: *alogos*
non-rationality: *alogia*
normal: *sunêthês*
not connected: *asunaptos*
not know: *agnoein*
notion: *ennoia*
number: *arithmos*
numerically: *kat' arithmon, tôi arithmôi*
nutrition: *trophê*
nutrition (faculty of nutrition), concerned with: *threptikos*
nutritive: *threptikos*

object: *pragma*
object, be: *antikeisthai*
obscure: *adêlos*
observe: *theôrein*
odd (number): *perittos*
old age: *gêras*
omnipotent: *pantodunamos*
one and the same kind, of: *homoeidês*

one as such, the: *autoeis*
opinion: *doxa*
opinion, be of an: *doxazein*
opinion, object of: *to doxaston*
opposites: *ta antikeimena*
opposition: *antidiastolê*
opposition, set in: *antidiairein*
optic: *optikos*
orderly arrangement: *taxis*
organ: *organon*
organ, of an: *organikos*
origin: *arkhê*
origin, of the (same): *sumphulos*
own: *idios, oikeios*
own, of its: *kath' hauto*
own, on its: *kath' hauto*

pain: *algunsis, lupê*
pain, cause: *algunein, lupein*
pale (pallor): *ôkhros*
paleness: *ôkhriasis*
palpitation: *palmos*
part: *merikos, meros, moira, morion, tmêma*
partake in: *metekhein*
participate in: *metekhein*
particular: *merikos*
particular, in: *exairetôs, idios*
particular case: *meros, en merei*
particular thing: *tode ti*
pass away: *aporrhein, phtheiresthai*
passing away: *phthora*
passive: *pathêtikos*
passive, be (v): *paskhein*
peculiar: *idios, oikeios*
peculiar nature, peculiarity: *idiotês*
penetrate: *diabainein, diadunein, dieisdunein*
perceive: *aisthanesthai, theôrein*
perceive, having the faculty to: *aisthêtikos*
perceptible: *aisthêtos*
perception: *to aisthanesthai, aisthêsis*
perfect: *telein, teleios*
perfected, being: *teleiôtikos*
perfection: *teleiôsis, teleiotês*
perish: *phtheiresthai*
perishable: *phthartos*
perishing: *phthora*
permeate: *diêkein*
perpendicular: *kathetos*
person: *anthrôpos*
persuasion: *pistis*

philosopher: *philosophos*
philosopher, first philosopher: *prôtos philosophos*
philosophy: *philosophia*
philosophy, first: *prôtê philosophia*
physical: *phusikos*
physics: *hê phusikê, phusiologia*
place: *khôra, topos*
place of punishment: *dikaiôtêrion*
place where X sets: *dusis*
plain: *prodêlos*
plane figure: *epipedos*
plant: *phuton*
plants, of: *phutikos*
plausible: *pithanos*
plausible conviction: *pistis*
pleasant: *hêdus*
pleasure: *hêdonê*
plurality: *plêthos*
pneuma: *pneuma*
pneumatic: *pneumatikos*
point: *sêmeion, stigmê*
political: *politeia*
posit: *hupotithenai*
position: *tropê*
position, as definition for *tropê*: *thesis*
possessing organs: *organikos*
possible: *dunatos*
posterior: *husteros*
posterior by nature, the: *to husteron têi phusei*
potentiality: *dunamis*
potentially: (*en*) *dunamei*
power: *dunamis*
powerful: *enargês*
practical: *praktikos*
precursors: *hoi proteroi*
premise: *protasis*
presence: *huparxis, parousia*
present: *prokeimenos*
present, be: *huphistanai*
present as attribute, be: *sumbainein*
present in, be: *huparkhein*
present subject: *prokeimenon*
preserve: *sôzein*
primarily: *prôtôs*
primary causes: *prôta aitia*
primary thoughts: *prôta noêmata*
principle: *arkhê*
prior: *proteros*
prior by nature, the: *to proteron têi phusei*
prior grasping: *prolêpsis*

problem: *aporia, problêma*
problematic: *aporos*
produce: *apotelein, poiein, tiktein*
producing effects: *poiêtikos*
productive: *poiêtikos*
project: *proballein*
prone: *epitêdeios*
prone to anger: *orgilos*
proof: *kataskeuê, pistis*
proper: *idios, kurios, oikeios*
proper attribute: *kath'hauto idion*
proper sense, in the: *kuriôs*
properly speaking: *kuriôs*
property: *pathos*
proportion: *logos*
protect: *skepein*
prove: *kataskeuazein, pisteuein*
Providence: *pronoia*
provoke: *erethizein*
proximate: *prosekhês*
pure: *katharos*
purgation: *katharsis*
purgative: *katharmos, kathartikos*
purification: *katharsis*
purify: *kathairein*
purifying: *kathartikos*
purpose: *telos*
pyramid: *puramis*
pyramidal: *puramoeidês*
pyramid-shaped: *puramoeidês*

quadrangle: *tetragônon*
qualitative sense, in the: *poios, epi tou poiou*
quality: *to poion, poiotês*
quality, in respect of: *kata poion*
quantity: *plêthos, to poson*
quantity, definite: *diôrismenon poion*
quantity, in respect of: *kata poson*
query: *aporein*
question: *to zêtein, zêtêma, zêtêsis*
question (raise the): *zêtein*

raise a problem/question/query: *aporein, diaporein*
raise problems prior: *proaporein*
rank (order): *taxis*
rank (v): *anagein*
rational: *logikos*
reach: *khôrein*
read: *anagignôskein*
reality: *alêtheia*
reason: *aitia, aition, logos*

English-Greek Glossary

reason, contrary to: *alogos*
reason, objects of: *ta dianoêta*
reason why: *dia ti*
reason why, the: *to dioti*
reasonable: *eulogos*
reasoning: *logos*
reasoning, correct: *orthos logos*
receive a share in: *metalambanein*
receive: *lambanein*
receptacle: *dekhas*
reckless: *thrasus*
recognise: *gnôrizein*
recollection: *anamnêsis*
rectilinear: *euthugrammos*
refer back: *anagein*
refer to: *paralambanein, sêmainein*
refutable: *lutos*
refutation: *elenkhos*
refute: *elenkhein*
regimen: *diaita*
reject: *katapsêphizesthai*
related objects: *ta hupokeimena*
relation: *logos, skhesis*
relative, (category of): *pros ti*
relationship: *skhesis*
remaining part: *to paraleleimmenon*
remind: *anamimnêskein*
repeat: *tautologein*
repetition: *tautologia*
report: *historein*
reproduce: *zôiopoiein*
reproduction: *to zôês poiêtikon, to zôiopoiein*
respect: *aidôs*
respiration: *anapnoê, eispnoê*
rest: *êremein*
restore to health: *hugiazein*
result: *apotelesma*
retaliate: *antilupein*
retaliation: *antilupêsis*
reverse: *antistrephein*
right angle: *orthia*
right proportion: *summetria*
rough outline, in: *holoskherês*
roughly: *holoskherês*
rule: *kanôn*

sameness: *tautotês*
scatter: *diaphorein*
science: *epistêmê, tekhnê*
scientific: *epistêmonikos*
scientific knowledge: *epistêmê*
scientific knowledge itself: *autoepistêmê*

scientific knowledge, objects of: *ta epistêta*
scientific understanding: *to epistasthai, epistêmê*
scientifically: *kat' epistêmên*
scientist: *tekhnitês*
sea: *thalatta*
search: *zêtêsis*
search (v): *ereunan, zêtein*
seed: *gonê, sperma*
seed-medley: *panspermia*
seeing: *to horan*
seek: *epizêtein, zêtein*
self, by itself: *kath' hauto, kath'heauto*
self, in itself: *kath' hauto*
self-moved: *autokinêtos*
self-movement: *to autokinêton*
self-moving: *autokinêtos*
semen, emit in sleep: *oneirôttein*
semicircle: *hêmisphairion*
semicircular: *dikhotomos*
sense: *aisthêsis*
sense organ: *aisthêtêrion*
sense perception: *aisthêsis*
sensitive: *aisthêtikos*
separable: *khôristos*
separate: *exêirêmenos, khôristos*
separate (v): *aphistanai, khôrizein*
separation: *diakrisis*
sequence, in a: *ephexês*
serious: *spoudaios*
servant: *hupêretês, sunergos*
sex: *gonê, mixis*
sexual activity: *aphrodisia*
shade: *skia*
shadowy: *skioeidês*
shame: *aidôs*
shape: *morphê, skhêma*
shape, give: *skhêmatizein*
shape with many/more angles: *polugônon*
share: *klêros*
share, designated: *lêxis*
share in: *metekhein*
sharp-witted: *oxus*
shipbuilder: *naupêgos*
show: *deiknunai*
sickening: *nosansis*
sign: *sêmeion*
signify: *sêmainein*
similar: *homoios*
similar, be: *homoiousthai*
similar way, in a: *homoiotropôs*

similarity: *homoiotês*
simple: *haplôs, haplous*
simply: *haplôs*
single way, in a: *monakhôs*
size: *megethos*
sketch, in rough: *tupôi*
skilful: *tekhnikos*
skin: *humên*
slip (away): *exolisthanein*
smell: *osphrêsis*
soft: *malakos*
soil: *gê*
solid: *pakhus, stereos*
solid figure: *stereon*
solidify: *pakhunein*
sophist: *sophistês*
soul: *psukhê*
soul, of the: *psukhikos*
sound: *phthongos*
sound (adj.): *hugiês*
source: *pêgê*
source of movement: *to kinoun*
spacious: *polukhôrêtos*
species: *eidos*
specific: *idikos*
specifically: *idikôs*
specify: *diorizein*
sphere: *sphaira*
spherical: *sphaira, sphairikos, sphairoeidês*
spirit, spirited part: *thumos*
spirited: *thumoeidês*
spontaneously: *automatôs*
spurious, be: *notheuesthai*
stability: *stasis*
stable: *hestôs*
stable, be: *hestanai*
stand: *anistanai*
standstill: *stasis*
star: *astron*
start: *arkhein*
starting point: *aphormê, arkhê*
state: *hexis, katastasis*
statement: *apodosis, logos, rhêtos*
steersman: *kubernêtês*
stick: *baktêria*
stimulate: *kinein*
stir up: *kinein*
straight: *euthus*
straight line: *eutheia*
straightforward: *haplous*
straightness: *to euthu, euthutês*
strictest sense, in the: *kuriôs*

Strife: *Neikos*
string: *khordos*
student of nature: *phusikos, phusiologos*
study: *theôria*
study (v): *episkeptein, theôrein, zêtein*
subdivide: *epidiairein, hupodiairein*
subject: *hupokeimenon, prokeimenos*
subject matter: *hupokeimenon*
subject-specific expert: *tekhnitês kata meros, tekhnitês kath' hekasta*
subordinated: *hupallêlos*
substance: *ousia, sustasis*
substance, in respect of: *kat' ousian*
substance, join with one's own: *sunousiousthai*
substrate: *hupokeimenon*
subsume: *perilambanein*
subtle: *leptos*
subtract: *aphairein*
succession: *diadokhê*
suffer: *paskhein*
suffer pain: *lupêisthai*
suit: *epharmozein*
suitability: *epitêdeiotês*
suitable: *skopimos*
sum up: *aparithmein, anakephalaiousthai, katarithmein*
summing up, a: *anakephalaiôsis*
superficial: *phainomenos*
superior: *epikratês*
supervene: *episumbainein*
suppose: *hupolambanein, huponoein, hupotithenai*
surface: *embadon, epipedon, epiphaneia*
surplus, be a result of: *pleonazein*
surround: *periekhein*
suspect: *eikasia*
suspect (v): *huponoein*
syllogism: *sullogismos*
syllogistic proof: *sullogismos*
symbolic language, in: *sumbolikos*
symbolic way, in a: *sumbolikôs*
sympathetic affection: *sumpatheia*
sympathetic relationship: *sumpatheia*
synthetic: *anagôgos*

take: *lambanein, eklambanein, paralambanein*
take account of: *perilambanein*
take into account: *hupologizesthai, paralambanein*

English-Greek Glossary

take note: *epistasthai*
take part in: *metalambanein, metekhein*
task: *ergon*
taste: *geusis*
teacher: *didaskalos*
teaching: *didaskalia*
temper: *kolazein*
tendency to, have a: *rhepein*
tepid: *khliaros*
terminate: *peratoun*
terminus: *peras*
terrestrial: *khthonios*
testimony: *marturia*
tetrad: *tetras*
tetradic: *tetradikos*
theological: *theologikos*
theology: *theologia*
theorem: *logos*
theoretical student: *theôrêtikos*
theoretical study: *theôria*
theory: *logos*
thing: *pragma*
things: *ta onta*
things surrounding: *ta parakeimena*
think: *dianoeisthai, ennoein, noein, nomizein, phronein*
thinkable: *noêtos*
thinking: *to dianoeisthai*
thinking (intuitive): *noêsis*
thought: *dianoia, noêma, phronêsis*
thought, object of: *dianoêtos*
thoughts, have/be with other: *allophronein*
three-dimensional: *stereos*
three-dimensional thing/figure/body: *stereos*
time: *aiôn*
tomb: *taphos*
tone: *phthongos*
tongue: *glôtta*
tongue, paternal: *patrikê glôtta*
touch: *haphê*
touch (v): *ephaptesthai, haptesthai*
trace: *ikhnos*
trace (v): *ikhnêlatein*
transcendent: *exeirêmenos*
transpose: *huperbibazein*
treatise: *pragmateia*
treble: *oxus*
tetrad as such, the: *autotetras*
triad as such, the: *autotrias*
triad: *trias*

triangle: *trigônon*
trivial: *idiôtikos*
true: *alêthês*
truly: *ontôs*
truth: *alêtheia*
tune: *melos*
turn: *trepein*
turn aside: *paraklinein*
turn in on: *epistrephesthai*
turn sideways: *epiklinein, klinein*
turn towards itself: *sunneuein pros (eis) heauton*
turning in on: *epistrophê*
two directions, go into: *epamphoterizein*

unchangeable: *atreptos*
unchanging: *ametablêtos*
unclear: *asaphês*
unconnected: *asunaptos*
unconscious: *anepaisthêtos*
undergo: *hupomenein*
underlying: *hupokeimenos*
understand: *eklambanein, lambanein*
understanding: *to epistasthai, epistêmê*
undertake: *lambanein*
underworld: *hupo gên*
undivided: *amerês, ameristos*
unensouled: *apsukhos*
unification: *henôsis*
uniform: *haplous*
unify: *henoun*
unilluminated: *aphôtistos*
union: *henôsis*
universal: *katholou*
universally: *holôs, katholou*
universe: *kosmos, to pan*
unmixed: *amigês, amiktos*
unmoved: *akinêtos*
unpurified: *akathartos*
unqualified: *haplôs*
unseparated: *akhôristos*
unsuitable: *anepitêdeios*
unwritten: *agraphos*
use: *paralambanein*
uterus: *mêtra*

vain, in: *kenôs, matên*
valuable: *axiologos, timios*
vapour: *anathumiasis, atmos*
vegetative: *phutikos*
vehicle: *okhêma*

verbal account: *logos*
vessel: *angeion*
view: *gnômê*
view (v): *theôrein*
virtue: *aretê*
visible: *emphanês, horatos*
vision: *opsis*
vital: *zôtikos*
void: *kenos*

walk: *badizein*
warm: *thermos*
wash: *plunein*
waste away: *marainein*
water: *hudôr*
way: *hodos, tropos*
weaken with: *sunamaurousthai*
weakness: *astheneia*
weave anew: *anuphainein*
weave to: *prosuphainein*
well talented: *euphuês*
what-it-is: *ti esti*
whole: *holos, to holon, holotês*
whole, as a: *holôs, holon di' holou, sunolos, to sunolon*
whole, on the: *katholou*

wholeness: *holotês*
widen: *manoun*
widening, capable of: *diakritikos*
width: *to manon, platos*
wild animal: *thêrion*
willing: *hekôn*
wisdom: *sophia*
wise person/man: *ho sophos*
wish: *boulêsis*
without angles: *agônios*
without being divided: *amerês*
without body: *asômatos*
without demonstration: *anapodeiktos*
without extension: *adiastatos*
without further qualification: *haplôs*
without giving shape: *askhêmatistos*
without lapse of time: *akhronôs*
without magnitude: *amegethês*
without matter: *aülos*
word: *logos, onoma, phônê*
work: *biblion, ergon*
world: *kosmos*
worth: *axios*

yearn for: *ephiesthai*
yearning: *ephesis*

Greek-English Index

abakion, (reckoning) board, 52,35; 58,12
aboulêtos, without wishing, 8,33
adêlos, obscure, 39,6.8.25; 40,31; 41,7; 42,2.27
adiairetos, indivisible, 79,23
adiastatos, without extension, 58,10
adunamos, without potentiality, 46,25
aeikinêtos, always in motion, 2,6; 18,29; 21,1; 70,35; 71,3; 75,12.13; 87,25; 88,13; 90,24
aêr, air, 17,22; 35,26; 66,1.5; 67,20.24; 69,23; 70,17.34; 84,4; 86,21.22; 87,1.3.7
aerios, airy, 9,9; 20,8; living in air, 11,34; 77,27
agathos, good, 3,21; 5,26.29; 18,18; 21,33.34; 22,3.5; 75,34; *beltiôn*, superior, 22,15; 24,9.13.15
agnoein, ignore, 60,15; not know, 4,5; 33,20; 43,7
agnôsia, ignorance, 22,2.4; 58,21
agônios, without angles, 56,11; 68,18; 69,3; 85,7
agraphos, unwritten, 75,35
aidêlos, destructive, 73,20
aidios, eternal, 7,17; 11,3; 16,11.12.13.25; 18,26.27.30.31; 21,3; 49,6; 56,20
aidiotês, eternity, 7,14.15.17
aidôs, respect, 86,29; shame, 50,19
ainittesthai, allude, 36,14.16; 37,18; 70,18; 71,6; 74,3
aiôn, time, 48,34
aisthanesthai, perceive, 11,4; 13,12; 27,6; 35,13; 39,29.30; 42,10; 65,13.14; 72,7.30;
  aisthanesthai, to, perception, 65,8.29; 89,6.14.20
aisthêsis, perception, 7,36; 10,21; 13,24; 19,12; 39,18.25.35.36; 40,1.2; 41,19; 42,3.16.23.26; 43,5.11; 44,23; 52,23; 65,22.29; 66,18; 71,27; 72,5.32; 76,30; 78,22.23.25; 79,19.31; 80,29; 81,6.9.10; 89,15.16.20; 90,19.22.26; sense, 6,9; 7,1; 19,5.32; 21,32; 27,15; sense perception, 2,8.14.21; 4,17; 5,3.15.35.36.37.38; 7,32.33; 10,21.24; 11,14.15; 12,35; 13,4.16; 14,34; 15,2; 18,37; 19,34; 39,12; 44,26; 45,19.20; 65,15; 67,4; 71,25
aisthêtêrion, sense organ, 19,6.34.35
aisthêtikos, (faculty) of sense perception, 11,18; 36,28; 39,30; having the faculty to perceive, 40,1.4; sensitive, 19,7.13.15; 89,17.22
aisthêtos, perceptible, 1,15; 2,26.27.29; 3,15; 4,6; 6,1; 10,21.24; 11,15; 39,13.17.35; 40,1.2; 50,4; 73,32; 74,9.21; 76,16; 77,1.5.21.27; 78,7.22
aisthêton, *(to)*, object of perception, 6,10; 19,33.36; 27,15; 57,30; 79,22; 80,27; 81,11
aithêr, aether, 73,20
aitherios, aethereal, 9,6
aitia, cause, 5,30; 14,5.8; 20,34. 36; 21,5; 30,12; 35,28; 40,7; 41,3.6; 51,3; 52,6.23; 54,20.23; 55,18.27; 56,2.5.19.22; 57,1.7.8.12.15.18.20.26.37; 58,1.3.25.30; 59,6.8.9.13.16.28; 60,1.7.8.20.21; 61,33; 62,16; 68,32; 70,10.34; 72,11; 73,30; 81,3; 83,6; 84,12; 87,25; 88,15.23; 92,7; reason, 14,20; 18,16; 21,19; 22,19; 64,24; 79,32; 84,9.17.21

aitiasthai, give as cause of, 57,9; 83,21
aitiaton, to, the thing caused, 30,12.21.24.26; 52,22; what is caused, 35,28; 50,24; 57,21.24.25
aition, cause, 15,24.26.32; 20,35; 30,15.21.25.26; 31,19; 33,29; 35,29; 42,25; 51,37; 52,22.24; 55,15.16; 56,24.35; 57,24.25; 69,14; 72,14; 83,18; 84,26; 85,21; 89,15.21; reason, 11,17
aitios, cause of, 85,20
akathartos, unpurified, 19,20
akhôristos, inseparable, 9,22; 10,2; 12,11.12.18; 15,30.31; 16,2.27.29; 17,5.7; 18,10.33; 19,17; 33,9; 46,22; 49,22.23; 51,19; 57,28; 61,18; 61,29; 62,24.28.31; 63,16; unseparated, 70,12
akhronôs, without lapse of time, 79,24
akinêsia, absence of movement, 76,18
akinêtos, difficult to move, 9,13; free from movement, 76,33; immobile, 19,9; unmoved, 20,37; 21,2; 35,29; 55,16; 66,26
akmazein, gain strength, 15,3
akoê, hearing, 7,3; 14,34
akoinônêtos, not having anything in common, 70,12; unsharing, 91,18
akolouthein, accompany, 27,3; follow, 29,10.12; 49,9; 65,29
akolouthos, in accordance with, 79,15
akolouthôs, accordingly, 82,2; 83,15; in accordance with, 33,26; 82,29
akribeia, exactness, 23,5
akribês, accurate, 59,11; 82,8; exact, 21,11.14; 22,14.20.22; 23,6; 24,3.5.11.19; 26,16
akroasis, lecture, 82,8
akron, extreme end, 2,13
aktis, sunbeam/ray of sun, 67,21.25; 69,25; 70,18
alêtheia, reality, 8,19; 72,6; 80,5; truth, 24,31.34.35; 25,1; 71,25; 72,25.26; 91,24
alêthês, correct, 34,3; 72,25; true, 1,8; 10,8; 36,11; 43,1.8; 71,24; 78,18; 79,27.30
alêtheuein, speak the truth, 5,10.11.14

algunein, cause pain, 17,34; 18,3.5
algunsis, pain, 17,33
alloiôsis, alteration, 76,34
allophronein, have/be with other thoughts, 72, 2.1.7
alogia, non-rationality, 5,31; 8,2
alogos, contrary to reason, 85,27; non-rational, 1,10.13; 2,21; 5,28.30.31.34; 6,25.33; 7,9.22.24.33; 8,19.21.24.25; 9,1.37; 10,1.4.6; 11,30; 12,7.18; 14,33; 15,11; 16,27; 17,19.23.26; 18,34.37; 19,3; 20,30.31; 35,18.29.30; 36,15; 37,3.4.5.8; 38,25; 52,26; 53,31; 54,26; 57,13; 61,34; 76,30; 89,32
alutos, irrefutable, 31,17
amauros, dull, 11,22
amegethês, without magnitude, 14,12; 22,27
amelein, neglect, 17,30
amerês, undivided, 13,21.25.34; 14,11.21; 35,9.10.12.22; 36,8; 56,31; 58,10; 76,17; 77,30; 78,10; without being divided, 13,10.17.27.33
ameristos, undivided, 38,29; 75,17
amesôs, immediately, 29,18
ametablêtos, free from change, 76,33; unchanging, 23,31; 24,22.24.26
ametros, immoderate, 18,3; 51,12
amigês, unmixed, 11,19; 86,2.3; 91,13.15.18
amiktos, unmixed, 70,15
ampelos, vine, 6,29
amphibolia, controversy, 32,31; wavering, 46,10
amphibolos, controversial, 33,6
amphikurtos, gibbous, 30,29
amphisbêtein, dispute, 30,7; 32,23
amudros, dull, 11,15
amuna, revenge, 55,5
amunein, attack, 64,10.11
anagein, lift up, 2,24.28; 20,33.35; 55,14; rank, 26,21.22; 32,12.23.31.32; 33,5; refer back, 90,26; 91,5
anagignôskein, read, 13,5
anagôgos, synthetic, 73,28.29; 74,2
anaidês, ruthless, 50,29
anaimos, bloodless, 89,14.18.19.20

Greek-English Index

anairein, abolish, 88,2.6; eliminate, 37,5
anaisthêtos, insensitive, 19,9.12.14; lacking perception, 52,25; 89,14
anakephalaiousthai, sum up, 6,31; ***anakephalaiôsis***, a summing up, 90,20
analambanein, adopt, 84,2
analogein, (give an) analogous account, 48,23
analogia, analogy, 37,14; 74,20; 78,3; 79,12; ***kat' analogian***, analogously, 77,9; 77,14.19; 78,30
analogos, as an analogy, 50,3; ***analogôs***, analogously, 38,23
analuein, break down, 79,7; dissolve, 46,29
anametrein, measure, 58,13
anamimnêskein, remind, 5,16; 63,25
anamnêsis, recollection, 58,22
anankaios, inevitable, 41,18; 43,10; must be, 64,18; necessary, 1,5; 12,35; 17,13; 32,26; 33,15; 44,20.34; 49,7; 64,27; ***anankaiôs***, of necessity, 54,23
anankê, have to be/has to be, 46,25.27.35; 49,22; 59,19.21; inevitable, 43,29.33; 57,24; must be, 18,2.10.32; 27,25; 55,12; necessarily, 4,24; 33,23; 54,22; necessary, 12,30; 21,1; 39,15; 44,28.33; 48,30; 54,19; 66,24; necessity, 10,20; 16,4.11.12.29; 17,1.15.16; ***ex anankês***, inevitably, 33,26; 46,22; necessarily, 6,32; 15,18.23; 17,32; 24,13; 26,31.33; 27,3; 29,7; 33,13; 45,29; 46,3; 51,29.34; necessity, 45,27; 46,28; ***pasa anankê***, absolutely necessary, 45,18; 47,1; 51,26
anaplattein, re-shape, 6,1
anapnein, breathe, 68,27
anapnoê, breathing, 68,27; respiration, 68,19.28; 69,4; 92,7.9
anapodeiktos, without demonstration, 3,18.30
anarmostia, lack of internal harmony, 16,20
anateinesthai, stretch itself, 74,3
anatellein, rise, 34,17; ***anatolê***, place where X rises, 76,36

anathumiasis, evaporation, 90,8; vapour, 83,19; 87,9.12
anatithenai, attribute, 79,22; 81,29
andreikelon, human-like shape, 19,37; 20,2
aneideos, formless, 52,33
anemos, wind, 59,25; 60,9; 70,36; 83,20
anenergêtos, numb, 19,8; unable to be activated, 46,35
anepaisthêtos, unconscious, 72,3; without perceiving, 8,6
anepistêmôn, uneducated, 74,21
anepitêdeios, unsuitable, 46,31
angeion, vessel, 20,5
angelos, angel, 79,16
anistanai, stand, 49,3
ankistroeidês, having a barbed shape, 84,28
anô, higher, 70,14
anoêtos, without intelligence, 85,26
anomoiotês, dissimilarity, 75,20
anousios, without essence, 46,25
anthrôpeios, human, 36,18; 89,5
anthrôpinos, human, 20,10; 22,22; 36,7.13; 57,5
anthrôpos, human, 6,32; 7,25; 9,21.39; 26,8; 34,13; 72,19; 89,13; human being, 1,17; 4,11; 6,31; 48,3.5.12; man, 3,31; 4,8; 5,23; 21,31; 29,15; 30,9; 33,13.19; 34,14.29.32; 36,22.27; 37,12; 38,4.7.9.24; 74,16; 79,16; 89,32; person, 21,14
antidiairein, set in opposition, 29,5
antidiastellein, contradistinguish, 6,12.17.19; contrast, 35,4
antidiastolê, opposition, 47,22
antikeimena, ta, opposites, 39,34.35; 46,15
antikeisthai, be object, 39,36
antikrus, openly, 71,24; 72,8
antilambanesthai, apprehend, 5,37; 13,5; 19,33.36; 50,5.6.7.10; grasp, 11,15.16.17; 78,24; 81,12
antilêpsis, apprehension, 78,10
antilêptikos, capable of apprehending, 13,2; having capacity to grasp, 79,23
antilupein, retaliate, 6,13.36; 17,3; 55,3; 57,23; 59,1.8
antilupêsis, retaliation, 44,3.8; 55,4.5; 57,16; 58,24.30.36.37

antistrephein, reverse, 29,19; 30,1; 46,17
antistrophê, conversion, 46,11.13.19
antiteinein, resist, 51,35
anuphainein, weave anew, 6,24
aoratos, invisible, 67,26
aoristos, indefinite, 76,5.20
aparithmein, enumerate, 6,32; 69,24; 73,3.5; 89,33; 90,23; list, 32,5; 61,17; 62,17; 64,31; sum up, 82,11
apathês, impassive, 11,5.7.8.19; 70,21; 83,35.36; 91,13
apeiron, infinite, 41,2; 42,1; 48,34; 67,6; 83,25; *eis apeira*, indefinitely, 12,26; *ep' apeiron*, ad infinitum, 12,30
apereidein, find support in, 43,35
apergazesthai, create, 12,6
aphairein, subject to abstraction, 57,34; subtract, 3,20
aphairesis, abstraction, 57,35; *ex aphaireseôs*, by (means of) abstraction, 62,23.27
aphanês, invisible, 11,32; 20,9; *aphanês ginesthai*, disappear, 20,8
aphantastos, not product of imagination, 45,24; without imagination, 2,14
aphistanai, separate, 77,14
aphorizein, mark out, 1,9
aphormê, starting point, 43,6
aphôtistos, unilluminated, 31,5
aphrodisia, sexual activity, 8,3
aphthartos, imperishable, 46,28
aplatês, without width, 77,31
apoblepein, concentrate on, 72,28; 81,17; 82,1.6; 86,14; 88,11; 91,5
apodeiknunai, demonstrate, 4,8.10.11.16; 14,38; 23,21.24; 24,4.6; 30,22
apodeiktikos, demonstrative, 31,24; 32,7; demonstrative knowledge, 42,17; *apodeiktikôs*, based on demonstration, 43,3
apodeixis, demonstration, 2,7.9.21; 3,18.23; 4,1; 5,18.20.21.22; 12,13; 30,2; 31,23; 32,3; 42,14.33; 43.28
apodosis, statement, 32,20
apoklêrôtikos, arbitrary, 84,27
apokruptein, keep secret, 69,28
apolambanein, adopt, 27,21

apologeisthai, speak in defence of, 36,17; 90,3
aponemein, attribute, 83,30; 86,33
apophasis, negation, 3,21; 78,18
aporein, be in doubt, 78,15.17.24; query, 46,12; raise a problem/question/query, 32,28.30; 39,33; 64,22; 83,28
aporia, difficulty, 8,16; 38,33; problem, 32,8; 44,18; raising the questions, 64,22
aporos, difficult, 44,24; problematic, 33,33
aporrhein, pass away, 6,24
aposbennunai, destroy, 46,31; *to aposbennusthai*, extinction, 46,30
aposkiasma, adumbration, 5,17
aposobein, scare away, 6,24
aposos, without quantity, 14,12
apostasis, distance, 77,14.15.19
aposulan, strip, 62,26
apotelein, produce, 53,3.4; 70,9.14
apotelesma, final result, 8,8; result, 51,26; 52,8.12
apoteleutêsis, final result, 1,21
apotemnein, cut away, 44,5
apothermainesthai, to, cooling, 49,2
apotrepein, discourage, 21,12.16; 28,1; *apotropê*, discouragement, 21,11
apousia, absence, 6,36
aproairetos, not of own accord, 20,17
apsukhos, unensouled, 35,28; 52,24; 65,11.13.14; 72,33; 75,10; 89,10
aptaistos, infallible, 23,3; 30,4
areskein, adhere to, 65,16
aretê, virtue, 15,6; 25,6
aristeuein, excel (in battle), 45,28.30
arithmêtikê, arithmetic, 23,7.8.24.25.28
arithmêtikos, arithmetical, 23,10
arithmos, number, 23,8; 28,10; 31,32; 32,11; 32,33; 33,11; 44,12; 71,13; 76,2; 78,32; 79,7.18; 80,15; 81,16; 82,19; *kat' arithmon*, numerically, 7,16; *tôi arithmôi*, numerically, 7,13
arkein, suffice, 60,10
arkhê, beginning, 53,24; 56,21; 60,24; 65,1; 69,8; origin, 51,7; 53,27; 65,32; principle, 4,1; 7,15; 9,7.12.18; 20,36; 21,3; 23,20;

Greek-English Index

24,4.6; 25,31.33; 26,12; 55,17.20;
65,33; 67,5.27; 72,31; 73,11;
73,21; 74,6.10.32.34; 75,6.26.27;
76,1; 79,8.9; 80,14;
81,23.28.29.32; 82,29.30.32; 83,1;
83,13; 84,13; 85,32.33.34;
86,7.9.14.22.35; 87,2.4.8;
89,4.5.25; 90,26.27; 91,5; 91,31;
92,3; starting point, 3,27.29.33;
4,3; 32,10; 33,21.26.29.31.32.33;
42,14.18.33; 43,2.8.28.31; 44,17;
64,22; 76,7; 83,3; 87,20
arkhein, start, 2,5; 32,29; 38,36;
39,1.7.11.16
arkhetupos, archetype, 58,17
artios, even number, 80,13
asaphês, unclear, 39,20; 49,18; 64,22
askhêmatistôs, without giving
shape, 6,4; without reference to
shape, 3,5
asômatos, incorporeal, 3,13; 9,3.21;
12,16; 13,11; 14,9.12.28.29.33.38;
16,19.23; 18,1.6; 21,2; 33,7.8;
34,6.7.9.21.34; 35,4.8; 46,32.34;
66,24; 70,21; 78,21; 82,16;
83,11.17.27.28; 87,23; 90,19;
91,13; without body, 22,27;
without reference to body, 3,4
aspondos, irreconcilable, 51,35
astheneia, weakness, 23,32; 24,1
astroeidês, astral, 18,23
astron, star, 4,22.24; 24,2
astronomia, astronomy, 22,20.23.24
asummetros, asymmetrical, 23,5
asunaptos, not connected, 9,5;
unconnected, 9,16
atelês, incomplete, 7,12; 11,35; 75,8
atenizein, look into, 23,34
athanasia, immortality, 40,14
athanatos, immortal, 1, 18.19;
2,1.2.4.6; 4,10; 5,21; 9,15.28;
11,6.8.28.30; 12,4.6.8.17; 15,15;
24,7.13.25.27.28; 25,10; 40,14;
42,27.29; 46,28; 47,4; 77,10.16;
78,20; 81,20; 88,12.14
atheos, atheist, 9,11; 88,23
atimos, of low value, 72,17; 85,30
atmos, vapour, 19,26.27.30.31
atomos, atom, 9,17.18.19; 67,6;
68,16.23.24.25.28; 69,8; 70,27;
84,14.16.22; 85,14; 86,21; atomic
body, 67,32; cannot be
divided/indivisible, 28,25.26;
38,5; 67,6; 82,23; individual
thing/object, 77,1.5
atreptos, unchangeable, 83,36
augoeidês, luminous, 18,22.27.28.31;
49,5
aülos, immaterial, 50,11; 55,11;
without matter, 2,28; 3,9.10;
16,16; 22,26; 23,1.9.27;
24,4.6.7.11.12; 35,4.7
authupostatos, in a mode of
existence of its own, 52,19.27.28
autoanthrôpos, man as such, 79,14
autoduas, the dyad as such, 77,8
autoeis, the one as such, 77,8; 78,28
autoenergeia, actuality itself, 35,1
autoepistêmê, scientific knowledge
itself, 81,10
autokalon, beauty as such, 79,14
autokhrêma, in very deed, 83,36
autokinêtos, self-moved, 2,5.6;
18,18; 40,13; 42,29; 75,24;
self-moving, 71,8.9.14; sets self
in motion, 81,19.22.30;
autokinêton, to, self-movement,
81,28
automatôs, spontaneously, 52,13.18
autonous, the intellect itself, 81,9
autotetrad, the tetrad as such, 77,9
autotriad, the triad as such, 77,9
autozôion, living being as such, 77,5;
78,29; 79,11.13; 81,2.9
auxanein, grow, 6,29.34; 8,32;
17,2.11; 65,26
auxêsis, growth, 7,20.21; 16,31;
(faculty of) 17,12.13; 42,25
auxêtikos, concerned with growth,
6,27; 8,32; 13,28.36;
axia, dignity, 37,7; 52,17
axiologos, valuable, 86,29
axios, important, 21,32; worth, 4,4;
21,11; 52,26
azôos, lifeless, 35,29; 52,24; 89,1

badizein, go down the road, 91,10;
walk, 47,11; 47,12
baktêria, stick, 66,23.31
barus, bass, 70,8; heavy, 9,13; 20,19;
61,29
basileus, ruler, 64,9.10
basis, base, 68,17
bathos, depth, 10,16; 26,9; 78,5.6.29;
79,4
bia, force, 66,5

biblion, work, 75,36
bios, life, 11,35; 12,14
bôlos, lump of earth, 65,34
boreas, north, 76,37
boulêsis, wish, 5,25.27.28; 26,1; 71,11
brôma, food, 16,35

daimôn, demon, 20,7.12
daktulos, finger, 13,2; 80,5
deiknunai, demonstrate, 4,25; 12,15; 13,1; 15,8.9.12; 16,24.25; 17,9; 21,17; 23,21.25.26; 30,14.23; 43,23; 49,24.33; 50,16; 52,2; 56,9; 84,23; show, 4,22; 10,1.8.11; 11,27; 13,25; 14,12.29; 16,3; 20,6; 21,17; 30,10; 48,22; 49,31; 55,25; 68,21; 70,20; 77,2; 81,19.31; 84,29; 86,14; 87,26; 88,2; 89,17
deiknusthai, be evident, 17,9
deilia, cowardice, 53,19.21
deilos, cowardly, 50,29
deixis, demonstration, 5,19; 31,15; 30,24; 40,23.24; 42,21; 43,14.22; 54,8
dekadikos/dekas, decadic/decad, 76,2; 79,7; 80,25.26
dekhas, receptacle, 76,11
dektikos, capable of receiving, 29,15.20; that which receives, 56,7
dêlos, evident, 39,6.7; 42,3; 73,21; 74,10
dêmiourgein, create, 52,21
dêmiourgia, creation, 12,2; 52,15.16
dêmiourgikos, creative, 38,15; 52,20; 58,9.15.17
dêmiourgos, the Craftsman, 11,31; 37,25
dendron, tree, 33,20
desmos, bondage, 18,5
dia ti, reason why, 1,18
diabainein, penetrate, 3,17; 35,20; 52,6; proceed, 2,5
diadokhê, succession, 8,12
diadunein, penetrate, 68,1.14.15; 84,18; 87,6.24
diairein, divide, 1,6.11.14; 5,24; 12,26; 28,16; 38,27; 75,2; 78,20
diairesis, division, 1,9.10; 32,4; 33,16; 34,3; 36,11; 38,21; 60,17.18
diairetikos, by means of division, 32,7
diaita, regimen, 19,23.28; 20,3; 51,8

diakeisthai, to be inclined, 53,18
diakosmêsis, arrangement, 11,34
diakrinein, differentiate between, 72,9; discern, 13,13.14; 44,26; distinguish, 11,14; 13,7.19.20; 23,18; 42,32; 62,3; 72,11; 85,22.27
diakrinesthai, undergo expansion, 18,2
diakrisis, analysis, 73,32; disintegration, 74,7; separation, 90,5.10
diakritikos, capable of widening, 1,16
dialambanein, analyse, 82,3; divide, 82,14; make distinction, 74,11
dialektikê, hê, dialectic, 55,28
dialektikos, dialectical, 43,26.33; 44,1; 57,23; 59,29
dialektikos, ho, dialectician, 55,21; 57,14.23; 58,24; 59,5; 60,24.29; 62,7
diallêlos, circular, 40,23.24.25; 42,21; 43,14.22
dialogos, dialogue, 1,20
diamartanein, fail completely, 33,23.27; 43,9
diametros, hypotenuse, 23,5; in diametrical opposition, 30,32
dianoeisthai, discursive thinking, 43,11; think, 11,12; *dianoeisthai, to*, discursive thought, 48,20; thinking, 65,28
dianoêta, ta, objects of reason, 1,17; 2,19; 3,7; 4,7.9
dianoêtos, object of thought, 39,13
dianoia, (discursive) thinking, 1,14.19.21; 2,2.4.19.22.24; 3,6.13; 4,1.9.11.16.21; 39,13; 44,1; 71,12; 78,11; idea, 22,17; 69,22; thought, 37,31; 70,1
diaphora, difference, 7,28; 33,10; 67,8; 84,3; differentia, 26,24; 28,15.17; 32,24; disagreement, 82,2
diaphorein, scatter, 69,11
diaphoros, different, 20,5; 35,15; 36,11; 37,12; 38,26; 49,19; 90,6.7
diaplastikos, concerned with formation, 13,28
diapnein, cause to evaporate, 89,1
diaporein, raise problems/questions, 64,18.28
diarrhêdên, explicitly, 91,28

diastasis, dissolution, 67,7; distance, 77,34
diastatos, extension, 58,10; extended, 58,12
diastellein, distinguish, 49,18
diastêma, distance, 58,13
diastrophos, distorted, 21,24
diathesis, disposition, 6,16; 53,12.27
diathigê, arrangement, 68,12.13
diatithenai, bring into a certain condition, 16,33; 19,5
diatribê, occupation, 51,31.32
didaskalia, exposition, 38,34; teaching, 69,28; 70,2; 73,22
didaskalos, teacher, 5,4
dieisdunein, penetrate, 85,15
diêkein, permeate, 75,4
dikaiôtêrion, place of punishment, 17,34; 18,15.19.23; 20,16.20
dikhotomos, semicircular, 30,29
diorganôsis, equipment with organic parts, 26,7
diorganousthai, be equipped with different organs, 19,31.36; 26,10
diorizein, determine, 90,28; give a definition, 59,22; specify, 39,24; *diôrismenon*, definite, 32,19; discrete, 79,7.9; *diôrismenon poion*, definite quantity, 32,15; *diôrismenon poson*, discrete quantity, 78,32
dioti, to, the reason why, 4,5
diplasios, twofold, 33,5.6
dipous, (having) two-feet, 1,17; 4,8.12; 5,15.16
diskoeidês, having the shape of a flat plate, 31,13
diskos, flat plate, 30,30
distazein, be in doubt, 78,13.20
dôdekaedron, dodecahedron, 56,17
dogma, doctrine, 12,14; 21,21; 69,28; 86,29
dokêsis, appearance, 83,35
dokounta, ta, the (things) that are believed, 65,1.7.20
dotikê ptôsis, dative, 34,22
doxa, appearance, 44,2; doctrine, 1,8; 10,3.8; 12,22.33; 20,24.25.26; 64,28.31; 65,18.24; 67,5.33; 68,21; 69,24; 73,15; 76,1; 81,33; 82,10.12.14.29; 86,13; 88,24; 89,33; 90,9.23.30; 92,5; opinion, 1,14.15.19; 2,1.20.21.22; 4,5.7.10.19; 5,3.14.20; 10,10; 20,24; 39,18; 65,17.21; 71,12; 73,3; 76,23.28.29.31; 78,13.16; 79,19; 80,29; 81,6.8.10; *doxasta, ta*, objects of opinion, 2,20.21; 76,22; 79,22; 80,27; 81,11; *doxaston, to*, object of opinion, 39,18; 76,30
doxazein, be of an opinion, 86,34; make a judgement, 78,13.16
duas, dyad, 76,12; 78,30.31; 79,12.33; 80,22
dunamis, faculty, 1,6.10.11.12.13; 2,21; 5,24.30.33.34; 6,18.25.32.38; 7,20; 8,1; 9,1; 10,31; 11,1.23; 12,27.30.34; 13,36; 14,9.19.28.33; 15,8.18.19; 17,8.14; 18,34.38; 19,7.13; 20,28; 25,4.7.18; 26,10; 33,10; 35,11.14; 36,19; 38,26.32; 39,3.4.5.9.10.28.29.31; 40,5; 50,32; 51,4.14.23.31; 53,35; 54,17.32; 65,27; 72,5; 73,3.23.24; 74,2.28.29; 86,9; 89,30.31; (faculty) of bodies, 25,18; potentiality, 16,17; 23,31; 24,23; 27,15; 34,10; 35,3; 46,24.27; 63,14; power, 12,3; 20,18; 66,26; 92,10; *dunamei*, potentially, 34,9; 48,24; *en dunamei*, potentially, 34,8.21.23.27; 35,6; *tôn en dunamei ontôn*, belong to what is potentially, 34,1.7; 35,5
dunasthai, be able, 44,14; 45,30; 51,32; 68,15; be capable, 2,17; 9,15; 16,16; can, 7,9; 11,15; 13,2.16; 14,23; 24,1; 25,8; 42,9.18; 44,17; 51,25; 52,33; 57,32; 61,20.22.23; 62,30; 63,1.28.32; 66,15; 68,14; 71,8; 85,15; have a particular ability, 68,1
dunatos, possible, 4,13.14.20.28; 6,38
dusis, place where X sets, 76,36; setting, 34,18
duskataplêktos, hardly impressed, 53,20
duskinêtôs, difficult to move, 53,15; not easily moved, 50,27

ear, spring, 41,4
ebenos, ebony, 61,11
eidenai, know, 1,6.7.18.20; 2,1.16;

3,30; 4,5.6; 5,18.19.20.22.38; 6,7.8; 9,39; 11,31; 13,6; 14,32.33.34; 15,28; 25,11; 33,22; 37,25; 39,2.15; 41,20; 43,11.13; 54,24; 57,12; 58,21; 63,4.5.26; 69,27; to be familiar with (the fact), 10,10.18.30; 11,30; to have knowledge, 43,3.9; *eidenai, to*, knowing, 21,31; 22,7.9.10 knowledge, 33,28; 39,22; 41,25; *eidôs*, the person who knows, 39,14
eidêsis, knowing, 21,8; 22,5.6; knowledge 21,33.34; 22,1; 51,9
eidikos, formative, 25,32; 26,1
eidopoiein, define the form, 26,2; inform by form, 61,27; make up the form, 57,33
eidos, form, 7,12; 9,27.34.35; 14,24; 16,20; 25,17.18; 26,4; 34,25.27.31.32; 35,1.7; 37,27.29.32; 38,7; 50,10; 52,18.21.30; 53,29; 54,15; 55,27; 57,6.11.14.16.28; 58,7; 58,29; 59,3; 59,15.20.30; 60,1.4; 60,20.21.24.28.29.31; 62,24.28.24; 63,5.11.12; 76,2; 80,15; 90,13.14; idea, 74,14.16; kind, 22,24; 31,32; 35,17; 77,25; species, 7,11; 33,11.12.14; 35,24; 36,2.10.12.27; 37,20; 38,20.27.29; 52,7; 75,3
eikasia, conjecture, 43,26.31; suspect, 44,13
eikôn, image, 56,25; 58,16; 66,28
einai, be, 37,8; 59,19; be composed of, 90,11; be made up of, 75,26; exist, 70,19; 75,26.29; 77,3; 83,17; to apply, 38,13; *dia ti esti*, through what it is, 43,16.19; *einai, to*, being, 15,10; 16,20; 17,19; 42,28; 44,5.32; 46,33; 52,6; 53,8; 54,16; 75,5; mode of being, 92,7; to be, 15,5; 42,25; to exist (have existence), 14,10; 37,34; 51,34; 52,27.28; 74,33; *hopoion ti esti*, of what nature it is, 43,16.19; *onta, ta*, beings, 32,13; 47,19; 76,1.24; things, 3,32; 4,3; 5,4.6; 9,8.12.18; 10,23; 11,13; 27,20; 28,6.8; 72,30; 74,35; 75,4; 78,8; 79,21; 80,15; 81,23.27; 82,6; 83,2.3.16; 86,22;

87,2.10.13.14.29; 91,14; things that exist, 88,2; *ti esti*, what-it-is, 33,17.18; 40,6; 43,16; *to ei esti*, whether it is 43,15; *to ti esti*, the what-it-is, 33,16; 42,14.33; 43,17.19.20.21; 43,28; *tôi tauta einai*, to be as it is, 29,12
eiskrinesthai, be taken in, 68,28
eispnein, inhale, 35,26; 68,25.33; 69,19
eispnoê, inhaling, 69,4.5; respiration, 68,25.30; 69,14
ekkaluptein, reveal, 65,21
ekkrinein, emit, 7,36; excrete, 68,31; 69,15; extrude, 68,32; 69,13
eklambanein, listen to, 70,3; take (to mean), 36,9; 70,28; understand, 35,14; 38,23.33; 89,31
ekphainein, bring to light, 5,5
ekpnein, exhale, 69,19
ekpnoê, exhaling, 69,4
ekpurênizein, squeeze out, 68,22
ekstasis, extension, 20,9
ekthesis, display, 21,21
ekthlibein, extrude, 69,9.10
ektithenai, expound, 81,33; 82,12.13; set out, 21,20; 65,24; 67,4; 83,24
ektos, external, 5,36; 6,2
elaia, olive tree, 6,29.30
elaion, olive oil, 47,15
elenkhein, refute, 5,8; 12,23.33; 27,22
elenkhos, refutation, 12,24
ellampein, illuminate, 19,6
ellampsis, illumination, 19,3
ellipês, elliptical, 21,25
embadon, surface, 56,15.18; 84,31; 85,2.5.10.11
emballein, meet, 78,15
empathês, subject to emotions, 23,33
emphainein, make manifest, 43,32
emphanês, visible, 11,32
emphutos, innate, 83,4.5; 89,2
empodizein, impede, 63,1; pose an obstacle, 68,17; prevent, 5,2
empsukhon, to, ensouled being, 65,10; 72,28.33; living being, 36,5.9; 38,24.30; 88,33; living thing, 92,5
empsukhos, ensouled, 6,32.33.34;

Greek-English Index

12,31; 26,2.3.5; 35,23; 36,28;
65,10.11.12; 86,17.25.26; 88,34;
89,3.22
enargeia, evidence, 19,18
enargês, evident, 40,28.30; 41,8;
42,15; powerful, 53,9; 54,8;
enargós, clearly, 10,11; 11,7;
12,8; 13,25; 14,38; 17,12; 45,21;
71,21; evidently, 3,25; manifest,
42,7; 43,17; manifestly visible,
41,31
endein, be deficient, 14,2.7
endiastrophos, distorted, 21,24
endon, within, 5,37
energeia, activity, 2,12; 7,30.35;
8,13.14; 10,13.14.26.27; 15,15;
16,3; 17,1.2.6; 35,20; 39,4; 40,3;
44,30.32.35; 45,5; 46,4.21; 49,22;
66,26; 75,8.9; 76,17; actuality,
11,13; 16,17; 23,31; 24,23.24.26;
27,16; 34,18; 35,3; 39,35; 63,14;
energeiâi (dative), actually,
34,24; 35,1.3
energein, activate, 3,6.10;
7,22.26.33; 8,1.35; 16,32; 41,11;
74,3; activity, 76,28; be active,
5,29; 7,23.25; 11,26; 18,30; 19,32;
39,26.27; 58,19; exercise, 48,3.11;
exercise activity, 58,13.18
enginesthai, to be engendered in,
76,5
enkatakhônnunai, encapsulate,
4,32
enkephalos, brain, 10,14; 19,6.10.13;
47,23; 51,5
enkhôrios, vernacular, 68,11
enkosmios, cosmic, 18,28
ennoein, think, 3,5
ennoêmatikos, existing in thought
only, 38,3.15
ennoia, insight, 3,17.24.28.29; 4,1;
5,13.17.18; 16,5; 19,2; 40,33;
41,1; 78,19; notion, 38,15; 57,17;
what someone has in mind, 43,24
ensômatos, embodied, 23,33
entelekheia, actuality, 9,26.33;
33,3.4; 34,1; 35,7; 48,24.25.26.27
entelekheiâi (dative), actually,
34,21.23.26.27
enthousiazein, to be inspired, 70,1
entoma, ta, insects, 89,19
enudros, that lives in water, 11,34;
77,27

enulos, enmattered, 54,12.15.18;
55,23; 58,8; 62,13; 63,19.21
epainos, praise, 21,18
epamphoterizein, go into two
directions, 5,26
epekhein, keep under control, 51,27
ephaptesthai, grasp, 87,18; touch,
43,34; 50,6; 57,20; 84,25; 85,16
epharmozein, coincide, 50,12;
connect, 82,13; fit, 36,28; 61,11;
suit, 40,35; 73,7; 87,18
ephesis, yearning, 8,11
ephexês, in a sequence, 50,12; in the
sequel, 66,19
ephiesthai, yearn for, 3,21; 7,14; 8,6;
15,5
ephodios, procedure, 44,25
epiballein, grasp, 6,2; 85,25; grasp
intuitively, 2,7; 26,15
epibolê, intuition, 78,10; 79,24 ;
(intuitive) apprehension,
2,7.10.11; 3,23; 79,20; 85,25
epidekhesthai, admit of, 1,10
epidiairein, subdivide, 34,6
epiistôr, inquirer, 24,20
epiklinein, turn sideways, 31,11
epikoinônein, have in common,
10,26
epikratein, master, 26,9; rule, 73,32
epikratês, superior, 92,10
epikrinein, give judgement, 65,24
epikrisis, concluding decision, 60,19
epimeleia, attention, 17,31
epinoiâi (dative), conceptually,
57,29; 61,22; 63,1.28.30.32; *kat'
epinoian*, conceptually, 57,31;
61,23.24.30; 62,30
epipan, generally speaking, 41,18
epipedon, plane (figure), 32,11;
13.15.16.18; 41,14.25.29;
49,24.32; 56,9; 63,18.29; 67,13;
77,28.32; 79,18; 80,1; 84,24; 85,16
epiphaneia, surface, 50,20; 78,33;
79,3.4.5
epiplein, float, 61,12
epiplokê, state of being interwoven
with, 5,31
episkeptein, investigate, 55,8; study,
25,5.8
episkopein, examine, 64,18.27
epistasthai, to, scientific
understanding, 33,28; take note
78,34; understanding, 22,10.11

epistêmê, knowledge, 2,13; 3,27.33; 4,3; 23,11; 29,15.20; 43,31; science, 23,19.27; 24,4; scientific knowledge, 3,26; 24,21; 30,4; 76,19.19; 79,17; 80,28; 81,6.8.11; scientific understanding, 22,6.10; understanding, 22,7; *kat' epistêmên*, scientifically, 58.20
epistêmonikos, having scientific knowledge, 76,19; scientific, 4,1; 42,18; 43,6.13; 79,25
epistêta, ta, objects of (scientific) knowledge, 79,22; 80,27
epistrephesthai, turn in to, 14,21; 18,20; 25,23.24.25; 58,19
epistrophê, turning in to, 56,33
episumbainein, supervene, 61,27
epitêdeios, inclined to, 54,3; prone, 50,26.30
epitêdeiotês, inclination, 54,10; suitability, 14,6.18; 52,11.21
epithumein, desire, 6,13.14; 27,7; 45,3
epithumia, desire, 6,11.12.15.18.23; 7,24.28; 8,5; 10,28; 15,2; 16,32.36; 17,3; 18,9.12.25.33; 19,4.17; 26,11; 38,28; 50,18; 52,23
epitrepein, instruct, 64,7.10
epizêtein, seek, 26,13; 28,3; inquire, 64,20
erastês, lover, 66,28
êremein, be at rest, 69,6
erethizein, provoke, 5,13.15
ereunan, search, 26,16
ergon, activity, 46,7; 48,28; 62,13.14; 65,15; 91,11; function(ing), 1,19; 2,2.7; 39,3.27; 62,2; task, 5,20; 25,17; 54,18; 55,14.31; 61,9; work, 7,18
eruthrainein, blush, 50,19; redden, 44,10
eruthros, red, 57,32
eskhatos, extreme, 4,2; 86,30; last, 2,22; lowest, 12,34.36; 25,26
êthikê, ethics, 25,21
êthikos, ethical, 25,3.21
êthikos, ho, the ethical philosopher, 25,5
êthos, character, 25,4.26
etumologein, to explain etymologically, 68,4.6.9.10; to provide an etymological basis, 92,4

euemptôtôs ekhein, be inclined to, 53,15
eukherês, easy, 44,34
eukinêtos, easily moved, 9,9.19; 53,25; 54,5; 67,15; 68,13; 84,19.22.23; 88,27; moving easily, 67,11; 68,31; 69,1.3.10; 84,25; 85,15; 87,13; 90,23
eulabeisthai, be careful, 36,20.24
eulogos, reasonable, 22,16; 24,16; 38,35; 74,17.18
euolisthos, easily slipping out, 68,3
euphuês, well talented, 51,12
euplastos, flexible, 20,12
euporein, be well supplied, 40,27; know the answers, 64,23.28; solve, 64,19
euporia, good position, 40,10; 44,22; knowing the answers, 64,22
eutaxis, fine arrangement, 25,7
euthruptos, brittle, 61,15
euthugrammos, having straight lines, 84,29; rectilinear, 29,29.30
euthus, straight, 41,13.26; 49,15.19.34; 61,10; straight line, 49,24; 50,6.8; 58,2; *eutheia*, straight line, 49,25.26.30; 50,13; 78,6; *eutheia (ptôsis)*, nominative, 34,22; *euthu, to*, straightness, 49,17; 50,1
euthutês, straightness, 49,20; 50,1.4; 62,20
euzôia, good life, 19,22
exairein, exairetos, in particular, 82,6; selected for example, 59,7; *exêirêmenos*, dissociated, 32,19; separate, 15,9; transcendent, 20,33; 21,5; 37,25; 55,15; 58,9
exallattein, change, 53,29
exêgeisthai, explain, 26,19; interpret, 21,25.28; 35,22; *exêgoumenos*, interpreter, 24,10
exêgêsis, interpretation, 79,16
exêgêtês, interpreter, 21,28; 46,10.18; 51,15
existanai, deviate, 66,2
exiskhuein, have the power, 23,33
exolisthanein, slip, 84,25; slip away, 68,17
exomoiôsis, assimilation, 56,30.34
exumnein, sing praise, 21,2

gaia, earth, 73,19

Greek-English Index

gastêr, belly, 51,10
gê, earth, 9,12.13; 20,16.20; 52,19; 61,6; 66,4; 71,11; 89,23; soil, 52,14; **hupo gên**, underworld, 17,34; 18,15.19.23
gêinos, earthy, 17,23
gelastikos, capable of laughing, 5,23
genesis, becoming, 5,28.29; (domain of); 18,13; 52,5; 57,9; coming into being, 12,3; 52,14; 90,10; coming to be, 34,11; 67,7; 76,24
genêtos, coming into being, 16,13
genikos, general, 28,25
gennan, generate, 6,29.34; 7,18.19; 7,3; 65,26; 77,31; yield, 32,18
gennêsis, generation, 7,19; 42,25
gennêtikos, concerned with generation, 6,27; 13,36; 16,31; faculty of generation, 17,15; generative, 7,19.29.30; 8,32.34
gennêtos, coming to be, 7,13
genos, genus, 26,20.21.24; 28,14.15.16.17.29; 30,11; 32,12.13.22.23.26.31; 33,6; 35,24; 36,2.10.24.26.29.32; 37,11.20; 38,2.17.21.29.31; 74,34; 75,1.3.15; kind, 8,12; 11,2.24.33; 38,27
geôdês, earthy, 64,14
geômetrês, geometrician, 3,32; 49,31; 58,11
geômetria, geometry, 22,25.26.27; 23,1.2.23.24; 49,24; 84,29
gêras, old age, 11,21
geusis, taste, 7,4
ginesthai, come into being, 76,24 *passim*
ginôskein, to, know, 72,30; 73,6.7.8; 75,30; 86,7; 87,15.17; 91,25; cognitive aspect, 91,1
glaphuros, ingenious, 84,7
gliskhrotês, fattiness, 47,14
glôtta, patrikê glôtta, paternal tongue, 68,9
glukutês, sweetness, 47,15.17.20
glukuthumia, indulge, 17,32
gnêsios, genuine, 75,36
gnômê, view, 21,24
gnôrimos, known, 42,26; 44,8
gnôrizein, get to know, 42,22; 43,26; 44,6; know, 70,19; 73,7; 74,25.34; 75,21; 81,13; recognise, 90,22
gnôsis, capacity/ability to know, 81,24; 88,15; cognition, 41,6; 78,23; knowing, 22,12; 40,20; knowledge, 1,16; 4,7; 5,4.21.37; 7,34; 12,15; 21,10; 22,2.4.9.17; 23,3.10; 24,20.31.33; 42,1.15.16.23; 43,6.13; 44,23; 52,25; 75,19.26; 79,25; 87,19; 88,18; 91,11; **gnôsin ekhein**, get to know, 42,23
gnôstikos, able to know, 75,19; capable of knowing, 75,28; 81,14; 91,8; capacity to know, 81,27; 82,2.6.31; cognitive, 1,13; 5,24.34.35; 12,34; 18,35.37; 51,4; 73,3.5; 81,18; 86,8; cognitive aspect, 81,22; 86,14; 88,14; 91,5; concerned with cognition, 1,12; providing knowledge, 58,16
gnôstos, object of knowledge, 6,2; 11,10
gonê, seed, 9,11; 88,30; sex, 8,6.9
gônia, angle, 23,4; 29,16.21; 30,17; 40,17; 41,15; 84,31
grammê, line, 32,17; 41,14.25; 58,2; 63,17.29.31; 64,3; 77,28.30.31; 78,33; 79,2.3
grammikos, geometrical, 12,35
graphein, write, 79,15; 89,11
gumnazein, exhibit, 65,21
gumnos, deprived, 34,31; 45,30

haima, blood, 9,20; 16,33; 19,4; 44,7.11; 50,18.19.21; 53,15.18; 54,32; 55,1.2; 57,22.23; 58,26; 59,8; 61,30.31; 64,3.9.16; 88,31.33; 89,6
hamartanein, err, 17,31; 85,23.26
haphê, touch, 7,4.5; 54,30
haplous, simple, 9,4.5.14; 12,23; 33,8; 39,2; 85,25; 86,1.4; straightforward, 2,7.10.11; 6,2; 8,9; 78,10; 85,25; 88,33; uniform, 33,8; generally, 9,17.29; 14,17.34; **haplôs**, generally speaking, 14,12; 50,21; 51,2; in general, 38,24; 48,12; simple, 42,11; 58,34; simply, 8,5.7.34; 13,15; 16,35; 26,2.17; 42,19; 44,2; 47,16; 52,8.19.36; 57,16.21; 58,27.31; 60,33; 73,26; 84,28; unqualified, 35,15; 36,5.9; 38,26.31; 65,16; without further qualification, 27,9.10; 37,32; 38,1; 61,2.4

haptesthai, touch, 49,16; 67,13; 84,24
harmonia, harmony, 16,21; 46,31; 52,8.10; 70,5
harmonikê, harmonics, 23,7.24.25
harmozein, fit, 38,9
hêdonê, pleasure, 8,10.16.28
hêdus, pleasant, 8,7; 17,4
hêgoumenon, antecedent, 46,12
hekôn, willing, 18,22
hêlikia, age, 53,28
hêlios, sun, 23,34; 30,31; 31,3; 34,17; 49,12
hêmiolios, one and a half, 33,5
hêmisphairion, hemisphere, 31,8.12.14; semicircle, 31,1
heneka, for the sake of, 26,5.6
henôsis, unification, 73,20; union, 70,8; 74,7.10
henoun, unify, 73,30
hêpar, liver, 10,14; 16,33; 19,5; 50,19
hepesthai, accompany, 26,28
hermêneuein, communicate, 2,17
heterogenês, heterogeneous, 36,23
heterotês, difference, 74,7.35; 75,6.7.16.20
hexagônon, figure with six angles, 84,33; 85,1.3; shape with six angles, 56,12.15.16
hexis, disposition, 39,7.8; state, 2,15; 6,17
hippos, horse, 4,12.14; 33,13; 36,21.27; 37,13; 38,5; 74,2.15
histanai, hestanai, be stable, 65,37; 66,26; 75,13
hestôs, stable, 23,30; 87,19
historein, give a report, 73,14; 75,35.36; provide information, 88,17; report, 86,16.19
historia, inquiry, 22,16; 24,16.20
hodeuein, be on the (/its) way, 3,5
hodos, direction, 66,6; journey, 2,2; way, 3,10; 66,11.14; 78,12.14; 79,27; *hodos skhistê*, cross-roads, 78,15
holôs, as a whole, 23,1; universally, 38,13
holos, holon di' holou, as a whole, 19,26.32.35; *holon, to*, whole, 27,4; 38,19.35.36; 47,11; 61,26.30; 66,12.23.32; 74,22; 87,6.24
holoskherês, in general, 42,6; in general outline, 22,8; in rough outline, 20,27; roughly, 26,15; 27,9; 59,10
holotês, whole, 38,31; wholeness, 47,25; main mass, 65,36.37; 66,7.8.9; 75,13
homoeidês, of one and the same kind, 36,1.2.3
homogenês, homogeneous, 36,23
homoiomereia, homoeomerous parts, 86,2; 91,14
homoiomerês, homoeomerous, 14,23.24.26; 82,22
homoios, like, 73,7.9; 74,26; 75,27.28.29.30; 80,29.32; 86,15.16; 88,1; 89,19; 91,6; similar, 73,6; 75,21; 79,24; 90,4; 92,1
homoiotês, similarity, 75,20
homoiotropôs, in a similar way, 79,10.11.15
homoiousthai, be similar, 56,24
homologein, agree on, 27,26; 30,8; 36,11; 41,3
homônumia, identical term, 49,18
homônumos, called by the same name, 12,4; identical in name, 24,25.27.28; *homônumos phônê*, homonymous term, 37,10.12
homoousios, identical in essence, 4,23.24
homophuês, of the same nature, 5,16
horan, to, seeing, 47,8
horatos, visible, 19,20; 20,9
horismos, definition, 26,21.25.29; 28,5; 28,23.24.30.32; 30,11; 31,25; 32,7.21.24.28.30; 33,15; 36,25.26.27.29; 37,11.12.14.16; 38,9.11.13; 40,9; 41,15; 42,10; 42,17; 43,25 44,22.25.31; 48,23; 54,20.27; 55,9.26; 56,35; 57,6.14.24.65.37; 59,11.12.16.17.20.27.29; 60,5.6.13.20.25.26.27.28; 61,34; 62,7; 63,22.23.26; 64,5; 65,4.5.6.7; 80,3; 81,22
horistikê (methodos), by means of definition, 32,8
horistikos, capable of determining, 76,5
horizein, define, 1,20; 2,18; 37,34; 38,4.5.8.14.15.16; 44,6; 54,29.30; 55,21; 57,37; 63,21; 70,7; 76,6;

Greek-English Index

81,19.25.31; 90,18.20.27; 91,1; determine, 76,4; *hôrismenon*, defined, 7,20; determinate, 76,20; finite, 22,28.30; *hôrismenôs*, in a determinate way, 76,19.31
horizesthai, be finite, 22,28.30
horman, take off, 78,13.19; urge away, 76,31
hormê, impulse, 51,16; 65,31; initiative, 18,21
horos, definition, 54,16; determining principle, 3,27.28.31.32; 4,2.4; 68,19
hoti, to hoti, the fact, 1,19; 2,1; the fact 'that', 4,5
hudôr, water, 9,10.12.24; 19,30; 52,19; 66,5; 73,19.24; 74,19; 84,4; 86,23; 88,21; 92,3.9
hudrelaion, diluted olive oil, 47,14
huetos, rain, 52,14
hugiainein, be healthy, 63,11
hugiansis, healing, 66,15
hugiazein, restore to health, 37,23
hugieia, hugeia, health, 37,22; 63,10
hugiês, sound, 41,1
hugrainein, cause moisture, 75,10
hugron, moisture, 88,28
hugros, moist, 9,11; 14,15; 51,2; 57,32; 88,30
hulê, material, 49,32.34; 61,14; matter, 3,11; 4,31; 9,35; 10,18.30.31; 14,5.6.7; 16,16.17; 28,30; 34,24.25.28.34; 35,2.6; 38,6; 52,30; 54,15; 55,9.11.24; 57,6.11.29; 58,7.27; 58,3.5.10.12; 59,18.19.22.30; 60,2.5; 60,14.20.23; 61,18; 62,2; 62,26.31; 63,1.13.16.21.32.33; 64,6; 70,11.12; 74,4; 76,5; 88,25
hulikos, material, 16,15; 35,4; 73,15; 91,26
hulôdestês, material, 88,25
humên, skin, 19,10
hupallêlos, subordinated, 75,3
huparkhein, be, 4,26; 65,36; 68,23; 84,20; be attribute of, 27,2; 29,26; 41,1.3; 91,4; be characterised by, 43,10; belong to, 26,32; 29,6; 30,3.8; 31,23; 41,17.23.24; 42,11.20; 62,32.33; 63,17; 64,1; 65,2; be present in, 72,18; 78,7; 92,8; present itself as, 69,7; *huparkhein, kath' hauto*, be an essential attribute, 40,14.18; 42,30.31; 43,30.32; 44,23;
huparkhonta, ta, attributes, 26,18; 40,21.33; 41.19; 42,9.5; things that belong to, 26,27; 41,22; 42,12; 43,12; 44,14.16; 65,19; *ta huparkhonta kat' ousian*, essential attributes, 43,3
huparkhesthai, initiate, 12,5
huparxis, existence, 3,10; 28,30.17.23; 63,19; 64,5; presence, 47,14
huperbibazein, transpose, 64,26; 80,17; 87,30
huperbolê, excess, 83,19; 87,11
hupêretês, servant, 8,15
huperoptikos, holding in contempt, 52,2
hupertera, ta, higher things, 56,33
huperzein, boil over, 53,18
huphistanai, be present, 29,5; consist of, 83,31; exist, 52,35; exist independently, 50,3; exist on own/have existence of own, 52,33.34.35
hupoballein, subject, 60,32
hupodiairein, subdivide, 34,4
hupographê, description, 28,12.25; 30,11
hupokeimena, ta, related objects, 76,4
hupokeimenon, subject, 22,21.26; 23,9.14.27; 24,4.6.11; 55,30; 52,27.30; 53,2.6; subject matter, 22,19.24; 23,1; 24,19; substrate, 9,27.33; 14,9; 15,3.4.7; 16,20.23; 17,20; 18,9; 37,6; 46,30; 50,2; 51,17.22; 52,3.6; 68,32
hupokeimenos, underlying, 42,32; 46,33; 58,35; 62,32
hupokeisthai, be assumed, 84,31.33.35
hupolambanein, assume, 38,35; conceive of, 70,34; 72,29; consider, 21,26.27.29; 22,18; 75,30; form beliefs, 11,12; hold, 71,7.20; 72,21; 88,9; suppose, 15,14; 82,34; 83,8.12.22; 87,32; 88,2; 89,7
hupologizesthai, take into account, 57,36
hupomenein, undergo, 66,12
hupomnêmatizein, comment, 21,23

huponoein, suppose, 3,3; 74,18; suspect, 31,23; 83,33
hupostasis, existence, 37,34; 38,3; 59,20
hupothesis, hypothesis, 78,16; *en hupothesei*, ex hypothesi, 32,5; hypothetical, 46,6; hypothetically, 41,26
hupotithenai, claim, 86,15; posit, 80,34; 83,20; 85,14; 86,15; 91,22; say, 86,2; suppose, 73,15; 74,6; 82,5; 83,9; 86,2; 89,26
husterogenês, that which comes into being later, 37,32; 38,16.17
husteron, posterior, 37,7.17; 38,2.12; *husteron têi phusei*, posterior by nature, 36,31; 37,2

iama, healing, 17,34
iatrikê, medicine, 22,20.23; 23,22
iatrikos, medical, 89,16
iatros, doctor, 19,8; 33,2; 37,23; 50,31; 51,14.30; 57,5.9; 62,20; 63,10; 67,27
idea, form, 63,4.12; 79,16; *Platonis*, 37,18; 77,6; 78,27; 80,23
idikos, specific, 6,16.19,
idikôs, specifically, 6,17
idios, own, 20,11; 21,21; 46,4; 52,3; 61,14; 66,7; 68,10; peculiar. 8, 5.13; 27,1; 41,11; 42,25; 44,19.27.30; 45,6.7.13.18; 46,8.14; 50,16.23; 53,11.25; 54,8.14; 56,26; 62,13; 63,27; 65,28; 72,20.32; 75,30; 76,15: 86,18; 87,15; 89,16; proper, 6,10; 26,27; 29,3.14.22; 31,22; *idiâi* (dative), individually, 77,3.4; in particular, 28,6.19; 40,9; *kath' hauto idia*, proper attribute, 28,26; 29,31
idiotês, peculiar nature, 26,7; peculiarity, 35,25.27
idiôtikos, trivial, 8,16
ikhnêlatein, trace, 42,9
ikhnos, trace, 3,16; 17,12.13.17; 18,38
indalma, manifestation, 3,17.24
isoperimetros, with equal circumference, 56,10; 84,30; 85,5.9.10
isos, equal, 3,19.20; 23,4; 29,16.21; 30,18.19; 40,17.34; 41,15; 58,6; 85,13

kakos, evil, 20,18.21; 21,34; 22.2.3.4
kalos, fine, 21,8; 22,18.19.21; 23,11.13.15; 24,18; 25,18; good, 33,22; 35,22; 43,8; 85,20;
kallistos, excellent, 42,8
kamnein, be ill, 62,21
kampsis, bending, 81,4
kampulos, curved, 41,13.26.28
kanôn, rod, 49,21; rule, 15,12.15.22.35; 16,28; 23,18; 24,12; 44,14; 46,20; 47,2.4.26
kapnos, smoke, 4,26.27; 31,15.16.17
kardia, heart, 10,13; 44,9; 53,15; 58,26.27.30; 59,8
karpos, fruit, 88,31
kataduein, descend, 4,31
katagein, drag down, 74,4; 88,25
katagôgos, analytic, 73,28.29; 74,3
katakosmein, adorn, 25,4; embellish, 6,20
katamênia, ta, menstrual blood, 14,7; 34,13
kataphasis, affirmation, 3,20; confirmation, 78,17
kataphronein, deprecate, 52,3
katapsêphizesthai, reject, 5,8
katarithmein, list, 65,17; sum up, 40,34
kataskeuazein, prove, 46,15; 51,18; 71,22; 80,21
kataskeuê, fitting, 61,10; proof, 3,22; 6,3
katastasis, state, 2,17
katêgorein, categorise (pass. to belong to the category of) 33,17.18; criticise, 86,28; designate, 36,32; 37,10; 38,8
katêgoria, category, 33,26; 34,5
kath' hauto, by itself, 3,14; 5,26; 14,12; 26,33; 29,14; 29,28.30.32; 30,3.7; 31,23; 38,4; 41,16; 52,34; 61,8; 62,27; 69,10; essential, 28,26; essentially, 40,21; 41,8.22.23; 42,8; 42,20; 43,2; 44,5.16; 61,3; in itself, 57,35.36; of its own, 52,34.35; on its own, 44,4; 49,27.28; 69,20; *auto kath'hauto*, in itself, 14,21; 18,6; 22,26; 24,33; 27,5; 49,33; *kath'hauto idia*, proper attribute, 29,31; *kath'heauto*, by itself, 29,5

Greek-English Index

kathairein, purify, 17,32.34; 18,17.19; 19,31
katharmos, purgative, 19,29.30
katharos, pure, 18,13; 35,2.7; 86,3; 91,13.15
katharsis, purgation, 58,20; purification, 2,13
kathartikos, purgative, 58,18.19; purifying, 2,13
kathêsthai, sitting, 49,2
kathetos, perpendicular, 31,4
katheudein, be asleep, 7,35
katholikos, general, 28,26; 30,10.16
katholou, general, 37,1; generally speaking, 34,9; in general, 37,17.33; 61,5; 65,25.27; 70,27; on the whole, 30,13; universal, 1,15; 4,6.7.13.19.21.29; 38,2.12; 70,28; 76,22.27; universally, 76,25; **katholou, to**, general kind, 37,34
katorthoun, to be correct, 91,18.23
kauma, heat, 59,25; 60,10
kausis, heat, 18,3
kekramenos, having a particular mixture, 50,24.27; 51,1.5.20.27; 53,34; 54,3
kenkhramis, kernel, 14,1
kenos, empty, 57,19; 59,21; void, 9,18; 41,2; 42,2; 43,34; 67,6.19; 82,24; **kenôs**, devoid, 43,27; in vain, 43,34
kephalê, head, 13,31
kerannunai, mix, 70,8.15
kêros, wax, 13,23
khalaza, hail, 61,5; hailstorm, 41,3
khalepos, difficult, 2,30; 11,22; 21,15.19; 23,29.32; 27,30; 28,2.3.6.18; 31,28; 39,24; 44,29
khalkos, bronze, 22,30; 23,1; 49,16; 62,25
kharaktêristikos, characteristic, 59,9
kharaktêrizein, characterise, 10,13; 26,10; 59,6; 89,14; 90,21
kheein, disperse, 50,20
kheimôn, winter, 41,4
kheir, hand, 14,32; 66,23.32
khersaios, land animal, 26,8; that live on land, 11,34
khiôn, snow, 61,5
khliaros, tepid, 9,32
khôra, place, 41,5

khordos, string, 16,21; 23,10; 46,31; 52,8.10.11; 70,6
khorêgein, supply, 19,7.13
khôrein, reach, 3,11.24
khôrion, passage, 24,8.10.18; 27,21; 35,14; 46,10
khôristos, separable, 9,22.35.36; 10,4; 11,9; 12,11.12.17.18; 15,17; 16,3; 18,35; 46,9; 46,14; 46,23; 51,20; 52,1; 54,16; 61,28; separate, 3,11; 11,5; 25,9; 27,12; 33,8; 58,7; 60,24; 61,1.16.20.21; 62,22; 63,5.11.12; 64,4.13.14; 70,11
khôrizein, distinguish, 62,5.7; separate, 11,2.25; 15,19; 16,8; 17,2; 35,18; 46,8; 49,17; 50,1.7.10; 57,29.31; 61,20.22.24.30; 62,30; 63,1.3.13.28.30.32
khrêma, money, 16,35
khriesthai, colour, 31,7
khthonios, terrestrial, 77,27
khumos, humour, 52,5; 57,10
kindunos, danger, 45,31
kinein, arouse, 7,34; cause movement/movement, 48,19; 67,14.15; 70,29.30; 71,8; 83,4.6.15; 84,11.14.19.20.26; 85,16.31; 87,23; move, 20,37; 21,1; 25,33; 32,33; 34,15; 50,25; 53,14; 55,25; 57,23; 59,7; 65,13; 66,31; 67,14.15; 68,15; 69,17; 70,32; 71,8.13.16.19; 75,14; 81,20; 83,4.5; 84,10.11.14.19.20; 85,29; 86,8.9; 87,6.21.22.24.28; 91,12; movement, 88,6; set in motion, 8,2; 48,17; 59,1; 64,8.11; 65,34; 71,2.16.17; 81,16.26; 83,6; stimulate, 50,31; stir up, 3,3; 16,33; 17,4; 19,4; 20,6; **kinein, to**, (the property of) causing movement/motion, 65,8; 84,10; 87,5.15; motion, 71,18; movement, 91,12; moving, 86,7; the capacity to cause movement, 71,7; **kinôn heauton**, self-moving, 44,12; **prôtôs kinoun**, the first mover, 20,37
kineisthai, to, movement, 72,28
kinêma, movement, 51,38
kinêsis, capacity to cause movement, 81,24; motion, 87,17.18.27.28;

movement, 19,5; 20,35.36; 35,20; 42,26; 44,11; 54,17.27.30; 55,16; 58,25; 65,15; 67,4.11; 69,16.17; 70,36; 71,1.11.19; 72,20.32; 73,1; 74,35; 75,7.8; 81,29; 83,3.5.18; 86,18.33; 87,14.25; 88,5.7.18; 90,19.21.25; *kinêsis, kata topon*, locomotion, 65,30; 66,21.25; movement in the local sense, 71,10
kinêtikon, to, kinetic aspect, 81,17.16; 86,19; locomotion, 39,26; 41,10; movement, 73,4; 83,20
kinêtikos, apt to move, 88,11.27; (capable of being) set in motion, 83,17.26; capable of causing/having capacity to cause movement, 72,29; 81,14.28; 82,1.32.34.36; 83,7.12.14.15; 86,11; kinetic, 84,17; 86,19; 87,33; move easily/easily set in motion, 87,4.21; producing movement, 83,1; that which causes movement, 21,2; that which has the capacity to move, 35,29; 83,2.8; to do with movement, 73,2
kinoumenon, to, what is in a state of motion, 87,19
kinoun, to, source of movement/that which moves/that which causes movement, 66,30.33; 69,23.26; 70,27; 71,2.5
kirnan, mix, 70,15
kisêrôdês lithos, pumice stone, 61,14
klados, branch, 13,36; 14,22
klêma, cutting, 13,36
klêros, share, 6,21.22; 8,11; 18,28
klinein, turn sideways, 31,10
koinos, common, 3,17.24.28.29; 4,1; 5,17.18; 12,24; 15,13; 19,2; 27,2.7.22.23; 31,27; 35,26; 36,26.29; 37,13.15.16; 38,5; 40,33.35; 44,19.27; 48,10.23; 57,30; 77,37; 83,31.33; general, 6,15; 14,30; 20,27.29; 28,6.7.18; 32,28; 40,8; 44,35; *koinôs*, common, 22,12; 76,15.16; commonly, 16,11; 36,32; 37,9; 41,3; 65,22; generally, 6,16.18; jointly, 23,25; 47,3
kolasis, chastisement, 18,1

kolazein, chastise, 18,2; temper, 92,9
kolobos, mutilated, 14,22
kôluein, prevent, 68,30; 69,12.15
kôlutikos, protecting against, 59,24.28; 60,9.10
koprizein, manure, 6,28
kosmos, adornment, 25,6.7; cosmos, 18,29; universe, 7,12; 37,24; 55,17; 77,26; world, 11,35; 21,4
kradiê, heart, 8,27
krasis, mixture, 9,23; 26,23; 33,2; 35,25.26; 50,25; 53,3.13.22.24.29; 54,4; 62,30; 90,6.13.14
kratein, control, 8,28; rule, 74,8.10
krinein, judge, 80,28.29; 81,5.13; 89,24; *krinein, to*, judging, 65,28
krios, Aries, 49,12
krisis, judgement, 24,15
kritêrion, criterion, 40,32
kritês, judge, 89,23.24
krustallos, ice, 20,4
kubernêtês, steersman, 48,1
kubos, cube, 56,16.18; 68,7
kuklos, circle, 14,11.15; 22,27.28.29.31; 49,25; 56,9.14.16.25; 58,2; 65,37; 66,2.4; 73,34; 85,4.6.7; circular, 56,29; 65,38; 66,11.13
kuôn, dog, 36,22; 37,13
kuparittos, cypress, 61,13
kurios, proper, 25,33; 30,12.20; *kuriôs*, in the literal sense, 83,27; in the proper sense, 29,12; 30,10; 90,24; in the strictest sense, 72,17; properly speaking, 19,34

lambanein, accept, 4,8.10; 86,6; adopt, 40,31; 43,32; 65,7; 77,27; gain, 22,7; get, 43,17; grasp, 2,1; 31,25.28; 32,1; 40,28; 41,7.19; 42,30; 44,13.20; have, 43,7.13; 53,27; learn, 33,17; 43,4; make an assumption/assume, 34,5; 36,10; 74,20; 78,19; 85,24; obtain, 21,16; 27,30; 28,18; 31,7; 33,15; receive, 5,38; take, 27,8; 34,4; 35,11; 45,32; 46,15.19; 49,13.19.30; 50,3; understand, 49,34; undertake, 44,25; use as basis, 46,20
lanthanein, escape notice, 86,31; cause to ignore, 36,20

Greek-English Index

lêpsis, establishing, 32,29; 44,34; grasping, 40,29; 41,9.30; 42,1; 44,22
leptomereia, delicacy of parts/particles, 87,5.22
leptomerês, composed/consisting of fine particles, 83,10; 87,5.6.13.24; consisting of delicate particles, 83,17.28; consisting of small particles, 90,25; fine 84,17
leptos, fine, 67,26; light, 19,27; slender, 31,11; subtle, 51,10
leptunesthai, become lighter, 19,29
lêros, babble, 70,4
leukos, white, 1,16; 2,8.10; 6,7; 9,32; 13,3; 26,28; 29,7.13; 31,8.10.12; 51,23; 53,6.8; 75,20.21;
  leleukasmenos, (being) white, 31,14
lêxis, designated share, 66,4
lithos, brick, 57,5; 59,26.29; 60,3.8; 61,19; 62,33; 84,5; stone, 33,14; 49,27; 86,17.25.26
logikos, rational, 1,10.11.13; 4,30; 5,24.27.33; 6,25.32.38; 7,10; 8,21.23.24.31; 9,1.36; 10,4; 11,28.29; 12,8.11.17; 14,29.36; 15,2.5.9; 16,1.2.22.26; 20,30.31; 27,5.10; 35,18; 37,3.5.8; 38,25; 42,28; 48,13.16.20; 52,1.17; 55,19; 58,11.14
logos, account, 1,18; 21,20; 28,20; 36,20; 37,14; 38,33; 48,23; 49,5; 78,34; 83,1; 85,33; 88,18; 91,18.23; argument, 14,30; 36,8; 46,6; 60,26; 85,8; book, 10,31; 11,3.11.20; 45,21; definition, 49,33; 59,4.14.24; 61,20.21.25.28.32; 72,25; 81,21; discourse, 61,7; discussion, 16,1; 37,32; 44,22; 55,16; 63,15.25; 64,21.30.32; formal principle, 4,30; 5,4.6.12; 13,25.27.31; 14,16.18; 37,25; 52,10.15.16.17.20; 54,12.15; 55,23; 63,19; formula, 38,14; 58,9; 64,12; 73,27; 74,13.16; 89,3; 91,27; lecture, 1,5; 21,18; proportion, 9,23.25.28.30; 26,23; 33,4; reason, 2,19; 5,31; 6,14; 7,25; 8,2; 12,7.9; 14,35; 35,19.21; 38,27; 51,36; 54,24; 63,6.7; 76,29; 84,27; reasoning, 5,21; relation, 9,39; 23,8; statement, 26,30; 59,16; 63,33; 65,16; 76,28; theorem, 23,6; theory, 63,10; 89,17; verbal account, 60,15; 62,16; word, 2,17; 91,27; *logon ekhein*, be reasonable, 83,1; *orthos logos*, correct reasoning, 71,27
lumainesthai, defile, 6,22.24
lupê, pain, 8,28
lupein, cause pain, 55,3.5; 58,34.35
lupêisthai, suffer pain, 45,3
lutos, refutable, 31,18.20

makhê, battle, 51,35
makhesthai, battle, 51,37.38; 52,1
malakos, soft, 57,32
manikôs, inclined to get beside oneself, 53,18
manon, to, width, 61,18.22.29
manos, loose, 61,12.25
manoun, widen, 20,8.9
marainein, waste away, 15,2
marturia, testimony, 63,7
matên, in vain, 15,20; 17,4.5; without purpose, 46,35; 47,1
mathêmata, ta, mathematical objects, 3,9; mathematics, 3,12; 41,13; 49,31; objects of learning, 6,14
mathêmatikos, mathematical form, 62,30; mathematical object, 61,21; (the study of) mathematics, 3,8; 41,18; 55,29; *mathêmatikos, ho*, mathematician, 57,28.35; 62,5.22.23
mathêsis, process of learning, 58,22
megethos, magnitude, 2,29; 3,4; 7,20; 14,13; 22,27.29; 23,2.7.10; 57,30; 79,1; size, 34,14
meignunai, mix, 75,23; 86,3; 91,15
mêkhanê, mechanism, 8,3
mêkhanikê, hê, mechanics, 22,25; 23,1.2.6.23
mêkos, length, 77,31.34.37; 78,28; 79,2.5; *kata mêkos*, lengthwise, 78,3
melankholikos, having a tendency to melancholic affections, 51,1
melas, black, 4,15.16; 9,22; 13,3; 29,7; 31,8; 51,23; 75,22
meli, honey, 47,15.18.20

melissa, bee, 17,18
melos, tune, 70,9
mên, month, 30,27
mêningophulax, membrane-protector, 19,9
mêninx, cerebral membrane, 19,9.10
mêniskos, crescent-shaped, 31,11
mênoeidês, crescent-shaped, 30,28
mênuein, indicate, 53,9
merikos, individual, 4,13.19; 6,7; 38,1; 66,4.5; 70,30; 78,23; part, 30,13; 62,4; particular, 57,4; 76,26; 77,1
meristos, divided, 35,9.10.22; 36,8; 38,29; 75,18; in individual parts, 58,13
merizein, divide, 35,15; 38,29
meros, part, 14,20.24.25; 27,19; 18,29; 19,11.15; 27,19; 31,2.11; 39,1; 44,10; 47,10.16.22.25; 54,17.28.31; 58,11; 66,10.12; 91,24; *en merei*, particular case, 61,5; *kata meros*, individual, 36,28; 55,28
mesos, intermediary, 70,13; intermediate, 3,7; middle, 2,22.23; middle position, 30,32; 31,5; *dia mesou*, middle (term), 30,14
mesouranêma, centre of the heavens, 34,17
metabainein, proceed, 78,12
metaballein, change, 20,12; 24,28; 53,33; 76,34.36
metabasis, passage, 76,20
metabolê, change, 34,11.16; 76,35
metadidonai, let share in, 70,16
metalambanein, receive a share in, 7,8; take part in, 13,3
metallon, metal, 61,6; 90,7
metapoieisthai, lay claim to, 51,9
metekhein, have a share in, 3,16; 7,1; partake in, 75,15; participate in, 49,19.20; share in, 89,20; take part in, 75,12
meteôrizein, cause to rise up, 78,6; throw up, 31,9
meteôros, higher region of the atmosphere, 61,5; high up in the sky, 44,1
metharmozein, adapt accordingly, 51,25
methistanai, move, 20,16

methodos, method, 28,8.9.13; 29,1; 31,24.25.27; 32,2.4.6; 33,29; 40,10.11; 55,28.30
methuein, to be drunk, 50,28; 51,11
metopôron, autumn, 41,4
mêtra, uterus, 13,29
metrein, measure, 76,5
metrêtikos, capable of measuring, 76,4
mikromereia, state of consisting of fine particles, 67,24; 84,18
mikromerês, consisting of small parts, 84,21.25.28; 85,14
miktos, mixed, 82,20.27
mimeisthai, imitate, 56,26.30.33
mimêma, imitation, 56,25
mixis, mixture, 9,31; 52,18; sex, 8,7
mnêmonikos, having a good memory, 51,4
moira, part, 83,36
mokhleia, dislodgement, 26,1
mokhthêros, bad, 20,2; 51,20; unhealthy, 19,23
monakhôs, in a single way, 79,18; 79,26.29
monas, monad, 32,16.22; 76,7; 78,30; 79,12.33; 80,22
monê, constancy, 88,6
monoeidês, having one form, 33,9
morion, bodily part, 89,14; part, 10,13.15.32; 11,22; 13,2; 14,3.4; 19,26; 38,18; 39,26.27; 47,12.13; 74,28
morphê, shape, 20,1
mousikos, musician, 52,9.10
muriakis, numerous, 51,24
muthos, myth, 69,30

naupêgos, shipbuilder, 61,11
neikos, strife, 73,16.27; 82,21; 91,34
nekros, corpse, 17,11; dead, 17,17; 89,1; *nekron sôma*, corpse, 17,18
nênemia, absence of wind, 70,33.36
neuron, nerve, 19,7.14; 47,23; 89,17
noein, know, 79,24; think, 11,3.13; 48,12; 78,6.20; *to noein*, (intuitive) thinking, 35,13; 39,28.29; 45,7; 48,20; 51,10.11; 57,33
noêma, thought, 9,21; 27,23.28; 45,10.12.22.24; 89,13
noeros, intellectual, 55,11; intelligible, 25,23

Greek-English Index

noêsis, intellect, 76,29; intellection, 2,19; (intuitive) thinking, 27,5; 39,12; 40,3; 45,17.18.22; 51,6
noêtikos, thought, 40,2.4
noêtos, intellectually, 74,3; intelligible, 2,11.18; 23,29; 24,30; 39,19.20.21.23; 40,1.2; 50,9.11; 55,13; 56,23; 76,24.29; 79,21; 81,11; thinkable, 39,12; **noêta, ta**, intelligible objects, 2,25.28; 3,14.31; 4,1.4; 10,20.22.24; 11,4.16 (objects of thought); 16,5; 24.3.22; 25,10.14.15.24.26; 45,24; 70,10; 73,30; 74,8; 76,15; 77,4.21.23; 78,10; 79,23; 80,27; objects of intellect, 76,17
nomizein, believe, 2,28; 3,26; 9,12;71,1; think, 46,11; 64,12; 65,19; 71,8; 74,17; 81,4; 88,29; 91,8
nosansis, sickening, 66,16
nosos, disease, 50,29
nôthês, dull-witted, 51,13
notheuein, be spurious, 27,22.26.27; 45,9
nôtiaios, back, 19,11
notios, south, 76,37
nous, intellect, 1,15; 2,7; 3,14; 4,3; 5,17; 6,2; 10,19; 11,7; 19,1 25,9.10.12.14.15; 39,19; 45,4; 55,13; 56,26.30; 58,9; 71,16; 72,8; 78,9.10; 79,17.22.34; 80,28; 81,6.8; 82,22; 84,14; 85,18; 91,11; mind, 51,11; **nous, ho kat' energeian**, active intellect, 37,27; **nous, ho theios**, divine intellect, 37,28; **tou nou dunamis**, intellectual faculty, 72,5

oenomeli, oenomel, 47,15.17
oikeios, appropriate, 2,23; 12,15; 57,33; 79,31; characteristic, 89,7; own, 20,26; 65,24; 66,3.4; 75,9; 92,5; peculiar, 71,1.7.18.20; proper, 7,15; 27,21; 32,24
oikeiotês, appropriateness, 79,34
oikhein, disappear, 50,8
oikodomos, architect, 61,13
oikos, house, 59,24.30; 60,2.7.11; 61,19
okhêma, vehicle, 17,20; 18,25
okhlos, audience, 88,25

ôkhriasis, paleness, 50,20
ôkhros, pale (pallor), 51,23; 53,23.24
oktaedron, octahedron, 56,17
oktagônon, figure with eight angles, 85,1.2; octagonal figure, 84,35
ombros, rain, 59,25; 60,9
omma, eye, 24,1
oneirôttein, emit semen in sleep, 8,33
onkos, mass, 85,14
onoma, name, 2,3; word, 27,12; 28,29; 29,11
onomasia, name, 1,7
onomazein, call, 71,12; use the name, 85,33
ontôs, genuine, 21,34; 25,1; truly, 58,20
onux, nail, 89,15
ophthalmos, eye, 47,7.9.21.24
opsis, vision, 1,16; 7,2.5; 13,8; 14,34;
optikos, optic, 47,23
oregesthai, long for, 21,31
orektikos, (concerned with) appetite, 1,12; 5,35; 6,11; (appetitive) 18,34
orektos, object of desire, 66,27
orexis, appetite, 7,34; 16,35; 17,4; desire, 44,3.7; 53,34; 55,4; 57,16.22; 58,24.30.36; 64,8; 66,28
organikos, of an organ, 54,28; possessing organs, 48,24; **organikôs**, as a kind of instrument, 46,4
organon, instrument, 8,23; 44,29; 45,28; 53,31.32.33; 70,28.29.30; organ, 19,13
orgê, anger, 8,28; 44,3.7; 50,18.30; 54,1; 54,31
orgilos, prone to anger, 50,23; 51,1
orgizein, be angry, 44,9.10; 45,3; 54,2.4.16
orthia, right angle, 23,4; 29,16.21; 30,18.19; 40,17; 41,14; 58,6
orthos, just, 85,20
osphrêsis, smell, 7,3
ostoun, bone, 57,31; 62,34; 89,15
ouranios, celestial, 9,7; 18,22; 56,23; 66,11; 76,35; 77,26; celestial body, 34,16.18; 56,3; heavenly, 22,21; 24,28; 88,12; heavenly body, 88,13
ouranos, the heavens, 21,4; 55,17; 56,7; 71,11
ousia, being, 3,9; 15,10.23; 23,31;

24,23.24.28; 25,25; 26,20.21;
28,28.29.31; 29,2.8; 53,3.6; 66,26;
70,20; 74,35; 75,4.16.17; 76,17;
essence, 15,16; 16,3.10.11.12;
17,1.5;26,14.18.25; 27.11; 28,4;
29,5.6; 39,6.9.10; 42,8;
44,4.29.31; 46,21; 47,28; 49,22;
57,16; 58,20.21; 59,17; 63,32;
64,20; 70,14; 73,2; 75,19; 81,21;
82,4.15.16; 91,24; mode of being,
91,26; substance, 9,11; 11,20;
26,21; 30,14; 30,14.15.16.17;
32,32; 33,7.24.25; 34,4.5; 36,28;
37,33; 38,6.8; 40,7.13; 42,16.19;
56,24; 63,13; true being, 70,23;
kat' ousian, essentially, 26,28;
29,19; in respect of substance,
34,10; in virtue of the essence,
29,24; *têi ousiai*, essentially,
11,19
ousiôdês, essential, 42,32; *ousiôdôs huparkhonta, ta*, essential attributes, 40,12
oxugônios, have sharp angles, 68,16
oxus, fast, 66,13; sharp-witted, 51,12; treble, 70,8

pais, child, 34,14
pakhumerês, broad/broadly speaking, 22,9; 23,4
pakhunein, solidify, 19,23.28; 20,3
pakhus, fat, 51,10; solid, 10,5; 12,18.21; 17,6; 18,11.36; 19,1; 20,19; 49,1; 52,7
palaioi, oi, the ancients, 64,23; 65,19.21.29; 66,17; 91,28
palmos, palpitation, 44,9
pan, to, the universe, 2,24; 7,12; 12,1; 67,6; 70,10; 71,16.17; 88,5
panselênos, full (moon), 30,29
panspermia, seed-medley, 67,29.30.32
pantelês, complete, 70,33
panteles, to, completeness, 63,13
pantelôs, altogether, 72,21; completely, 3,11
pantodunamos, omnipotent, 21,3
paraballein, compare, 5,10.13
paradeigma, example, 41,16.21.26; 49,21; 59,27; model, 76,6; 79,13; 80,23; 81,2
paraisthanesthai, to be deranged, 72,3; to ill perceive, 72,7

parakeimena, ta, things surrounding, 75,10
paraklinein, turn aside, 31,9
parakolouthein, accompany, 29,8; 41,8.17; 44,9; apply to, 28,19; follow, 41,21;
parakolouthounta, ta, attributes, 44,6.8
paralambanein, add, 49,32; adopt, 19,29; 22,13; 65,18; 67,3; cover, 60,7; include, 57,38; 61,25; 62,6; refer to, 69,5; take, 46,2; take into account, 55,9; use, 61,14
paraleipein, leave out, 78,25;
paraleleimmenon, to, remaining part, 60,17
parallêlos, pleonastically, 26,19
paraplêsiôs, very similar, 88,9; 91,2
parastasis, establishing, 60,11
parathesis, juxtaposition, 75,21
parempiptein, come in between, 3,2
parempodizein, be an impediment/impede, 45,30.32; 46,1
parousia, presence, 6,36
paroxunein, to paroxunesthai, excitement, 53,10; *ta paroxunonta*, exciting factors, 53,14.16
paskhein, be acted upon, 62,14; be affected, 11,4; 18,1.6; 19,7.11.12.14; 27,13.14.17.20; 49,26.27.28.29; 50,2; be passive, 88,29; experience, 45,1; suffer, 18,5; 54,10; to have happen to, 23,34
pathêma, affection, 27,13; 45,10.12; 46,6; 48,29; 53,9.11
pathêtikos, passive, 6,1.4; 11,7.9.10; 88,27.28
pathos, affection, 10,27; 18,13.14.16; 27,1; 44,18; 45,8.14; 46,14.16.18; 47,7; 48,13; 50,14; 53,16; 54,7.8.9.12.14; 55,23; 61,1.3.8; 62,7.15.23.25.29; 63,1.16; 70,22.24; attribute, 60,21; 61,3.9; emotion, 19,24; 58,21; 59,7; property, 49,26; 61,13; 62,2.13.14
pêgê, source, 81,29
pêkhuaios, a cubit (in size), 22,28.29; 56,13;
pêkhus, cubit, 84,32; *dipêkhus*, two

Greek-English Index

cubits, 22,28; *tripêkhus*, three cubits, 22,29
peras, limit, 3,32.33; 4,4; terminus, 77,36.37
peratoun, terminate, 77,31
periekhein, encompass, 40,33; 56,7; 58,2; 76,9; surround, 20,3; 68,21
periergazesthai, have concern with, 61,13; have particular concern with, 61,8
perigraphein, describe, 76,6; 90,21
perikardios, in the region of the heart, 9,21; 19,4; 44,7; 50,18; 53,17; 54,31.32; 55,1; 57,22.23; 58,32; 61,31; 64,3.8.16; 89,13; 92,9
perilambanein, encompass, 42,31; subsume, 78,25; take account of, 57,6
perilêptos, grasp (to be grasped), 2,19; 76,29
perimetros, circumference, 56,13.14; 84,32
periolkê, distraction, 3,1
peripherês, circular, 56,14
periphora, circular, 66,13
perittos, odd number, 80,13
phainomenos, apparent, 70,3; 74,14; superficial, 70,4; *phainomena, ta*, appearances, 42,6; 74,19; *phainomenon, to*, outward appearance, 69,31; what is apparent, 71,24; 71,29; 72,6
phaios, grey, 9,33
phaneros, apparent, 42,7; clear, 4,18; 11,1.24; 32,3.6; 54,6; 72,22
phantasia, appearance, 42,4.6.7; imagination, 3,3.15; 4,17; 5,35.37.38; 6,5.9; 7,36; 11,9; 13,21; 16,9; 18,37; 20,6; 39,13.25; 45,15; 51,7; 52,23; 58,10.12.13; 71,28; 78,25
phantasiousthai, imagining, 27,6; 43,10
phantasma, image, 45,23
phantastikon, imagination, 39,26; 41,9
phantastos, what can be imagined, 39,13
phantazein, imagine, 2,29
phaostasia, bringing to a halt of light, 6,5
phasma, appearance, 19,19

pherein, tend to, 71,4
Philia, Love, 73,17.28; 82,21; 91,35
philoneikein, have ambition, 51,37
philosophia, philosophy, 24,35; 25,2; 51,21.24.31.32; *philosophia, prôtê*, first philosophy, 23,26; 25,16; 55,29
philosophos, philosopher, 15,13; 46,11.12; 63,4; *prôtos philosophos*, first philosopher, 10,22; 55,12; 58,7.14;62,7; 63,3.6
phlox, flame, 83,19; 87,11
phobeisthai, be afraid, 54,7; be frightened, 45,4; fear, 53,10
phoberos, fearful, 54,6
phobos, fear, 50,20; 53,20.21.22; 54,11; 63,17
phônê, word, 68,10
phortikos, vulgar, 86,28; 88,21.24
phôs, light, 23,33; 24,2; 45,26; 70,18.19.20
phôtismos, illumination, 30,22.26; 31,2
phôtizein, illuminate, 30,24.30.31; 31,1.6.18
phronein, think, 70,8.13
phronêsis, intelligence, 72,18; thought, 72,5
phrontizein, be careful, 51,9
phthartos, perishable, 11,3.7.9.25; subject to passing away, 6,23; 7,13; 16,13
phtheirein, cause to perish, 7,11; 11,21; destroy, 15,4
phtheiresthai, pass away, 16,18.22; 68,24; perish, 46,29.34
phthongos, sound, 23,10; tone, 70,8
phthora, decay, 59,25; 60,9.10; destruction, 27,13.14; passing away, 34,11; 57,9; 67,8; 90,10; perishing, 46,32
phuein, grow, 52,13; *pephukenai*, naturally, 20,12; in their nature, 8,25
phukion, sea-weed, 70,24
phusikê, hê, physics, 55,28
phusikos, based on nature, 44,4; concerned with the study of nature, 25,16; in accordance with nature, 44,1; natural, 7,18; 20,32.33; 21,5; 25,3; 26,4; 42,32; 48,24; 54,28; 55,8.9.19; 56,1.19.22; 61,27.28; 63,16;

65,32; 67,5.8.27; 76,22; 89,3;
natural philosopher, 36,16;
82,8.18; of nature,
10,16.19.23.29; physical, 18,5;
54,26; student of nature,
25,13.16; 54,18.19.24; 55,6;
55,24.25.31; 56,34; 57,3; 58,26;
59,5.10.11; 60,13.14.20.25.26;
61,3; 62,1.9; 63,20.22; *phusika,
ta*, natural kinds, 55,8; natural
objects, 76,16.22.32; 77,4.21.25;
natural things, 55,15.26; 56,34;
76,22.25.26
phusiologia, physics, 23,21.22
phusiologos, student of nature, 21,4
phusis, natural capacity, 82,36;
83,13; natural entity, 82,22;
85,19; nature, 3,13; 5,7.9; 6,23;
7,18; 8,13.14; 11,32; 12,2.25;
14,8.35; 15,21; 17,30; 24,15;
25,8.19.20.29; 26,12.13.18.20;
28,4; 43,12.35; 47,1; 49,2.7.10 ;
65,2; 67,29; 75,23; 82,34; 83,6;
85,23; *kata phusin*, natural,
65,35; *phusei*, naturally, 21,31;
50,24.26; 65,34; 69,3; 83,35;
phusis tis, natural being, 38,6
phutikos, of plants, 35,17.20;
vegetative, 6,26.27.33;
7,10.22.29.31.33.35; 8,1; 9,2.36;
10,4.6; 13,24.25.26.30; 15,11;
16,27; 17,6; 20,29; 37,4.5.7;
38,24; 52,26; 53,31; 65,23; 89,32
phuton, plant, 6,28.34; 7,23.8; 19,24
pisteuein, prove, 4,13.24; 30,13.21;
65,8f
pistis, persuasion, 3,22; plausible
conviction, 21,16; 27,31; proof,
31,6
pithanos, plausible, 68,5; 84,9.12;
89,28
plagios, sideways, 42,26
plassein, mould, 20,15
platos, width, 10,16; 77,35.37;
78,4.29; 79,3.5
plêgê, blow, 72,3
pleonazein, be a result of surplus,
14,2; be in excess, 14,7; 17,22.23
pleonektein, exceed, 79,2.3
plêrôma, fullness, 7,12; 56,28; 58,22
plêthos, plurality, 32,22; 38,6; 67,30;
75,6.7; 80,4.5; quantity, 82,25

pleura, side, 23,5; 29,17.21; 30,18;
31,5; 40,16; 84,32.35
plinthos, mortar, 59,29; 60,3.8
ploion, ship, 48,1; 61,18
plôtêr, sailor, 48,26
plunein, wash, 19,30
pneuma, pneuma, 12,18; 15,11;
17,26; 18,26.35; 19,21.23.28.35;
20,11; 47,23; 52,6; 64,6.8.13
pneumatikos, pneumatic, 10,8;
12,19; 17,8.21.24; 18,8.32; 19,16;
20,13
poiein, produce, make, act, *passim*;
be active, 83,15; 88,29
poiêtês, poet, 72,4
poiêtikos, active, 88,27; creative,
58,17; 73,16; 74,6; producing
effects, 83,1; productive,
25,32.33; 37,24; 63,9.10; 86,1;
poiêtikos, ho, poet, 69,30
poikilôs, manifold, 79,26; various,
19,36
poios, kind, 55,25; 63,22; of a certain
nature, kind, 28,11; 31,26.32;
53,12; *epi tou poiou*, in the
qualitative sense, 34,14; *kata
poion*, in respect of quality,
34,10; *poion, to*, quality, 26,22;
33,2.25; 34,4; 82,15.16
poiotes, quality, 9,31; 60,12
politeia, political, 89,11
pollaplasiazein, multiply, 80,6.8.10
poludunamos, having many
(different) faculties, 33,10;
35,11.12
polugônios, having many angles,
56,10.12
polugônon, polygone, 56,18; shape
with many angles, 56,17; shape
with more angles, 85,4
polukhôrêtos, having a large
surface, 85,4.5.9; spacious,
56,8.10.11
polumigês, heterogeneous, 70,7
poson, quantity, 26,22.23; 32,32;
33,1.24.25; 34,4; 79,6; 82,15.17;
diôrismenon poson, discrete
quantity, 78,32; *kata to poson*,
quantitatively, 9,29
poton, drink, 51,9
pous, foot, 13,32; 47,11.12
pragma, fact, 19,18; object, 3,7;
23,30; 24,14; 81,12; 87,17; thing,

Greek-English Index

2,8; 4,31; 5,7.9.12; 8,18; 12,13; 16,35; 26,25; 28,13.15.23; 29,6.14.18.32; 31,32; 32,2.31; 37,26.27.30; 38,16; 39,6; 40,11; 41,17.32; 42,9.10.30; 43,2.4.5.7; 43,29; 53,3; 55,26; 56,1; 57,4.16.19.21.27; 59,14.17.21; 65,13; 73,18; 74,25; 75,25; 78,11; 79,24; 80,28; 85,23.25; 86,15; 87,17; 89,26; *prokeimenon pragma*, present object, 40,20; present subject, 28,16; 32,12
pragmateia, treatise, 10,11.12.25; 20,32.33; 21,23; 25,13.21; 37,26
pragmateuesthai, to pragmateuthênai, discussion, 31,28
praktikos, practical, 5,24
prepôdês, appropriate, 56,20
proairesis, deliberate choice, 5,25.26.27.31
proairetôs, of own accord, 20,15
proaporein, raise problems prior, 64,20
proballein, project, 5,3
problêma, problem, 21,19; 40,8; 43,15.21; 44,21; 45,21
prodêlos, obvious, 75,25; plain, 40,29; very clear, 4,17; 71,23
proerkhesthai, originate, 52,15; proceed, 3,10; 35,13
prokatalegein, sum up already, 82,14
prokeimenos, subject, 25,22; present, 46,2; 64,30; 86,13; present subject, 31,14; 32,23; 55,30; *prokeimenon pragma*, present thing, 28,15; present subject, 28,16; *prokeimenos pragmateia*, present discussion, 63,23
prolambanein, accept (in advance), 15,12; establish in advance, 44,28
prolêpsis, prior grasping, 41,31
prolupein, to cause pain previously, 6,13; 57,18; 59,2
pronoia, Providence, 6,20; 17,29; 20,17; 86,30
prophasis, causal trigger, 58,32
pros ti, (category of) relative, 33,5; 54,22; relational, 25,10; 39,12.14.36
prosballein, come into contact with, 31,1; dash through, 67,25; grasp, 2,8; 13,15.16.17; 26,17
prosbolê, apprehension, 6,2
prosêkein, be appropriate, 12,4; 17,31; 88,29
prosekhês, adjoining, 24,18; connected, 8,21; proximate, 26,12; 52,35; 56,23.24; 57,8; 58,35; 60,1; 62,13
proskhrêsthai, also to refer to, 44,30.33
proskrinein, assimilate, 68,29
prosphuês, germane, 5,16;
prosphuôs, not suitable, 86,13
prostatês, champion, 89,24
prosuphainein, weave to, 12,6.7
protasis, premise, 2,3; 26,32; 29,8.9; 78,12; 79,28; 85,24
proteroi, hoi, precursors, 64,28.31
proteron, prior, 15,26.27.33; 36,30; 37,7.8; *proteron kai husteron*, prior and posterior, 36,31; 37,9; *proteron têi phusei*, prior by nature, 36,32; 37,2.7
prôtos, prôta aitia, primary causes, 57,9; *prôta noêmata*, primary thoughts, 45,22.24; *prôta pragmata*, first things, 58,16
prôtôs, primarily, 40,21; 41,8.22.23; 42,9.20; 66,24.29.31.32.33; 78,28; 83,4.18; 84,11
protrepein, encourage, 21,12.14.17; 28,1
protropê, encouragement, 21,9.10.18
proüphistasthai, exist before, 52,20
pseudês, false, 12,23; 79,30
pseudesthai, speak falsehood, 5,14
pseudos, falsehood, 25,1
psilos, bare, 90,16
psukhê, soul, 1,5; 2,1; 3,5.8.31; 4,10.30; 5,8.21.27.28.33.34; 6,19.25.36; 8,17.18.25.31; 9,1.3; 10,10; 11,1; 12,7.10; 13,24; 14,35; 15,2.5.9.14; 16,1.3.5.22.26; 17,9.20.26.30; 18,1.4.5.11.38; 19,19.20.24; 20,6.10.14.24.25.26.29; 21,9; 22,16; 23,12; 24,5.7.11.12.13.16.24.33; 25,5.6.7.13.18.23.26.29; 26,3; 27,1; 28,3.5.7.19.20; 32,29.30.33; 33,9; 35,11.15.16.23.28; 36,1.4.6.8.10.12.18.23.25;

37,2.10.12.14.15.27; 38,11.18;
40,9.13.14; 41,7.11; 42,2.25.28;
43,10.14; 44,12.13.18;
45,10.14.18.; 46,7.14.16.33;
47,4.6; 48,14.16.23.26.27.28;
49,28; 50,3.5.6.10.14.16.22.32;
51,14.16.27.29.31.33;
52,1.4.5.17.25.26.29.31;
53,11.25.31; 54,8.14;
55,6.10.11.19.23.24.26; 58,8;
63,16; 64,18; 65,4; 66,29.33;
67,4.11.14; 68,14.23; 69,22;
70,34; 71,1.2.4; 71,15; 72,8;
72,29; 73,23; 74,31.33;
75,15.18.26.29.30; 77,22;
78,7.19.23; 79,21.32; 80,23.31;
81,11.14; 81,33; 82,4.12.14.28;
83,7.12; 84,11.13.15;
85,17.22.28.30; 86,12;
87,2.4.8.16.19.33; 88,10.11.14.26;
89,7; 89,25; 90,17.18.22.28; 91,4;
91,32
psukhein, cause cold, 75,10
psukhesthai, become cold, 13,4
psukhikos, of the soul, 1,9; 10,28;
 15,8; 14,28; 20,28; 36,18; 51,38;
 65,31; 72,13; 89,30; 92,10
psukhron, to, (the) cold, 9,32; 69,16;
 91,35; 92,3.6.8
psukhros, cold, 34,15; 68,21; 92,11
psuxis, being cooled, 92,7; cooling,
 18,3; 68,32; 69,2; cooling effect,
 92,9
ptênos, bird, 26,8
puknon, to, density, 61,19.23
puknos, compact, 61,12; 68,22
puknôsis, (process of) condensation,
 69,2.9
puknousthai, become more compact,
 20,8.9; be made compact, 68,22
pur, fire, 4,26.27.28; 9,7.8.24; 27,14;
 31,16.17; 52,32; 66,5; 67,1.11;
 73,20.24; 74,19; 83,2.9.10;
 84,10.12; 86,22; 87,10.11.12; 92,2
puramis, pyramid, 78,1
puramoeidês, pyramidal, 84,28;
 pyramid-shaped, 68,16
purios, fiery, 9,9; 65,38

rhadios, easy, 23,29.32; 44,20;
 53,21.25; 84,18.25
rhein, move, 77,31
rhepein, have a tendency to, 51,2

rhêseidion, passage, 63,4
rhêtos, statement, 49,18
rheustos, subject to change, 6,23
rhuiskesthai, flow, 68,4.7; flux, 32,17
rhumê, force, 68,30
rhusis, state of flux, 76,32
rhusmos, rhusmos/shape, 68,2

saphês, clear, 2,4; 10,1; 30,25.26;
 38,36; 39,26.27; 40,27; 71,10;
 80,17; 86,9; 87,30; evident, 65,6.9
sarx, flesh, 14,25; 52,32; 53,4.5;
 57,30.33; 62,28.33; 90,14
sbennunai, extinguish, 50,31
seira, line, 75,2
seismos, earthquake, 83,20; 87,26
selênê, moon, 4,23.25; 30,22.25; 31,17
sêmainein, have meaning, 28,29;
 indicate, 82,31; mean, 32,1;
 62,27; 64,1; 68,3.12; refer to,
 59,2; 90,13; signify, 26,25.32;
 28,25.32; 30,12; 55,2.4.5;
 sêmainomena, meanings, 34,12;
 49,19
sêmantikos, indicative of, 40,3.4
sêmeion, point, 32,17; 49,23.25.32;
 50,12; 67,13; 77,28; 79,3; 84,24;
 85,10; sign, 21,31; 31,17.18.21.22
semnos, profound, 70,4
sidêreos, made of iron, 22,30
sidêron, iron, 86,17.24
sition, food, 50,30; 51,8
skedastos, dissoluble, 12,26
skênê, tent, 60,12
skeparnon, axe, 44,32
skepasma, shelter, 59,24.28; 60,10
skepein, protect, 19,10
skhêma, definition for *rhusmos*,
 68,3.12; figure, 56,8; 56,19; 58,5;
 61,21.26; 62,6.31; 77,33; 78,1;
 84,30; geometrical figure, 22,26;
 mathematical figure, 14,11;
 63,31; shape, 2,9; 3,4; 20,2.5;
 29,27.28.29; 30,9; 31,12; 57,30;
 58,1.2; 67,7.8.13.30.32; 68,5.6;
 84,19
skhêmatizein, give shape, 19,19
skhesis, relation, 9,30; 56,5.22;
 84,1.3; relationship, 48,31; 49,3;
 91,19
skhistos, twofold, 78,14; *hodos
 skhistê*, cross-roads, 78,15
skholazein, be free from, 3,2

Greek-English Index

skholê, freedom, 3,1
skia, shade, 45,26.27
skioeidês, shadowy, 19,18
skopimos, suitable, 7,18
skopos, aim, 64,30
skotos, dark, 70,21
skutotomos, cobbler, 69,29
smikros, small, 14,14; 35,7; 67,26
sôma, body, 2,28; 3,1.3; 7,8.9; 8,18; 9,3; 10,5.7.29; 11,13.18.26.29; 12,11; 13,1.14.22.31; 14,10; 15,1.3.5.7.8.10; 16,3; 17,1; 18,2.4.7.11.12.27.30.32.36; 19,1; 20,3.13.19; 22,22.30.31; 23,2.6.9; 25,17.18; 26,6.28; 27,4; 29,7; 31,21; 34,9.11.19.20; 35,5.28; 37,23.24; 41,12; 42,24; 44,30; 45,16.26.27; 46,5.21; 49,21; 50,4.7.10.15; 52,27; 53,31.34; 54,1.3.10.17.28.29.30; 56,4; 57,5; 61,26.27.28; 62,1; 62,22.25.29.32.34; 63,11.30; 64,17; 65,32; 66,23.32; 67,5.6.8.9.18.26; 68,22; 70,22.25.31; 75,17; 77,29; 78,22.24; 82,24; 83,6; 84,15; 86,2; 87,23; 88,11; 89,5; 90,1; 91,25; corporeal, 13,22; 33,7.8; 34,6.7.8; 35,8; 66,22; 78,21; 83,28
sômatikos, corporeal, 82,16.17.25; 91,10.22; of the body, 10,26; 16,35
sômatoeidês, corporeal, 78,23
sophia, wisdom, 25,1; 69,30
sophistês, sophist, 89,10
sophos, ho, wise person/man, 70,3.4; 74,17
sôstikos, that which preserves, 51,36
sôzein, preserve, 6,21
spêlaion, cave, 60,11
sperma, seed, 7,36; 13,26.27.28; 14,2; 34,13.32; 67,31; 88,31; 89,4
sphaira, ball, 31,7.9.10.12.13; sphere, 49,16; 56,9.17.18; 65,38; 84,24; 85,8.12; spherical, 67,12.15
sphairikos, spherical, 4,22.25; 9,19; 30,22.23; 31,17; 56,4.6.20.29; 67,12.28; 68,5.13.17.23; 84,13; 86,21; spherical atom, 83,21
sphairoeidês, spherical, 30,27.29; 84,16.23
spoudaios, ho, serious, 19,27; 21,10.17; 28,1
stasis, stability, 65,38; 74,35; 75,25; 76,18.21; 87,14; 88,2.5.6.7; standstill, 6,6
stereos, solid, 77,29; 78,1; 79,5.19; solid thing/figure/body, 56,9.16; 79,4; 85,8.9
stêthos, breast, 8,26
stigmê, point, 49,16
stoikheiôdes, elementary, 32,19
stoikheion, element, 9,16.35; 16,19; 33,5.30; 46,29; 52,21; 53,5; 56,3; 57,10; 62,29; 67,28.29; 73,16.23; 74,31; 75,29; 80,16.24.30.31.36; 82,21; 83,11; 86,20; 89,23; 90,11.15.16; 91,1.2.33
stratêgos, commander, 37,21.22; 63,8; 64,9.10.11
stratiôtês, soldier, 37,21.22; 64,9.11
stratos, army, 63,8.9
sullambanein, assume, 88,13
sullogismos, (syllogistic) proof, 2,10; syllogism, 3,28.29; 26,29.30; 71,22; 79,25; 85,23
sullogizesthai, conclude, 1,21; 4,26; 40,13; 41,20; 44,17; draw conclusions, 3,13.15; 4,21.29; infer, 42,27.29; 91,21.29.30
sumbainein, be an attribute, 29,8; belong to, 61,3,8; be present as attribute, 49,15; 50,11; follow, 26,31; 43,25; 85,26; happen, 20,2.4; 54,7; 68,29; **sumbainein, kath' hauto**, essential attributes, 65,3.5; (be) accidental, dist. from **kata sumbebêkos**, 29,4.9.10.12; 30,2.5
sumbebêkenai, (be an) attribute, 26,26.29; 28,27; 29,3.4.7.14.22; 31,32; 40,7; 41,22.30; 42,1.5.16; 43,25; 65,6.15; 68,20; essential attribute, 40,21; 41,17;
sumbebêkos, kata, accidentally, 26,27.32
sumballesthai, contribute, 24,32; 25,20.21.22.29; 32,20; 40,11; 40,20; 41,25.27.29
sumbolikôs, in a symbolic way, 73,22; 74,11; in symbolic language, 69,28; 73,21
summetaballein, cause to change accordingly, 53,29.33.35; change, 53,29
summetria, moderation, 51,9; right proportion, 57,9.10

summetros, commensurate, 14,10.13; 24,2; *summetrôs*, moderately, 51,11
sumparalambanein, call to aid, 64,29.31
sumparathein, run parallel, 87,18
sumpatheia, sympathetic affection, 8,22; 18,4.6.22; sympathetic relationship, 35,19
sumperainein, draw conclusion(s), 33,27
sumperasma, conclusion, 1,18; 2,1.3; 4,7.9.10; 5,20; 26,30.32; 29,9; 78,12; 79,28
sumphônos, consonant, 68,21; *sumphônôs*, in accordance, 5,9
sumphtheirein, cause to perish together with, 12,21; 17,7
sumphuia, kinship, 35,19
sumphulos, of the (same) origin, 2,26
sumplekein, combine, 28,17; connect, 60,19; construct, 81,15; intertwine, 3,14.15; 5,27.30
sumplêroun, complete, 44,31
sumptôma, concomitant attribute, 58,4
sunagein, fit, 41,6
sunagesthai, correspond, 80,4
sunaisthesthai, be aware, 5,6
sunaisthêsis, state of consciousness, 20,20
sunakmazein, gain strength with, 15,1
sunamaurousthai, weaken with, 15,1
sunamphoteron, composite, 27,7; 44,26.33; 45,6.18.20; 47,20.27; 48,17; 49,20.29; 50,4.17.23; 53,11.30; 54,15; 63,27
sunanairein, eliminate, 88,6; eliminate together, 29,15; 37,1.5
sunapheia, connection, 8,20.22
sunaptein, *sunêmmenos*, conditional, 46,19
sundesmos, connecting, 59,15
sundiatithenai, bring into a certain condition as well, 45,4; 50,18.22; bring into harmony, 35,21
sundiatupoun, compress, 20,3.4
sundromê, configuration, 62,29
sunduazein, couple with, 53,2.4
suneispherein, bring into the common stock, 37,1

sunekheia, continuum, 8,20
sunekhein, hold together, 12,26.27.29
sunekhês, constant, 87,14; continuous, 32,15.19; 67,18.19; 78,33.78; 79,6.9; *sunekhôs*, continuously, 70,32
sunektikos, that holds together, 12,30.31
sunepinoein, to think about at the same time, 57,33
sunepipherein, adduce, 63,6
sunepispan, draw in along with, 69,16.18.20
sunergia, assistance, 20,7
sunergos, servant, 16,7
sunêthês, normal, 21,29; ordinary, 81,4
sunethismos, being accustomed, 2,27; 3,13
sunethizein, make accustomed, 2,14; 3,10
sunistanai, compose, 81,23; 91,32; hold together, 87,9; *sunistasthai*, consist, 77,7; 79,6; constitute, 73,2; exist, 63,2
sunkataspan, distort, 21,22
sunkeisthai, consist, 80,26; 91,34
sunkhein, confuse, 72,15
sunkinein, move together, 45,4; 66,1; (mid.) to be accompanied by a movement, 50,17.18.22
sunkrinesthai, undergo contraction, 18,3
sunkrisis, mixture, 90,5.8.9
sunneuein pros (eis) heauton, turn towards itself, 56,21.26
sunodos, conjunction, 30,28; gathering, 67,7
sunolos, *to sunolon*, as a whole, 15,6
sunousia, conversation, 75,35
sunousiastikos, having desire for/prone to sexual intercourse, 50,30; 51,2
sunousiousthai, join with one's own substance, 4,30
suntattein, *suntetagmenos*, connected, 32,18.20
suntaxis, syntax, 64,26
suntelein, contribute, 63,24; co-operate, 53,7
sunthesis, combination, 9,34; 60,2.8.12; 83,34; 89,28; 90,16

sunthetos, composite, 9,4.16; 12,23; 33,8; 35,4; 39,2; 67,27; 79,25
suntithenai, add, 80,7.10; combine, 76,13
suntithesthai, assent, 5,9
suntrekhein, accompany, 34,26
suntrophos, same kin, 2,26
suntupoun, mould, 20,6
sustasis, substance, 47,26; 75,23
sustatikos, constitutive, 26,24; 28,17
sustellein, contract, 20,8; 53,23
sustoikhos, belonging to the same series, 17,16; corresponding, 15,16; 56,5
sustolê, contraction, 50,20

taphos, tomb, 19,18.22.37; 20,11
tautologein, repeat, 82,10
tautologia, repetition, 82,11
tautotês, sameness, 73,34; 74,7.35; 75,5.16.20
taxis, as definition for *diathigê*, 68,13; hierarchical position, 25,27; orderly arrangement, 37,20.22.24.25; 63,7.10; rank, 2,22; 15,29; 24,30; 25,25; rank order, 25,24
tekhnê, expertise, 54,24.25; 57,12; science, 55,28; 60,30; 61,32.33
tekhnikos, skilful, 70,9
tekhnitês, craftsman, 53,32.34; expert, 54,24; 61,7.8; practitioner of a discipline, 61,2; scientist, 60,28; 61,15; *tekhnitês, kata meros*, subject-specific expert, 57,3; 62,17; *tekhnitês, kath' hekasta*, subject-specific expert, 62,3.19
tekmairesthai, infer, 43,18; *tekmêriôdês*, inferential, 30,20; 31,15
tekmêrion, indication, 31,16.18.21
tektôn, carpenter, 44,31; 57,5; 61,9; 62,20
telein, perfect, 27,15
teleios, complete, 55,14; 59,22; perfect, 2,15; 13,29; 44,17; 76,9
teleiôsis, fulfilment, 56,33; perfection, 27,13
teleiotês, perfection, 2,25; 3,6; 9,27.33; 27,21; 76,9
teleiôtikos, being perfected, 27,18
telikos, final, 25,32; 26,5; 58,30; 59,29

telos, end, 56,21; 58,25; 79,28; purpose, 8,10.13.14.25
temnein, cut, 68,16; divide, 58,13
teras, monstrosity, 14,2.5.8
tetrad, tetrad, 76,13; 79,6.8.12.33; 80,22
tetradikos, tetradic, 76,14; 77,3.20
tetragônon, quadrangle, 84,31; 85,1.3
tetragônos, having four angles, 56,11
tetrapleuros, having four sides, 56,15
tetrapous, (having) four feet, 4,14
thalatta, sea, 71,11
thanatos, death, 6,36; 17,12
tharsein, be courageous, 45,3
tharsos, recklessness, 53,19
thateron, difference, 74,1
thaumasios, admirable, 22,15; 24,10.14.15.33
theios, divine, 3,2.4.11; 10,26; 11,32; 12,4. 8; 23,31; 25,24.26; 33,21; 34,33; 63,13; 66,25; 70,21; 72,14; 74,4; 77,16.17
thêlus, female, 7,34
theologia, theology, 23,28; 25,9.12.15.22.23; 55,9; 77,24
theologikos, theological, 25,3
theôrein, find, 17,8; 36,18; observe, 34,19; perceive, 65,27; 75,12; study, 10,29; 40,7; 55,6.24; view, 26,13.15.17; 28,3; 52,34; 61,23; 62,14; 76,18; 77,3.4; 78,33
theôrêma, object of theoretical study, 6,15
theôrêtikos, of contemplation, 11,1.23; theoretical student, 58,18
theôria, contemplation, 2,25.27; 3,2; study, 3,8; 21,9; 23,13; 24,6.11.19.22; 25,11.22.23; 27,32; 28,3; 44,24; theoretical study, 38,34
theos, god, 3,5; 12,1; 15,21; 16,5; 36,22; 47,1; 73,33
thêrion, wild animal, 8,29
thermainein, cause heat, 75,10; cause to become hot, 13,3; heat, 68,31; *thermainesthai, to*, heating, 49,2
thermos, hot, 51,2; 67,1; warm, 34,15; *thermon, to*, (the) hot, 9,32; 91,35; 92,1.6; the heat,

53,23; 55,1.2; 58,26.27; 69,16; 83,4.5; 92,10
thermotês, heat, 44,9; ***emphutos thermotês***, natural heat, 89,2
thesis, position, 67,9; as definition for ***tropê***, 68,12
thnêtos, mortal, 9,39; 10,2; 11,30.33; 12,1.2.6.7.8; 15,14; 47,3; 77,10.17; 78,20
thrasus, reckless, 50,29
threptikos, concerned with nutrition, 6,27; 7,21; 13,27.35; 16,31; faculty of nutrition, 17,13; nutritive, 7,26.29; 8,31; 74,29
thrix, hair, 89,15
thumikos, inclined to anger, 51,27
thumoeidês, spirited, 74,28
thumos, anger, 44,4.6.34; 50,26; 51,27; 52,23; 53,17; 54,27; 57,16.17; 58,29; 59,7.9.17; 61,30.31; 63,17.32; 64,2.6.12.16; spirit, 6,11.13.19.23; 7,24; 10,28; 14,2; 16,32.36; 18,9.11.32; 19,1.17; 38,27; spirited part, 26,10
thumousthai, being angry, 27,6
thura, door, 61,10; 66,23.31
thuris, window, 69,25
thurôma, window, 67,21.22.25
tiktein, give birth, 31,20.21; produce, 51,10
timios, of high value, 72,17; valuable, 21,8.13.25.27.29.33; 22,18.21.23.25; 23,2.13.14.16; 24,18.34; 85,30
tmêma, part, 60,18
to pothen poi, the 'from where to what', 78,11
tode ti, particular thing, 62,12
topos, environment, 66,7; location, 74,14; place, 4,14.27.28; 34,11.16; 37,27; 40,31.33; 41,1; 42,1; 65,13.36; 66,3.8; 76,36
trepein, turn, 78,14.16.17
trephein, feed, 6,28.34; 8,32; 17,2
trephesthai, be fed, 65,25; be nourished, 19,25.31
trias, triad, 76,12; 78,31; 79,12.33; 80,22
trigônon, triangle, 23,3; 29,16; 30,9; 40,15; 41,15; 58,1.6; 64,4; 77,33; 78,2
tropê, position, 68,11.12

trophê, eating, 51,12; food, 7,30; 8,3.6.7.9; nutrition, 7,21; 17,14; 42,25;
tropos, method, 31,29; 32,1; way, 16,18.22.23; 46,29.34; 74,30
tupos, impression, 6,1.4.9; 11,11; 13,22.23; 45,20; ***tupôi***, in rough sketch, 54,26

xêrainein, cause dryness, 75,11
xêros, dry, 19,28; 51,5; 61,29; 83,19; 87,12
xêrotês, dryness, 62,20
xulon, timber, 57,5; 59,26.30; 60,2.8; (planks of) 61,10; 61,18.23.25; 62,20.26.28.33; 84,5; wood, 22,31; 27,13; 52,35.36.37; 53,4
xusma, mote, 67,20; 69,23; 70,17.34; 86,21

zein, boil, 53,17; 58,33; the boiling, 92,6
zên, be alive, 92,5; live, 6,35; 52,2; 64,7.17; 65,25.26; 68,26; ***zên, to***, life, 68,19.23; 88,32; living, 65,25; 69,15
zesis, boiling, 19,4; 44,7; 54,27; 57,22; 58,25; 61,29.31; 64,2.15
zêtein, ask, 4,5; 6,12; 10,15; 17,25; 21,32; 48,28; 56,6; 60,27; 68,33; examine, 21,20; 25,9.24; 28,7; 33,15; 36,12.25; 38,19.24; 39,4.15; 40,8; 43,13; 44,21; 55,29; 59,11; find out, 28,10; 31,26; 33,31; inquiry, 32,10; 33,23; investigate, 36,6.7; 52,26; look for, 26,27; 32,22; 33,27; 61,9.11; 88,20; raise the question/question, 28,14; 31,31; 32,30; 33,7; 84,21; search, 41,3; 70,4; seek, 2,4.5; 14,34.35.36; 16,7; 20,35; 39,34; 41,7; 48,25; 70,1; study, 39,27; ***zêtein, to***, question, 36,3
zêtêma, question, 28,22
zêtêsis, question, 28,13; 31,30.33; search, 28,5.23
zôê, life, 6,35.37; 17,26; 19,3; 19,24; 35,21.29; 42,24; 48,24; 52,24.24; 65,27; 92,8; ***to zôês poiêtikon***, reproduction, 41,10
zôion, animal, 7,24; 10,13; 12,2.8; 19,10; 20,1; 42,26; 61,6; 65,23.28;

89,18.22; living being, 6,31.33;
13,29.30; 14,7; 17,18; 25,31;
26,1.7.12; 27,2.4; 29,25.26;

30,9.14.16.19; 33,14; 35,27;
36,20.26.28; 37,17.33.34; 38,1;
44,14.27; 48,13; 52,31; 55,20;
63,16; 64,9.13; 68,15.20.23.24;
69,9.12; 70,30; 72,16.18.19;
77,6.10.16.26; 78,27; 81,1; 83,5;
84,2; 85,29.31

zôiopoiein, cause to live, 69,8; keep alive, 18,30; reproduce, 48,19;
zôiopoiein, to, reproduction, 48,17
zôtikos, (concerned with) life, 1,12; 5,35; 6,11; vital, 10,13; 18,34

Index of Names

This index lists names that appear in the Translation. References are to the page and line numbers of the *CAG* edition, which appear in the margins of the Translation. Names in the Preface, Introduction and Notes are listed in the Subject Index.

Abderite: 68,3
Achilles: 45,28
Alcmaeon: 71,6; 88,9
Alexander (of Aphrodisias): 10,2; 21,21.27; 24,7.17; 35,10; 36,13; 38,10; 43,1; 62,15; 89,10
Ammonius: 1,2
Anaxagoras: 71,15; 72,9.23.27; 82,7.22; 85,17.28.34; 91,9.20.30
Anaximander: 82,18
Anaximenes: 9,9; 82,18; 87,2
Andronicus of Rhodes: 27,22.24; 45,8.11
Archelaus: 71,18
Aristotle: 3,25; 4,22; 6,2; 10,3.9; 11,28; 12,10.32; 15,12.35; 19,33; 21,22.30; 23,17; 24,12; 26,4; 27,23.27; 33,4.28; 38,10; 39,22; 43,24; 44,15; 45,10; 47,6.19; 48,22; 56,19; 74,14; 75,8.35; 83,21; 86,4; 87,11.26; 88,3.16; 90,9; 91,17; *Ethics* 25,6; *Metaphysics* 19,34; 21,30; 22,12; 23,28; 37,20.28; 88,4; *Meteorologica* 41,2; 83,21; *On Coming to Be and Perishing* 21,6; 90,8; *On Demonstration* 3,25; 23,17; 30,1; *On Generation* 55,18; *On Interpretation* 27,22.26.27.29; 35,2; 45,9; 49,11; *On the Heavens* 30,22; 88,4; *On the Parts of Animals* 10,11.25; 25,13; 55,12; *On the Soul* 27,24.25.26; 45,10.11; *Physics* 20,34; 22,9; 33,28; 55,15; 67,10; 82,8; *On Philosophy* 75,32.34; *On the Good* 75,34

Critias: 9,19; 89,6.8.9

Democritus: 9,17; 35,12; 36,16; 67,1.4.11.17.19.21.33; 68,11.21; 70,26; 71,21.23.30; 72,8.21.22.27; 82,18.23; 83,24; 84,2.7.9.12.21; 85,13.33; 86,20; 91,30
Diogenes (of Apollonia): 87,1.2

Eleatic Stranger, the: 1,21
Empedocles: 73,15.21; 74,5.11.17.21; 82,20; 89,27; 91,33
Ethiopian: 4,15.16

Glaucus (the sea god): 70,23

Hades: 17,28
Hector: 72,1.3
Heraclides of Pontus: 9,7
Heraclitus: 9,7; 67,17; 82,19; 83,22.23; 87,8; 92,2
Hermias, 1,3
Hippasus: 83,23
Hippo: 9,10; 86,34; 88,22; 92,2
Homer: 72,1.8

Leucippus: 9,17; 67,33

Numenius: 9,37

Peripatetics: 75,2
Plato: 2,30; 9,38; 10,8; 11,29; 12,10;

Index of Names

22,1.6; 24,25; 27,16; 33,21; 36,14; 37,18; 54,25; 56,6; 57,12; 61,33; 69,29.30; 70,22; 71,6.9; 73,34; 74,30.32; 75,15.35.36; 76,23; 81,18.24; 82,20; 88,3; *Gorgias* 22,8; *Laws* 71,10; *Phaedo* 2,30; 9,38; 22,6; *Phaedrus* 33,21; 74,1; 81,20; *The Sophist* 1,21; 27,16; *Theaetetus* 88,3; *Timaeus* 11,31; 36,15; 56,6; 73,34; 74,30; 76,23; 81,23
Plotinus: 2,15; 3,12; 7,25; 56,21
Plutarch: 21,21
Protagoras: 71,26; 87,15

Pythagoreans: 69,21.24.28; 70,2.7.25.35; 73,21.22; 75,36; 81,27; 82,19; 86,21; 88,11

Roman: 68,9

Socrates: 89,8
Stoics: 9,10

Thales: 9,10; 82,18; 86,11.13.16.22.24
Timaeus: 2,18.20

Xenocrates: 32,33; 44,11; 71,6.13; 81,25; 82,20

Subject Index

This Index is complementary to the English-Greek Glossary and is restricted to the Preface, Introduction and Notes. It does not cover the Translation, which can be searched by using the English-Greek Glossary and the Greek-English Index in combination with each other; and it lists only those discussions in Preface, Introduction and Notes that cannot be found through the Translation. References are to the page and note numbers in this volume.

accidental: 129 nn.263.277
Achilles: 117 n.47
affections (*pathê*): 4, 122 n.162; see also *pathos*
Alexander of Aphrodisias: commentary on Arist. *DA*: 1-2, 121 n.121, 127 nn.221.223, 140 n.492; own views on the soul: 121 n.121; on dematerialisation of senses: viii; on independence of mental states from the body: ix
Alexandria: 1, 5; teaching of philosophy in: 121 n.126; 122 n.151
Ammonius: vii; relationship to Philoponus: 1, 115 n.1
anatomical experiments: 125 n.201
Anaxagoras: 6
anger (*thumos*): 4, 5, 119 n.75, 131 n.341
animals, species of: 121 n.127
Aristotle: view that soul is *entelekheia* of the body: 121 n.117; on inference: vii; on choice: viii; Platonism of: ix, 3; method in *DA* 1: 3, 6-7; *On Philosophy*: 6, 139 n.492, 140 n.495; *On Generation of Animals*: 7 n. 2; *On the Good*: 139 n.492, 140 n.494; *On Youth and Old Age*: 142 n.528; *On Memory and Recollection*: 134 n.373; as quoted by Galen: 133 n.371
astral body: 123 n.183

astronomy: 117 n.49
atoms: 137 n.441
Attic interpreters: 2, 5, 135 n.384
bile, black: 133 n.369, 134 n.372
bile, yellow: 133 n.369
bilious constitution: 133 n.369
blood: 4, 133 n.369
body: 119 n.80; influence on soul: 4, 125 n.203; impeding the working of *dianoia*: 116 n.17, 117 n.54, 118 n.64; unable to turn in on itself: 122 n.162; solid b.: 121 n.122, 123 n.165, 132 n.361; pneumatic b.: see *pneuma*
brain: 4; role in perception: 142 n.561; damage of: 125 n.201; seat of memory: 134 n.373; seat of consciousness ix

choice (*proairesis*): viii
Christianity: 123 n.183; of Philoponus: ix, 2
commentary, nature of Philoponus': 3
common insights: 117 n.38; 131 n.331
common sense faculty: vii, 119 n.74; objects of: 136 n.415
composite (*sunamphoteron*), of soul and body: 116 n.17; 129 n.267; 132 n.360, 133 n.367
conflict, between soul and body: 122 n.162; 135 n.380
constitution, natural (*phusis*) 4; c. types: 133 n.369, 134 n.372

contemplation: 3, 118 n.64
control, within human: 5
cooling, in the body: 124 n.186
corporeality of mental processes: 4
cosmology: 137 n.436
Craftsman (in Plato's *Timaeus*): 3, 122 n.146, 141 n.508

Damascius: 2, 127 n.224
death, life after: ix, 2
definition: 5, 117 n.41
Democritus: 6
demons: ix, 124 n.183, 126 n.212, 127 n.213
desire: 119 n.76-7
determinism: 136 n.396
diet: ix; see also regimen
discursive thought (*dianoia*): vii, 115 n.11, 116 n.17, 117 nn.35.54, 135 n.382; susceptible to bodily influence: 5, 133-4 n.371
disease: 133 n.369
disposition: 133 n.369
division of soul faculties: 115 nn.3-6; 131 n.310, 139 n.481, 142 n.565
doctors: 4, 121 n.116, 125 n.200, 128 n.237, 130 n.305, 134 n.371, 135 n.378
doxography: 6
dura mater: 125 n.201

elementary qualities: 133 n.369
emotions: 122 n.162; 123 n.180, 133 n.369
Empedocles: 121 n.116; element theory of: 138 n.443
envelope (*okhêma*) of soul: see vehicle
epistrophê: 122 n.161
essence: 129 n.261
etymology: 143 n.569
Euryalus: 139 n.471
evil: 2
exactness: 128 n.232

female contribution to reproduction: 130 n.295
fever: 4
fiery sphere: 137 nn.435-6
fluids, bodily: 133 n.369
form and matter: 3, 4; in definition: 5
Forms: 122 n.159
formula, formal principles: 136 nn.401.418

functions (*erga*), of bodily parts: 121 n.126

Galen: 4; on the nerves: 142 n.561; *On the Elements according to Hippocrates*: 138 n.443; *That the Faculties of the Soul follow the Mixture of the Body*: ix, 133 n.371, 134 n.374; *On Simple Medicines*: 133 n.371; *On the Usefulness of the Parts* commented upon by Philoponus: 5, 134 n.371; *On the Affected Parts*: 134 n.371; *On Demonstration*: 134 n.371; *Therapeutics to Glauco* commented upon by Stephanus of Alexandria: 5
Galenic medicine: 124 n.199, 125 n.200, 130 n.295, 137 n.428
generation, female contribution to: 130 n.295
Gennadius: 6
gods, lower (in Plato's *Timaeus*): 122 n.146, 141 n.508
growth: 120 n.84

Hades: 125 n.203
harmonia theory: 121 n.115, 123 n.176
health: 131 n.312
heart: ix, 4
heating, in the body: 124 n.186
heavenly bodies: 116 n.17; 117 n.49
Herophilus: 142 n.561
hierarchy: 135 n.392; of sciences: 128 n.232; of soul functions: 6, 116 n.27, 129 n.258, 131 n.311, 141 n.515; of senses: 120 n.86
Hierocles: 118 n.67, 119 n.79; on vehicles of soul: 124 n.183; on return of the soul after death: 124 n.191
Hippocrates: *Aphorisms*: 5; *Prognosticon*: 5; as quoted by Galen: 133 n.371; *On the Nature of Man*: 138 n.443; Hippocratic medicine: 124 n.185
hylomorphism: 135 n.396

Iamblichus: on choice: viii; on demons: 126 n.212; on luminous

Subject Index

body: 132 n.362; on vehicles of soul: 123 n.183
imagination: vii; equated with passive intellect: vii-viii, 2; see also *phantasia*
immortality: 121 nn.118.121.124; 122 n.144; of rational soul: ix, 2-3
impression (*tupos*): vii, 119 n.70, 141 n.516
inclination, to disease: 133 n.369
incorporeality, of soul: vii, 115 n.5
innate knowledge: 117 n.52
intellect (*nous*): 131 n.326.328; independent of the body: 5; as distinct from *dianoia*: 116 n.17; 117 nn.35.54; capacity to turn in on itself: 122 n.162; passive: vii, 119 n.71; Aristotle on: 3
intelligible objects: 116 nn.20.28; world: 141 nn.506.508
intuition: 116 nn.17-18

John of Alexandria, as distinct from John Philoponus: 5
knowledge: scientific: 127 n.218; perceptual: 127 n.218

krasis: 133 n.369; see also mixture

location of mental functions in the body: 4
logos: 116 n.17
luminous body: ix, 2, 123 n.183, 124 nn.193-4, 132 n.362

mass, main: 137 n.435
materialisation, of cognitive processes: 4
materialism: 5
mathematical objects: 117 n.32
mathematics: 136 n.416, 140 n.497
matter: 122 n.159
medical ideas: ix, 4-5, 9 n.34, 121 n.116, 125 n.200, 128 n.237, 132 n.355, 133 n.369, 134 n.371, 135 n.378
melancholics: 134 n.372; melancholic constitution: 133 n.369
membrane protector: 125 n.201
memory: 134 n.373
Michael of Ephesus: 7 n. 2
Michael Psellus: 7
mixture (*krasis*): 4-5, 120 n.115, 129 n.262, 130 nn.287.305, 133 nn.369.371, 136 nn.396.398
Moerbeke, William of: 6
Moon: 117 n.49; sphericity of: vii
mortal life: 128 n.235

nature, human: 133 n.369
nature, study of: 5, 129 n.255
Neo-Pythagoreanism: 140 n.495
nerves: 4, 125 n.200, 142 n.561
non-rational soul: 124 n.183, 135 n.396
nutrition: 120 n.84

One, the (in Plotinus): 116 n.23, 122 n.161
opinion (*doxa*): vii, 115 nn.9-10, 141 n.506
opposite qualities: viii
Origen, on vehicles of soul: 123 n.183

parts (*moria*), of the body (in Aristotle's *PA*): 121 n.126
pathos: 129 n.266, 133 nn.365-6
phantasia: 117 nn.30.35, 119 n.70-2, 136 n.416, 141 n.515; as passive intellect: 119 n.71
phantasma: 116 n.22
Philistion of Locri, his theory of elements: 138 n.443
philosophy, life according to: 5
phlegm: 133 n.369; phlegmatic constitution: 133 n.369
phronêsis: 116 n.17
physiognomy: 4, 133 n.369; 134 n.371
plants: 120 n.82, 123 n.180
Plato, theory of recollection: vii, 118 n.56; unwritten doctrines: 6, 140 n.495; theory of elements in *Timaeus*: 138 n.443; *Timaeus*, Philoponus' interpretation of: 2; as quoted by Galen: 133 n.371
Pletho: 6
Plotinus, on vehicles of soul: 123 n.183
Plutarch of Athens: 2, 127 nn. 220.224; on self-awareness: viii
pneuma, as vehicle for the soul: 121 nn.122.153; as vehicle for emotions: 2, 137 nn.427-8; expansion and contraction of: 124 n.186; 126 n.209; pneumatic body: ix, 123 nn.180.183, 124

nn.193-4; seat of memory: 134 n.373; thickening of pneuma giving rise to ghost-like phantasms around tombs: 125 n.203
pollution, of soul by body: 125 n.203
Porphyry: on self-awareness: viii; on demons: 126 n.212; on ghost-like phantasms around tombs: 125 n.203; on vehicles of soul: 123 n.183, 124 n.183; on return of the soul after death: 124 n.191
pre-existence, of soul: 2, 118 n.65
Presocratics: 6
Proclus: on opinion: vii; on projection of concepts: vii; on passive intellect: viii; influence on Philoponus' *in DA*: 2, 127 n.224, 140 n.495; on vehicles of soul: 123 n.183; on return of the soul after death: 124 n.191; on ghost-like phantasms around tombs: 125 n.203
projection (*proballein*): vii, 118 n.55
Prooemium, to Philoponus' *in DA*: vii-ix; relationship with Commentary: 3, 5, 115 n.2; 135 nn.384-8
Providence: 119 n.79, 127 n.213
pulse: 4
purgatives: 126 nn.203.206-7
purification, of soul from bodily affections: 2, 116 n.21, 125 n.203

qualities, elementary: 133 n.369

rational soul: 121 n.124; 122 n.144; vs. non-rational faculties of soul: 115 n.6; 118 n.61; 119 n.68
recollection, Plato's theory of: vii, 118 n.56
regimen: 133 n.369, 134 n.374
reproduction: 120 n.84
respiration, Democritus' theory of: 138 n.450

sciences, hierarchy of: 128 n.232
self-awareness: viii
sense-perception: 123 n.180; physiology of: 124 n.199, 142 n.561; loss of: 125 n.201, 126 n.209

separateness, of soul functions from body: 3, 122 n.162
shadows, of soul: 125 n.203
sight: 120 n.86; anatomy of: 132 n.356; physiology of: 132 n.356
Simplicius, (Ps.?), *in DA*: 2, 6, 140 n.495, 141 n.507; on luminous body: 132 n.362
solid body: see body
Sophonias: 6, 7 n. 3
spirit (*thumos*): 131 n.341, 137 n.428
splenetic constitution: 133 n.369
spokesmen, anonymous, referred to by Philoponus: 124 n. 191; 126 n.203.212
steersman: 132 n.358
Stephanus of Alexandria: 5
Stoics, on *phantasia*: 117 n.39; on the soul: 120 n.115; on expansion and contraction of *pneuma*: 124 n.186
suitability (*epitêdeiotês*): 122 n.159, 133 n.370
sumpatheia: 120 n.100, 124 n.187
supernatural beings: see demons
sympathetic reaction (*sumpatheia*): 2
Synesius: on vehicles of soul: 124 n.183
Syrianus: 2

temperament: 133 n.369
Themistius: *in DA*: 2, 6, 140 n.495, 141 n.507; on passive intellect: vii-viii; criticism of Galen: 134 n.371
Thirty, oligarchs: 120 n.113
Thomas Aquinas: 6
tombs: 125 n.203
touch: 120 n.86
transcendent world, hierarchy of: 128 n.235
transmigration of souls: 124 n.192, 132 n.361
trepanning: 125 n.201
Trincavelli, V.: 7
tripartition, of soul in Plato: 119 n.77
turning in on itself (*epistrophê*:): 122 n.161

universals, as ideas in the mind of the Craftsman: 3
Unmoved Mover: 3

vapours, arising from foods influencing the soul: 126 n.203
vehicle (*okhêma*) of soul: ix, 2, 123 n.183; see also *pneuma*
virtue: 116 n.21

vision, see sight
vivisection: 125 n.202
voluntary motion, loss of: 125 n.201

wish (*boulêsis*): viii

Index of Passages

This Index lists the passages cited in the Preface, the Introduction and the Notes to the Translation (the lemmas of Aristotle's *DA* as cited in the Translation itself are not included). References are to the page and note numbers of this volume.

ALCMAEON
Fragmenta **DK 24 A 12**: 138 n.461, 142 n.533
ALEXANDER
de Anima **25,2-9**: 120 n.115; **86,14-23**: viii
AMMONIUS
in Aristotelis de Interpretatione **5, 24-7,14**: 129 n.271; **6,4-22**: 119 n.71
in Porphyrii Isagogen **12,20-33**: 117 n.34
ANAXAGORAS
Fragmenta **DK 59 A 99**: 138 n.464; **DK 59 A 100**: 139 n.470, 142 n.535; **DK 59 B 12**: 142 n.538
ANAXIMENES
Fragmenta **DK 13 A 5**: 142 n.545; **DK 13 A 6**: 142 n.545; **DK 13 A 7**: 142 n.545
ANONYMUS LONDINIENSIS
16.3: 134 n.374; **20.25ff.**: 138 n.443
ARCHELAUS
Fragmenta **DK 60 A 18**: 139 n.466; **DK 68 A 113**: 139 n.467
ARISTOTLE
Analytica Posteriora **72b23**: 117 n.41; **75a28ff.**: 130 n.280; **75b16**: 128 n.234; **1.9**: 128 n.232; **76a10**: 128 n.234; **76a24**: 128 n.233, 128 n.234; **76a37-b2**: 117 n.38; **1.13**: 128 n.232; **78b35**: 128 n.236; **78b37**: 128 n.233; **78b37-79a2**: 128 n.232; **79a14**: 128 n.232; **87a34**: 128 n.234; **87a31-5**: 128 n.232; **88a12-17**: vii, 117 n.49; **89b7**: 116 n.17; **89b23-5**: 131 n.339; **90a26**: vii; **90a26**: 117 n.49; **100a1ff.**: 141 n.500; **100a15**: 141 n.500; **100b10-15**: 142 n.537
Analytica Priora **24b18**: 129 n.264; **25a38**: 133 n.364; **32a18**: 133 n.363
de Anima **402a10-11**: 127 n.219; **402a13**: 129 n.272; **402b5**: 131 n.321; **402b21-403a12**: 123 n.166; **403a16ff.**: 4; **403a25**: 4; **403a27**: 122 n.132; **403a30-1**: 119 n.77, 123 n.178, 131 n.340; **403b9**: 4; **403b23**: 142 n.540; **403b31**: 120 n.112; **404b1ff.**: 142 n.536; **404b13**: 142 n.564; **404b18-27**: 6; **405a5**: 129 n.253; **405a5ff.**: 120 n.105; **405a8**: 120 n.112; **405a29**: 138 n.461; **405b1-3**: 142 n.543; **405b8**: 120 n.111; **407a32-3**: 141 n.500; **408b18**: 122 n.141; **408b32**: 130 n.286; **408b32ff.**: 138 n.460; **411b18**: 122 n.142; **2.1-2**: 131 n.313; **412a10.21.27**: 121 n.117; **412a13ff.**: 137 n.433; **412a15ff.**: 129 n.256; **413a8-9**: 132 n.358; **413b5-7**: 120 n.86; **413b24**: 122 n.133, 122 n. 143; **414a2-3**: 120 n.86; **414b3**: 120 n.86; **414b19**: 126 n.212; **414b28-415a11**: 131 n.311; **415a1ff.**: 120 n.85; **415a3-5**: 120 n.86; **415a25-b7**: 120 n.91; **417b2-7**: 129 n.268; **417b15-16**: 119 n.78; **418a10ff.**: 119 n.74, 136 n.415; **422b15**: 133 n.371; **424b27**: 136 n.401;

Index of Passages

425a14ff.: 136 n.415; **426b19**: 122 n.157; **426b29ff.**: 122 n.155; **426b30ff.**: 122 n.154; **427b15**: 116 n.17; **428a13-14**: 115 n.11; **428a27**: 115 n.9; **428b11ff.**: 141 n.516; **428b22**: 136 n.415; **429a1-2**: 141 n.516; **3.4-5**: 131 n.326; **3.4–8**: 1; **429a13**: 122 n.134; **429a18-19**: 142 n.539; **429a22**: 122 n.137; **429a23**: 116 n.17; **429a27**: 131 n.318; **429a27-8**:139 n.480; **429a31-b4**: 122 n.138; **429b4-5**: 122 n.139; **430a2-4**: vii; **430a14-15**: 131 n.317; **430a17**: 122 n.140; **430a18**: 142 n.539; **430a22**: 122 n.135; **3.6**: 131 n.326; **431a1**: 131 n.317; **431a4-7**: 129 n.268; **431a14**: 116 n.17; **432a2**: 136 n.413; **432a12**: 132 n.348; **432a31-b2**: 141 n.516; **434a1**: 120 n.86; **435a12-14**: 120 n.86
de Bono **fr. 84-97 Gigon**: 140 n.492
de Caelo **1.3**: 142 n.551; **271a33**: 123 n.169; **1.9**: 142 n.551; **286b10ff.**: 136 n.409; **2.6**: 142 n.551; **288a27ff.**: 142 n.551; **291b17ff.**: 117 n.49; **291b18**: 130 n.281; **311b21ff.**: 137 n.436
Categoriae **1.4**: 130 n.284; **8b27**: 119 n.78
Ethica Eudemia **1248a39**: 134 n.372
Ethica Nicomachea **1102a18ff.**: 128 n.249; **1102a23-8**: 115 n.6; **1102b25-1103a10**: 120 n.101; **1104b17**: 124 n.185; **1139b5**: viii; **1142a25-6**:116 n.17; **1143a35-6**: 116 n.17; **1147a26**: 115 n.9; **1147b17-18**: 115 n.9; **1150b25.27**: 134 n.372; **1152a19.28**: 134 n.372; **1154b11**: 134 n.372; **1154b11-14**: 9 n.30
de Generatione Animalium **2.1**: 120 n.91; **731b25-35**: 120 n.91; **736b27ff.**: 121 n. 131, 123 n.183; **744a30-2**: 9 n.30
de Generatione et Corruptione **1.2**: 142 n.566; **331b25**: 142 n.547; **2.9-11**: 127 n.217; **2.10**: 136 n.407
de Insomniis **458b4-6**: 119 n.74, 136 n.415; **458b10-13**: 115 n.9;

459a16-17: 141 n.516; **460b21-2**: 120 n.86
de Interpretatione **16a6**: 132 n.346; **16b20**: 141 n.500; **23a23**: 130 n.300, 137 n.426
Magna Moralia **1203b1**: 134 n.375
de Memoria **449b7-8**: 134 n.373; **450a1-10**: 116 n.22, 119 n.72; **450a9**: 136 n.415; **450a10-11**: 119 n.74; **450a31**: 119 n.70, 134 n.373; **450b5**: 119 n.70
Metaphysica **980a22**: 128 n.225; **980a22-3**: 120 n.86; **982a25-8**: 128 n.232; **984a7**: 142 n.531; **985b16**: 138 n.447; **985b16-17**: 138 n.449; **992a10ff.**:140 n.493; **992b13ff.**:140 n.493; **995a27-b4**: 137 n.430; **4.1**: 131 n.312; **1003a34-b3**: 131 n.316; **1009b28**: 139 n.471; **1036b13**:140 n.493; **1042b14**: 138 n.447, 138 n.449; **1051a22-1052a11**: 142 n.537; **1057b8**: 115 n.10; **1060b36-1061a6**: 131 n.316; **1072a9ff.**: 142 n.551; **1072b1-14**: 120 n.89; **1072b3**: 137 n.439; **1072b5-7**: 128 n.248; **1072b13**: 127 n.216, 136 n.406; **1072b19-21**: viii; **1074b33ff.**: 131 n.319; **1075a11**: 137 n.425; **1075a11ff.**: 137 n.429; **1075a13-15**: 131 n.315; **1085a7ff.**:140 n.493; **1090b2ff.**:140 n.493
Meteorologica **340b21ff.**: 137 n.436; **347b34**: 131 n.334; **2.4**: 142 n.529; **2.8**: 142 n.529; **2.9**: 142 n.529
de Motu Animalium **701a27**: 141 n.500
de Partibus Animalium **640b28-9**: 129 n.256; **641a17ff.**: 121 n.125; **641a18ff.**: 129 n.256; **641a18-b10**: 129 n.255; **641a32**: 136 n.404; **641a33ff.**: 121 n.128, 128 n.252; **641b8-10**: 129 n.255; **645b20-646a3**: 121 n.126; **2-4**: 129 n.257; **656b19ff.**: 142 n.562; **666a17ff.**: 142 n.562
Physica **184a1-2**: 130 n.293; **184a10**: 128 n.231; **188b22-6**: 137 n.442; **193b13**: 137 n.438;

Index of Passages

201b31:139 n.486; **203b15ff.**: 131 n.333; **210b32**: 131 n.332; **213a19**: 131 n.333; **217b30**: 131 n.333; **246b4-5**: 9 n.30; **8.6**: 127 n.215, 136 n.406
Physiognomonica **805a1**: 134 n.371; **805a1-3**: 9 n.32
Poetica **1451b18-19**: 123 n.174; **1455a32**: 134 n.375
Politica **1327b35**: 9 n.30
Problemata physica **954a15**: 9 n.30; **954a32**: 134 n.375
de Respiratione **471b30-472b5**: 138 n.450; **480b22-31**: 128 n.237
de Sensu et Sensibilibus **436a18-b2**: 128 n.237; **437a3**: 120 n.86; **437a8-9**: 136 n.415; **442b4ff.**: 136 n.415
de Somno et Vigilia **455a14ff.**: 136 n.415; **455a15-22**: viii; **455a20**: 126 n.209; **456a7**: 123 n.183, 126 n.209; **456a13-18**: 123 n.183, 126 n.209

CAELIUS AURELIANUS
de Morbis Chronicis **2.12.137**: 135 n.378

CRITIAS
Fragmenta **DK 88 A 22**: 142 n.558; **DK 88 A 23**: 120 n.114, 142 n.557

DAMASCIUS
in Platonis Phaedonem **1.3**: 135 n.390; **1.177**: 121 n.118

DEMOCRITUS
Fragmenta **DK 68 A 101**: 138 n.465, 142 n.532, 534; **DK 68 A 105**: 130 n.302

DIOGENES APOLLONIATES
Fragmenta **DK 64 A 20**: 412 n.544

EMPEDOCLES
Fragmenta **DK 31 B 109**: 139 n.474; **DK 31 B 115,13-14**: 139 n.476

EUCLID
Elementa **1.3**: 117 n.38; **1.13**: 117 n.45

GALEN
de Anatomicis Administrationibus **9.11-13**: 125 n.202
de Instrumento Odoratus **6 (2.886 K)**: 125 n.202
de Locis Affectis **2.5 (8.128 K)**: 125 n.202; **2.10 (8.128 K)**: 125 n.201;
4.3 (8.230-3K): 125 n.202; **4.3 (8.232 K)**: 125 n.201
de Placitis Hippocratis et Platonis **1.6.4-6 (5.185-6 K)**: 125 n.202; **1.6 (5.186 K)**: 125 n.201; **7.7.20-6 (5.643-4 K)**: 123 n.183; *Thrasybulus* **38 (5.878 K)**: 134 n.374

HERACLITUS
Fragmenta **DK 22 A 15**: 142 n.546; **DK 22 B 118**: 142 n.530

HIPPASUS
DK 18 A 7: 142 n.531

HIPPO
DK 38 A 8: 142 n.554; **DK 38 A 10**: 143 n.570

HIPPOCRATES
de Flatibus **1.5 (6.92 L.)**: 124 n.185

HOMER
Iliad **3.35**: 136 n.399; **16.149**: 117 n.47; **23.698**: 139 n.471
Odyssey **20.17**: 120 n.102; **20.18**: 120 n.103

IAMBLICHUS
de Mysteriis **1.10, 36,1-5**: viii, 118 n.63, 128 n.246; **1.12, 41,3-4**: viii, 118 n.63
Theologoumena Arithmeticae **59**: 141 n.498

LEUCIPPUS
DK 67 A 6: 138 n.447; **DK 67 A 28**: 137 n.440, 138 n.445

MICHAEL PSELLUS
PG 122, col. 1030-1076: 7

NEMESIUS
de Natura Hominis **8 (64,1-15 Morani)**: 125 n.201, 142 n.561; **13 (69,17-71,4 Morani)**: 125 n.201

NUMENIUS
Fragmenta **47 des Places**: 121 n.118

OLYMPIODORUS
in Aristotelis Categorias **8, 120,33**: 127 n.224
in Platonis Phaedonem **83,31**: 127 n.224; **94,12**: 127 n.224
Prolegomena **8,29-9,13**: 117 n.34

ORIGEN
Contra Celsum **2.60 (1,183,5 Koetschau = 425,10 Crouzel-Simonetti)**: 125 n.203

PHILOLAUS
DK 44 B 10: 138 n.456
PHILOPONUS
de Aeternitate Mundi Contra Proclum **319,5-8**: 134 n.371; **600,2**: 134 n.371
in Aristotelis Analytica Posteriora **34,24-35,1**: 128 n.237; **100,25-31**: 128 n.237; **146,17-25**: 128 n.237
in Aristotelis de Anima **1,9-9,2**: 115 n.3; **1,12**: 118 n.61; **1,13-5,23**: 141 n.513; **1,16**: 141 n.501, n.504; **2,2**: 117 n.46; **2,2-3**: 141 n.514; **2,22-4**: 141 n.506; **3,16-17**: 117 n.42; **3,17**: 124 n.197, 131 n.331; **4,20-1**: 117 n.50; **4,22**: vii, 130 n.281; **4,31**: 124 n.189; **5,3**: vii; **5,16**: vii; **5,17**: 117 n.38; **5,24ff.**: 115 n.7; **5,24-33**: viii; **5,27-8**: 118 n.61; **5,34**: 131 n.310; **5,34ff.**: 115 n.8; **5,34-6,10**: vii; **5,35ff.**: 117 n.48; **5,35-6,10**: 141 n.515; **5,36ff.**: 117 n.30; **6,1-2**: 8 n.14, 122 n.136; **6,9-10**: 141 n.516; **6,11**: 131 n.341, 139 n.481; **6,13-14**: 131 n.340; **6,20-6**: 118 n.66, 124 n.189, n.190; **6,21**: 2; **6,21-2**: 120 n.96; **6,25**: 118 n.61, 122 n.158; **6,26**: 131 n.310, 139 n.481; **6,26-7**: 143 n.565; **8,8**: 135 n.378; **8,22-3**: 8 n.16; **9,3**: 143 n.564; **9,3ff.**: 6; **9,3-12,9**: 115 n.4; **9,10-11**: 142 n.555; **9,12-13**: 143 n.563; **9,16**: 143 n.564; **9,19**: 143 n.558, n.560; **9,23-6**: 129 n.262, 130 n.287, n.305; **9,26**: 133 n.369; **9,29-30**: 132 n.359; **10,1-3**: 128 n.243; **10,7**: 122 n.153; **10,7-8**: 137 n.427; **10,8**: 123 n.164; **10,9-11,29**: 3, 128 n.242; **10,11ff.**: 128 n.252, 129 n.253, 136 n.404; **10,12-13**: 127 n.221; **10,16**: 129 n.255, n.258; **10,31-11,3**: 122 n.143; **11,5-11**: 119 n.71; **11,29ff.**: 121 n.120; **11,33**: 141 n.508; **12,6-9**: 124 n.189, n.190; **12,10-15,8**: 10 n.46, 122 n.150; **12,12**: 115 n.5; **12,15**: 9 n.26; **12,18**: 123 n.164; **12,19**: 121 n.123; **12,20ff.**: 121 n.122; **12,34-13,20**: viii; **13,24-14,1**: 130 n.304; **13,26**: 122 n.158; **13,30**: 122 n.158; **14,5-28**: 8 n.17; **14,6**: 133 n.370; **14,18**: 133 n.370; **14,31-2**: viii; **14,35-8**: 136 n.411; **14,36ff.**: viii; **15,5**: 135 n.380; **15,11**: 121 n.123, 137 n.427; **15,12-35**: 132 n.352; **15,15-22**: 128 n.242, 131 n.325; **15,20-1**: 132 n.354; **15,22-34**: 135 n.395; **16,2-12**: 10 n.46; **16,3ff.**: 130 n.289; **16,19-21**: 132 n.353; **16,20-1**: 135 n.388; **17,6-20**: 10 n.46; **17,17**: 121 n.123; **17,17ff.**: 122 n.153; **17,19ff.**: ix; **17,22**: 10 n.46; **17,26-18,16**: 135 n.385, 138 n.457; **17,29**: 119 n.79; **18,9**: 137 n.427; **18,11**: 135 n.387; **18,11ff.**: 132 n.361; **18,16-24**: 116 n.21; **18,17-28**: 8 n.15; **18,18**: 2; **18,21**: 135 n.377; **18,26.32.33**: 137 n.427; **18,27ff.**: 133 n.362; **18,27-8**: 123 n.183; **19,2**: 117 n.38; **19,8-10**: 9 n.34; **19,17-18**: 126 n.213; **19,18**: 126 n.203; **19,19ff.**: ix; **19,20ff.**: 124 n.192; **19,27**: ix; **19,34**: 133 n.369; **20,4**: 133 n.369; **20,7**: 126 n.203; **20,7-8**: 127 n.213; **20,10**: 126 n.203, n.213; **20,12**: 124 n.183; **20,14**: 127 n.213; **20,17**: 119 n.79; **20,31ff.**: ix; **21,4**: 136 n.406; **21,4-6**: 136 n.405; **1.1-2**: 8 n.3; **21,10**: 127 n.218; **21,16**: 127 n.219; **21,21**: 8 n.10; **21,22-3**: 121 n.121; **21,28**: 8 n.11, 132 n.351, 134 n.376; **22,9**: 127 n.218; **22,11**: 127 n.218; **22,12**: 127 n.218; **23,26**: 119 n.79; **24,12**: 123 n.170, 131 n.325, 132 n.352; **24,26**: 128 n.240; **24,32**: 129 n.253; **25,9-16**: 9 n.26, 9 n.27; **25,10ff.**: 121 n.129; **25,13**: 136 n.404; **26,9**: 121 n.127; **26,21**: 129 n.261; **26,21-2**: 129 n.261; **26,22-3**: 130 n.287, n.305; **26,22-4**: 121 n.116; **26,25**: 129 n.261; **26,27ff.**: 130 n.277; **27,21ff.**: 132 n.345; **29,4**: 129 n.263; **29,6**: 129 n.277; **29,11**: 129 n.277; **29,12**: 129 n.277; **29,14**: 131 n.330; **30,20-2**: 117 n.49; **32,33**: 132 n.342, 138 n.460; **33,1-5**: 121 n.116; **33,1-6**: 129 n.262, 130 n.305; **33,4**: 121 n.117; **34,5**: 130 n.289; **35,2**: 137 n.426;

Index of Passages

35,10: 2; **35,25-6**: 120 n.115, 133 n.369; **36,30-37,17**: 9 n.28; **37,7**: 135 n.392; **37,19ff.**: 3; **37,21-2**: 137 n.425, n.429; **38,14-15**: 135 n.391, 136 n.418; **38,27**: 131 n.341; **39,3ff.**: 123 n.170; **40,17-22**: 137 n.432; **40,18ff.**: 9 n.29; **44,1**: 138 n.460; **44,3**: 132 n.343; **44,3-4**: 119 n.77, 131 n.340; **44,7-8**: 123 n.178; **44,11**: 130 n.286; **44,18-63,14**: 4; **44,21ff.**: 137 n.431; **45,8ff.**: 129 n.270; **46,18**: 127 n.224; **46,20-49,14**: 123 n.170; **46,28**: 123 n.175; **49,5**: 123 n.183; **49,5-6**: 124 n.193; **50,14-52,25**: 10 n.46; **50,19**: 123 n.178; **50,25**: 9 n.33; **50,25ff.**: 4; **50,31ff.**: 121 n.115, 130 n.287, n.305; **51,5**: 133 n.369; **51,7-8**: 133 n.369; **51,15**: 127 n.224; **51,13-52,1**: ix; **51,15ff.**: 5; **51,16ff.**: 117 n.52; **51,18**: 135 n.395; **51,20ff.**: 5; **51,21**: 135 n.377; **51,28**: 135 n.377; **51,33**: 135 n.377; **51,35**: 5; **51,35-52,4**: 122 n.163; **52,2ff.**: 116 n.21; **52,3-4**: 119 n.80; **52,4ff.**: 5; **52,4-5**: 138 n.458; **52,6**: 137 n.427; **52,8-11**: 123 n.176, 132 n.353; **52,15-16**: 131 n.322; **52,16**: 142 n.556; **52,20**: 136 n.418; **53,18**: 133 n.369; **54,20-1**: 5; **54,25**: 137 n.422; **54,26**: 136 n.414; **55,3-5**: 119 n.77, 313 n.340; **55,17**: 127 n.216; **57,12**: 137 n.422; **57,16-17**: 119 n.77, 131 n.340; **58,19-21**: 116 n.21, n.22; **58,24-5**: 119 n.77, 131 n.340; **59,8**: 119 n.77, 131 n.340; **61,33**: 136 n.414; **64,14-15**: 137 n.428; **1.2**: 120 n.105; **65,31**: 135 n.377; **65,32-66,14**: 10 n.46; **65,36-8**: 139 n.487; **67,11ff.**: 120 n.112; **70,10-16**: 138 n.457; **70,10-17**: 139 n.479; **71,13**: 130 n.286; **71,22ff.**: 130 n.302; **71,26**: 142 n.548; **72,8-9**: 139 n.468; **74,1**: 141 n.525; **74,30ff.**: 139 n.477; **75,11-15**: 10 n.46; **75,13**: 142 n.552; **75,32ff.**: 6; **76,2**: 141 n.523; **76,2ff.**: 140 n.495; **76,4ff.**: 140 n.495; **76,11**: 140 n.495;

76,14-77,5: 140 n.495; **76,22ff.**: 141 n.520; **76,23-5**: 140 n.495; **76,28-30**: 140 n.495; **77,1ff.**: 141 n.521; **77,10.16.17**: 140 n.495; **77,26-7**: 140 n.495; **77,30-1**: 140 n.495; **77,32**: 140 n.495; **77,33-7**: 140 n.495; **78,3-5**: 140 n.495; **78,25**: 9 n.44; **80,2**: 140 n.497; **81,25**: 130 n.286, 138 n.460; **82,12ff.**: 6; **82,18**: 120 n.109; **82,20**: 138 n.460; **82,30**: 130 n.286; **83,10**: 120 n.105; **83,22**: 120 n.107; **84,9ff.**: 120 n.112; **86,34**: 120 n.110; **88,9-12**: 138 n.461; **88,23**: 120 n.110; **89,3**: 122 n.158; **89,8ff.**: 120 n.113; **89,16-17**: 9 n.34, 125 n.200; **89,24ff.**: 120 n.111; **90,10**: 120 n.105; **1.3**: 8 n.22; **95,27**: 119 n.78; **115,4-35**: 116 n.17; **138,5**: 133 n.371; **138,9**: 124 n.193; **1.4**: 121 n.115; **150,3ff.**: 121 n.116; **155,4ff.**: 135 n.382; **155,4-35**: 9 n.41, 117 n.35, 118 n.54, 134 n.371; **155,11-12**: 132 n.360; **155,22-3**: 9 n.33, 134 n.371; **155,28-9**: 134 n.373; **155,33-4**: 133 n.371, 134 n.371; **158,8-22**: 134 n.373; **158,16-17**: 123 n.183; **159,5**: 121 n.121; **162,2-27**: 124 n.193; **162,17-24**: 122 n.162; **162,20**: 135 n.380; **164,8-13**: 123 n.183; **164,8-28**: 134 n.373; **165,18ff.**: 130 n.286; **172,22ff.**: 138 n.460; **186,25**: 139 n.492; **200,2**: 9 n.24; **203,5**: 9 n.24; **222,15**: 123 n.183; **224,12ff.**: 132 n.358; **226,1-3**: 131 n.339; **229,29-32**: 116 n.17; **232,5**: 127 n.224; **237,11**: 121 n.118; **239,7-9**: 126 n.211; **239,8-9**: 126 n.204; **239,8-12**: 125 n.203; **239,12**: 126 n.206; **239,15**: 126 n.203; **239,15ff.**: 126 n.203; **241,7-9**: 118 n.64; **241,27-8**: 122 n.144, 123 n.177; **241,36**: 9 n.24; **242,16-19**: 123 n.177; **242,18**: 122 n.144; **249,15**: 118 n.63; **249,16-18**: 119 n.78; **250,17**: 124 n.185; **251,12-13**: 119 n.78; **254,10**: 124 n.185; **255,6-15**: 126 n.212; **255,9-15**: 8 n.21; **258,36-259,2**: 116 n.17;

Index of Passages

260,18-25: 116 n.17; **261,1-262,4**: 122 n.152; **261,28**: 121 n.128; **268,33**: 135 n.390; **274,8-10**: 134 n.371; **293,22**: 118 n.57; **296,30-2**: 119 n.78; **336,29ff.**: 132 n.356; **408,25**: 8 n.12; **410,1**: 8 n.12; **418,25**: 8 n.12

(PS.?-)PHILOPONUS
in Aristotelis de Anima 3 **3.2**: 122 n.154; **464,24-465,31**: viii; **491,21-7**: 117 n.35; **501-4 passim**: 115 n.9; **533,26**: 8 n.13; **578,12-13**: 118 n.61
de Intellectu **4,70-2**: 121 n.121; **13,1-4**: 119 n.71; **20,71-88**: 116 n.17, 117 n.54; **24,60-5**: 124 n.193; **35,21-7**: 123 n.167; **39,21-7**: 121 n.124, 128 n.250; **40,36**: vii, 118 n.56; **48,42**: 120 n.83; **49,55-50,77**: 121 n.124, 128 n.250; **49,56**: 122 n.144; **52,35**: 130 n.295; **53,64**: 138 n.459; **78,13-80,56**: 8 n.12; **83,42-4**: 117 n.52; **84,24**: 130 n.299; **88,61-3**: 142 n.537; **89,96-9**: 116 n.20; **91,62-5**: 116 n.19; **107,51-5**: 118 n.64; **111-112,67-8**: 136 n.412; **119,42-9**: 132 n.349
in Aristotelis de Generatione et Corruptione **169,5-6**: 135 n.378; **169,7**: 135 n.390; **226,17-30**: 140 n.492
in Aristotelis Meteorologica **12,25-6**: 136 n.411
in Aristotelis Physica **316,25**: 136 n.417
Corollaries on Place **576,13-21**: 133 n.371
in Nicomachi Arithmeticam Introductio **1, λσ, 4**: 136 n.417

PLATO
Cratylus **399Dff.**:143 n.571
Epistulae **2, 314A**: 138 n.454
Gorgias **454E3-9**: 128 n.230; **465A5-6**: 136 n.403, n.414, 137 n.422; **525B-C**: 124 n.184
Leges **896E8-897A2**: 138 n.462; **898E**: 123 n.183
Meno **81C9-D5**: 137 n.419
Phaedrus **237B**: 131 n.338; **237B7**: 130 n.292; **245C**: 131 n.329; **245C5**: 121 n.119; **245C5ff.**:139 n.490; **245C5-246A2**: 116 n.16; **245E2-4**: 141 n.524; **246Bff.**:139 n.478; **247B**: ix, 123 n.183; **249A**: 124 n.184
Phaedo **66D2-7**: 117 n.29; **69C**: 116 n.21; **75D8-10**: 128 n.229; **81C-D**: 125 n.203; **81E**: 126 n.210; **86B-C**: 124 n.186; **87D-E**: 120 n.81; **96B8**: 141 n.500; **113D**: ix, 123 n.183
Philebus **31C**: 124 n.185
Protagoras **357Dff.**: 128 n.227
Republic **511D6-E2**: 116 n.17; **611D**: 138 n.459; **615A-616B**: 124 n.184; **620A-D**: 126 n.210
Sophist **244Dff.**: 129 n.269; **249Bff.**: 142 n.550; **251A-259B**:139 n.484; **254D4**:139 n.485; **264A10**: 116 n.13
Theaetetus **180D**: 138 n.453; **180Dff.**: 142 n.550; **181Dff.**: 142 n.550
Timaeus **27D**: 140 n.495; **27D6**: 141 n.502; **28A**: 140 n.495, 141 n.505; **28A1-2**: 116 n.25; **28A1-3**: 141 n.503; **28A2-3**: 116 n.26; **30B**: 119 n.79; **33B**: 136 n.408; **34Cff.**:139 n.483; **34C3-35A8**:139 n.488; **35A**:139 n.484; **35Aff.**: 141 n.525; **35A4ff.**: 139 n.477; **37A-C**:139 n.477, n.483; **37A3-C5**:139 n.489; **37A7-8**:139 n.490; **39E-40A**: 119 n.79, 141 n.507; **41Bff.**: 122 n.145; **41C6ff.**: 128 n.247; **41D4ff.**:139 n.483; **41D-E**: ix, 123 n.183; **67E5**: 115 n.10; **69C**: 123 n.183; **70B-D**: 124 n.198; **71B**: 123 n.179, 124 n.198; **74A-75C**: 134 n.374; **76E-77C5**: 131 n.307; **86B-87B**: 4; **90E-92C**: 126 n.210; **91D6-92C9**: 131 n.307

PLOTINUS
1.1.9: 142 n.537; **1.1.12**: 138 n.459; **1.2.3,8-10**: 116 n. 21; **1.2.4**: 116 n. 21; **1.3.3,5-10**: 117 n.34; **2.2.1**: 136 n.410; **3.1.34-6**: 4; **3.4.2**: 120 n.93; **3.6.3,27-34**: 128 n.246; **3.7.11,35-6**: 116 n.17; **4.5.2**: 138 n.449; **4.5.6**: 138 n.449; **4.8.1,41**: 119 n.79; **5.3.3,23-9**: 116 n.17; **5.3.5,42-8**: viii; **5.3.8,47**: 117 n.37; **5.3.14**: 116 n.23;

5.3.14,129: 116 n.23; **5.3.17**: 116 n.23; **5.8.1**: 116 n.20; **5.8.1,1-6**: 116 n.23; **6.4.3,17-23**: 120 n.100; **6.8.18,27**: 116 n.37; **6.9.11,26**: 116 n.23

PLUTARCH OF ATHENS
Fragmenta **fr. 18 Taormina**: 127 n.220

PORPHYRY
de Abstinentia (ed. Nauck) **2.39**: 126 n.212; **2.42, 172,2-6**: 126 n.207; **3.8.6**: 128 n.246
de Antro Nympharum (ed. Nauck) **11, 64,13-22**: 126 n.207; **11, 64,15-21**: 125 n.203; **11**: 126 n.212
ad Gaurum **6.1, 42,6-11 Kalbfleisch**: 126 n.212
Isagoge **2,16**: 130 n.290
Sententiae (ed. Lamberz) **29, 17,11-18,13**: 125 n.203; **41, 52,7-53,5**: viii, 122 n.161

PRISCIANUS
Metaphrasis in Theophrastum **21,32-22,23**, ix

PROCLUS
Elementatio Theologica **16**: 8 n.18; **44**: 8 n.18; **83**: 122 n.161; **171**: 122 n.161; **177 (156,1 Dodds)**: 136 n.412; **186**: 8 n.18; **196**: ix, 124 n.183; **207-9**: ix, 124 n.183; **209**: 137 n.437
in Euclidis Elementa **1, 51,10-52,20**: viii, 119 n.71; **1, 121,1-7**: vii, 118 n.55; **1, 141,2-19**: vii; **1, 141,2-19**: 118 n.55
de Malorum Subsistentia **21,22-8 Boese**: 128 n.246
in Platonis Rem publicam (ed. Kroll) **2, 156,25-157,8**: 125 n.203; **2, 164,19-27**: 125 n.203
in Platonis Timaeum (ed. Diehl) **1, 251,4-9**: vii, 118 n.55; **1, 254,31-255,20**: viii; **1, 446,1-7**: 135 n.390; **3, 53,6-9**: 135 n.390; **3, 234,8-235,9**, ix; **3, 236,31ff.**, ix, 124 n.183; **3, 237,24-7**: 124 n.195; **3, 238,18-21**: 124 n.183; **3, 298,12ff.**: ix, 124 n.183; **3, 335,23-336,2**: 128 n.246; **3, 338,6-13**: 128 n.246; **3, 340,14-17**: 128 n.246; **3, 349,21-350,8**: 135 n.380; **3, 349,22**: 134 n.371
Theologia Platonica **3.5**: ix; **3.5, 18,24-19,15**: 124 n.183

PROTAGORAS
Fragmenta **DK 80 B 1**: 139 n.469

PYTHAGORAS
Fragmenta **DK 58 B 40**: 138 n.452

SEXTUS EMPIRICUS
Adversus Mathematicos **10.281**: 140 n.493

(PS.?-)SIMPLICIUS
in Aristotelis de Anima **1,25-3,2**: 121 n.128; **7,1-14**: 128 n.232; **17,3-5**: 132 n.347; **19,4-11**: 134 n.376; **19,39**: 134 n.372; **27,20**: 119 n.71; **28,7-9**:140 n.492; **30,33ff.**: 141 n.527; **106,24-30**: 126 n.212; **173,3-7**: ix; **187,27-188,35**, ix; **214,1-2**: 121 n.122; **237,8-9**: 115 n.9
in Aristotelis Physica **1,6-11**: 115 n.6; **722,30**: 130 n.285

SOPHONIAS
in Aristotelis de Anima Paraphrasis **121,19-20**: 119 n.73

STOICI
SVF 2.774,885: 123 n.183

SYNESIUS
de Insomniis **5,564,14 Garzya**: 126 n.208; **5,564,17-18 Garzya**: 125 n.199

THALES
Fragmenta **DK 11 A 1**: 142 n.541; **DK 11 A 22**: 142 n.541

THEMISTIUS
in Aristotelis Analytica Posteriora **25,25**: 128 n.237
in Aristotelis de Anima **1,11-23**: 128 n.232; **11,30**:140 n.493; **12,1**: 141 n.509; **13,7**: 141 n.527; **19,33**: 124 n.193; **98,35-99,10**: viii